CONQUEST OF MEXICO

ARREST OF THE EMPEROR MONTEZUMA

CONQUEST OF MEXICO

BY
WILLIAM H. PRESCOTT

WITH AN INTRODUCTION BY
CARL VAN DOREN

THE BOOK LEAGUE OF AMERICA

New York

CL

MANUFACTURED IN THE UNITED STATES OF AMERICA

PREFACE

As THE Conquest of Mexico has occupied the pens of Solís and of Robertson, two of the ablest historians of their respective nations, it might seem that little could remain at the present day to be gleaned by the historical inquirer. But Robertson's narrative is necessarily brief, forming only part of a more extended work; and neither the British nor the Castilian author was provided with the important materials for relating this event, which have been since assembled by the industry of Spanish scholars. The scholar who led the way in these researches was Don Juan Baptista Muñoz, the celebrated historiographer of the Indies, who, by a royal edict, was allowed free access to the national archives, and to all libraries, public, private, and monastic, in the kingdom and its colonies. The result of his long labours was a vast body of materials, of which unhappily he did not live to reap the benefit himself. His manuscripts were deposited, after his death, in the archives of the Royal Academy of History at Madrid; and that collection was subsequently augmented by the manuscripts of Don Vargas Ponce, President of the Academy, obtained, like those of Muñoz, from different quarters, but especially from the Archives of the Indies at Seville.

On my application to the Academy, in 1838, for permission to copy that part of this inestimable collection relating to Mexico and Peru, it was freely acceded to, and an eminent German scholar, one of their own number, was appointed to superintend the collation and transcription of the manuscripts; and this, it may be added, before I had any claim on the courtesy of that respectable body, as one of its associates. This conduct shows the advance of a liberal spirit in the Peninsula since the time of Dr. Robertson, who complains that he was denied admission to the most important public repositories. The favour with which my own application was regarded, however, must chiefly be attributed to the kind offices of the venerable President of the Academy, Don Martin Fernandez de Navarrete; a scholar whose personal character has secured to him the same high consideration at home, which his literary labours have obtained abroad. To this eminent person I am under still further obligations, for the free use which he has allowed me to make of his own manuscripts—the fruits of a life of accumulation, and the basis of those valuable publications with which he has at different times illustrated Spanish colonial history.

From these three magnificent collections, the result of half a century's careful researches, I have obtained a mass of unpublished documents, relating to the Conquest and Settlement of Mexico and of Peru, comprising altogether about eight thousand folio pages. They consist of instructions of the Court, military and private journals, correspondence of the great actors in the scenes, legal instruments, contemporary chronicles, and the like, drawn from all the principal places in the extensive colonial empire of Spain, as well as from the public archives in the Peninsula.

I have still further fortified the collection, by gleaning such materials from Mexico itself as had been overlooked by my illustrious predecessors in these researches. For these I am indebted to the courtesy of Count Cortina, and, yet more, to that of Don Lucas Alaman, Minister of Foreign Affairs in Mexico; but, above all, to my excellent friend Don Angel Calderon de la Barca, late Minister Plenipotentiary to that country from the Court of Madrid—a gentleman whose high and estimable qualities, even more than his station, secured him the public confidence, and gained him free access to every place of interest and importance in Mexico.

I have also to acknowledge the very kind offices rendered to me by the Count Camaldoli at Naples; by the Duke of Serradifalco in Sicily, a nobleman whose science gives additional lustre to his rank; and by the Duke of Monteleone, the present representative of Cortés, who has courteously opened the archives of his family to my inspection. To these names must also be added that of Sir Thomas Phillips, Bart., whose precious collection of manuscripts probably surpasses in extent that of any private gentleman in Great Britain, if not in Europe; that of Mons. Ternaux-Compans, the proprietor of the valuable literary collection of Don Antonio Uguina, including the papers of Muñoz, the fruits of which he is giving to the world in his excellent translations; and, lastly, that of my friend and countryman, Arthur Middleton, Esq., late Chargé d'Affaires from the United States at the Court of Madrid, for the efficient aid he has afforded me in prosecuting my inquiries in that capital.

In addition to this stock of original documents obtained through these various sources, I have diligently provided myself with such printed works as have reference to the subject, including the magnificent publications which have appeared both in France and England on the Antiquities of Mexico, which, from their cost and colossal dimensions, would seem better suited to a public than to a private library.

Having thus stated the nature of my materials, and the sources whence they are derived, it remains for me to add a few observations on the general plan and composition of the work. Among the remarkable achievements of the Spaniards in the sixteenth century, there is no one more striking to the imagination than the Conquest of Mexico. The subversion of a great empire by a handful of adventurers, taken with all its strange and picturesque accompaniments, has the air of romance rather than of sober history; and it is not easy to treat such a theme according to the severe rules prescribed by historical criticism. But, notwithstanding the seductions of the subject, I have conscientiously endeavoured to distinguish fact from fiction, and to establish the narrative on as broad a basis as possible of contemporary evidence; and I have taken occasion to corroborate the text by ample citations from authorities, usually in the original, since few of them can be very accessible to the reader. In these extracts I have scrupulously conformed to the ancient orthography, however obsolete and even barbarous, rather than impair in any degree the integrity of the original document.

The distance of the present age from the period of the narrative might be presumed to secure the historian from undue prejudice or partiality. Yet to the American and the English reader, acknowledging so different a moral standard from that of the sixteenth century, I may possibly be thought too indulgent to the errors of the Conquerors; while to a Spaniard, accustomed to the undiluted panegyric of Solís, I may be deemed to have dealt too hardly with them. To such I can only say that, while, on the one hand, I have not hesitated to expose in their strongest colours the excesses of the Conquerors; on the other, I have given them the benefit of such mitigating reflections as might be suggested by the circumstances and the period in which they lived. I have endeavoured not only to present a picture true in itself, but to place it in its proper light, and to put the spectator in a proper point of view for seeing it to the best advantage. I have endeavoured, at the expense of some repetition, to surround him with the spirit of the times, and, in a word, to make him, if I may so express myself, a contemporary of the sixteenth century. Whether, and how far, I have succeeded in this, he must determine.

For one thing, before I conclude, I may reasonably ask the reader's indulgence. Owing to the state of my eyes, I have been obliged to use a writing-case made for the blind, which does not permit the writer to see his own manuscript. Nor have I ever corrected, or even read, my own original draft. As the chirography, under these disadvantages, has been too often careless and obscure, occasional errors, even with the utmost care of my secretary, must have necessarily occurred in the transcription, somewhat increased by the barbarous phraseology imported from my Mexican authorities. I cannot expect that these errors have always been detected even by the vigilant eye of the perspicacious critic to whom the proof-sheets have been subjected.

In the preface to *The History of Ferdinand and Isabella,* I lamented that, while occupied with that subject, two of its most attractive parts had engaged the attention of the most popular of American authors, Washington Irving. By a singular chance, something like the reverse of this has taken place in the composition of the present history, and I have found myself unconsciously taking up ground which he was preparing to occupy. It was not till I had become master of my rich collection of materials, that I was acquainted with this circumstance; and had he persevered in his design, I should unhesitatingly have abandoned my own, if not from courtesy, at least from policy; for, though armed with the weapons of Achilles, this could give me no hope of success in a competition with Achilles himself. But no sooner was that distinguished writer informed of the preparations I had made, than, with the gentlemanly spirit which will surprise no one who has the pleasure of his acquaintance, he instantly announced to me his intention of leaving the subject open to me. While I do but justice to Mr. Irving by this statement, I feel the prejudice it does to myself in the unavailing regret I am exciting in the bosom of the reader.

I must not conclude this Preface, too long protracted as it is already, without a word of acknowledgment to my friend George Ticknor, Esq. —the friend of many years—for his patient revision of my manuscript; a labour of love, the worth of which those only can estimate who are acquainted with his extraordinary erudition and his nice critical taste. If I have reserved his name for the last in the list of those to whose good offices I am indebted, it is most assuredly not because I value his services least.

WILLIAM H. PRESCOTT.

BOSTON, *October* 1, 1843.

CONTENTS

DISCOVERY OF MEXICO

MARCH TO MEXICO

SIEGE AND SURRENDER OF MEXICO

INTRODUCTION

ONE HISTORIAN of the conquest of Mexico was as heroic as the conqueror. While Prescott was still at Harvard he was struck in the eye by a crust of bread thrown by a skylarking student in the Commons. The accident not only made the victim almost blind but gave his nervous system such a shock that he was never able to enter upon any active career. Although his grandfather had commanded the Americans at Bunker Hill and his father was an eminent lawyer in Boston, Prescott had to become a secluded scholar, seldom well enough to leave his native city or even his house, dependent on the eyes of others for most of his enormous reading, and strictly limited to at most a few hours' work a day. Yet with magnificent courage he undertook to become the historian of Spain during its most splendid period. As an American he found himself particularly interested in the exploits of Spain in the New World. Besides his *History of the Reign of Ferdinand and Isabella,* he wrote also the *History of the Conquest of Mexico* and the *History of the Conquest of Peru.* Fortunately he was enabled by his wealth to obtain the countless books he needed and to have many manuscripts copied for him in Spain, as well as to engage the services of skilful assistants. All this, however, would not have made him the great historian he became if he had not had the audacity and persistence which carried him along as the same qualities carried Cortez to the City of Mexico.

Ever since 1843 when the *Conquest of Mexico* was first published, it has been praised and honored by all good judges and has been a stirring experience to many readers. Only its length has kept it from being still more widely read. Prescott made it long by including a first part on Aztec civilization and a third part on the subsequent career of Cortez. These parts are not necessary to the larger body of readers for whom this present book has been undertaken. Although Prescott put as much into his account of Aztec life and customs as anybody in his day knew or could know, so much has since then been discovered about them that his first part is no longer so valuable as it was. His narrative of Cortez's later life does not belong to the story of the conquest. Leaving these parts out therefore subtracts nothing from the book so far as its essential subject is concerned. The second part, here reprinted as Prescott wrote it, may still accurately be called a true history of the conquest of Mexico.

CARL VAN DOREN.

DISCOVERY OF MEXICO

CHAPTER I

Spain under Charles V—Progress of Discovery—Colonial Policy—Conquest of Cuba—Expeditions to Yucatan

1516–1518

IN THE beginning of the sixteenth century, Spain occupied perhaps the most prominent position on the theatre of Europe. The numerous states, into which she had been so long divided, were consolidated into one monarchy. The Moslem crescent, after reigning there for eight centuries, was no longer seen on her borders. The authority of the crown did not, as in later times, overshadow the inferior orders of the state. The people enjoyed the inestimable privilege of political representation, and exercised it with manly independence. The nation at large could boast as great a degree of constitutional freedom as any other, at that time, in Christendom. Under a system of salutary laws and an equitable administration, domestic tranquillity was secured, public credit established, trade, manufactures, and even the more elegant arts, began to flourish; while a higher education called forth the first blossoms of that literature, which was to ripen into so rich a harvest, before the close of the century. Arms abroad kept pace with arts at home. Spain found her empire suddenly enlarged, by important acquisitions, both in Europe and Africa, while a New World beyond the waters poured into her lap treasures of countless wealth, and opened an unbounded field for honourable enterprise.

Such was the condition of the kingdom at the close of the long and glorious reign of Ferdinand and Isabella, when, on the 23rd of January, 1516, the sceptre passed into the hands of their daughter Joanna, or rather their grandson, Charles the Fifth, who alone ruled the monarchy during the long and imbecile existence of his unfortunate mother. During the two years following Ferdinand's death, the regency, in the absence of Charles, was held by Cardinal Ximenes, a man whose intrepidity, extraordinary talents, and capacity for great enterprises, were accompanied by a haughty spirit, which made him too indifferent as to the means of their execution. His administration, therefore, notwithstanding the uprightness of his intentions, was, from his total disregard of forms, unfavourable to constitutional liberty; for respect of forms is an essential element of freedom. With all his faults, however, Ximenes was a Spaniard; and the object he had at heart was the good of his country.

It was otherwise on the arrival of Charles, who, after a long absence, came as a foreigner into the land of his fathers. (November, 1517.) His manners, sympathies, even his language, were foreign, for he spoke the Castilian with difficulty. He knew little of his native country, of the character of the people or their institutions. He seemed to care still less for them; while his natural reserve precluded that freedom of communication which might have counteracted, to some extent at least, the errors of education. In everything, in short, he was a foreigner; and resigned himself to the direction of his Flemish counsellors with a docility that gave little augury of his future greatness.

On his entrance into Castile, the young monarch was accompanied by a swarm of courtly sycophants, who settled, like locusts, on every place of profit and honour throughout the kingdom. A Fleming was made grand chancellor of Castile; another Fleming was placed in the archiepiscopal see of Toledo. They even ventured to profane the sanctity of the Cortés by intruding themselves on its deliberations. Yet that body did not tamely submit to these usurpations, but gave vent to its indignation in tones becoming the representatives of a free people.

The deportment of Charles, so different from that to which the Spaniards had been accustomed under the benign administration of Ferdinand and Isabella, closed all hearts against him; and, as his character came to be understood, instead of the spontaneous outpourings of loyalty, which usually greet the accession of a new and youthful sovereign, he was everywhere encountered by opposition and disgust. In Castile, and afterwards in Aragon, Catalonia, and Valencia, the commons hesitated to confer on him the title of *King* during the lifetime of his mother; and, though they eventually yielded this point, and associated his name with hers in the sovereignty, yet they reluctantly granted the supplies he demanded, and, when they did so, watched over their appropriation with a vigilance which left little to gratify the cupidity of the Flemings. The language of the legislature on these occasions, though temperate and respectful, breathes a spirit of resolute independence not to be found, probably, on the parliamentary records of any other nation at that period. No wonder that Charles should have early imbibed a disgust for these popular assemblies—the only bodies whence truths so unpalatable could find their way to the ears of the sovereign! Unfortunately, they had no influence on his conduct; till the discontent, long allowed to fester in secret, broke out into that sad war of the *comunidades,* which shook the state to its foundations, and ended in the subversion of its liberties.

The same pestilent foreign influence was felt, though much less sensibly, in the Colonial administration. This had been placed, in the preceding reign, under the immediate charge of the two great tribunals, the Council of the Indies, and the *Casa de Contratacion,* or India House at Seville. It was their business to further the progress of discovery, watch over the infant settlements, and adjust the disputes, which grew up in them. But the licences granted to private adventurers did more for the cause of discovery than the patronage of the crown or its officers. The long peace, enjoyed with slight interruption by Spain in the early part of the sixteenth century, was most auspicious for this; and the restless cavalier, who could no longer win laurels on the fields of Africa and Europe, turned with eagerness to the brilliant career opened to him beyond the ocean.

It is difficult for those of our time, as familiar from childhood with the most remote places on the globe as with those in their own neighbourhood, to picture to themselves the feelings of the men who lived in the sixteenth century. The dread mystery, which had so long hung over the great deep, had indeed been removed. It was no longer beset with the same undefined horrors as when Columbus launched his bold bark on its dark and unknown waters. A new and glorious world had been thrown open. But as to the precise spot where that world lay, its extent, its history, whether it were island or continent—of all this, they had very vague and confused conceptions. Many, in their ignorance, blindly adopted the erroneous conclusion into which the great Admiral had been led by his superior science—that the new countries were a part of Asia; and, as the mariner wandered among the Bahamas, or steered his caravel across the Caribbean seas, he fancied he was inhaling the rich odours of the spice-islands in the Indian Ocean. Thus every fresh discovery, interpreted by this previous delusion, served to confirm him in his error, or, at least, to fill his mind with new perplexities.

The career thus thrown open had all the fascinations of a desperate hazard, on which the adventurer staked all his hopes of fortune, fame, and life itself. It was not often, indeed, that he won the rich prize which he most coveted; but then he was sure to win the meed of glory, scarcely less dear to his chivalrous spirit; and, if he survived to return to his home, he had wonderful stories to recount, of perilous chances among the strange people he had visited, and the burning climes, whose rank fertility and magnificence of vegetation so far surpassed anything he had witnessed in his own. These reports added fresh fuel to imaginations already warmed by the study of those tales of chivalry which formed the favourite reading of the Spaniards at that period. Thus romance and reality acted on each other, and the soul of the Spaniard was exalted to that pitch of enthusiasm, which enabled him to encounter the terrible trials that lay in the path of the discoverer. Indeed, the life of the cavalier of that day was romance put into action. The story of his adventures in the New World forms one of the most remarkable pages in the history of man.

Under this chivalrous spirit of enterprise, the progress of discovery had extended, by the beginning of Charles the Fifth's reign, from the Bay of Honduras, along the winding shores of Darien, and the South American continent, to the Rio de la Plata. The mighty barrier of the Isthmus had been climbed, and the Pacific described, by Nuñez de Balboa, second only to Columbus in this valiant band of "ocean chivalry." The Bahamas and Caribbee Islands had been explored, as well as the Peninsula of Florida on the northern continent. To this latter point Sebastian Cabot had arrived in his descent along the coast from Labrador, in 1497. So that before 1518, the period when our narrative begins, the eastern borders of both the great continents had been surveyed through nearly their whole extent. The shores of the great Mexican Gulf, however, sweeping with a wide circuit far into the interior, remained still concealed, with the rich realms that lay beyond, from the eye of the navigator. The time had now come for their discovery.

The business of colonisation had kept pace with that of discovery. In several of the islands, and in various parts of Terra Firma, and in Darien, settlements had been established, under the control of governors who affected the state and authority of viceroys. Grants of land were assigned to the colonists, on which they raised the natural products of the soil, but gave still more attention to the sugar-cane, imported from the Canaries. Sugar, indeed, together with the beautiful dye-woods of the country and the precious metals, formed almost the only articles of export in the infancy of the colonies, which had not yet introduced those other staples of the West Indian commerce, which, in our day, constitute its principal wealth. Yet the precious metals, painfully gleaned from a few scanty sources, would have made poor returns, but for the gratuitous labour of the Indians.

The cruel system of *repartimientos,* or distribution of the Indians as slaves among the conquerors, had been suppressed by Isabella. Although subsequently countenanced by the government, it was under the most careful limitations. But it is impossible to licence crime by halves—to authorise injustice at all, and hope to regulate the measure of it. The eloquent remonstrances of the Dominicans—who devoted themselves to the good work of conversion in the New World with the same zeal that they showed for persecution in the Old—but, above all, those of Las Casas, induced the regent Ximenes to send out a commission with full powers to inquire into the alleged grievances, and to redress them. It had authority, moreover, to investigate the conduct of the civil officers, and to reform any abuses in their administration. This extraordinary commission consisted of three Hieronymite friars and an eminent jurist, all men of learning and unblemished piety.

They conducted the inquiry in a very dispassionate manner; but, after long deliberation, came to a conclusion most unfavourable to the demands of Las Casas, who insisted on the entire freedom of the natives. This conclusion they justified on the grounds that the Indians would not labour without compulsion, and that, unless they laboured, they could not be brought into communication with the whites, nor be converted to Christianity. Whatever we may think of this argument, it was doubtless urged with sincerity by its advocates, whose conduct through their whole administration places their motives above suspicion. They accompanied it with many careful provisions for the protection of the natives—but in vain. The simple people, accustomed all their days to a life of indolence and ease, sunk under the oppressions of their masters, and the population wasted away with even more frightful rapidity than did the aborigines in our own country, under the operation of other causes. It is not necessary to pursue these details further, into which I have been led by the desire to put the reader in possession of the general policy and state of affairs in the New World, at the period when the present narrative begins.

Of the islands, Cuba was the second discovered; but no attempt had been made to plant a colony there during the lifetime of Columbus; who, indeed, after skirting the whole extent of its southern coast, died in the conviction that it was part of the continent. At length, in 1511, Diego, the son and successor of the "Admiral," who still maintained the seat of government in Hispaniola, finding the mines much exhausted there, proposed to occupy the neighbouring island of Cuba, or Fernandina, as it was called, in compliment to the Spanish monarch. He prepared a small force for the conquest, which he placed under the command of Don Diego Velasquez; a man described by a contemporary, as "possessed of considerable experience in military affairs, having served seventeen years in the European wars; as honest, illustrious by his lineage and reputation, covetous of glory, and somewhat more covetous of wealth." The portrait was sketched by no unfriendly hand.

Velasquez, or rather his lieutenant Narvaez, who took the office on himself of scouring the country, met with no serious opposition from the inhabitants, who were of the same family with the effeminate natives of Hispaniola. The conquest, through the merciful interposition of Las Casas, "the protector of the Indians," who accompanied the army in its march, was effected without much bloodshed. One chief, indeed, named Hatuey, having fled originally from St. Domingo to escape the oppression of its invaders, made a desperate resistance, for which he was condemned by Velasquez to be burned alive. It was he who made that memorable reply, more eloquent than a volume of invective. When urged at the stake to embrace Christianity, that his soul might find admission into heaven, he inquired if the white men would go there. On being answered in the affirmative, he exclaimed, "Then I will not be a Christian; for I would not go again to a place where I must find men so cruel!"

After the conquest, Velasquez, now appointed governor, diligently occupied himself with measures for promoting the prosperity of the island. He formed a number of settlements, bearing the same names with the modern towns, and made St. Jago, on the south-east corner, the seat of government. He invited settlers by liberal grants of land and slaves. He encouraged them to cultivate the soil, and gave particular attention to the sugar-cane, so profitable an article of commerce in later times. He was, above all, intent on working the gold mines, which promised better returns than those in Hispaniola. The affairs of his government did not prevent him, meanwhile, from casting many a wistful glance at the discoveries going forward on the continent, and he longed for an opportunity to embark in these golden adventures himself. Fortune gave him the occasion he desired.

An *hidalgo* of Cuba, named Hernandez de Cordova, sailed with three vessels on an expedition to one of the neighbouring Bahama Islands, in quest of Indian slaves (February 8, 1517). He encountered a succession of heavy gales which drove him far out of his course, and at the end of three weeks he found himself on a strange but unknown coast. On landing and asking the name of the country, he was answered by the natives, *"Tectetan,"* meaning, "I do not understand you"—but which the Spaniards, misinterpreting into the name of the place, easily corrupted into Yucatan. Some writers give a different etymology. Such mistakes, however, were not uncommon with the early discoverers, and have been the origin of many a name on the American continent.

Cordova had landed on the north-eastern end of the peninsula, at Cape Catoche. He was astonished at the size and solid material of the buildings constructed of stone and lime, so different from the frail tenements of reeds and rushes which formed the habitations of the islanders. He was struck, also, with the higher cultivation of the soil, and with the delicate texture of the cotton garments and gold ornaments of the natives. Everything indicated a civilisation far superior to anything he had before witnessed in the New World. He saw the evidence of a different race, moreover, in the warlike spirit of the people. Rumours of the Spaniards had, perhaps, preceded them, as they were repeatedly asked if they came from the east; and wherever they landed, they were met with the most deadly hostility. Cordova himself, in one of his skirmishes with the Indians, received more than a dozen wounds, and one only of his party escaped unhurt. At length, when he had coasted the peninsula as far as Campeachy, he returned to Cuba, which he reached after an absence of several months, having suffered all the extremities of ill, which these pioneers of the ocean were sometimes called to endure, and which none but the most courageous spirit could have survived. As it was, half the original number, consisting of one hundred and ten men, perished, including their brave commander, who died soon after his return. The reports he had brought back of the country, and still more, the specimens of curiously wrought gold, convinced Velasquez of the importance of this discovery, and he prepared with all dispatch to avail himself of it.

He accordingly fitted out a little squadron of four vessels for the newly discovered lands, and placed it under the command of his nephew, Juan de Grijalva, a man on whose probity, prudence, and attachment to himself he knew he could rely. The fleet left the port of St. Jago de Cuba, May 1, 1518. It took the course pursued by Cordova, but was driven somewhat to the south, the first land that it made being the island of Cozumel. From this quarter Grijalva soon passed over to the continent and coasted the peninsula, touching at the same places as his predecessor. Everywhere he was struck, like him, with the evidences of a higher civilisation, especially in the architecture; as he well might be, since this was the region of those extraordinary remains which have become recently the subject of so much speculation. He was astonished, also, at the sight of large stone crosses, evidently objects of worship, which he met with in various places. Reminded by these circumstances of his own country, he gave the peninsula the name "New Spain," a name since appropriated to a much wider extent of territory.

Wherever Grijalva landed, he experienced the same unfriendly reception as Cordova, though he suffered less, being better prepared to meet it. In the *Rio de Tabasco* or *Grijalva,* as it is often called, after him, he held an amicable conference with a chief, who gave him a number of gold plates fashioned into a sort of armour. As he wound round the Mexican coast, one of his captains, Pedro de Alvarado, afterwards famous in the Conquest, entered a river, to which he also left his own name. In a neighbouring stream, called the *Rio de Vanderas,* or "River of Banners," from the ensigns displayed by the natives on its borders, Grijalva had the first communication with the Mexicans themselves.

The cacique who ruled over this province had received notice of the approach of the Europeans, and of their extraordinary appearance. He was anxious to collect all the information he could respecting them, and the motives of their visit, that he might transmit them to his master, the Aztec emperor. A friendly conference took place between the parties on shore, where Grijalva landed with all his force, so as to make a suitable impression on the mind of the barbaric chief. The interview lasted some hours, though, as there was no one on either side to interpret the language of the other, they could communicate only by signs. They, however, interchanged presents, and the Spaniards had the satisfaction of receiving, for a few worthless toys and trinkets, a rich treasure of jewels, gold ornaments and vessels, of the most fantastic forms and workmanship.

Grijalva now thought that in this successful traffic—successful beyond his most sanguine expectations—he had accomplished the chief object of his mission. He steadily refused the solicitations of his followers to plant a colony on the spot—a work of no little difficulty in so populous and powerful a country as this appeared to be. To this, indeed, he was inclined, but deemed it contrary to his instructions, which limited him to barter with the natives. He therefore despatched Alvarado in one of the caravels back to Cuba, with the treasure and such intelligence as he had gleaned of the great empire in the interior, and then pursued his voyage along the coast.

He touched at St. Juan de Ulua, and at the *Isla de los Sacrificios,* so called by him from the bloody remains of human victims found in one of the temples. He then held on his course as far as the province of Panuco, where finding some difficulty in doubling a boisterous headland, he returned on his track, and after an absence of nearly six months, reached Cuba in safety. Grijalva has the glory of being the first navigator who set foot on the Mexican soil, and opened an intercourse with the Aztecs.

On reaching the island, he was surprised to learn that another and more formidable armament had been fitted out to follow up his own discoveries, and to find orders at the same time from the governor, couched in no very courteous language, to repair at once to St. Jago. He was received by that personage, not merely with coldness, but with reproaches for having neglected so fair an opportunity of establishing a colony in the country he had visited. Velasquez was one of those captious spirits, who, when things do not go exactly to their minds, are sure to shift the responsibility of the failure from their own shoulders, where it should lie, to those of others. He had an ungenerous nature, says an old writer, credulous, and easily moved to suspicion. In the present instance it was most unmerited. Grijalva, naturally a modest, unassuming person, had acted in obedience to the instructions of his commander, given before sailing; and had done this in opposition to his own judgment and the importunities of his followers. His conduct merited anything but censure from his employer.

When Alvarado had returned to Cuba with his golden freight, and the accounts of the rich empire of Mexico which he had gathered from the natives, the heart of the governor swelled with rapture as he saw his dreams of avarice and ambition so likely to be realised. Impatient of the long absence of Grijalva, he despatched a vessel in search of him under the command of Olid, a cavalier, who took an important part afterwards in the Conquest. Finally he resolved to fit out another armament on a sufficient scale to insure the subjugation of the country.

He previously solicited authority for this from the Hieronymite commission in St. Domingo. He then despatched his chaplain to Spain with the royal share of the gold brought from Mexico, and a full account of the intelligence gleaned there. He set forth his own manifold services, and solicited from the court full powers to go on with the conquest and colonisation of the newly discovered regions. Before receiving an answer, he began his preparations for the armament, and, first of all, endeavoured to find a suitable person to share the expense of it, and to take the command. Such a person he found, after some difficulty and delay, in Hernando Cortés; the man of all others best calculated to achieve this great enterprise—the last man to whom Velasquez, could he have foreseen the results, would have confided it.

CHAPTER II

Hernando Cortés—His Early Life—Visits the New World—
His Residence in Cuba—Difficulties with Velasquez—
Armada Intrusted to Cortés

1518

HERNANDO CORTÉS was born at Medellin, a town in the south-east corner of Estremadura, in 1485. He came of an ancient and respectable family; and historians have gratified the national vanity by tracing it up to the Lombard kings, whose descendants crossed the Pyrenees, and established themselves in Aragon under the Gothic monarchy. This royal genealogy was not found out till Cortés had acquired a name which would confer distinction on any descent, however noble. His father, Martin Cortés de Monroy, was a captain of infantry, in moderate circumstances, but a man of unblemished honour; and both he and his wife, Doña Catalina Pizarro Altamirano, appear to have been much regarded for their excellent qualities.

In his infancy Cortés is said to have had a feeble constitution, which strengthened as he grew older. At fourteen, he was sent to Salamanca, as his father, who conceived great hopes from his quick and showy parts, proposed to educate him for the law, a profession which held out better inducements to the young aspirant than any other. The son, however, did not conform to these views. He showed little fondness for books, and after loitering away two years at college, returned home, to the great chagrin of his parents. Yet his time had not been wholly misspent, since he had laid up a little store of Latin, and learned to write good prose, and even verses "of some estimation, considering"—as an old writer quaintly remarks—"Cortés as the author." He now passed his days in the idle, unprofitable manner of one who, too wilful to be guided by others, proposes no object to himself. His buoyant spirits were continually breaking out in troublesome frolics and capricious humours, quite at variance with the orderly habits of his father's household. He showed a particular inclination for the military profession, or rather for the life of adventure to which in those days it was sure to lead. And when, at the age of seventeen, he proposed to enrol himself under the banners of the Great Captain, his parents, probably thinking a life of hardship and hazard abroad preferable to one of idleness at home, made no objection.

The youthful cavalier, however, hesitated whether to seek his fortunes under that victorious chief, or in the New World, where gold as well as glory was to be won, and where the very dangers had a mystery and romance in them inexpressibly fascinating to a youthful fancy. It was in this direction, accordingly, that the hot spirits of that day found a vent, especially from that part of the country where Cortés lived, the neighbourhood of Seville and Cadiz, the focus of nautical enterprise. He decided on this latter course, and an opportunity offered in the splendid armament fitted out under Don Nicolas de Ovando, successor to Columbus. An unlucky accident defeated the purpose of Cortés.

As he was scaling a high wall, one night, which gave him access to the apartment of a lady with whom he was engaged in an intrigue, the stones gave way, and he was thrown down with much violence and buried under the ruins. A severe contusion, though attended with no other serious consequences, confined him to his bed till after the departure of the fleet.

Two years longer he remained at home, profiting little, as it would seem, from the lesson he had received. At length he availed himself of another opportunity presented by the departure of a small squadron of vessels bound to the Indian islands. He was nineteen years of age when he bade adieu to his native shores in 1504—the same year in which Spain lost the best and greatest in her long line of princes, Isabella the Catholic.

The vessel in which Cortés sailed was commanded by one Alonso Quintero. The fleet touched at the Canaries, as was common in the outward passage. While the other vessels were detained there taking in supplies, Quintero secretly stole out by night from the island, with the design of reaching Hispaniola, and securing the market, before the arrival of his companions. A furious storm which he encountered, however, dismasted his ship, and he was obliged to return to port and refit. The convoy consented to wait for their unworthy partner, and after a short detention they all sailed in company again. But the faithless Quintero, as they drew near the islands, availed himself once more of the darkness of the night, to leave the squadron with the same purpose as before. Unluckily for him, he met with a succession of heavy gales and head winds, which drove him from his course, and he wholly lost his reckoning. For many days the vessel was tossed about, and all on board were filled with apprehensions, and no little indignation against the author of their calamities. At length they were cheered one morning with the sight of a white dove, which, wearied by its flight, lighted on the topmast. The biographers of Cortés speak of it as a miracle. Fortunately it was no miracle, but a very natural occurrence, showing incontestably that they were near land. In a short time, by taking the direction of the bird's flight, they reached the island of Hispaniola; and, on coming into port, the worthy master had the satisfaction to find his companions arrived before him, and their cargoes already sold.

Immediately on landing, Cortés repaired to the house of the governor, to whom he had been personally known in Spain. Ovando was absent on an expedition into the interior, but the young man was kindly received by the secretary, who assured him there would be no doubt of his obtaining a liberal grant of land to settle on. "But I came to get gold," replied Cortés, "not to till the soil like a peasant."

On the governor's return, Cortés consented to give up his roving thoughts, at least for a time, as the other laboured to convince him that he would be more likely to realise his wishes from the slow, indeed, but sure, returns of husbandry, where the soil and the labourers were a free gift to the planter, than by taking his chance in the lottery of adventure, in which there were so many blanks to a prize. He accordingly received a grant of land, with a *repartimiento* of Indians, and was appointed notary of the town or settlement of Açua. His graver pursuits, however, did not prevent his indulgence of the amorous propensities which belong to the sunny clime where he was born; and this frequently involved him in affairs of honour, from which, though an expert swordsman, he carried away scars that accompanied him to his grave. He occasionally, moreover, found the means of breaking up the monotony of his way of life by engaging in the military expeditions which, under the command of Ovando's lieutenant, Diego Velasquez, were employed to suppress the insurrections of the natives. In this school the young adventurer first studied the wild tactics of Indian warfare; he became familiar with toil and danger, and with those deeds of cruelty which have too often, alas! stained the bright scutcheons of the Castilian chivalry in the New World. He was only prevented by illness—a most fortunate one, on this occasion—from embarking in Nicuessa's expedition, which furnished a tale of woe, not often matched in the annals of Spanish discovery. Providence reserved him for higher ends.

At length, in 1511, when Velasquez undertook the conquest of Cuba, Cortés willingly abandoned his quiet life for the stirring scenes there opened, and took part in the expedition. He displayed throughout the invasion an activity and courage that won him the approbation of the commander; while his free and cordial manners, his good humour, and lively sallies of wit made him the favourite of the soldiers. "He gave little evidence," says a contemporary, "of the great qualities which he afterwards showed." It is probable these qualities were not known to himself; while to a common observer his careless manners and jocund repartees might well seem incompatible with anything serious or profound; as the real depth of the current is not suspected under the light play and sunny sparkling of the surface.

After the reduction of the island, Cortés seems to have been held in great favour by Velasquez, now appointed its governor. According to Las Casas, he was made one of his secretaries. He still retained the same fondness for gallantry, for which his handsome person afforded obvious advantages, but which had more than once brought him into trouble in earlier life. Among the families who had taken up their residence in Cuba was one of the name of Xuarez, from Granada in Old Spain. It consisted of a brother, and four sisters remarkable for their beauty. With one of them, named Catalina, the susceptible heart of the young soldier became enamoured. How far the intimacy was carried is not quite certain. But it appears he gave his promise to marry her—a promise which, when the time came, and reason, it may be, had got the better of passion, he showed no alacrity in keeping. He resisted, indeed, all remonstrances to this effect from the lady's family, backed by the governor, and somewhat sharpened, no doubt, in the latter by the particular interest he took in one of the fair sisters, who is said not to have repaid it with ingratitude.

Whether the rebuke of Velasquez, or some other cause of disgust, rankled in the breast of Cortés, he now became cold toward his patron, and connected himself with a disaffected party tolerably numerous in the island. They were in the habit of meeting at his house and brooding over their causes of discontent, chiefly founded, it would appear, on what they conceived an ill requital of their services in the distribution of lands and offices. It may well be imagined, that it could have been no easy task for the ruler of one of these colonies, however discreet and well intentioned, to satisfy the indefinite cravings of speculators and adventurers, who swarmed, like so many famished harpies, in the track of discovery in the New World.

The malcontents determined to lay their grievances before the higher authorities in Hispaniola, from whom Velasquez had received his commission. The voyage was one of some hazard, as it was to be made in an open boat, across an arm of the sea, eighteen leagues wide; and they fixed on Cortés, with whose fearless spirit they were well acquainted, as the fittest man to undertake it. The conspiracy got wind, and came to the governor's ears before the departure of the envoy, whom he instantly caused to be seized, loaded with fetters, and placed in strict confinement. It is even said, he would have hung him, but for the interposition of his friends. The fact is not incredible. The governors of these little territories, having entire control over the fortunes of their subjects, enjoyed an authority far more despotic than that of the sovereign himself. They were generally men of rank and personal consideration; the distance from the mother country withdrew their conduct from searching scrutiny, and, when that did occur, they usually had interest and means of corruption at command, sufficient to shield them from punishment. The Spanish colonial history, in its earlier stages, affords striking instances of the extraordinary assumption and abuse of powers by these petty potentates; and the sad fate of Vasquez Nuñez de Balboa, the illustrious discoverer of the Pacific, though the most signal, is by no means a solitary example that the greatest services could be requited by persecution and an ignominious death.

The governor of Cuba, however, although irascible and suspicious in his nature, does not seem to have been vindictive, nor particularly cruel. In the present instance, indeed, it may well be doubted whether the blame would not be more reasonably charged on the unfounded expectations of his followers than on himself.

Cortés did not long remain in durance. He contrived to throw back one of the bolts of his fetters; and, after extricating his limbs, succeeded in forcing open a window with the irons so as to admit of his escape. He was lodged on the second floor of the building, and was able to let himself down to the pavement without injury, and unobserved. He then made the best of his way to a neighbouring church, where he claimed privilege of sanctuary.

Velasquez, though incensed at his escape, was afraid to violate the sanctity of the place by employing force. But he stationed a guard in the neighbourhood, with orders to seize the fugitive, if he should forget himself so far as to leave the sanctuary. In a few days this happened. As Cortés was carelessly standing without the walls in front of the building, an *alguacil* suddenly sprung on him from behind and pinioned his arms, while others rushed in and secured him. This man, whose name was Juan Escudero, was afterwards hung by Cortés for some offence in New Spain.

The unlucky prisoner was again put in irons, and carried on board a vessel to sail the next morning for Hispaniola, there to undergo his trial. Fortune favoured him once more. He succeeded after much difficulty and no little pain, in passing his feet through the rings which shackled them. He then came cautiously on deck, and, covered by the darkness of the night, stole quietly down the side of the ship into a boat that lay floating below. He pushed off from the vessel with as little noise as possible. As he drew near the shore, the stream became rapid and turbulent. He hesitated to trust his boat to it; and, as he was an excellent swimmer, prepared to breast it himself, and boldly plunged into the water. The current was strong, but the arm of a man struggling for life was stronger; and after buffeting the waves till he was nearly exhausted, he succeeded in gaining a landing; when he sought refuge in the same sanctuary which had protected him before. The facility with which Cortés a second time effected his escape, may lead one to doubt the fidelity of his guards; who perhaps looked on him as the victim of persecution, and felt the influence of those popular manners which seem to have gained him friends in every society into which he was thrown.

For some reason not explained—perhaps from policy—he now relinquished his objections to the marriage with Catalina Xuarez. He thus secured the good offices of her family. Soon afterwards the governor himself relented, and became reconciled to his unfortunate enemy. A strange story is told in connection with this event. It is said, his proud spirit refused to accept the proffers of reconciliation made him by Velasquez; and that one evening, leaving the sanctuary, he presented himself unexpectedly before the latter in his own quarters, when on a military excursion at some distance from the capital. The governor, startled by the sudden apparition of his enemy completely armed before him, with some dismay inquired the meaning of it. Cortés answered by insisting on a full explanation of his previous conduct. After some hot discussion the interview terminated amicably; the parties embraced, and, when a messenger arrived to announce the escape of Cortés, he found him in the apartments of his Excellency, where, having retired to rest, both were actually sleeping in the same bed! The anecdote is repeated without distrust by more than one biographer of Cortés. It is not very probable, however, that a haughty irascible man like Velasquez should have given such uncommon proofs of condescension and familiarity to one, so far beneath him in station, with whom he had been so recently in deadly feud; nor, on the other hand, that Cortés should have had the silly temerity to brave the lion in his den, where a single nod would have sent him to the gibbet— and that too with as little compunction or fear of consequences as would have attended the execution of an Indian slave.

The reconciliation with the governor, however brought about, was permanent. Cortés, though not re-established in the office of secretary, received a liberal *repartimiento* of Indians, and an ample territory in the neighbourhood of St. Jago, of which he was soon after made *alcalde*. He now lived almost wholly on his estate, devoting himself to agriculture, with more zeal than formerly. He stocked his plantation with different kinds of cattle, some of which were first introduced by him into Cuba. He wrought, also, the gold mines which fell to his share, and which in this island promised better returns than those in Hispaniola. By this course of industry he found himself in a few years master of some two or three thousand *castellanos,* a large sum for one in his situation. "God, who alone knows at what cost of Indian lives it was obtained," exclaims Las Casas, "will take account of it!" His days glided smoothly away in these tranquil pursuits, and in the society of his beautiful wife, who, how-ever ineligible as a connection, from the inferiority of her condition, appears to have fulfilled all the relations of a faithful and affectionate partner. Indeed, he was often heard to say at this time, as the good bishop above quoted remarks, "that he lived as happily with her as if she had been the daughter of a duchess." Fortune gave him the means in after life of verifying the truth of his assertion.

Such was the state of things, when Alvarado returned with the tidings of Grijalva's discoveries, and the rich fruits of his traffic with the natives. The news spread like wildfire throughout the island; for all saw in it the promise of more important results than any hitherto obtained. The gov-ernor, as already noticed, resolved to follow up the track of discovery with a more considerable armament; and he looked around for a proper person to share the expense of it, and to take the command.

Several hidalgos presented themselves, whom, from want of proper qualifications, or from his distrust of their assuming an independence of their employer, he, one after another, rejected. There were two persons in St. Jago in whom he placed great confidence—Amador de Lares, the *contador,* or royal treasurer, and his own secretary, Andres de Duero. Cortés was also in close intimacy with both these persons, and he availed himself of it to prevail on them to recommend him as a suitable person to be intrusted with the expedition. It is said, he reinforced the proposal by promising a liberal share of the proceeds of it. However this may be, the parties urged his selection by the governor with all the eloquence of which they were capable. That officer had had ample experience of the capacity and courage of the candidate. He knew, too, that he had acquired a fortune which would enable him to co-operate materially in fitting out the armament. His popularity in the island would speedily attract followers to his standard. All past animosities had long since been buried in oblivion, and the confidence he was now to repose in him would insure his fidelity and gratitude. He lent a willing ear, therefore, to the recommendation of his counsellors, and, sending for Cortés, announced his purpose of making him captain-general of the armada.

Cortés had now attained the object of his wishes—the object for which his soul had panted, ever since he had set foot in the New World. He was no longer to be condemned to a life of mercenary drudgery; nor to be cooped up within the precincts of a petty island; but he was to be placed on a new and independent theatre of action, and a boundless perspective was opened to his view, which might satisfy not merely the wildest cravings of avarice, but, to a bold aspiring spirit like his, the far more important cravings of ambition. He fully appreciated the importance of the late discoveries, and read in them the existence of the great empire in the far West, dark hints of which had floated from time to time in the islands, and of which more certain glimpses had been caught by those who had reached the continent. This was the country intimated to the "Great Admiral" in his visit to Honduras in 1502, and which he might have reached, had he held on a northern course, instead of striking to the south in quest of an imaginary strait. As it was, "he had but opened the gate," to use his own bitter expression, "for others to enter." The time had at length come when they were to enter it; and the young adventurer, whose magic lance was to dissolve the spell which had so long hung over these mysterious regions, now stood ready to assume the enterprise.

From this hour the deportment of Cortés seemed to undergo a change. His thoughts, instead of evaporating in empty levities or idle flashes of merriment, were wholly concentrated on the great object to which he was devoted. His elastic spirits were shown in cheering and stimulating the companions of his toilsome duties, and he was roused to a generous enthusiasm, of which even those who knew him best had not conceived him capable. He applied at once all the money in his possession to fitting out the armament. He raised more by the mortgage of his estates, and by giving his obligations to some wealthy merchants of the place, who relied for their reimbursement on the success of the expedition; and, when his own credit was exhausted, he availed himself of that of his friends.

The funds thus acquired he expended in the purchase of vessels, provisions, and military stores, while he invited recruits by offers of assistance to such as were too poor to provide for themselves, and by the additional promise of a liberal share of the anticipated profits.

All was now bustle and excitement in the little town of St. Jago. Some were busy in refitting the vessels and getting them ready for the voyage; some in providing naval stores; others in converting their own estates into money in order to equip themselves; every one seemed anxious to contribute in some way or other to the success of the expedition. Six ships, some of them of a large size, had already been procured; and three hundred recruits enrolled themselves in the course of a few days, eager to seek their fortunes under the banner of this daring and popular chieftain.

How far the governor contributed towards the expenses of the outfit is not very clear. If the friends of Cortés are to be believed, nearly the whole burden fell on him; since, while he supplied the squadron without remuneration, the governor sold many of his own stores at an exorbitant profit. Yet it does not seem probable that Velasquez, with such ample means at his command, should have thrown on his deputy the burden of the expedition; nor that the latter, had he done so, could have been in a condition to meet these expenses, amounting, as we are told, to more than twenty thousand gold ducats. Still it cannot be denied that an ambitious man like Cortés, who was to reap all the glory of the enterprise, would very naturally be less solicitous to count the gains of it, than his employer, who, inactive at home, and having no laurels to win, must look on the pecuniary profits as his only recompense. The question gave rise, some years later, to a furious litigation between the parties, with which it is not necessary at present to embarrass the reader.

It is due to Velasquez to state, that the instructions delivered by him for the conduct of the expedition cannot be charged with a narrow or mercenary spirit. The first object of the voyage was to find Grijalva, after which the two commanders were to proceed in company together. Reports had been brought back by Cordova, on his return from the first visit to Yucatan, that six Christians were said to be lingering in captivity in the interior of the country. It was supposed they might belong to the party of the unfortunate Nicuessa, and orders were given to find them out, if possible, and restore them to liberty. But the great object of the expedition was barter with the natives. In pursuing this, special care was to be taken that they should receive no wrong, but be treated with kindness and humanity. Cortés was to bear in mind, above all things, that the object which the Spanish monarch had most at heart was the conversion of the Indians. He was to impress on them the grandeur and goodness of his royal master, to invite them "to give in their allegiance to him, and to manifest it by regaling him with such comfortable presents of gold, pearls, and precious stones as, by showing their own good will, would secure his favour and protection." He was to make an accurate survey of the coast, sounding its bays and inlets for the benefit of future navigators. He was to acquaint himself with the natural products of the country, with the character of its different races, their institutions and progress in civilisation; and he was to send home minute accounts of all these, together with such articles as he should obtain in his intercourse with them. Finally, he was to take *the most careful care* to omit nothing that might redound to the service of God or his sovereign.

Such was the general tenor of the instructions given to Cortés, and they must be admitted to provide for the interests of science and humanity, as well as for those which had reference only to a commercial speculation. It may seem strange, considering the discontent shown by Velasquez with his former captain, Grijalva, for not colonising, that no directions should have been given to that effect here. But he had not yet received from Spain the warrant for investing his agents with such powers; and that which had been obtained from the Hieronymite fathers in Hispaniola conceded only the right to traffic with the natives. The commission at the same time recognised the authority of Cortés as captain-general of the expedition.

CHAPTER III

1519

THE IMPORTANCE given to Cortés by his new position, and perhaps a somewhat more lofty bearing, gradually gave uneasiness to the naturally suspicious temper of Velasquez, who became apprehensive that his officer, when away where he would have the power, might also have the inclination, to throw off his dependence on him altogether. An accidental circumstance at this time heightened these suspicions. A mad fellow, his jester, one of those crack-brained wits—half wit, half fool—who formed in those days a common appendage to every great man's establishment, called out to the governor, as he was taking his usual walk one morning with Cortés towards the port, "Have a care, master Velasquez, or we shall have to go a-hunting, some day or other, after this same captain of ours!" "Do you hear what the rogue says?" exclaimed the governor to his companion. "Do not heed him," said Cortés, "he is a saucy knave, and deserves a good whipping." The words sunk deep, however, in the mind of Velasquez—as, indeed, true jests are apt to stick.

There were not wanting persons about his Excellency, who fanned the latent embers of jealousy into a blaze. These worthy gentlemen, some of them kinsmen of Velasquez, who probably felt their own deserts somewhat thrown into the shade by the rising fortunes of Cortés, reminded the governor of his ancient quarrel with that officer, and of the little probability that affronts so keenly felt at the time could ever be forgotten. By these and similar suggestions, and by misconstructions of the present conduct of Cortés, they wrought on the passions of Velasquez to such a degree, that he resolved to intrust the expedition to other hands.

He communicated his design to his confidential advisers, Lares and Duero, and these trusty personages reported it without delay to Cortés,

23

although, "to a man of half his penetration," says Las Casas, "the thing would have been readily divined from the governor's altered demeanour." The two functionaries advised their friend to expedite matters as much as possible, and to lose no time in getting his fleet ready for sea, if he would retain the command of it. Cortés showed the same prompt decision on this occasion, which more than once afterwards in a similar crisis gave the direction to his destiny.

He had not yet got his complement of men, nor of vessels; and was very inadequately provided with supplies of any kind. But he resolved to weigh anchor that very night. He waited on his officers, informed them of his purpose, and probably of the cause of it; and at midnight, when the town was hushed in sleep, they all went quietly on board, and the little squadron dropped down the bay. First, however, Cortés had visited the person whose business it was to supply the place with meat, and relieved him of all his stock in hand, notwithstanding his complaint that the city must suffer for it on the morrow, leaving him, at the same time, in payment, a massive gold chain of much value, which he wore round his neck.

Great was the amazement of the good citizens of St. Jago, when, at dawn, they saw that the fleet, which they knew was so ill prepared for the voyage, had left its moorings and was busily getting under way. The tidings soon came to the ears of his Excellency, who, springing from his bed, hastily dressed himself, mounted his horse, and, followed by his retinue, galloped down to the quay. Cortés, as soon as he descried their approach, entered an armed boat, and came within speaking distance of the shore. "And is it thus you part from me!" exclaimed Velasquez; "a courteous way of taking leave, truly!" "Pardon me," answered Cortés, "time presses, and there are some things that should be done before they are even thought of. Has your Excellency any commands?" But the mortified governor had no commands to give; and Cortés, politely waving his hand, returned to his vessel, and the little fleet instantly made sail for the port of Macaca, about fifteen leagues distant. (November 18, 1516.) Velasquez rode back to his house to digest his chagrin as he best might; satisfied, probably, that he had made at least two blunders; one in appointing Cortés to the command—the other in attempting to deprive him of it. For, if it be true, that by giving our confidence by halves, we can scarcely hope to make a friend, it is equally true, that, by withdrawing it when given, we shall make an enemy.

This clandestine departure of Cortés has been severely criticised by some writers, especially by Las Casas. Yet much may be urged in vindication of his conduct. He had been appointed to the command by the voluntary act of the governor, and this had been fully ratified by the authorities of Hispaniola. He had at once devoted all his resources to the undertaking, incurring, indeed, a heavy debt in addition. He was now to be deprived of his commission, without any misconduct having been alleged or at least proved against him. Such an event must overwhelm him in irretrievable ruin, to say nothing of the friends from whom he had so largely borrowed, and the followers who had embarked their fortunes in the expedition on the faith of his commanding it. There are few persons, probably, who under these circumstances would have felt called tamely to acquiesce in the sacrifice of their hopes to a groundless and arbitrary whim. The most to have been expected from Cortés was that he should feel obliged to provide faithfully for the interests of his employer in the conduct of the enterprise. How far he felt the force of this obligation will appear in the sequel.

From Macaca, where Cortés laid in such stores as he could obtain from the royal farms, and which, he said, he considered as "a loan from the king," he proceeded to Trinidad; a more considerable town, on the southern coast of Cuba. Here he landed, and erecting his standard in front of his quarters, made proclamation, with liberal offers to all who would join the expedition. Volunteers came in daily, and among them more than a hundred of Grijalva's men, just returned from their voyage, and willing to follow up the discovery under an enterprising leader. The fame of Cortés attracted, also, a number of cavaliers of family and distinction, some of whom, having accompanied Grijalva, brought much information valuable for the present expedition. Among these hidalgos may be mentioned Pedro de Alvarado and his brothers, Cristoval de Olid, Alonso de Avila, Juan Velasquez de Leon, a near relation of the governor, Alonso Hernandez de Puertocarrero, and Gonzalo de Sandoval— all of them men who took a most important part in the Conquest. Their presence was of great moment, as giving consideration to the enterprise; and, when they entered the little camp of the adventurers, the latter turned out to welcome them amidst lively strains of music and joyous salvos of artillery.

Cortés meanwhile was active in purchasing military stores and provisions. Learning that a trading vessel laden with grain and other commodities for the mines was off the coast, he ordered out one of his caravels to seize her and bring her into port. He paid the master in bills for both cargo and ship, and even persuaded this man, named Sedeño, who was wealthy, to join his fortunes to the expedition. He also despatched one of his officers, Diego de Ordaz, in quest of another ship, of which he had tidings, with instructions to seize it in like manner, and to meet him with it off Cape St. Antonio, the westerly point of the island. By this he effected another object, that of getting rid of Ordaz, who was one of the governor's household, and an inconvenient spy on his own actions.

While thus occupied, letters from Velasquez were received by the commander of Trinidad, requiring him to seize the person of Cortés, and to detain him, as he had been deposed from the command of the fleet, which was given to another. This functionary communicated his instructions to the principal officers in the expedition, who counselled him not to make the attempt, as it would undoubtedly lead to a commotion among the soldiers, that might end in laying the town in ashes. Verdugo thought it prudent to conform to this advice.

As Cortés was willing to strengthen himself by still further reinforcements, he ordered Alvarado with a small body of men to march across the country to the Havana, while he himself would sail round the westerly point of the island, and meet him there with the squadron. In this port he again displayed his standard, making the usual proclamation. He caused all the large guns to be brought on shore, and with the small arms and cross bows, to be put in order. As there was abundance of cotton raised in this neighbourhood, he had the jackets of the soldiers thickly quilted with it, for a defence against the Indian arrows, from which the troops in the former expeditions had grievously suffered. He distributed his men into eleven companies, each under the command of an experienced officer; and it was observed that, although several of the cavaliers in the service were the personal friends and even kinsmen of Velasquez, he appeared to treat them all with perfect confidence.

His principal standard was of black velvet embroidered with gold, and emblazoned with a red cross amidst flames of blue and white, with this motto in Latin beneath: "Friends, let us follow the Cross; and under this sign, if we have faith, we shall conquer." He now assumed more state in his own person and way of living, introducing a greater number of domestics and officers into his household, and placing it on a footing becoming a man of high station. This state he maintained through the rest of his life.

Cortés at this time was thirty-three, or perhaps thirty-four years of age. In stature he was rather above the middle size. His complexion was pale; and his large dark eyes gave an expression of gravity to his countenance, not to have been expected in one of his cheerful temperament. His figure was slender, at least until later life; but his chest was deep, his shoulders broad, his frame muscular and well-proportioned. It presented the union of agility and vigour which qualified him to excel in fencing, horsemanship, and the other generous exercises of chivalry. In his diet he was temperate, careless of what he ate, and drinking little; while to toil and privation he seemed perfectly indifferent. His dress, for he did not disdain the impression produced by such adventitious aids, was such as to set off his handsome person to advantage; neither gaudy nor striking, but rich. He wore few ornaments, and usually the same; but those were of great price. His manners, frank and soldier-like, concealed a most cool and calculating spirit. With his gayest humour there mingled a settled air of resolution, which made those who approached him feel they must obey; and which infused something like awe into the attachment of his most devoted followers. Such a combination, in which love was tempered by authority, was the one probably best calculated to inspire devotion in the rough and turbulent spirits among whom his lot was to be cast.

The character of Cortés seems to have undergone some change with change of circumstances; or to speak more correctly, the new scenes in which he was placed called forth qualities which before lay dormant in his bosom. There are some hardy natures that require the heats of excited action to unfold their energies; like the plants, which, closed to the mild influence of a temperate latitude, come to their full growth, and give forth their fruits, only in the burning atmosphere of the tropics. Such is the portrait left to us by his contemporaries of this remarkable man; the instrument selected by Providence to scatter terror among the barbarian monarchs of the Western world, and lay their empires in the dust!

Before the preparations were fully completed at the Havana, the commander of the place, Don Pedro Barba, received despatches from Velasquez ordering him to apprehend Cortés and to prevent the departure of his vessels; while another epistle from the same source was delivered to Cortés himself, requesting him to postpone his voyage till the governor could communicate with him, as he proposed, in person. "Never," exclaims Las Casas, "did I see so little knowledge of affairs shown, as in this letter of Diego Velasquez—that he should have imagined that a man, who had so recently put such an affront on him, would defer his departure at his bidding!" It was, indeed, hoping to stay the flight of the arrow by a word, after it had left the bow.

The captain-general, however, during his short stay had entirely conciliated the good will of Barba. And, if that officer had had the inclination, he knew he had not the power, to enforce his principal's orders, in the face of a resolute soldiery, incensed at this ungenerous persecution of their commander, and "all of whom," in the words of the honest chronicler who bore part in the expedition, "officers and privates, would have cheerfully laid down their lives for him." Barba contented himself, therefore, with explaining to Velasquez the impracticability of the attempt, and at the same time endeavoured to tranquillise his apprehensions by asserting his own confidence in the fidelity of Cortés. To this the latter added a communication of his own, couched "in the soft terms he knew so well how to use," in which he implored his Excellency to rely on his devotion to his interests, and concluded with the comfortable assurance that he and the whole fleet, God willing, would sail on the following morning.

Accordingly, on February 10, 1519, the little squadron got under way, and directed its course towards Cape St. Antonio, the appointed place of rendezvous. When all were brought together, the vessels were found to be eleven in number; one of them, in which Cortés himself went, was of a hundred tons' burden, three others were from seventy to eighty tons, the remainder were caravels and open brigantines. The whole was put under the direction of Antonio de Alaminos, as chief pilot; a veteran navigator, who had acted as pilot to Columbus in his last voyage, and to Cordova and Grijalva in the former expeditions to Yucatan.

Landing on the Cape and mustering his forces, Cortés found they amounted to one hundred and ten mariners, five hundred and fifty-three soldiers, including thirty-two crossbow-men, and thirteen arquebusiers, besides two hundred Indians of the island, and a few Indian women for menial offices. He was provided with ten heavy guns, four lighter pieces called falconets, and with a good supply of ammunition. He had, besides, sixteen horses. They were not easily procured; for the difficulty of transporting them across the ocean in the flimsy craft of that day made them rare and incredibly dear in the islands. But Cortés rightfully estimated the importance of cavalry, however small in number, both for their actual service in the field, and for striking terror into the savages. With so paltry a force did he enter on a conquest which even his stout heart must have shrunk from attempting with such means, had he but foreseen half its real difficulties!

Before embarking, Cortés addressed his soldiers in a short but animated harangue. He told them they were about to enter on a noble enterprise, one that would make their name famous to after ages. He was leading them to countries more vast and opulent than any yet visited by Europeans. "I hold out to you a glorious prize," continued the orator, "but it is to be won by incessant toil. Great things are achieved only by great exertions and glory was never the reward of sloth. If I have laboured hard and staked my all on this undertaking, it is for the love of that renown, which is the noblest recompense of man. But, if any among you covet riches more, be but true to me, as I will be true to you and to the occasion, and I will make you masters of such as our countrymen have never dreamed of! You are few in number, but strong in resolution; and, if this does not falter, doubt not but that the Almighty, who has never deserted the Spaniard in his contest with the infidel, will shield you, though encompassed by a cloud of enemies; for your cause is a *just cause,* and you are to fight under the banner of the Cross. Go forward then," he concluded, "with alacrity and confidence, and carry to a glorious issue the work so auspiciously begun."

The rough eloquence of the general, touching the various chords of ambition, avarice, and religious zeal, sent a thrill through the bosoms of his martial audience; and, receiving it with acclamations, they seemed eager to press forward under a chief who was to lead them not so much to battle, as to triumph.

Cortés was well satisfied to find his own enthusiasm so largely shared by his followers. Mass was then celebrated with the solemnities usual with the Spanish navigators, when entering on their voyages of discovery. The fleet was placed under the immediate protection of St. Peter, the patron saint of Cortés; and, weighing anchor, took its departure on February 18, 1519, for the coast of Yucatan.

CHAPTER IV

Voyage to Cozumel—Conversion of the Natives—Jeronimo de Aguilar—Army Arrives at Tabasco—Great Battle with the Indians—Christianity Introduced

1519

ORDERS WERE GIVEN for the vessels to keep as near together as possible, and to take the direction of the *capitana,* or admiral's ship, which carried a beacon-light in the stern during the night. But the weather, which had been favourable, changed soon after their departure, and one of those tempests set in, which at this season are often found in the latitudes of the West Indies. It fell with terrible force on the little navy, scattering it far asunder, dismantling some of the ships, and driving them all considerably south of their proposed destination.

Cortés, who had lingered behind to convoy a disabled vessel, reached the island of Cozumel last. On landing, he learned that one of his captains, Pedro de Alvarado, had availed himself of the short time he had been there to enter the temples, rifle them of their few ornaments, and, by his violent conduct, so far to terrify the simple natives, that they had fled for refuge into the interior of the island. Cortés, highly incensed at these rash proceedings, so contrary to the policy he had proposed, could not refrain from severely reprimanding his officer in the presence of the army. He commanded two Indian captives, taken by Alvarado, to be brought before him, and explained to them the pacific purpose of his visit. This he did through the assistance of his interpreter, Melchorejo, a native of Yucatan, who had been brought back by Grijalva, and who, during his residence in Cuba, had picked up some acquaintance with the Castilian. He then dismissed them loaded with presents, and with an invitation to their countrymen to return to their homes without fear of further annoyance. This humane policy succeeded. The fugitives, reassured, were not slow in coming back; and an amicable intercourse was established, in which Spanish cutlery and trinkets were exchanged for

31

the gold ornaments of the natives; a traffic in which each party congratulated itself—a philosopher might think with equal reason—on out-
witting the other.

The first object of Cortés was to gather tidings of the unfortunate
Christians who were reported to be still lingering in captivity on the
neighbouring continent. From some traders in the islands he obtained
such a confirmation of the report, that he sent Diego de Ordaz with
two brigantines to the opposite coast of Yucatan, with instructions to
remain there eight days. Some Indians went as messengers in the vessels,
who consented to bear a letter to the captives, informing them of the
arrival of their countrymen in Cozumel, with a liberal ransom for their
release. Meanwhile the general proposed to make an excursion to the
different parts of the island, that he might give employment to the restless
spirits of the soldiers, and ascertain the resources of the country.

It was poor and thinly peopled. But everywhere he recognised the
vestiges of a higher civilisation than what he had before witnessed in the
Indian islands. The houses were some of them large, and often built
of stone and lime. He was particularly struck with the temples, in which
were towers constructed of the same solid materials, and rising several
stories in height.

In the court of one of these he was amazed by the sight of a cross,
of stone and lime, about ten palms high. It was the emblem of the God
of rain. Its appearance suggested the wildest conjectures, not merely to
the unlettered soldiers, but subsequently to the European scholar, who
speculated on the character of the races that had introduced there the
sacred symbol of Christianity. But no such inference, as we shall see hereafter, could be warranted. Yet it must be regarded as a curious fact, that
the Cross should have been venerated as the object of religious worship
both in the New World and in regions of the Old, where the light of
Christianity had never risen.

The next object of Cortés was to reclaim the natives from their gross
idolatry, and to substitute a purer form of worship. In accomplishing
this he was prepared to use force, if milder measures should be ineffectual.
There was nothing which the Spanish government had more earnestly at
heart, than the conversion of the Indians. It forms the constant burden
of their instructions, and gave to the military expeditions in this Western
Hemisphere somewhat of the air of a crusade. The cavalier who embarked
in them entered fully into these chivalrous and devotional feelings. No
doubt was entertained of the efficacy of conversion, however sudden might

be the change, or however violent the means. The sword was a good argument when the tongue failed; and the spread of Mohometanism had shown that seeds sown by the hand of violence, far from perishing in the ground, would spring up and bear fruit to after time. If this were so in a bad cause, how much more would it be true in a good one! The Spanish cavalier felt he had a high mission to accomplish as a soldier of the Cross. However unauthorised or unrighteous the war into which he had entered may seem to us, to him it was a holy war. He was in arms against the infidel. Not to care for the soul of his benighted enemy was to put his own in jeopardy. The conversion of a single soul might cover a multitude of sins. It was not for morals that he was concerned, but for *the faith*. This, though understood in its most literal and limited sense, comprehended the whole scheme of Christian morality. Whoever died in the faith, however immoral had been his life, might be said to die in the Lord. Such was the creed of the Castilian knight of that day, as imbibed from the preachings of the pulpit, from cloisters and colleges at home, from monks and missionaries abroad—from all save one, whose devotion, kindled at a purer source, was not, alas! permitted to send forth its radiance far into the thick gloom by which he was encompassed.

No one partook more fully of the feelings above described than Hernando Cortés. He was, in truth, the very mirror of the times in which he lived, reflecting its motley characteristics, its speculative devotion, and practical licence—but with an intensity all his own. He was greatly scandalised at the exhibition of the idolatrous practices of the people of Cozumel, though untainted, as it would seem, with human sacrifices. He endeavoured to persuade them to embrace a better faith, through the agency of two ecclesiastics who attended the expedition—the licentiate Juan Diaz and Father Bartolomé de Olmedo. The latter of these godly men afforded the rare example—rare in any age—of the union of fervent zeal with charity, while he beautifully illustrated in his own conduct the precepts which he taught. He remained with the army through the whole expedition, and by his wise and benevolent counsels was often enabled to mitigate the cruelties of the Conquerors, and to turn aside the edge of the sword from the unfortunate natives.

These two missionaries vainly laboured to persuade the people of Cozumel to renounce their abominations, and to allow the Indian idols, in which the Christians recognised the true lineaments of Satan, to be thrown down and demolished. The simple natives, filled with horror at the proposed profanation, exclaimed that these were the gods who sent them the sunshine and the storm, and, should any violence be offered, they would be sure to avenge it by sending their lightnings on the heads of its perpetrators.

Cortés was probably not much of a polemic. At all events, he preferred on the present occasion action to argument; and thought that the best way to convince the Indians of their error was to prove the falsehood of the prediction. He accordingly, without further ceremony, caused the venerated images to be rolled down the stairs of the great temple, amidst the groans and lamentations of the natives. An altar was hastily constructed, an image of the Virgin and Child placed over it, and mass was performed by Father Olmedo and his reverend companion for the first time within the walls of a temple in New Spain. The patient ministers tried once more to pour the light of the gospel into the benighted understandings of the islanders, and to expound the mysteries of the Catholic faith. The Indian interpreter must have afforded rather a dubious channel for the transmission of such abstruse doctrines. But they at length found favour with their auditors, who, whether overawed by the bold bearing of the invaders, or convinced of the impotence of deities that could not shield their own shrines from violation, now consented to embrace Christianity.

While Cortés was thus occupied with the triumphs of the Cross, he received intelligence that Ordaz had returned from Yucatan without tidings of the Spanish captives. Though much chagrined, the general did not choose to postpone longer his departure from Cozumel. The fleet had been well stored with provisions by the friendly inhabitants, and, embarking his troops, Cortés, in the beginning of March, took leave of its hospitable shores. The squadron had not proceeded far, however, before a leak in one of the vessels compelled them to return to the same port. The detention was attended with important consequences; so much so, indeed, that a writer of the time discerns in it "a great mystery and a miracle."

Soon after landing, a canoe with several Indians was seen making its way from the neighbouring shores of Yucatan. On reaching the island, one of the men inquired, in broken Castilian, "if he were among Christians"; and, being answered in the affirmative, threw himself on his knees and returned thanks to Heaven for his delivery. He was one of the unfortunate captives for whose fate so much interest had been felt. His name was Jeronimo de Aguilar, a native of Ecija, in Old Spain, where he had been regularly educated for the church. He had been established with the colony at Darien, and on a voyage from that place to Hispaniola, eight years previous, was wrecked near the coast of Yucatan. He escaped with several of his companions in the ship's boat, where some perished from hunger and exposure, while others were sacrificed, on their reaching land, by the cannibal natives of the peninsula. Aguilar was preserved from the same dismal fate by escaping into the interior, where he fell into the hands of a powerful cacique, who, though he spared his life, treated him at first with great rigour. The patience of the captive, however, and his singular humility, touched the better feelings of the chieftain, who would have persuaded Aguilar to take a wife among his people, but the ecclesiastic steadily refused, in obedience to his vows. This admirable constancy excited the distrust of the cacique, who put his virtue to a severe test by various temptations, and much of the same sort as those with which the devil is said to have assailed St. Anthony. From all these fiery trials, however, like his ghostly predecessor, he came out unscorched. Continence is too rare and difficult a virtue with barbarians not to challenge their veneration, and the practice of it has made the reputation of more than one saint in the Old as well as the New World. Aguilar was now intrusted with the care of his master's household and his numerous wives. He was a man of discretion, as well as virtue; and his counsels were found so salutary that he was consulted on all important matters. In short, Aguilar became a great man among the Indians.

It was with much regret, therefore, that his master received the proposals for his return to his countrymen, to which nothing but the rich treasure of glass beads, hawk bells, and other jewels of like value, sent for his ransom, would have induced him to consent. When Aguilar reached the coast, there had been so much delay that the brigantines had sailed, and it was owing to the fortunate return of the fleet to Cozumel that he was enabled to join it.

On appearing before Cortés, the poor man saluted him in the Indian style, by touching the earth with his hand, and carrying it to his head. The commander, raising him up, affectionately embraced him, covering him at the same time with his own cloak, as Aguilar was simply clad in the habiliments of the country, somewhat too scanty for a European eye. It was long, indeed, before the tastes which he had acquired in the freedom of the forest could be reconciled to the constraints either of dress or manners imposed by the artificial forms of civilisation. Aguilar's long residence in the country had familiarised him with the Mayan dialects of Yucatan, and, as he gradually revived his Castilian, he became of essential importance as an interpreter. Cortés saw the advantage of this from the first, but he could not fully estimate all the consequences that were to flow from it.

The repairs of the vessels being at length completed, the Spanish commander once more took leave of the friendly natives of Cozumel, and set sail on March 4. Keeping as near as possible to the coast of Yucatan, he doubled Cape Catoche, and with flowing sheets swept down the broad bay of Campeachy, fringed with the rich dye-woods which have since furnished so important an article of commerce to Europe. He passed Potonchan, where Cordova had experienced a rough reception from the natives; and soon after reached the mouth of the *Rio de Tabasco,* or *Grijalva,* in which that navigator had carried on so lucrative a traffic. Though mindful of the great object of his voyage—the visit to the Aztec territories—he was desirous of acquainting himself with the resources of this country, and determined to ascend the river and visit the great town on its borders.

The water was so shallow, from the accumulation of sand at the mouth of the stream, that the general was obliged to leave the ships at anchor, and to embark in the boats with a part only of his forces. The banks were thickly studded with mangrove trees, that, with their roots shooting up and interlacing one another, formed a kind of impervious screen or network, behind which the dark forms of the natives were seen glancing to and fro with the most menacing looks and gestures. Cortés, much surprised at these unfriendly demonstrations, so unlike what he had reason to expect, moved cautiously up the stream. When he had reached an open place, where a large number of Indians were assembled, he asked, through his interpreter, leave to land, explaining at the same time his amicable intentions. But the Indians, brandishing their weapons, answered only with gestures of angry defiance. Though much chagrined, Cortés thought it best not to urge the matter further that evening, but withdrew to a neighbouring island, where he disembarked his troops, resolved to effect a landing on the following morning.

When day broke the Spaniards saw the opposite banks lined with a much more numerous array than on the preceding evening, while the canoes along the shore were filled with bands of armed warriors. Cortés now made his preparations for the attack. He first landed a detachment of a hundred men under Alonso de Avila, at a point somewhat lower down the stream, sheltered by a thick grove of palms, from which a road, as he knew, led to the town of Tabasco, giving orders to his officer to march at once on the place, while he himself advanced to assault it in front.

Then embarking the remainder of his troops, Cortés crossed the river in face of the enemy; but, before commencing hostilities, that he might "act with entire regard to justice, and in obedience to the instructions of the Royal Council," he first caused proclamation to be made through the interpreter, that he desired only a free passage for his men; and that he proposed to revive the friendly relations which had formerly subsisted between his countrymen and the natives. He assured them that if blood were spilt, the sin would lie on their heads, and that resistance would be useless, since he was resolved at all hazards to take up his quarters that night in the town of Tabasco. This proclamation, delivered in lofty tone, and duly recorded by the notary, was answered by the Indians—who might possibly have comprehended one word in ten of it—with shouts of defiance and a shower of arrows.

Cortés, having now complied with all the requisitions of a loyal cavalier, and shifted the responsibility from his own shoulders to those of the Royal Council, brought his boats alongside of the Indian canoes. They grappled fiercely together and both parties were soon in the water, which rose above the girdle. The struggle was not long, though desperate. The superior strength of the Europeans prevailed, and they forced the enemy back to land. Here, however, they were supported by their countrymen, who showered down darts, arrows, and blazing billets of wood on the heads of the invaders. The banks were soft and slippery, and it was with difficulty the soldiers made good their footing. Cortés lost a sandal in the mud, but continued to fight barefoot, with great exposure of his person, as the Indians, who soon singled out the leader, called to one another, "Strike at the chief!"

At length the Spaniards gained the bank, and were able to come into something like order, when they opened a brisk fire from their arquebuses and crossbows. The enemy, astounded by the roar and flash of the firearms, of which they had had no experience, fell back, and retreated behind a breastwork of timber thrown across the way. The Spaniards, hot in the pursuit, soon carried these rude defences, and drove the Tabascans before them towards the town, where they again took shelter behind their palisades.

Meanwhile Avila had arrived from the opposite quarter, and the natives taken by surprise made no further attempt at resistance, but abandoned the place to the Christians. They had previously removed their families and effects. Some provisions fell into the hands of the victors, but little gold, "a circumstance," says Las Casas, "which gave them no particular satisfaction." It was a very populous place. The houses were mostly of mud; the better sort of stone and lime; affording proofs in the inhabitants of a superior refinement to that found in the islands, as their stout resistance had given evidence of superior valour.

Cortés, having thus made himself master of the town, took formal possession of it for the crown of Castile. He gave three cuts with his sword on a large *ceiba* tree, which grew in the place, and proclaimed aloud that he took possession of the city in the name and on behalf of the Catholic sovereigns, and would maintain and defend the same with sword and buckler against all who should gainsay it. The same vaunting declaration was also made by the soldiers, and the whole was duly recorded and attested by the notary. This was the usual simple but chivalric form with which the Spanish cavaliers asserted the royal title to the conquered territories in the New World. It was a good title, doubtless, against the claims of any other European potentate.

The general took up his quarters that night in the courtyard of the principal temple. He posted his sentinels, and took all the precautions practised in wars with a civilised foe. Indeed, there was reason for them. A suspicious silence seemed to reign through the place and its neighbourhood; and tidings were brought that the interpreter, Melchorejo, had fled, leaving his Spanish dress hanging on a tree. Cortés was disquieted by the desertion of this man who would not only inform his countrymen of the small number of the Spaniards, but dissipate any illusions that might be entertained of their superior natures.

On the following morning, as no traces of the enemy were visible, Cortés ordered out a detachment under Alvarado and another under Francisco de Lujo, to reconnoitre. The latter officer had not advanced a league before he learned the position of the Indians, by their attacking him in such force that he was fain to take shelter in a large stone building, where he was closely besieged. Fortunately the loud yells of the assailants, like most barbarous nations, seeking to strike terror by their ferocious cries, reached the ears of Alvarado and his men, who, speedily advancing to the relief of their comrades, enabled them to force a passage through the enemy. Both parties retreated, closely pursued, on the town, when Cortés, marching out to their support, compelled the Tabascans to retire.

A few prisoners were taken in this skirmish. By them Cortés found his worst apprehensions verified. The country was everywhere in arms. A force consisting of many thousands had assembled from the neighbouring provinces, and a general assault was resolved on for the next day. To the general's inquiries why he had been received in so different a manner from his predecessor, Grijalva, they answered, that "the conduct of the Tabascans then had given great offence to the other Indian tribes, who taxed them with treachery and cowardice; so that they had promised, on any return of the white men, to resist them in the same manner as their neighbours had done."

Cortés might now well regret that he had allowed himself to deviate from the direct object of his enterprise, and to become entangled in a doubtful war which could lead to no profitable result. But it was too late to repent. He had taken the step, and had no alternative but to go forward. To retreat would dishearten his own men at the outset, impair their confidence in him as their leader, and confirm the arrogance of his foes, the tidings of whose success might precede him on his voyage, and prepare the way for greater mortifications and defeats. He did not hesitate as to the course he was to pursue; but, calling his officers together, announced his intention to give battle the following morning.

He sent back to the vessels such as were disabled by their wounds, and ordered the remainder of the forces to join the camp. Six of the heavy guns were also taken from the ships, together with all the horses. The animals were stiff and torpid from long confinement on board; but a few hours' exercise restored them to their strength and usual spirit. He gave the command of the artillery—if it may be dignified with the name—to a soldier named Mesa, who had acquired some experience as an engineer in the Italian wars. The infantry he put under the orders of Diego de Ordaz, and took charge of the cavalry himself. It consisted of some of the most valiant gentlemen of his little band, among whom may be mentioned Alvarado, Velasquez de Leon, Avila, Puertocarrero, Olid, Montejo. Having thus made all the necessary arrangements and settled his plan of battle, he retired to rest—but not to slumber. His feverish mind, as may well be imagined, was filled with anxiety for the morrow, which might decide the fate of his expedition; and as was his wont on such occasions, he was frequently observed, during the night, going the rounds, and visiting the sentinels, to see that no one slept upon his post.

At the first glimmering of light he mustered his army, and declared his purpose not to abide, cooped up in the town, the assault of the enemy, but to march at once against him. For he well knew that the spirits rise with action, and that the attacking party gathers a confidence from the very movement, which is not felt by the one who is passively, perhaps anxiously, awaiting the assault. The Indians were understood to be encamped on level ground a few miles distant from the city, called the plain of Ceutla. The general commanded that Ordaz should march with the foot, including the artillery, directly across the country, and attack them in front, while he himself would fetch a circuit with the horse, and turn their flank when thus engaged, or fall upon their rear.

These dispositions being completed, the little army heard Mass and then sallied forth from the wooden walls of Tabasco. It was Lady Day, March 25—long memorable in the annals of New Spain. The district around the town was chequered with patches of maize, and, on the lower level, with plantations of cacao—supplying the beverage, and perhaps the coin of the country, as in Mexico. These plantations, requiring constant irrigation, were fed by numerous canals and reservoirs of water, so that the country could not be traversed without great toil and difficulty. It was, however, intersected by a narrow path or causeway, over which the cannon could be dragged.

The troops advanced more than a league on their laborious march, without descrying the enemy. The weather was sultry, but few of them were embarrassed by the heavy mail worn by the European cavaliers at that period. Their cotton jackets, thickly quilted, afforded a tolerable protection against the arrows of the Indian, and allowed room for the freedom and activity of movement essential to a life of rambling adventure in the wilderness.

At length they came in sight of the broad plains of Ceutla, and beheld the dusky lines of the enemy stretching, as far as the eye could reach, along the edge of the horizon. The Indians had shown some sagacity in the choice of their position; and, as the weary Spaniards came slowly on, floundering through the morass, the Tabascans set up their hideous battle-cries, and discharged volleys of arrows, stones, and other missiles, which rattled like hail on the shields and helmets of the assailants. Many were severely wounded before they could gain the firm ground, where they soon cleared a space for themselves, and opened a heavy fire of artillery and musketry on the dense columns of the enemy, which presented a fatal mark for the balls. Numbers were swept down at every discharge; but the bold barbarians, far from being dismayed, threw up dust and leaves to hide their losses, and, sounding their war instruments, shot off fresh flights of arrows in return.

They even pressed closer on the Spaniards, and, when driven off by a vigorous charge, soon turned again, and, rolling back like the waves of the ocean, seemed ready to overwhelm the little band by weight of numbers. Thus cramped, the latter had scarcely room to perform their necessary evolutions, or even to work their guns with effect.

The engagement had now lasted more than an hour, and the Spaniards, sorely pressed, looked with great anxiety for the arrival of the horse—which some unaccountable impediments must have detained—to relieve them from their perilous position. At this crisis, the furthest columns of the Indian army were seen to be agitated and thrown into a disorder that rapidly spread through the whole mass. It was not long before the ears of the Christians were saluted with the cheering war-cry of "San Jago and San Pedro," and they beheld the bright helmets and swords of the Castilian cavalry flashing back the rays of the morning sun, as they dashed through the ranks of the enemy, striking to the right and left, and scattering dismay around them. The eye of faith, indeed, could discern the patron Saint of Spain himself, mounted on his grey war-horse, heading the rescue and trampling over the bodies of the fallen infidels.

The approach of Cortés had been greatly retarded by the broken nature of the ground. When he came up, the Indians were so hotly engaged, that he was upon them before they observed his approach. He ordered his men to direct their lances at the faces of their opponents, who, terrified at the monstrous apparition—for they supposed the rider and the horse, which they had never before seen, to be one and the same—were seized with a panic. Ordaz availed himself of it to command a general charge along the line, and the Indians, many of them throwing away their arms, fled without attempting further resistance.

Cortés was too content with the victory, to care to follow it up by dipping his sword in the blood of the fugitives. He drew off his men to a copse of palms which skirted the place, and, under their broad canopy, the soldiers offered up thanksgivings to the Almighty for the victory vouchsafed them. The field of battle was made the site of a town, called in honour of the day on which the action took place, *Santa Maria de la Vitoria,* long afterwards the capital of the Province. The number of those who fought or fell in the engagement is altogether doubtful. Nothing, indeed, is more uncertain than numerical estimates of barbarians.

And they gain nothing in probability, when they come, as in the present instance, from the reports of their enemies. Most accounts, however, agree that the Indian force consisted of five squadrons of eight thousand men each. There is more discrepancy as to the number of slain, varying from one to thirty thousand! In this monstrous discordance, the common disposition to exaggerate may lead us to look for truth in the neighbourhood of the smallest number. The loss of the Christians was inconsiderable; not exceeding—if we receive their own reports, probably, from the same causes, much diminishing the truth—two killed, and less than a hundred wounded! We may readily comprehend the feelings of the Conquerors, when they declared that "Heaven must have fought on their side, since their own strength could never have prevailed against such a multitude of enemies!"

Several prisoners were taken in the battle, among them two chiefs. Cortés gave them their liberty, and sent a message by them to their countrymen, "that he would overlook the past, if they would come in at once, and tender their submission. Otherwise he would ride over the land, and put every living thing in it, man, woman, and child, to the sword!" With this formidable menace ringing in their ears, the envoys departed.

But the Tabascans had no relish for further hostilities. A body of inferior chiefs appeared the next day, clad in dark dresses of cotton, intimating their abject condition, and implored leave to bury their dead. It was granted by the general, with many assurances of his friendly disposition; but at the same time he told them he expected their principal caciques, as he would treat with none other. These soon presented themselves, attended by a numerous train of vassals, who followed with timid curiosity to the Christian camp. Among their propitiatory gifts were twenty female slaves, which, from the character of one of them, proved of infinitely more consequence than was anticipated by either Spaniards or Tabascans. Confidence was soon restored; and was succeeded by a friendly intercourse, and the interchange of Spanish toys for the rude commodities of the country, articles of food, cotton, and a few gold ornaments of little value. When asked where the precious metal was procured, they pointed to the west, and answered "Culhua," "Mexico." The Spaniards saw this was no place for them to traffic, or to tarry in. Yet here, they were not many leagues distant from a potent and opulent city, or what once had been so, the ancient Palenque. But its glory may have even then passed away, and its name have been forgotten by the surrounding nations.

Before his departure the Spanish commander did not omit to provide for one great object of his expedition, the conversion of the Indians. He first represented to the caciques, that he had been sent thither by a powerful monarch on the other side of the water, to whom he had now a right to claim their allegiance. He then caused the reverend fathers Olmedo and Diaz to enlighten their minds, as far as possible, in regard to the great truths of revelation, urging them to receive these in place of their own heathenish abominations. The Tabascans, whose perceptions were no doubt materially quickened by the discipline they had undergone, made but a faint resistance to either proposal. The next day was Palm Sunday, and the general resolved to celebrate their conversion by one of those pompous ceremonials of the Church, which should make a lasting impression on their minds.

A solemn procession was formed of the whole army with the ecclesiastics at their head, each soldier bearing a palm-branch in his hand. The concourse was swelled by thousands of Indians of both sexes, who followed in curious astonishment at the spectacle. The long files bent their way through the flowery savannas that bordered the settlement, to the principal temple, where an altar was raised, and the image of the presiding deity was deposed to make room for that of the Virgin with the infant Saviour. Mass was celebrated by Father Olmedo, and the soldiers who were capable joined in the solemn chant. The natives listened in profound silence and, if we may believe the chronicler of the event who witnessed it, were melted into tears; while their hearts were penetrated with reverential awe for the God of those terrible beings who seemed to wield in their own hands the thunder and the lightning.

The Roman Catholic communion has, it must be admitted, some decided advantages over the Protestant, for the purpose of proselytism. The dazzling pomp of its service and its touching appeal to the sensibilities affect the imagination of the rude child of nature much more powerfully than the cold abstractions of Protestantism, which, addressed to the reason, demand a degree of refinement and mental culture in the audience to comprehend them. The respect, moreover, shown by the Catholic for the material representations of Divinity greatly facilitates the same object. It is true, such representations are used by him only as incentives, not as the objects of worship. But this distinction is lost on the savage, who finds such forms of adoration too analogous to his own to impose any great violence on his feelings. It is only required of him to transfer his homage from the image of Quetzalcoatl, the benevolent deity who walked among men, to that of the Virgin or the Redeemer; from the Cross, which he has worshipped as the emblem of the God of rain, to the same Cross, the symbol of salvation.

These solemnities concluded, Cortés prepared to return to his ships, well satisfied with the impression made on the new converts, and with the conquests he had thus achieved for Castile and Christianity. The soldiers, taking leave of their Indian friends, entered the boats with the palm branches in their hands, and descending the river, re-embarked on board their vessels, which rode at anchor at its mouth. A favourable breeze was blowing, and the little navy, opening its sails to receive it, was soon on its way again to the golden shores of Mexico.

CHAPTER V

*Voyage along the Coast—Doña Marina—Spaniards Land in
Mexico—Interview with the Aztecs*

1519

THE FLEET HELD ITS COURSE so near the shore, that the inhabitants
could be seen on it; and, as it swept along the winding borders of the
gulf, the soldiers, who had been on the former expedition with Grijalva,
pointed out to their companions the memorable places on the coast. Here
was the *Rio de Alvarado,* named after the gallant adventurer, who was
present, also, in this expedition; there the *Rio de Vanderas,* in which
Grijalva had carried on so lucrative a commerce with the Mexicans;
and there the *Isla de los Sacrificios,* where the Spaniards first saw the
vestiges of human sacrifice on the coast. Puertocarrero, as he listened
to these reminiscences of the sailors, repeated the words of the old ballad
of Montesinos, "Here is France, there is Paris, and there the waters of
the Duero," etc. "But I advise you," he added, turning to Cortés, "to look
out only for the rich lands, and the best way to govern them." "Fear
not," replied his commander, "if Fortune but favours me as she did
Orlando, and I have such gallant gentlemen as you for my companions,
I shall understand myself very well."

The fleet had now arrived off St. Juan de Ulua, the island so named
by Grijalva. The weather was temperate and serene, and crowds of
natives were gathered on the shore of the main land, gazing at the
strange phenomenon, as the vessels glided along under easy sail on the
smooth bosom of the waters. It was the evening of Thursday in Passion
Week. The air came pleasantly off the shore, and Cortés, liking the spot,
thought he might safely anchor under the lee of the island, which
would shelter him from the *nortes* that sweep over these seas with fatal
violence in the winter, sometimes even late in the spring.

The ships had not been long at anchor, when a light pirogue, filled
with natives, shot off from the neighbouring continent, and steered for

the general's vessel, distinguished by the royal ensign of Castile floating from the mast. The Indians came on board with a frank confidence, inspired by the accounts of the Spaniards spread by their countrymen who had traded with Grijalva. They brought presents of fruits and flowers and little ornaments of gold, which they gladly exchanged for the usual trinkets. Cortés was baffled in his attempts to hold a conversation with his visitors by means of the interpreter, Aguilar, who was ignorant of the language; the Mayan dialects, with which he was conversant, bearing too little resemblance to the Aztec. The natives supplied the deficiency, as far as possible, by the uncommon vivacity and significance of their gestures—the hieroglyphics of speech—but the Spanish commander saw with chagrin the embarrassments he must encounter in future for want of a more perfect medium of communication. In this dilemma, he was informed that one of the female slaves given to him by the Tabascan chiefs was a native Mexican, and understood the language. Her name—that given to her by the Spaniards—was Marina; and, as she was to exercise a most important influence on their fortunes, it is necessary to acquaint the reader with something of her character and history.

She was born at Painalla, in the province of Coatzacualco, on the south-eastern borders of the Mexican empire. Her father, a rich and powerful cacique, died when she was very young. Her mother married again, and, having a son, she conceived the infamous idea of securing to this offspring of her second union Marina's rightful inheritance. She accordingly feigned that the latter was dead, but secretly delivered her into the hands of some itinerant traders of Xicallanco. She availed herself, at the same time, of the death of a child of one of her slaves, to substitute the corpse of that of her own daughter, and celebrated the obsequies with mock solemnity. These particulars are related by the honest old soldier, Bernal Diaz, who knew the mother, and witnessed the generous treatment of her afterwards by Marina. By the merchants the Indian maiden was again sold to the cacique of Tabasco, who delivered her, as we have seen, to the Spaniards.

From the place of her birth she was well acquainted with the Mexican tongue, which, indeed, she is said to have spoken with great elegance. Her residence in Tabasco familiarised her with the dialects of that country, so that she could carry on a conversation with Aguilar, which he in turn rendered into the Castilian. Thus a certain, though somewhat circuitous, channel was opened to Cortés for communicating with the Aztecs; a circumstance of the last importance to the success of his enterprise. It was not very long, however, before Marina, who had a lively genius, made herself so far mistress of the Castilian as to supersede the necessity of any other linguist. She learned it the more readily, as it was to her the language of love.

Cortés, who appreciated the value of her services from the first, made her his interpreter, then his secretary, and, won by her charms, his mistress. She had a son by him, Don Martin Cortés, *comendador* of the Military Order of St. James, less distinguished by his birth than his unmerited persecutions.

Marina was at this time in the morning of life. She is said to have possessed uncommon personal attractions, and her open, expressive features indicated her generous temper. She always remained faithful to the countrymen of her adoption; and her knowledge of the language and customs of the Mexicans, and often of their designs, enabled her to extricate the Spaniards, more than once, from the most embarrassing and perilous situations. She had her errors, as we have seen; but they should be rather charged to the defects of early education, and to the evil influence of him to whom in the darkness of her spirit she looked with simple confidence for the light to guide her. All agree that she was full of excellent qualities, and the important services which she rendered the Spaniards have made her memory deservedly dear to them; while the name of Malinche—the name by which she is still known in Mexico—was pronounced with kindness by the conquered races, with whose misfortunes she showed an invariable sympathy.

With the aid of his two intelligent interpreters, Cortés entered into conversation with his Indian visitors. He learned that they were Mexicans, or rather subjects of the great Mexican empire, of which their own province formed one of the comparatively recent conquests. The country was ruled by a powerful monarch, called Moctheuzoma, or by Europeans more commonly Montezuma, who dwelt on the mountain plains of the interior, nearly seventy leagues from the coast; their own province was governed by one of his nobles, named Teuhtlile, whose residence was eight leagues distant. Cortés acquainted them in turn with his own friendly views in visiting their country, and with his desire of an interview with the Aztec governor. He then dismissed them loaded with presents, having first ascertained that there was abundance of gold in the interior, like the specimens they had brought.

Cortés, pleased with the manners of the people, and the goodly reports of the land, resolved to take up his quarters here for the present. The

next morning, April 21, being Good Friday, he landed with all his force
on the very spot where now stands the modern city of Vera Cruz. Little
did the Conqueror imagine that the desolate beach, on which he first
planted his foot, was one day to be covered by a flourishing city, the great
mart of European and Oriental trade, the commercial capital of New
Spain.

It was a wide and level plain, except where the sand had been drifted
into hillocks by the perpetual blowing of the *norte*. On these sand-hills
he mounted his little battery of guns, so as to give him the command of
the country. He then employed the troops in cutting down small trees
and bushes which grew near, in order to provide a shelter from the
weather. In this he was aided by the people of the country, sent, as it
appeared, by the governor of the district, to assist the Spaniards. With
their help stakes were firmly set in the earth, and covered with boughs,
and with mats and cotton carpets, which the friendly natives brought
with them. In this way they secured, in a couple of days, a good defence
against the scorching rays of the sun, which beat with intolerable fierce-
ness on the sands. The place was surrounded by stagnant marshes, the
exhalations from which, quickened by the heat into the pestilent malaria,
have occasioned in later times wider mortality to Europeans than all the
hurricanes on the coast. The bilious disorders, now the terrible scourge
of the *tierra caliente,* were little known before the Conquest. The seeds
of the poison seem to have been scattered by the hand of civilisation; for
it is only necessary to settle a town, and draw together a busy European
population, in order to call out the malignity of the venom which had
before lurked in the atmosphere.

While these arrangements were in progress, the natives flocked in
from the adjacent district, which was tolerably populous in the interior,
drawn by a natural curiosity to see the wonderful strangers. They
brought with them fruits, vegetables, flowers in abundance, game, and
many dishes cooked after the fashion of the country, with little articles
of gold and other ornaments. They gave away some as presents, and
bartered others for the wares of the Spaniards; so that the camp, crowded
with a motley throng of every age and sex, wore the appearance of a
fair. From some of the visitors Cortés learned the intention of the
governor to wait on him the following day.

This was Easter. Teuhtlile arrived, as he had announced, before noon.
He was attended by a numerous train, and was met by Cortés, who conducted him with much ceremony to his tent, where his principal officers

were assembled. The Aztec chief returned their salutations with polite, though formal courtesy. Mass was first said by Father Olmedo, and the service was listened to by Teuhtlile and his attendants with decent reverence. A collation was afterwards served, at which the general entertained his guest with Spanish wines and confections. The interpreters were then introduced, and a conversation commenced between the parties.

The first inquiries of Teuhtlile were respecting the country of the strangers, and the purport of their visit. Cortés told him that "he was the subject of a potent monarch beyond the seas, who ruled over an immense empire, and had kings and princes for his vassals! that, acquainted with the greatness of the Mexican emperor, his master had desired to enter into a communication with him, and had sent him as his envoy to wait on Montezuma with a present in token of his good will, and a message which he must deliver in person." He concluded by inquiring of Teuhtlile when he could be admitted to his sovereign's presence.

To this the Aztec noble somewhat haughtily replied: "How is it, that you have been here only two days, and demand to see the emperor?" He then added, with more courtesy, that "he was surprised to learn there was another monarch as powerful as Montezuma; but that if it were so, he had no doubt his master would be happy to communicate with him. He would send his couriers with the royal gift brought by the Spanish commander, and, so soon as he had learned Montezuma's will, would communicate it."

Teuhtlile then commanded his slaves to bring forward the present intended for the Spanish general. It consisted of ten loads of fine cotton, several mantles of that curious featherwork whose rich and delicate dyes might vie with the most beautiful painting, and a wicker basket filled with ornaments of wrought gold, all calculated to inspire the Spaniards with high ideas of the wealth and mechanical ingenuity of the Mexicans.

Cortés received these presents with suitable acknowledgments, and ordered his own attendants to lay before the chief the articles designed for Montezuma. These were an arm-chair richly carved and painted, a crimson cap of cloth, having a gold medal emblazoned with St. George and the dragon, and a quantity of collars, bracelets, and other ornaments of cut glass, which, in a country where glass was not to be had, might claim to have the value of real gems, and no doubt passed for such with the inexperienced Mexicans. Teuhtlile observed a soldier in the camp with a shining gilt helmet on his head, which he said reminded him of one worn by the god Quetzalcoatl in Mexico; and he showed a desire that Montezuma should see it. The coming of the Spaniards, as the reader will soon see, was associated with some traditions of this same deity. Cortés expressed his willingness that the casque should be sent to the emperor, intimating a hope that it would be returned filled with the gold dust of the country, that he might be able to compare its quality with that in his own! He further told the governor, as we are informed by his chaplain, "that the Spaniards were troubled with a disease of the heart, for which gold was a specific remedy!" "In short," says Las Casas, "he contrived to make his want of gold very clear to the governor."

While these things were passing, Cortés observed one of Teuhtlile's attendants busy with a pencil, apparently delineating some object. On looking at his work, he found that it was a sketch on canvas of the Spaniards, their costumes, arms, and, in short, different objects of interest, giving to each its appropriate form and colour. This was the celebrated picture-writing of the Aztecs, and, as Teuhtlile informed him, this man was employed in portraying the various objects for the eye of Montezuma, who would thus gather a more vivid notion of their appearance than from any description by words. Cortés was pleased with the idea; and, as he knew how much the effect would be heightened by converting still life into action, he ordered out the cavalry on the beach, the wet sands of which afforded a firm footing for the horses. The bold and rapid movements of the troops, as they went through their military exercises; the apparent ease with which they managed the fiery animals on which they were mounted; the glancing of their weapons, and the shrill cry of the trumpet, all filled the spectators with astonishment; but when they heard the thunders of the cannon, which Cortés ordered to be fired at the same time, and witnessed the volumes of smoke and flame issuing from these terrible engines, and the rushing sound of the balls, as they dashed through the trees of the neighbouring forest, shivering their branches into fragments, they were filled with consternation, from which the Aztec chief himself was not wholly free.

Nothing of all this was lost on the painters, who faithfully recorded, after their fashion, every particular; not omitting the ships—"the water-houses," as they called them, of the strangers—which, with their dark hulls and snow-white sails reflected from the water, were swinging lazily at anchor on the calm bosom of the bay. All was depicted with a fidelity that excited in their turn the admiration of the Spaniards, who, doubtless unprepared for this exhibition of skill, greatly over-estimated the merits of the execution.

These various matters completed, Teuhtlile with his attendants withdrew from the Spanish quarters, with the same ceremony with which he had entered them; leaving orders that his people should supply the troops with provisions and other articles requisite for their accommodation, till further instructions from the capital.

CHAPTER VI

Account of Montezuma—State of His Empire—Strange Prognostics—Embassy and Presents—Spanish Encampment

1519

WE MUST NOW TAKE LEAVE of the Spanish camp in the *tierra caliente,* and transport ourselves to the distant capital of Mexico, where no little sensation was excited by the arrival of the wonderful strangers on the coast. The Aztec throne was filled at that time by Montezuma the Second, nephew of the last, and grandson of a preceding monarch. He had been elected to the regal dignity in 1502, in preference to his brothers, for his superior qualifications, both as a soldier and a priest—a combination of offices sometimes found in the Mexican candidates, as it was, more frequently, in the Egyptian. In early youth he had taken an active part in the wars of the empire, though of late he had devoted himself more exclusively to the services of the temple; and he was scrupulous in his attentions to all the burdensome ceremonial of the Aztec worship. He maintained a grave and reserved demeanour, speaking little and with prudent deliberation. His deportment was well calculated to inspire ideas of superior sanctity.

When his election was announced to him, he was found sweeping down the stairs in the great temple of the national war-god. He received the messengers with a becoming humility, professing his unfitness for so responsible a station. The address, delivered as usual on the occasion, was made by his relative Nezahualpilli, the wise king of Tezcuco. It has fortunately been preserved, and presents a favourable specimen of Indian eloquence. Towards the conclusion the orator exclaims, "Who can doubt that the Aztec empire has reached the zenith of its greatness, since the Almighty has placed over it one whose very presence fills every beholder with reverence? Rejoice, happy people, that you have now a sovereign who will be to you a steady column of support: a father in distress, a more than brother in tenderness and sympathy; one whose aspiring soul will

disdain all the profligate pleasures of the senses, and the wasting indulgence of sloth. And thou, illustrious youth, doubt not that the Creator,
who has laid on thee so weighty a charge, will also give strength to sustain it; that He, who has been so liberal in times past, will shower yet
more abundant blessings on thy head, and keep thee firm in thy royal
seat through many long and glorious years." These golden prognostics,
which melted the royal auditor into tears, were not destined to be
realised.

Montezuma displayed all the energy and enterprise in the commencement of his reign, which had been anticipated from him. His first expedition against a rebel province in the neighbourhood was crowned with
success, and he led back in triumph a throng of captives for the bloody
sacrifice that was to grace his coronation. This was celebrated with uncommon pomp. Games and religious ceremonies continued for several
days, and among the spectators who flocked from distant quarters were
some noble Tlascalans, the hereditary enemies of Mexico. They were
in disguise, hoping thus to elude detection. They were recognised, however, and reported to the monarch. But he only availed himself of the
information to provide them with honourable entertainment, and a
good place for witnessing the games. This was a magnanimous act, considering the long cherished hostility between the nations.

In his first years, Montezuma was constantly engaged in war, and
frequently led his armies in person. The Aztec banners were seen in
the farthest provinces on the Gulf of Mexico, and the distant regions
of Nicaragua and Honduras. The expeditions were generally successful; and the limits of the empire were more widely extended than at any
preceding period.

Meanwhile the monarch was not inattentive to the interior concerns
of the kingdom. He made some important changes in the courts of justice; and carefully watched over the execution of the laws, which he
enforced with stern severity. He was in the habit of patrolling the streets
of his capital in disguise, to make himself personally acquainted with the
abuses in it. And with more questionable policy, it is said, he would
sometimes try the integrity of his judges by tempting them with large
bribes to swerve from their duty, and then call the delinquent to strict
account for yielding to the temptation.

He liberally recompensed all who served him. He showed a similar
munificent spirit in his public works, constructing and embellishing the
temples, bringing water into the capital by a new channel, and establish-

ing a hospital, or retreat for invalid soldiers, in the city of Colhuacan.

These acts, so worthy of a great prince, were counterbalanced by others of an opposite complexion. The humility, displayed so ostentatiously before his elevation, gave way to an intolerable arrogance. In his pleasure-houses, domestic establishment, and way of living, he assumed a pomp unknown to his predecessors. He secluded himself from public observation, or, when he went abroad, exacted the most slavish homage; while in the palace he would be served only, even in the most menial offices, by persons of rank. He, further, dismissed several plebeians, chiefly poor soldiers of merit, from the places they had occupied near the person of his predecessor, considering their attendance a dishonour to royalty. It was in vain that his oldest and sagest counsellors remonstrated on a conduct so impolitic.

While he thus disgusted his subjects by his haughty deportment, he alienated their affections by the imposition of grievous taxes. These were demanded by the lavish expenditure of his court. They fell with peculiar heaviness on the conquered cities. This oppression led to frequent insurrection and resistance; and the latter years of his reign present a scene of unintermitting hostility, in which the forces of one half of the empire were employed in suppressing the commotions of the other. Unfortunately there was no principle of amalgamation by which the new acquisitions could be incorporated into the ancient monarchy, as parts of one whole. Their interests, as well as sympathies, were different. Thus the more widely the Aztec empire was extended, the weaker it became; resembling some vast and ill-proportioned edifice, whose disjointed materials, having no principle of cohesion, and tottering under their own weight, seem ready to fall before the first blast of the tempest.

In 1516, died the Tezcucan king, Nezahualpilli, in whom Montezuma lost his most sagacious counsellor. The succession was contested by his two sons, Cacama and Ixtlilxochitl. The former was supported by Montezuma. The latter, the younger of the princes, a bold, aspiring youth, appealing to the patriotic sentiment of his nation, would have persuaded them that his brother was too much in the Mexican interests to be true to his own country. A civil war ensued, and ended by a compromise, by which one half of the kingdom, with the capital, remained to Cacama, and the northern portion to his ambitious rival. Ixtlilxochitl became from that time the mortal foe of Montezuma.

A more formidable enemy still was the little republic of Tlascala, lying midway between the Mexican Valley and the coast. It had maintained its independence for more than two centuries against the allied forces of the empire. Its resources were unimpaired, its civilisation scarcely below that of its great rival states, and for courage and military prowess it had established a name inferior to none other of the nations of Anahuac.

Such was the condition of the Aztec monarchy, on the arrival of Cortés—the people disgusted with the arrogance of the sovereign; the provinces and distant cities outraged by fiscal exactions; while potent enemies in the neighbourhood lay watching the hour when they might assail their formidable rival with advantage. Still the kingdom was strong in its internal resources, in the will of its monarch, in the long habitual deference to his authority—in short, in the terror of his name, and in the valour and discipline of his armies, grown grey in active service, and well drilled in all the tactics of Indian warfare. The time had now come when these imperfect tactics and rude weapons of the barbarian were to be brought into collision with the science and enginery of the most civilised nations of the globe.

During the latter years of his reign, Montezuma had rarely taken part in his military expeditions, which he left to his captains, occupying himself chiefly with his sacerdotal functions. Under no prince had the priesthood enjoyed greater consideration and immunities. The religious festivals and rites were celebrated with unprecedented pomp. The oracles were consulted on the most trivial occasions; and the sanguinary deities were propitiated by hecatombs of victims dragged in triumph to the capital from the conquered or rebellious provinces. The religion, or to speak correctly the superstition, of Montezuma proved a principal cause of his calamities.

In a preceding chapter I have noticed the popular traditions respecting Quetzalcoatl, that deity with a fair complexion and flowing beard, so unlike the Indian physiognomy, who, after fulfilling his mission of benevolence among the Aztecs, embarked on the Atlantic Sea for the mysterious shores of Tlapallan. He promised, on his departure, to return at some future day with his posterity, and resume the possession of his empire. That day was looked forward to with hope or with apprehension, according to the interest of the believer, but with general confidence throughout the wide borders of Anahuac. Even after the Conquest, it still lingered among the Indian races, by whom it was as fondly cherished as the advent of their king Sebastian continued to be by the Portuguese, or that of the Messiah by the Jews.

A general feeling seems to have prevailed in the time of Montezuma, that the period for the return of the deity, and the full accomplishment of his promise, was near at hand. This conviction is said to have gained ground from various preternatural occurrences, reported with more or less detail by all the most ancient historians. In 1510, the great lake of Tezcuco, without the occurrence of a tempest, or earthquake, or any other visible cause, became violently agitated, overflowed its banks, and, pouring into the streets of Mexico, swept off many of the buildings by the fury of the waters. In 1511, one of the turrets of the great temple took fire, equally without any apparent cause, and continued to burn in defiance of all attempts to extinguish it. In the following years, three comets were seen; and not long before the coming of the Spaniards a strange light broke forth in the east. It spread broad at its base on the horizon, and, rising in a pyramidal form, tapered off as it approached the zenith. It resembled a vast sheet or flood of fire, emitting sparkles, or, as an old writer expresses it, "seemed thickly powdered with stars." At the same time, low voices were heard in the air, and doleful wailings, as if to announce some strange, mysterious calamity! The Aztec monarch, terrified at the apparitions in the heavens, took counsel of Nezahualpilli, who was a great proficient in the subtle science of astrology. But the royal sage cast a deeper cloud over his spirit, by reading in these prodigies the speedy downfall of the empire.

Such are the strange stories reported by the chroniclers, in which it is not impossible to detect the glimmerings of truth. Nearly thirty years had elapsed since the discovery of the islands by Columbus, and more than twenty since his visit to the American continent. Rumours, more or less distinct, of this wonderful appearance of the white men, bearing in their hands the thunder and the lightning, so like in many respects to the traditions of Quetzalcoatl, would naturally spread far and wide among the Indian nations. Such rumours, doubtless, long before the landing of the Spaniards in Mexico, found their way up the grand plateau, filling the minds of men with anticipations of the near coming of the period when the great deity was to return and receive his own again.

In the excited state of their imaginations, prodigies became a familiar occurrence. Or rather, events not very uncommon in themselves, seen through the discoloured medium of fear, were easily magnified into prodigies; and the accidental swell of the lake, the appearance of a comet, and the conflagration of a building, were all interpreted as the special annunciations of Heaven. Thus it happens in those great political convulsions which shake the foundations of society—the mighty events that cast their shadows before them in their coming. Then it is that the atmosphere is agitated with the low, prophetic murmurs, with which nature, in the moral as in the physical world, announces the march of the hurricane:

> "When from the shores
> And forest-rustling mountains comes a voice,
> That, solemn sounding, bids the world prepare!"

When tidings were brought to the capital of the landing of Grijalva on the coast, in the preceding year, the heart of Montezuma was filled with dismay. He felt as if the destinies which had so long brooded over the royal line of Mexico were to be accomplished, and the sceptre was to pass away from his house for ever. Though somewhat relieved by the departure of the Spaniards, he caused sentinels to be stationed on the heights; and when the Europeans returned under Cortés, he doubtless received the earliest notice of the unwelcome event. It was by his orders, however, that the provincial governor had prepared so hospitable a reception for them. The hieroglyphical report of these strange visitors, now forwarded to the capital, revived all his apprehensions. He called without delay a meeting of his principal counsellors, including the kings of Tezcuco, and Tlacopan, and laid the matter before them.

There seems to have been much division of opinion in that body. Some were for resisting the strangers at once, whether by fraud, or by open force. Others contended that, if they were supernatural beings, fraud and force would be alike useless. If they were, as they pretended, ambassadors from a foreign prince, such a policy would be cowardly and unjust. That they were not of the family of Quetzalcoatl was argued from the fact that they had shown themselves hostile to his religion; for tidings of the proceedings of the Spaniards in Tabasco, it seems, had already reached the capital. Among those in favour of giving them a friendly and honourable reception was the Tezcucan king, Cacama.

But Montezuma, taking counsel of his own ill-defined apprehensions, preferred a half-way course—as usual, the most impolitic. He resolved to send an embassy, with such a magnificent present to the strangers, as should impress them with high ideas of his grandeur and resources; while at the same time, he would forbid their approach to the capital. This was to reveal, at once, both his wealth and his weakness.

While the Aztec court was thus agitated by the arrival of the Spaniards, they were passing their time in the *tierra caliente,* not a little annoyed by the excessive heats and suffocating atmosphere of the sandy waste on which they were encamped. They experienced every alleviation that could be derived from the attentions of the friendly natives. These, by the governor's command, had constructed more than a thousand huts or booths of branches and matting which they occupied in the neighbourhood of the camp. Here they prepared various articles of food for the tables of Cortés and his officers, without any recompense; while the common soldiers easily obtained a supply for themselves, in exchange for such trifles as they brought with them for barter. Thus the camp was liberally provided with meat and fish dressed in many savoury ways, with cakes of corn, bananas, pine-apples, and divers luscious vegetables of the tropics, hitherto unknown to the Spaniards. The soldiers contrived, moreover, to obtain many little bits of gold, of no great value, indeed, from the natives; a traffic very displeasing to the partisans of Velasquez, who considered it an invasion of his rights. Cortés, however, did not think it prudent in this matter to baulk the inclinations of his followers.

At the expiration of seven, or eight days at most, the Mexican embassy presented itself before the camp. It may seem an incredibly short space of time, considering the distance of the capital was near seventy leagues. But it may be remembered that tidings were carried there by means of posts, as already noticed, in the brief space of four-and-twenty hours; and four or five days would suffice for the descent of the envoys to the coast, accustomed as the Mexicans were to long and rapid travelling. At all events, no writer states the period occupied by the Indian emissaries on this occasion as longer than that mentioned.

The embassy, consisting of two Aztec nobles, was accompanied by the governor, Teuhtlile, and by a hundred slaves, bearing the princely gifts of Montezuma. One of the envoys had been selected on account of the great resemblance which, as appeared from the painting representing the camp, he bore to the Spanish commander. And it is a proof of the fidelity of the painting, that the soldiers recognised the resemblance, and always distinguished the chief by the name of the "Mexican Cortés."

On entering the general's pavilion, the ambassadors saluted him and his officers, with the usual signs of reverence to persons of great consideration, touching the ground with their hands and then carrying them to their heads, while the air was filled with clouds of incense, which rose up from the censers borne by their attendants. Some delicately wrought mats of the country (*petates*) were then unrolled, and on them the slaves displayed the various articles they had brought. They were of the most miscellaneous kind; shields, helmets, cuirasses, embossed with plates and ornaments of pure gold; collars and bracelets of the same metal, sandals, fans, *panaches* and crests of variegated feathers, intermingled with gold and silver thread, and sprinkled with pearls and precious stones; imitations of birds and animals in wrought and cast gold and silver, of exquisite workmanship; curtains, coverlets, and robes of cotton, fine as silk, of rich and various dyes, interwoven with featherwork that rivalled the delicacy of painting. There were more than thirty loads of cotton cloth in addition. Among the articles was the Spanish helmet sent to the capital, and now returned filled to the brim with grains of gold. But the things which excited the most admiration were two circular plates of gold and silver, "as large as carriage-wheels." One, representing the sun, was richly carved with plants and animals—no doubt denoting the Aztec century. It was thirty palms in circumference, and was valued at twenty thousand *pesos de oro*. The silver wheel, of the same size, weighed fifty marks.

The Spaniards could not conceal their rapture at the exhibition of treasures which so far surpassed all the dreams in which they had indulged. For, rich as were the materials, they were exceeded—according to the testimony of those who saw these articles afterwards in Seville, where they could coolly examine them—by the beauty and richness of the workmanship.

When Cortés and his officers had completed their survey, the ambassadors courteously delivered the message of Montezuma. "It gave their master great pleasure," they said, "to hold this communication with so powerful a monarch as the King of Spain, for whom he felt the most profound respect. He regretted much that he could not enjoy a personal interview with the Spaniards, but the distance of his capital was too great; since the journey was beset with difficulties, and with too many dangers from formidable enemies, to make it possible. All that could be done, therefore, was for the strangers to return to their own land, with the proofs thus afforded them of his friendly disposition."

Cortés, though much chagrined at this decided refusal of Montezuma to admit his visit, concealed his mortification as he best might, and politely expressed his sense of the emperor's munificence. "It made him only the more desirous," he said, "to have a personal interview with him. He should feel it, indeed, impossible to present himself again before his own sovereign, without having accomplished this great object of his voyage; and one who had sailed over two thousand leagues of ocean held lightly the perils and fatigues of so short a journey by land." He once more requested them to become the bearers of his message to their master, together with a slight additional token of his respect.

This consisted of a few fine Holland shirts, a Florentine goblet, gilt and somewhat curiously enamelled, with some toys of little value—a sorry return for the solid magnificence of the royal present. The ambassadors may have thought as much. At least, they showed no alacrity in charging themselves either with the present or the message; and, on quitting the Castilian quarters, repeated their assurance that the general's application would be unavailing.

The splendid treasure, which now lay dazzling the eyes of the Spaniards, raised in their bosoms very different emotions, according to the difference of their characters. Some it stimulated with the ardent desire to strike at once into the interior, and possess themselves of a country which teemed with such boundless stores of wealth. Others looked on it as the evidence of a power altogether too formidable to be encountered with their present insignificant force. They thought, therefore, it would be most prudent to return and report their proceedings to the governor of Cuba, where preparations could be made commensurate with so vast an undertaking. There can be little doubt as to the impression made on the bold spirit of Cortés, on which difficulties ever operated as incentives rather than discouragements to enterprise. But he prudently said nothing—at least in public—preferring that so important a movement should flow from the determination of his whole army, rather than from his own individual impulse.

Meanwhile the soldiers suffered greatly from the inconveniences of their position amidst burning sands and the pestilent effluvia of the neighbouring marshes, while the venomous insects of these hot regions left them no repose, day or night. Thirty of their number had already sickened and died; a loss that could ill be afforded by the little band. To add to their troubles, the coldness of the Mexican chiefs had extended to their followers; and the supplies for the camp were not only much diminished, but the prices set on them were exorbitant. The position was equally unfavourable for the shipping, which lay in an open roadstead, exposed to the fury of the first *norte* which should sweep the Mexican Gulf.

The general was induced by these circumstances to despatch two vessels, under Francisco de Montejo, with the experienced Alaminos for his pilot, to explore the coast in a northerly direction, and see if a safer port and more commodious quarters for the army could not be found there.

After the lapse of ten days the Mexican envoys returned. They entered the Spanish quarters with the same formality as on the former visit, bearing with them an additional present of rich stuffs and metallic ornaments, which, though inferior in value to those before brought, were estimated at three thousand ounces of gold. Besides these, there were four precious stones of a considerable size, resembling emeralds, called by the natives *chalchuites,* each of which, as they assured the Spaniards, was worth more than a load of gold, and was designed as a mark of particular respect for the Spanish monarch. Unfortunately they were not worth as many loads of earth in Europe.

Montezuma's answer was in substance the same as before. It contained a positive prohibition for the strangers to advance nearer to the capital; and expressed the confidence that, now they had obtained what they had most desired, they would return to their own country without unnecessary delay. Cortés received this unpalatable response courteously, though somewhat coldly, and, turning to his officers, exclaimed, "This is a rich and powerful prince indeed; yet it shall go hard, but we will one day pay him a visit in his capital!"

While they were conversing, the bell struck for vespers. At the sound, the soldiers, throwing themselves on their knees, offered up their orisons before the large wooden cross planted in the sands. As the Aztec chiefs gazed with curious surprise, Cortés thought it a favourable occasion to impress them with what he conceived to be a principal object of his visit to the country. Father Olmedo accordingly expounded, as briefly and clearly as he could, the great doctrines of Christianity, touching on the atonement, the passion, and the resurrection, and concluding with assuring his astonished audience that it was their intention to extirpate the idolatrous practices of the nation, and to substitute the pure worship of the true God. He then put into their hands a little image of the Virgin with the infant Redeemer, requesting them to place it in their temples instead of their sanguinary deities. How far the Aztec lords comprehended the mysteries of the Faith, as conveyed through the double version of Aguilar and Marina, or how well they perceived the subtle distinctions between their own images and those of the Roman Church, we are not informed. There is reason to fear, however, that the seed fell on barren ground; for, when the homily of the good father ended, they withdrew with an air of dubious reserve very different from their friendly manners at the first interview. The same night every hut was deserted by the natives, and the Spaniards saw themselves suddenly cut off from supplies in the midst of a desolate wilderness. The movement had so suspicious an appearance that Cortés apprehended an attack would be made on his quarters, and took precautions accordingly. But none was meditated.

The army was at length cheered by the return of Montejo from his exploring expedition, after an absence of twelve days. He had run down the Gulf as far as Panuco, where he experienced such heavy gales, in attempting to double that headland, that he was driven back, and had nearly foundered. In the whole course of the voyage he had found only one place tolerably sheltered from the north winds. Fortunately, the adjacent country, well watered by fresh running streams, afforded a favourable position for the camp; and thither, after some deliberation, it was determined to repair.

CHAPTER VII

Troubles in the Camp—Plan of a Colony—Management of Cortés—March to Cempoalla—Proceedings with the Natives—Foundation of Vera Cruz

1519

THERE IS NO SITUATION which tries so severely the patience and discipline of the soldier as a life of idleness in camp, where his thoughts, instead of being bent on enterprise and action, are fastened on himself and the inevitable privations and dangers of his condition. This was particularly the case in the present instance, where, in addition to the evils of a scanty subsistence, the troops suffered from excessive heat, swarms of venomous insects, and the other annoyances of a sultry climate. They were, moreover, far from possessing the character of regular forces, trained to subordination under a commander whom they had long been taught to reverence and obey. They were soldiers of fortune, embarked with him in an adventure in which all seemed to have an equal stake, and they regarded their captain—the captain of a day—as little more than an equal.

There was a growing discontent among the men at their longer residence in this strange land. They were still more dissatisfied on learning the general's intention to remove to the neighbourhood of the port discovered by Montejo. "It was time to return," they said, "and report what had been done to the governor of Cuba, and not linger on these barren shores until they had brought the whole Mexican empire on their heads!" Cortés evaded their importunities as well as he could, assuring them there was no cause for despondency. "Everything so far had gone on prosperously, and, when they had taken up a more favourable position, there was no reason to doubt they might still continue the same profitable intercourse with the natives."

While this was passing, five Indians made their appearance in the camp one morning, and were brought to the general's tent. Their dress and whole appearance were different from those of the Mexicans. They wore rings of gold and gems of a bright blue stone in their ears and nostrils, while a gold leaf delicately wrought was attached to the under lip. Marina was unable to comprehend their language; but, on her addressing them in Aztec, two of them, it was found, could converse in that tongue. They said they were natives of Cempoalla, the chief town of the Totonacs, a powerful nation who had come upon the great plateau many centuries back, and descending its eastern slope, settled along the sierras and broad plains which skirt the Mexican Gulf towards the north. Their country was one of the recent conquests of the Aztecs, and they experienced such vexatious oppressions from their conquerors as made them very impatient of the yoke. They informed Cortés of these and other particulars. The fame of the Spaniards had reached their master, who sent these messengers to request the presence of the wonderful strangers in his capital.

This communication was eagerly listened to by the general, who, it will be remembered, was possessed of none of those facts, laid before the reader, respecting the internal condition of the kingdom, which he had no reason to suppose other than strong and united. An important truth now flashed on his mind, as his quick eye descried in this spirit of discontent a potent lever by the aid of which he might hope to overturn this barbaric empire. He received the mission of the Totonacs most graciously, and, after informing himself, as far as possible, of their dispositions and resources, dismissed them with presents, promising soon to pay a visit to their lord.

Meanwhile, his personal friends, among whom may be particularly mentioned Alonso Hernandez Puertocarrero, Christoval de Olid, Alonso de Avila, Pedro de Alvarado and his brothers, were very busy in persuading the troops to take such measures as should enable Cortés to go forward in those ambitious plans for which he had no warrant from the powers of Velasquez. "To return now," they said, "was to abandon the enterprise on the threshold, which, under such a leader, must conduct to glory and incalculable riches." To return to Cuba would be to surrender to the greedy governor the little gains they had already got. The only way was to persuade the general to establish a permanent colony in the country, the government of which would take the conduct of matters into its own hands, and provide for the interests of its members. It was true, Cortés had no such authority from Velasquez. But the interests of the Sovereigns, which were paramount to every other, imperatively demanded it.

These conferences could not be conducted so secretly, though held by night, as not to reach the ears of the friends of Velasquez. They remonstrated against the proceedings, as insidious and disloyal. They accused the general of instigating them; and, calling on him to take measures without delay for the return of the troops to Cuba, announced their own intention to depart, with such followers as still remained true to the governor.

Cortés, instead of taking umbrage at this high-handed proceeding, or even answering in the same haughty tone, mildly replied, "that nothing was further from his desire than to exceed his instructions. He, indeed, preferred to remain in the country and continue his profitable intercourse with the natives. But, since the army thought otherwise, he should defer to their opinion, and give orders to return, as they desired." On the following morning, proclamation was made for the troops to hold themselves in readiness to embark at once on board the fleet, which was to sail for Cuba.

Great was the sensation caused by their general's order. Even many of those before clamorous for it, with the usual caprice of men whose wishes are too easily gratified, now regretted it. The partisans of Cortés were loud in their remonstrances. "They were betrayed by the general," they cried, and thronging round his tent, called on him to countermand his orders. "We came here," said they, "expecting to form a settlement, if the state of the country authorised it. Now it seems you have no warrant from the governor to make one. But there are interests, higher than those of Velasquez, which demand it. These territories are not his property, but were discovered for the Sovereigns; and it is necessary to plant a colony to watch over their interests, instead of wasting time in idle barter, or, still worse, of returning, in the present state of affairs, to Cuba. If you refuse," they concluded, "we shall protest against your conduct as disloyal to their Highnesses."

Cortés received this remonstrance with the embarrassed air of one by whom it was altogether unexpected. He modestly requested time for deliberation, and promised to give his answer on the following day. At the time appointed, he called the troops together, and made them a brief address. "There was no one," he said, "if he knew his own heart, more deeply devoted than himself to the welfare of his sovereigns, and the glory of the Spanish name. He had not only expended his all, but incurred heavy debts, to meet the charges of this expedition, and had hoped to reimburse himself by continuing his traffic with the Mexicans. But, if the soldiers thought a different course advisable, he was ready to postpone his own advantage to the good of the state." He concluded by declaring his willingness to take measures for settling a colony *in the name of the Spanish Sovereigns,* and to nominate a magistracy to preside over it.

For the *alcaldes* he selected Puertocarrero and Montejo, the former cavalier his fast friend, and the latter the friend of Velasquez, and chosen for that very reason; a stroke of policy which perfectly succeeded. The *regidores, alguacil,* treasurer, and other functionaries, were then appointed, all of them his personal friends and adherents. They were regularly sworn into office, and the new city received the title of *Villa Rica de Vera Cruz,* "The Rich Town of the True Cross"; a name which was considered as happily intimating that union of spiritual and temporal interests to which the arms of the Spanish adventurers in the New World were to be devoted. Thus, by a single stroke of the pen, as it were, the camp was transformed into a civil community, and the whole framework and even title of the city were arranged before the site of it had been settled.

The new municipality were not slow in coming together; when Cortés presented himself, cap in hand, before that august body, and, laying the powers of Velasquez on the table, respectfully tendered the resignation of his office of captain-general, "which, indeed," he said, "had necessarily expired, since the authority of the governor was now superseded by that of the magistracy of Villa Rica de Vera Cruz." He then, with a profound obeisance, left the apartment.

The council, after a decent time spent in deliberation, again requested his presence. "There was no one," they said, "who, on mature reflection, appeared to them so well qualified to take charge of the interests of the community, both in peace and in war, as himself; and they unanimously named him, in behalf of their Catholic Highnesses, Captain General and Chief Justice of the colony." He was further empowered to draw, on his own account, one-fifth of the gold and silver which might hereafter be obtained by commerce or conquest from the natives. Thus clothed with supreme civil and military jurisdiction, Cortés was not backward in exerting his authority. He found speedy occasion for it.

The transactions above described had succeeded each other so rapidly, that the governor's party seemed to be taken by surprise, and had formed no plan of opposition. When the last measure was carried, however, they broke forth into the most indignant and opprobrious invectives, denouncing the whole as a systematic conspiracy against Velasquez. These accusations led to recrimination from the soldiers of the other side, until from words they nearly proceeded to blows. Some of the principal cavaliers, among them Velasquez de Leon, a kinsman of the governor, Escobar his page, and Diego de Ordaz, were so active in instigating these turbulent movements that Cortés took the bold measure of putting them all in irons, and sending them on board the vessels. He then dispersed the common file by detaching many of them, with a strong party under Alvarado, to forage the neighbouring country, and bring home provisions for the destitute camp.

During their absence, every argument that cupidity or ambition could suggest was used to win the refractory to his views. Promises, and even gold, it is said, were liberally lavished; till, by degrees, their understandings were opened to a clearer view of the merits of the case. And when the foraging party re-appeared with abundance of poultry and vegetables, and the cravings of the stomach—that great laboratory of disaffection, whether in camp or capital—were appeased, good humour returned with good cheer, and the rival factions embraced one another as companions in arms, pledged to a common cause. Even the high-mettled hidalgos on board the vessels did not long withstand the general tide of reconciliation, but one by one gave in their adhesion to the new government. What is more remarkable is that this forced conversion was not a hollow one, but from this time forward several of these very cavaliers became the most steady and devoted partisans of Cortés.

Such was the address of this extraordinary man, and such the ascendency which in a few months he had acquired over these wild and turbulent spirits! By this ingenious transformation of a military into a civil community, he had secured a new and effectual basis for future operations. He might now go forward without fear of check or control from a superior—at least from any other superior than the crown, under which alone he held his commission. In accomplishing this, instead of incurring the charge of usurpation, or of transcending his legitimate powers, he had transferred the responsibility, in a great measure, to those who had imposed on him the necessity of action. By this step, moreover, he had linked the fortunes of his followers indissolubly with his own. They had taken their chance with him, and, whether for weal or for woe, must abide the consequences. He was no longer limited to the narrow concerns of a sordid traffic, but sure of their co-operation, might now boldly meditate, and gradually disclose, those lofty schemes which he had formed in his own bosom for the conquest of an empire.

Harmony being thus restored, Cortés sent his heavy guns on board the fleet, and ordered it to coast along the shore to the north as far as Chiahuitsala, the town near which the destined port of the new city was situated; proposing, himself, at the head of his troops, to visit Cempoalla, on the march. The road lay for some miles across the dreary plains in the neighbourhood of the modern Vera Cruz. In this sandy waste no signs of vegetation met their eyes, which, however, were occasionally refreshed by glimpses of the blue Atlantic, and by the distant view of the magnificent Orizaba, towering with his spotless diadem of snow far above his colossal brethren of the Andes. As they advanced, the country gradually assumed a greener and richer aspect. They crossed a river, probably a tributary of the *Rio de la Antigua,* with difficulty, on rafts, and on some broken canoes that were lying on the banks. They now came in view of very different scenery—wide-rolling plains covered with a rich carpet of verdure, and overshadowed by groves of cocoas and feathery palms, among whose tall, slender stems were seen deer, and various wild animals with which the Spaniards were unacquainted. Some of the horsemen gave chase to the deer, and wounded, but did not succeed in killing them. They saw, also, pheasants and other birds; among them the wild turkey, the pride of the American forest, which the Spaniards described as a species of peacock.

On their route they passed through some deserted villages in which were Indian temples, where they found censers, and other sacred utensils, and manuscripts of the *agave* fibre, containing the picture-writing, in which, probably, their religious ceremonies were recorded. They now beheld, also, the hideous spectacle, with which they became afterwards familiar, of the mutilated corpses of victims who had been sacrificed to the accursed deities of the land. The Spaniards turned with loathing and indignation from a display of butchery, which formed so dismal a contrast to the fair scenes of nature by which they were surrounded.

They held their course along the banks of the river, towards its source, when they were met by twelve Indians, sent by the cacique of Cempoalla to show them the way to his residence. At night they bivouacked in an open meadow, where they were well supplied with provisions by their new friends. They left the stream on the following morning, and, striking northerly across the country, came upon a wide expanse of luxuriant plains and woodland, glowing in all the splendour of tropical vegetation. The branches of the stately trees were gaily festooned with clustering vines of the dark-purple grape, variegated convolvuli, and other flowering parasites of the most brilliant dyes. The undergrowth of prickly aloe, matted with wild rose and honeysuckle, made in many places an almost impervious thicket. Amid this wilderness of sweet-smelling buds and blossoms fluttered numerous birds of the parrot tribe, and clouds of butterflies, whose gaudy colours, nowhere so gorgeous as in the *tierra caliente*, rivalled those of the vegetable creation; while birds of exquisite song, the scarlet cardinal and the marvellous mocking-bird, that comprehends in his own notes the whole music of a forest, filled the air with delicious melody. The hearts of the stern Conquerors were not very sensible to the beauties of nature. But the magical charms of the scenery drew forth unbounded expressions of delight, and as they wandered through this "terrestrial paradise," as they called it, they fondly compared it to the fairest regions of their own sunny land.

As they approached the Indian city, they saw abundant signs of cultivation in the trim gardens and orchards that lined both sides of the road. They were now met by parties of the natives of either sex, who increased in numbers with every step of their progress. The women, as well as men, mingled fearlessly among the soldiers, bearing bunches and wreaths of flowers, with which they decorated the neck of the general's charger, and hung a chaplet of roses about his helmet. Flowers were the delight of this people. They bestowed much care in their cultivation, in which they were well seconded by a climate of alternate heat and moisture, stimulating the soil to the spontaneous production of every form of vegetable life. The same refined taste, as we shall see, prevailed among the warlike Aztecs, and has survived the degradation of the nation in their descendants of the present day.

Many of the women appeared, from their richer dress and numerous attendants, to be persons of rank. They were clad in robes of fine cotton, curiously coloured, which reached from the neck—in the inferior orders, from the waist—to the ankles. The men wore a sort of mantle of the same material, *à la Morisca,* in the Moorish fashion, over their shoulders, and belts or sashes about the loins. Both sexes had jewels and ornaments of gold round their necks, while their ears and nostrils were perforated with rings of the same metal.

Just before reaching the town, some horsemen who had ridden in advance returned with the amazing intelligence, "that they had been near enough to look within the gates, and found the houses all plated with burnished silver!" On entering the place, the silver was found to be nothing more than a brilliant coating of stucco, with which the principal buildings were covered; a circumstance which produced much merriment among the soldiers at the expense of their credulous comrades. Such ready credulity is a proof of the exalted state of their imaginations, which were prepared to see gold and silver in every object around them. The edifices of the better kind were of stone and lime, or bricks dried in the sun; the poorer were of clay and earth. All were thatched with palm-leaves, which, though a flimsy roof, apparently, for such structures, were so nicely interwoven as to form a very effectual protection against the weather.

The city was said to contain from twenty to thirty thousand inhabitants. This is the most moderate computation, and not improbable. Slowly and silently the little army paced the narrow and now crowded streets of Cempoalla, inspiring the natives with no greater wonder than they themselves experienced at the display of a policy and refinement so far superior to anything they had witnessed in the New World. The cacique came out in front of his residence to receive them. He was a tall and very corpulent man, and advanced leaning on two of his attendants. He received Cortés and his followers with great courtesy; and, after a brief interchange of civilities, assigned the army its quarters in a neighbouring temple, into the spacious courtyard of which a number of apartments opened, affording excellent accommodations for the soldiery.

Here the Spaniards were well supplied with provisions, meat cooked after the fashion of the country, and maize made into bread-cakes. The general received, also, a present of considerable value from the cacique, consisting of ornaments of gold and fine cottons. Notwithstanding these friendly demonstrations, Cortés did not relax his habitual vigilance, nor neglect any of the precautions of a good soldier. On his route, indeed, he had always marched in order of battle, well prepared against surprise. In his present quarters, he stationed his sentinels with like care, posted his small artillery so as to command the entrance, and forbade any soldier to leave the camp without orders, under pain of death.

The following morning, Cortés, accompanied by fifty of his men, paid a visit to the lord of Cempoalla in his own residence. It was a building of stone and lime, standing on a steep terrace of earth, and was reached by a flight of stone steps. It may have borne resemblance in its structure to some of the ancient buildings found in Central America. Cortés, leaving his soldiers in the courtyard, entered the mansion with one of his officers, and his fair interpreter, Doña Marina. A long conference ensued, from which the Spanish general gathered much light respecting the state of the country. He first announced to the chief that he was the subject of a great monarch who dwelt beyond the waters; that he had come to the Aztec shores, to abolish the inhuman worship which prevailed there, and to introduce the knowledge of the true God. The cacique replied that their gods, who sent them the sunshine and the rain, were good enough for them; that he was the tributary of a powerful monarch also, whose capital stood on a lake far off among the mountains; a stern prince, merciless in his exactions, and, in case of resistance, or any offence, sure to wreak his vengeance by carrying off their young men and maidens to be sacrificed to his deities. Cortés assured him that he would never consent to such enormities; he had been sent by his sovereign to redress abuses and to punish the oppressor; and, if the Totonacs would be true to him, he would enable them to throw off the detested yoke of the Aztecs.

The cacique added that the Totonac territory contained about thirty towns and villages, which could muster a hundred thousand warriors— a number much exaggerated. There were other provinces of the empire, he said, where the Aztec rule was equally odious; and between him and the capital lay the warlike republic of Tlascala, which had always maintained its independence of Mexico. The fame of the Spaniards had gone before them, and he was well acquainted with their terrible victory at Tabasco. But still he looked with doubt and alarm to a rupture with "the great Montezuma," as he always styled him; whose armies, on the least provocation, would pour down from the mountain regions of the west, and, rushing over the plains like a whirlwind, sweep off the wretched people to slavery and sacrifice!

Cortés endeavoured to reassure him, by declaring that a single Spaniard was stronger than a host of Aztecs. At the same time, it was desirable to know what nations would co-operate with him, not so much on his account, as theirs, that he might distinguish friend from foe, and know whom he was to spare in this war of extermination. Having raised the confidence of the admiring chief by this comfortable and politic vaunt, he took an affectionate leave, with the assurance that he would shortly return and concert measures for their future operations, when he had visited his ships in the adjoining port, and secured a permanent settlement there.

The intelligence gained by Cortés gave great satisfaction to his mind. It confirmed his former views, and showed, indeed, the interior of the monarchy to be in a state far more distracted than he had supposed. If he had before scarcely shrunk from attacking the Aztec empire in the true spirit of a knight-errant, with his single arm, as it were, what had he now to fear, when one-half of the nation could be thus marshalled against the other? In the excitement of the moment, his sanguine spirit kindled with an enthusiasm which over-leaped every obstacle. He communicated his own feelings to the officers about him, and, before a blow was struck, they already felt as if the banners of Spain were waving in triumph from the towers of Montezuma! But many a bloody field was to be fought, many a peril and privation to be encountered, before that consummation could be attained.

Taking leave of the hospitable Indian on the following day, the Spaniards took the road to Chiahuitzlan, about four leagues distant, near which was the port discovered by Montejo, where their ships were now riding at anchor. They were provided by the cacique with four hundred Indian porters, *tamenes,* as they were called, to transport the baggage. These men easily carried fifty pounds' weight five or six leagues in a day. They were in use all over the Mexican empire, and the Spaniards found them of great service, henceforth, in relieving the troops from this part of their duty. They passed through a country of the same rich, voluptuous character as that which they had lately traversed; and arrived early next morning at the Indian town, perched like a fortress on a bold, rocky eminence that commanded the Gulf. Most of the inhabitants had fled, but fifteen of the principal men remained, who received them in a friendly manner, offering the usual compliments of flowers and incense. The people of the place, losing their fears, gradually returned. While conversing with the chiefs, the Spaniards were joined by the worthy cacique of Cempoalla, borne by his men on a litter. He eagerly took part in their deliberations. The intelligence gained here by Cortés confirmed the accounts already gathered of the feelings and resources of the Totonac nation.

In the midst of their conference, they were interrupted by a movement among the people, and soon afterwards five men entered the great square or market-place, where they were standing. By their lofty port, their peculiar and much richer dress, they seemed not to be of the same race as these Indians. Their dark glossy hair was tied in a knot on the top of the head. They had bunches of flowers in their hands, and were followed by several attendants, some wearing wands with cords, others fans, with which they brushed away the flies and insects from their lordly masters. As these persons passed through the place, they cast a haughty look on the Spaniards, scarcely deigning to return their salutations. They were immediately joined, in great confusion, by the Totonac chiefs, who seemed anxious to conciliate them by every kind of attention.

The general, much astonished, inquired of Marina what it meant. She informed him they were Aztec nobles, empowered to receive the tribute for Montezuma. Soon after, the chiefs returned with dismay painted on their faces. They confirmed Marina's statement, adding that the Aztecs greatly resented the entertainment afforded the Spaniards without the emperor's permission; and demanded in expiation twenty young men and women for sacrifice to the gods. Cortés showed the strongest indignation at this insolence. He required the Totonacs not only to refuse the demand, but to arrest the persons of the collectors, and throw them into prison. The chiefs hesitated, but he insisted on it so peremptorily, that they at length complied, and the Aztecs were seized, bound hand and foot, and placed under a guard.

In the night, the Spanish general procured the escape of two of them, and had them brought secretly before him. He expressed his regret at the indignity they had experienced from the Totonacs; told them he would provide means for their flight, and to-morrow would endeavour to obtain the release of their companions. He desired them to report this to their master, with assurances of the great regard the Spaniards entertained for him, notwithstanding his ungenerous behaviour in leaving them to perish from want on his barren shores. He then sent the Mexican nobles down to the port, whence they were carried to another part of the coast by water, for fear of the violence of the Totonacs. These were greatly incensed at the escape of the prisoners, and would have sacrificed the remainder at once, but for the Spanish commander, who evinced the utmost horror at the proposal, and ordered them to be sent for safe custody on board the fleet. Soon after, they were permitted to join their companions. This artful proceeding, so characteristic of the policy of Cortés, had, as we shall see hereafter, all the effect intended on Montezuma. It cannot be commended, certainly, as in the true spirit of chivalry; yet it has not wanted its panegyrist among the national historians!

By order of Cortés, messengers were despatched to the Totonac towns, to report what had been done, calling on them to refuse the payment of further tribute to Montezuma. But there was no need of messengers. The affrighted attendants of the Aztec lords had fled in every direction, bearing the tidings, which spread like wildfire through the country, of the daring insult offered to the majesty of Mexico. The astonished Indians, cheered with the sweet hope of regaining their ancient liberty, came in numbers to Chiahuitzlan, to see and confer with the formidable strangers. The more timid, dismayed at the thoughts of encountering the power of Montezuma, recommended an embassy to avert his displeasure by timely concessions. But the dexterous management of Cortés had committed them too far to allow any reasonable expectation of indulgence from this quarter. After some hesitation, therefore, it was determined to embrace the protection of the Spaniards, and to make one bold effort for the recovery of freedom. Oaths of allegiance were taken by the chiefs to the Spanish sovereigns, and duly recorded by Godoy, the royal notary. Cortés, satisfied with the important acquisition of so many vassals to the crown, set out soon after for the destined port, having first promised to revisit Cempoalla, where his business was but partially accomplished.

The spot selected for the new city was only half a league distant, in a wide and fruitful plain, affording a tolerable haven for the shipping. Cortés was not long in determining the circuit of the walls, and the sites of the fort, granary, town-house, temple, and other public buildings. The friendly Indians eagerly assisted, by bringing materials, stone, lime, wood, and bricks dried in the sun. Every man put his hand to the work. The general laboured with the meanest of the soldiers, stimulating their exertions by his example, as well as voice. In a few weeks the task was accomplished, and a town rose up, which, if not quite worthy of the aspiring name it bore, answered most of the purposes for which it was intended. It served as a good *point d'appui* for future operations; a place of retreat for the disabled, as well as for the army in case of reverses; a magazine for stores, and for such articles as might be received from or sent to the mother country; a port for the shipping; a position of sufficient strength to overawe the adjacent country.

It was the first colony—the fruitful parent of so many others—in New Spain. It was hailed with satisfaction by the simple natives, who hoped to repose in safety under its protecting shadow. Alas! they could not read the future, or they would have found no cause to rejoice in this harbinger of a revolution more tremendous than any predicted by their bards and prophets. It was not the good Quetzalcoatl who had returned to claim his own again, bringing peace, freedom, and civilisation in his train. Their fetters, indeed, would be broken, and their wrongs be amply avenged on the proud head of the Aztec; but it was to be by that strong arm which should bow down equally the oppressor and the oppressed. The light of civilisation would be poured on their land; but it would be the light of a consuming fire, before which their barbaric glory, their institutions, their very existence and name as a nation, would wither and become extinct! Their doom was sealed when the white man had set his foot on their soil.

CHAPTER VIII

Another Aztec Embassy—Destruction of the Idols—Despatches Sent to Spain—Conspiracy in the Camp—The Fleet Sunk

1519

WHILE the Spaniards were occupied with their new settlement, they were surprised by the presence of an embassy from Mexico. The account of the imprisonment of the royal collectors had spread rapidly through the country. When it reached the capital, all were filled with amazement at the unprecedented daring of the strangers. In Montezuma every other feeling, even that of fear, was swallowed up in indignation; and he showed his wonted energy in the vigorous preparations which he instantly made to punish his rebellious vassals, and to avenge the insult offered to the majesty of the empire. But when the Aztec officers liberated by Cortés reached the capital and reported the courteous treatment they had received from the Spanish commander, Montezuma's anger was mitigated, and his superstitious fears, getting the ascendency again, induced him to resume his former timid and conciliatory policy. He accordingly sent an embassy, consisting of two youths, his nephews, and four of the ancient nobles of his court, to the Spanish quarters. He provided them, in his usual munificent spirit, with a princely donation of gold, rich cotton stuffs, and beautiful mantles of the *plumaje,* or feather embroidery. The envoys, on coming before Cortés, presented him with the articles, at the same time offering the acknowledgments of their master for the courtesy he had shown in liberating his captive nobles. He was surprised and afflicted, however, that the Spaniards should have countenanced his faithless vassals in their rebellion. He had no doubt they were the strangers whose arrival had been so long announced by the oracles, and of the same lineage with himself. From deference to them he would spare the Totonacs, while they were present. But the time for vengeance would come.

Cortés entertained the Indian chieftains with frank hospitality. At the same time he took care to make such a display of his resources, as, while it amused their minds, should leave a deep impression of his power. He then, after a few trifling gifts, dismissed them with a conciliatory message to their master, and the assurance that he should soon pay his respects to him in his capital, where all misunderstanding between them would be readily adjusted.

The Totonac allies could scarcely credit their senses, when they gathered the nature of this interview. Notwithstanding the presence of the Spaniards, they had looked with apprehension to the consequences of their rash act; and their feelings of admiration were heightened into awe for the strangers who, at this distance, could exercise so mysterious an influence over the terrible Montezuma.

Not long after, the Spaniards received an application from the cacique of Cempoalla to aid him in a dispute in which he was engaged with a neighbouring city. Cortés marched with a part of his forces to his support. On the route, one Morla, a common soldier, robbed a native of a couple of fowls. Cortés, indignant at this violation of his orders before his face, and aware of the importance of maintaining a reputation for good faith with his allies, commanded the man to be hung up at once by the roadside, in face of the whole army. Fortunately for the poor wretch, Pedro de Alvarado, the future conqueror of Quiché, was present, and ventured to cut down the body while there was yet life in it. He, probably, thought enough had been done for example, and the loss of a single life, unnecessarily, was more than the little band could afford. The anecdote is characteristic, as showing the strict discipline maintained by Cortés over his men and the freedom assumed by his captains, who regarded him on terms nearly of equality—as a fellow-adventurer with themselves. This feeling of companionship led to a spirit of insubordination among them, which made his own post as commander the more delicate and difficult.

On reaching the hostile city, but a few leagues from the coast, they were received in an amicable manner; and Cortés, who was accompanied by his allies, had the satisfaction of reconciling these different branches of the Totonac family with each other, without bloodshed. He then returned to Cempoalla, where he was welcomed with joy by the people, who were now impressed with as favourable an opinion of his moderation and justice, as they had before been of his valour. In token of his gratitude, the Indian cacique delivered to the general eight Indian maidens, richly dressed, wearing collars and ornaments of gold, with a number of female slaves to wait on them. They were daughters of the principal chiefs, and the cacique requested that the Spanish captains might take them as their wives. Cortés received the damsels courteously, but told the cacique they must first be baptised, as the sons of the Church have no commerce with idolaters. He then declared that it was a great object of his mission to wean the natives from their heathenish abominations, and besought the Totonac lord to allow his idols to be cast down, and the symbols of the true faith to be erected in their place.

To this the other answered as before, that his gods were good enough for him; nor could all the persuasion of the general, nor the preaching of father Olmedo, induce him to acquiesce. Mingled with his polytheism, he had conceptions of a Supreme and Infinite Being, Creator of the Universe, and his darkened understanding could not comprehend how such a Being could condescend to take the form of humanity, with its infirmities and ills, and wander about on earth, the voluntary victim of persecution from the hands of those whom his breath had called into existence. He plainly told the Spaniards that he would resist any violence offered to his gods, who would, indeed, avenge the act themselves, by the instant destruction of their enemies.

But the zeal of the Christians had mounted too high to be cooled by remonstrance or menace. During their residence in the land, they had witnessed more than once the barbarous rites of the natives, their cruel sacrifices of human victims, and their disgusting cannibal repasts. Their souls sickened at these abominations, and they agreed with one voice to stand by their general, when he told them that "Heaven would never smile on their enterprise, if they countenanced such atrocities; and that, for his own part, he was resolved the Indian idols should be demolished that very hour, if it cost him his life." To postpone the work of conversion was a sin. In the enthusiasm of the moment, the dictates of policy and ordinary prudence were alike unheeded.

Scarcely waiting for his commands, the Spaniards moved towards one of the principal *teocallis,* or temples, which rose high on a pyramidal foundation, with a steep ascent of stone steps in the middle. The cacique, divining their purpose, instantly called his men to arms. The Indian warriors gathered from all quarters, with shrill cries and clashing of weapons; while the priests, in their dark cotton robes, with dishevelled tresses matted with blood, flowing wildly over their shoulders, rushed frantic among the natives, calling on them to protect their gods from violation! All was now confusion, tumult, and warlike menace, where so lately had been peace and the sweet brotherhood of nations.

Cortés took his usual prompt and decided measures. He caused the cacique and some of the principal inhabitants and priests to be arrested by his soldiers. He then commanded them to quiet the people, for, if an arrow was shot against a Spaniard, it should cost every one of them his life. Marina, at the same time, represented the madness of resistance, and reminded the cacique that, if he now alienated the affections of the Spaniards, he would be left without a protector against the terrible vengeance of Montezuma. These temporal considerations seem to have had more weight with the Totonac chieftain than those of a more spiritual nature. He covered his face with his hands, exclaiming that the gods would avenge their own wrongs.

The Christians were not slow in availing themselves of his tacit acquiescence. Fifty soldiers, at a signal from their general, sprang up the great stairway of the temple, entered the building on the summit, the walls of which were black with human gore, tore the huge wooden idols from their foundations, and dragged them to the edge of the terrace. Their fantastic forms and features, conveying a symbolic meaning, which was lost on the Spaniards, seemed in their eyes only the hideous lineaments of Satan. With great alacrity they rolled the colossal monsters down the steps of the pyramid, amidst the triumphant shouts of their own companions, and the groans and lamentations of the natives. They then consummated the whole by burning them in the presence of the assembled multitude.

The same effect followed as in Cozumel. The Totonacs, finding their deities incapable of preventing or even punishing this profanation of their shrines, conceived a mean opinion of their power, compared with that of the mysterious and formidable strangers. The floor and walls of the *teocalli* were then cleansed, by command of Cortés, from their foul impurities; a fresh coating of stucco was laid on them by the Indian masons; and an altar was raised, surmounted by a lofty cross, and hung with garlands of roses. A procession was next formed, in which some of the principal Totonac priests, exchanging their dark mantles for robes of white, carried lighted candles in their hands; while an image of the Virgin, half smothered under the weight of flowers, was borne aloft, and, as the procession climbed the steps of the temple, was deposited above the altar. Mass was performed by Father Olmedo, and the impressive character of the ceremony and the passionate eloquence of the good priest touched the feelings of the motley audience, until Indians as well as Spaniards, if we may trust the chronicler, were melted into tears and audible sobs. The Protestant missionary seeks to enlighten the understanding of his convert by the pale light of reason. But the bolder Catholic, kindling the spirit by the splendour of the spectacle and by the glowing portrait of an agonised Redeemer, sweeps along his hearers in a tempest of passion, that drowns everything like reflection. He has secured his convert, however, by the hold on his affections—an easier and more powerful hold with the untutored savage, than reason.

An old soldier named Juan de Torres, disabled by bodily infirmity, consented to remain and watch over the sanctuary and instruct the natives in its services. Cortés then embracing his Totonac allies, now brothers in religion as in arms, set out once more for the Villa Rica, where he had some arrangements to complete, previous to his departure for the capital.

He was surprised to find that a Spanish vessel had arrived there in his absence, having on board twelve soldiers and two horses. It was under the command of a captain named Saucedo, a cavalier of the ocean, who had followed in the track of Cortés in quest of adventure. Though a small, they afforded a very seasonable, body of recruits for the little army. By these men, the Spaniards were informed that Velasquez, the governor of Cuba, had lately received a warrant from the Spanish government to establish a colony in the newly discovered countries.

Cortés now resolved to put a plan in execution which he had been some time meditating. He knew that all the late acts of the colony, as well as his own authority, would fall to the ground without the royal sanction. He knew, too, that the interest of Velasquez, which was great at court, would, as soon as he was acquainted with his secession, be wholly employed to circumvent and crush him. He resolved to anticipate his movements, and to send a vessel to Spain, with despatches addressed to the emperor himself, announcing the nature and extent of his discoveries, and to obtain, if possible, the confirmation of his proceedings. In order to conciliate his master's good will, he further proposed to send him such a present as should suggest lofty ideas of the importance of his own services to the crown. To effect this, the royal fifth he considered inadequate. He conferred with his officers, and persuaded them to relinquish their share of the treasure. At his instance, they made a similar application to the soldiers; representing that it was the earnest wish of the general, who set the example by resigning his own fifth, equal to the share of the crown. It was but little that each man was asked to surrender, but the whole would make a present worthy of the monarch for whom it was intended. By this sacrifice they might hope to secure his indulgence for the past, and his favour for the future; a temporary sacrifice, that would be well repaid by the security of the rich possessions which awaited them in Mexico. A paper was then circulated among the soldiers, which all, who were disposed to relinquish their shares, were requested to sign. Those who declined should have their claims respected, and receive the amount due to them. No one refused to sign; thus furnishing another example of the extraordinary power obtained by Cortés over these rapacious spirits, who, at his call, surrendered up the very treasures which had been the great object of their hazardous enterprise!

He accompanied this present with a letter to the emperor, in which he gave a full account of all that had befallen him since his departure from Cuba; of his various discoveries, battles, and traffic with the natives; their conversion to Christianity; his strange perils and sufferings; many particulars respecting the lands he had visited, and such as he could collect in regard to the great Mexican monarchy and its sovereign. He stated his difficulties with the governor of Cuba, the proceedings of the army in reference to colonisation, and besought the emperor to confirm their acts, as well as his own authority, expressing his entire confidence that he should be able, with the aid of his brave followers, to place the Castilian crown in possession of this great Indian empire.

This was the celebrated *First Letter,* as it is called, of Cortés, which has hitherto eluded every search that has been made for it in the libraries of Europe. Its existence is fully established by references to it, both in his own subsequent letters, and in the writings of contemporaries. Its general purport is given by his chaplain, Gomara. The importance of the document has doubtless been much overrated; and, should it ever come to light, it will probably be found to add little of interest to the matter contained in the letter from Vera Cruz, which has formed the basis of the preceding portion of our narrative. He had no sources of information beyond those open to the authors of the latter document. He was even less full and frank in his communications, if it be true, that he suppressed all notice of the discoveries of his two immediate predecessors.

The magistrates of the Villa Rica, in their epistle, went over the same ground with Cortés; concluding with an emphatic representation of the misconduct of Velasquez, whose venality, extortion, and selfish devotion to his personal interests, to the exclusion of those of his sovereign as well as of his own followers, they placed in a most clear and unenviable light. They implored the government not to sanction his interference with the new colony, which would be fatal to its welfare, but to commit the undertaking to Hernando Cortés, as the man most capable, by his experience and conduct, of bringing it to a glorious termination.

With this letter went also another in the name of the citizen-soldiers of Villa Rica, tendering their dutiful submission to the sovereign, and requesting the confirmation of their proceedings, above all that of Cortés as their general.

The selection of the agents for the mission was a delicate matter, as on the result might depend the future fortunes of the colony and its commander. Cortés intrusted the affair to two cavaliers on whom he could rely: Francisco de Montejo, the ancient partisan of Velasquez, and Alonso Hernandez de Puertocarrero. The latter officer was a near kinsman of the Count of Medellin, and it was hoped his high connections might secure a favourable influence at court.

Together with the treasure, which seemed to verify the assertion that "the land teemed with gold as abundantly as that whence Solomon drew the same precious metal for his temple," several Indian manuscripts were sent. Some were of cotton, others of the Mexican *agave*. Their unintelligible characters, says a chronicler, excited little interest in the Conquerors. As evidence of intellectual culture, however, they formed higher objects of interest to a philosophic mind, than those costly fabrics which attested only the mechanical ingenuity of the nation. Four Indian slaves were added as specimens of the natives. They had been rescued from the cages in which they were confined for sacrifice. One of the best vessels of the fleet was selected for the voyage, manned by fifteen seamen, and placed under the direction of the pilot Alaminos. He was directed to hold his course through the Bahama channel, north of Cuba, or Fernandina, as it was then called, and on no account to touch at that island, or any other in the Indian Ocean. With these instructions, the good ship took its departure on July 26, freighted with the treasures and the good wishes of the community of the Villa Rica de Vera Cruz.

After a quick run the emissaries made the island of Cuba, and, in direct disregard of orders, anchored before Marien on the northern side of the island. This was done to accommodate Montejo, who wished to visit a plantation owned by him in the neighbourhood. While off the port, a sailor got on shore, and, crossing the island to St. Jago, the capital, spread everywhere tidings of the expedition, until they reached the ears of Velasquez. It was the first intelligence which had been received of the armament since its departure; and, as the governor listened to the recital, it would not be easy to paint the mingled emotions of curiosity, astonishment, and wrath, which agitated his bosom. In the first sally of passion, he poured a storm of invective on the heads of his secretary and treasurer, the friends of Cortés, who had recommended him as the leader of the expedition. After somewhat relieving himself in this way, he despatched two fast-sailing vessels to Marien with orders to seize the rebel ship, and, in case of her departure, to follow and overtake her.

But before the ships could reach that port, the bird had flown, and was far on her way across the broad Atlantic. Stung with mortification at this fresh disappointment, Velasquez wrote letters of indignant complaint to the government at home, and to the fathers of St. Jerome, in Hispaniola, demanding redress. He obtained little satisfaction from the last. He resolved, however, to take it into his own hands, and set about making formidable preparations for another squadron, which should be more than a match for that under his rebellious officer. He was indefatigable in his exertions, visiting every part of the island, and straining all his resources to effect his purpose. The preparations were on a scale that necessarily consumed many months.

Meanwhile the little vessel was speeding her prosperous way across the waters; and, after touching at one of the Azores, came safely into the harbour of St. Lucar, in the month of October. However long it may appear in the more perfect nautical science of our day, it was reckoned a fair voyage for that. Of what befell the commissioners on their arrival, their reception at court, and the sensation caused by their intelligence, I defer the account to a future chapter.

Shortly after the departure of the commissioners, an affair occurred of a most unpleasant nature. A number of persons, with the priest Juan Diaz at their head, ill-affected, from some cause or other, towards the administration of Cortés, or not relishing the hazardous expedition before them, laid a plan to seize one of the vessels, make the best of their way to Cuba, and report to the governor the fate of the armament. It was conducted with so much secrecy, that the party had got their provisions, water, and everything necessary for the voyage, on board, without detection; when the conspiracy was betrayed on the very night they were to sail by one of their own number, who repented the part he had taken in it. The general caused the persons implicated to be instantly apprehended. An examination was instituted. The guilt of the parties was placed beyond a doubt. Sentence of death was passed on two of the ringleaders; another, the pilot, was condemned to lose his feet, and several others to be whipped. The priest, probably the most guilty of the whole, claiming the usual benefit of clergy, was permitted to escape. One of those condemned to the gallows was named Escudero, the very alguacil who, the reader may remember, so stealthily apprehended Cortés before the sanctuary in Cuba. The general on signing the death-warrants was heard to exclaim, "Would that I had never learned to write!" It was not the first time, it was remarked, that the exclamation had been uttered in similar circumstances.

The arrangements being now fully settled at the Villa Rica, Cortés sent forward Alvarado, with a large part of the army to Cempoalla, where he soon after joined them with the remainder. The late affair of the conspiracy seems to have made a deep impression on his mind. It showed him that there were timid spirits in the camp on' whom he could not rely, and who, he feared, might spread the seeds of disaffection among their companions. Even the more resolute, on any occasion of disgust or disappointment hereafter, might falter in purpose, and, getting possession of the vessels, abandon the enterprise. This was already too vast, and the odds were too formidable, to authorise expectation of success with diminution of numbers. Experience showed that this was always to be apprehended, while means of escape were at hand. The best chance for success was to cut off these means. He came to the daring resolution to destroy the fleet, without the knowledge of his army.

When arrived at Cempoalla, he communicated his design to a few of his devoted adherents, who entered warmly into his views. Through them he readily persuaded the pilots, by means of those golden arguments which weigh more than any other with ordinary minds, to make such a report of the condition of the fleet as suited his purpose. The ships, they said, were grievously racked by the heavy gales they had encountered, and, what was worse, the worms had eaten into their sides and bottoms until most of them were not seaworthy, and some, indeed, could scarcely now be kept afloat.

Cortés received the communication with surprise; "for he could well dissemble," observes Las Casas, with his usual friendly comment, "when it suited his interests." "If it be so," he exclaimed, "we must make the best of it! Heaven's will be done!" He then ordered five of the worstconditioned to be dismantled, their cordage, sails, iron, and whatever was moveable, to be brought on shore, and the ships to be sunk. A survey was made of the others, and, on a similar report, four more were condemned in the same manner. Only one small vessel remained!

When the intelligence reached the troops in Cempoalla, it caused the deepest consternation. They saw themselves cut off by a single blow from friends, family, country! The stoutest hearts quailed before the prospect of being thus abandoned on a hostile shore, a handful of men arrayed against a formidable empire. When the news arrived of the destruction of the five vessels first condemned, they had acquiesced in it, as a necessary measure, knowing the mischievous activity of the insects in these tropical seas. But, when this was followed by the loss of the remaining four, suspicions of the truth flashed on their minds. They felt they were betrayed. Murmurs, at first deep, swelled louder and louder, menacing open mutiny. "Their general," they said, "had led them like cattle to be butchered in the shambles!" The affair wore a most alarming aspect. In no situation was Cortés ever exposed to greater danger from his soldiers.

His presence of mind did not desert him at this crisis. He called his men together, and employing the tones of persuasion rather than authority, assured them that a survey of the ships showed they were not fit for service. If he had ordered them to be destroyed, they should consider, also, that his was the greatest sacrifice, for they were his property—all, indeed, he possessed in the world. The troops, on the other hand, would derive one great advantage from it, by the addition of a hundred able-bodied recruits, before required to man the vessels. But, even if the fleet had been saved, it could have been of little service in their present expedition; since they would not need it if they succeeded, while they would be too far in the interior to profit by it if they failed. He besought them to turn their thoughts in another direction. To be thus calculating chances and means of escape was unworthy of brave souls. They had set their hands to the work; to look back, as they advanced, would be their ruin. They had only to resume their former confidence in themselves and their general, and success was certain. "As for me," he concluded, "I have chosen my part. I will remain here, while there is one to bear me company. If there be any so craven, as to shrink from sharing the dangers of our glorious enterprise, let them go home, in God's name. There is still one vessel left. Let them take that and return to Cuba. They can tell there how they deserted their commander and their comrades, and patiently wait till we return loaded with the spoils of the Aztecs."

The politic orator had touched the right chord in the bosoms of the soldiers. As he spoke, their resentment gradually died away. The faded visions of future riches and glory, rekindled by his eloquence, again floated before their imaginations. The first shock over, they felt ashamed of their temporary distrust. The enthusiasm for their leader revived, for they felt that under his banner only they could hope for victory; and they testified the revulsion of their feelings by making the air ring with their shouts, "To Mexico! to Mexico!"

The destruction of his fleet by Cortés is, perhaps, the most remarkable passage in the life of this remarkable man. History, indeed, affords examples of a similar expedient in emergencies somewhat similar; but none where the chances of success were so precarious, and defeat would be so disastrous. Had he failed, it might well seem an act of madness. Yet it was the fruit of deliberate calculation. He had set fortune, fame, life itself, all upon the cast, and must abide the issue. There was no alternative in his mind but to succeed or perish. The measure he adopted greatly increased the chance of success. But to carry it into execution, in the face of an incensed and desperate soldiery, was an act of resolution that has few parallels in history.

MARCH TO MEXICO

CHAPTER I

*Proceedings at Cempoalla—The Spaniards Climb the Table-
land—Picturesque Scenery—Transactions with the
Natives—Embassy to Tlascala*

1519

WHILE AT CEMPOALLA, Cortés received a message from Escalante, his commander at Villa Rica, informing him there were four strange ships hovering off the coast, and that they took no notice of his repeated signals. This intelligence greatly alarmed the general, who feared they might be a squadron sent by the governor of Cuba to interfere with his movements. In much haste, he set out at the head of a few horsemen, and, ordering a party of light infantry to follow, posted back to Villa Rica. The rest of the army he left in charge of Alvarado and of Gonzalo de Sandoval, a young officer, who had begun to give evidence of the uncommon qualities which have secured to him so distinguished a rank among the conquerors of Mexico.

Escalante would have persuaded the general, on his reaching the town, to take some rest, and allow him to go in search of the strangers; but Cortés replied with the homely proverb, "A wounded hare takes no nap," and, without stopping to refresh himself or his men, pushed on three or four leagues to the north, where he understood the ships were at anchor. On the way, he fell in with three Spaniards, just landed from them. To his eager inquiries whence they came, they replied that they belonged to a squadron fitted out by Francisco de Garay, governor of Jamaica. This person, the year previous, had visited the Florida coast, and obtained from Spain—where he had some interest at court—authority over the countries he might discover in that vicinity. The three men, consisting of a notary and two witnesses, had been sent on shore to warn their countrymen under Cortés to desist from what was considered an encroachment on the territories of Garay. Probably neither the governor of Jamaica,

93

nor his officers, had any very precise notion of the geography and limits of these territories.

Cortés saw at once there was nothing to apprehend from this quarter. He would have been glad, however, if he could, by any means, have induced the crews of the ships to join his expedition. He found no difficulty in persuading the notary and his companions. But when he came in sight of the vessels, the people on board, distrusting the good terms on which their comrades appeared to be with the Spaniards, refused to send their boat ashore. In this dilemma, Cortés had recourse to a stratagem.

He ordered three of his own men to exchange dresses with the new comers. He then drew off his little band in sight of the vessels, affecting to return to the city. In the night, however, he came back to the same place, and lay in ambush, directing the disguised Spaniards, when the morning broke, and they could be discerned, to make signals to those on board. The artifice succeeded. A boat pulled off, filled with armed men, and three or four leaped on shore. But they soon detected the deceit, and Cortés, springing from his ambush, made them prisoners. Their comrades in the boat, alarmed, pushed off at once for the vessels, which soon got under weigh, leaving those on shore to their fate. Thus ended the affair. Cortés returned to Cempoalla, with the addition of half a dozen able-bodied recruits, and, what was of more importance, relieved in his own mind from the apprehension of interference with his operations.

He now made arrangements for his speedy departure from the Totonac capital. The forces reserved for the expedition amounted to about four hundred foot and fifteen horse, with seven pieces of artillery. He obtained, also, thirteen hundred Indian warriors, and a thousand *tamanes,* or porters, from the cacique of Cempoalla, to drag the guns, and transport the baggage. He took forty more of their principal men as hostages, as well as to guide him on the way, and serve him by their counsels among the strange tribes he was to visit. They were, in fact, of essential service to him throughout the march.

The remainder of his Spanish force he left in garrison at Villa Rica de Vera Cruz, the command of which he had intrusted to the alguacil, Juan de Escalante, an officer devoted to his interests. The selection was judicious. It was important to place there a man who would resist any hostile interference from his European rivals, on the one hand, and maintain the present friendly relations with the natives, on the other. Cortés recommended the Totonac chiefs to apply to this officer, in case of any difficulty, assuring them that, so long as they remained faithful to their new sovereign and religion, they should find a sure protection in the Spaniards.

Before marching, the general spoke a few words of encouragement to his own men. He told them they were now to embark in earnest on an enterprise which had been the great object of their desires; and that the blessed Saviour would carry them victorious through every battle with their enemies. "Indeed," he added, "this assurance must be our stay, for every other refuge is now cut off, but that afforded by the providence of God, and your own stout hearts." He ended by comparing their achievements to those of the ancient Romans, "in phrases of honeyed eloquence far beyond anything I can repeat," says the brave and simple-hearted chronicler who heard them. Cortés was, indeed, master of that eloquence which went to the soldiers' hearts. For their sympathies were his, and he shared in that romantic spirit of adventure which belonged to them. "We are ready to obey you," they cried as with one voice. "Our fortunes, for better or worse, are cast with yours." Taking leave, therefore, of their hospitable Indian friends, the little army, buoyant with high hopes and lofty plans of conquest, set forward on the march to Mexico.

It was August 16, 1519. During the first day their road lay through the *tierra caliente,* the beautiful land where they had been so long lingering; the land of the vanilla, cochineal, cacao (not till later days of the orange, and the sugar-cane), products which, indigenous to Mexico, have now become the luxuries of Europe; the land where the fruits and the flowers chase one another in unbroken circle through the year; where the gales are loaded with perfumes till the sense aches at their sweetness; and the groves are filled with many-coloured birds, and insects whose enamelled wings glisten like diamonds in the bright sun of the Tropics. Such are the magical splendours of this paradise of the senses. Yet nature, who generally works in a spirit of compensation, has provided one here; since the same burning sun which quickens into life these glories of the vegetable and animal kingdoms calls forth the pestilent *malaria,* with its train of bilious disorders, unknown to the cold skies of the North. The season in which the Spaniards were there, the rainy months of summer, was precisely that in which the *vomito* rages with greatest fury; when the European stranger hardly ventures to set his foot on shore, still less to linger there a day. We find no mention made of it in the records of the Conquerors, nor any notice, indeed, of an uncommon mortality. The fact doubtless corroborates the theory of those who postpone the appearance of the yellow fever till long after the occupation of the country by the whites. It proves, at least, that, if existing before, it must have been in a very much mitigated form.

After some leagues of travel over the roads made nearly impassable by the summer rains, the troops began the gradual ascent—more gradual on the eastern than the western declivities of the Cordilleras—which leads up to the tableland of Mexico. At the close of the second day, they reached Xalapa, a place still retaining the same Aztec name that it has communicated to the drug raised in its environs, the medicinal virtues of which are now known throughout the world. This town stands midway up the long ascent at an elevation where the vapours from the ocean, touching in their westerly progress, maintain a rich verdure throughout the year. Though somewhat infected with these marine fogs, the air is usually bland and salubrious. The wealthy resident of the lower regions retires here for safety in the heats of summer, and the traveller hails its groves of oak with delight, as announcing that he is above the deadly influence of the *vomito*. From this delicious spot the Spaniards enjoyed one of the grandest prospects in nature. Before them was the steep ascent —much steeper after this point—which they were to climb. On the right rose the *Sierra Madre,* girt with its dark belt of pines, and its long lines of shadowy hills stretching away in the distance. To the south, in brilliant contrast, stood the mighty Orizaba, with his white robe of snow descending far down his sides towering in solitary grandeur, the giant spectre of the Andes. Behind them, they beheld, unrolled at their feet, the magnificent *tierra caliente,* with its gay confusion of meadows, streams, and flowering forests, sprinkled over with shining Indian villages; while a faint line of light on the edge of the horizon told them that there was the ocean, beyond which were the kindred and country—they were many of them never more to see.

Still winding their way upward, amidst scenery as different as was the temperature from that of the regions below, the army passed through settlements containing some hundreds of inhabitants each, and on the fourth day reached a "strong town," as Cortés terms it, standing on a rocky eminence, supposed to be that now known by the Mexican name of Naulinco. Here they were hospitably entertained by the inhabitants, who were friends of the Totonacs. Cortés endeavoured, through Father Olmedo, to impart to them some knowledge of Christian truths, which were kindly received, and the Spaniards were allowed to erect a cross in the place, for the future adoration of the natives. Indeed, the route of the army might be tracked by these emblems of man's salvation, raised wherever a willing population of Indians invited it, suggesting a very different idea from what the same memorials intimate to the traveller in these mountain solitudes in our day.

The troops now entered a rugged defile, the Bishop's Pass, as it is called, capable of easy defence against an army. Very soon they experienced a most unwelcome change of climate. Cold winds from the mountains mingled with rain, and, as they rose still higher, with driving sleet and hail, drenched their garments, and seemed to penetrate to their very bones. The Spaniards, indeed, partially covered by their armour and thick jackets of quilted cotton, were better able to resist the weather, though their long residence in the sultry regions of the valley made them still keenly sensible to the annoyance. But the poor Indians, natives of the *tierra caliente,* with little protection in the way of covering, sank under the rude assault of the elements, and several of them perished on the road.

The aspect of the country was as wild and dreary as the climate. Their route wound along the spur of the huge Cofre de Perote, which borrows its name, both in Mexican and Castilian, from the cofferlike rock on its summit. It is one of the great volcanoes of New Spain. It exhibits now, indeed, no vestige of a crater on its top, but abundant traces of volcanic action at its base, where acres of lava, blackened scoriæ, and cinders, proclaim the convulsions of nature, while numerous shrubs and mouldering trunks of enormous trees, among the crevices, attest the antiquity of these events. Working their toilsome way across this scene of desolation, the path often led them along the borders of precipices, down whose sheer depths of two or three thousand feet the shrinking eye might behold another climate, and see all the glowing vegetation of the Tropics choking up the bottom of the ravines.

After three days of this fatiguing travel, the way-worn army emerged through another defile, the *Sierra del Agua.* They soon came upon an open reach of country, with a genial climate, such as belongs to the temperate latitudes of southern Europe. They had reached the level of more than seven thousand feet above the ocean, where the great sheet of tableland spreads out for hundreds of miles along the crests of the Cordilleras. The country showed signs of careful cultivation, but the products were, for the most part, not familiar to the eyes of the Spaniards. Fields and hedges of the various tribes of the cactus, the towering organum, and plantations of aloes with rich yellow clusters of flowers on their tall stems, affording drink and clothing to the Aztec, were everywhere seen. The plants of the torrid and temperate zones had disappeared, one after another, with the ascent into these elevated regions. The glossy and dark-leaved banana, the chief, as it is the cheapest, aliment of the countries below, had long since faded from the landscape. The hardy maize, however, still shone with its golden harvests in all the pride of cultivation, the great staple of the higher equally with the lower traces of the plateau.

Suddenly the troops came upon what seemed the environs of a populous city, which, as they entered it, appeared to surpass even that of Cempoalla in the size and solidity of its structures. These were of stone and lime, many of them spacious and tolerably high. There were thirteen *teocallis* in the place; and in the suburbs they had seen a receptacle, in which, according to Bernal Diaz, were stored a hundred thousand skulls of human victims, all piled and ranged in order! He reports the number as one he had ascertained by counting them himself. Whatever faith we may attach to the precise accuracy of his figures, the result is almost equally startling. The Spaniards were destined to become familiar with this appalling spectacle, as they approached nearer to the Aztec capital.

The lord of the town ruled over twenty thousand vassals. He was tributary to Montezuma, and a strong Mexican garrison was quartered in the place. He had probably been advised of the approach of the Spaniards, and doubted how far it would be welcome to his sovereign. At all events, he gave them a cold reception, the more unpalatable after the extraordinary sufferings of the last few days. To the inquiry of Cortés, whether he were subject to Montezuma, he answered with real or affected surprise, "Who is there that is not a vassal to Montezuma?" The general told him, with some emphasis, that *he* was not. He then explained whence and why he came, assuring him that he served a monarch who had princes for his vassals as powerful as the Aztec monarch himself.

The cacique in turn fell nothing short of the Spaniard in the pompous display of the grandeur and resources of the Indian emperor. He told his guest that Montezuma could muster thirty great vassals, each master of a hundred thousand men! His revenues were immense, as every subject, however poor, paid something. They were all expended on his magnificent state, and in support of his armies. These were continually in the field, while garrisons were maintained in most of the large cities of the empire. More than twenty thousand victims, the fruit of his wars, were annually sacrificed on the altars of his gods! His capital, the cacique said, stood in a lake in the centre of a spacious valley. The lake was commanded by the emperor's vessels, and the approach to the city was by means of causeways, several miles long, connected in parts by wooden bridges, which, when raised, cut off all communication with the country. Some other things he added, in answer to queries of his guest, in which as the reader may imagine, the crafty or credulous cacique varnished over the truth with a lively colouring of romance. Whether romance or reality, the Spaniards could not determine. The particulars they gleaned were not of a kind to tranquillise their minds, and might well have made bolder hearts than theirs pause, ere they advanced. But far from it. "The words which we heard," says the stout old cavalier, so often quoted, "however they may have filled us with wonder, made us—such is the temper of the Spaniard—only the more earnest to prove the adventure, desperate as it might appear."

In a further conversation Cortés inquired of the chief whether his country abounded in gold, and intimated a desire to take home some, as specimens to his sovereign. But the Indian lord declined to give him any, saying it might displease Montezuma. "Should he command it," he added, "my gold, my person, and all I possess, shall be at your disposal." The general did not press the matter further.

The curiosity of the natives was naturally excited by the strange dresses, weapons, horses, and dogs of the Spaniards. Marina, in satisfying their inquiries, took occasion to magnify the prowess of her adopted countrymen, expatiating on their exploits and victories, and stating the extraordinary marks of respect they had received from Montezuma. This intelligence seems to have had its effect; for soon after, the cacique gave the general some curious trinkets of gold, of no great value, indeed, but as a testimony of his good will. He sent him, also, some female slaves to prepare bread for the troops, and supplied the means of refreshment and repose, more important to them, in the present juncture, than all the gold of Mexico.

The Spanish general, as usual, did not neglect the occasion to inculcate the great truths of revelation on his host, and to display the atrocity of the Indian superstitions. The cacique listened with civil, but cold, indifference. Cortés, finding him unmoved, turned briskly round to his soldiers, exclaiming that now was the time to plant the Cross! They eagerly seconded his pious purpose, and the same scenes might have been enacted as at Cempoalla, with, perhaps, very different results, had not Father Olmedo, with better judgment, interposed. He represented that to introduce the Cross among the natives, in their present state of ignorance and incredulity, would be to expose the sacred symbol to desecration, so soon as the backs of the Spaniards were turned. The only way was to wait patiently the season when more leisure should be afforded to instil into their minds a knowledge of the truth. The sober reasoning of the good father prevailed over the passions of the martial enthusiasts.

It was fortunate for Cortés that Olmedo was not one of those frantic friars who would have fanned his fiery temper on such occasions into a blaze. It might have had a most disastrous influence on his fortunes; for he held all temporal consequences light in comparison with the great work of conversion, to effect which the unscrupulous mind of the soldier, trained to the stern discipline of the camp, would have employed force, whenever fair means were ineffectual. But Olmedo belonged to that class of benevolent missionaries—of whom the Roman Catholic Church, to its credit, has furnished many examples—who rely on spiritual weapons for the great work, inculcating those doctrines of love and mercy which can best touch the sensibilities and win the affections of their rude audience. These, indeed, are the true weapons of the church, the weapons employed in the primitive ages, by which it has spread its peaceful banners over the farthest regions of the globe. Such were not the means used by the conquerors of America, who, rather adopting the policy of the victorious Moslems in their early career, carried with them the sword in one hand and the Bible in the other. They imposed obedience in matters of faith, no less than of government, on the vanquished, little heeding whether the conversion were genuine, so that it conformed to the outward observances of the church. Yet the seeds thus recklessly scattered must have perished but for the missionaries of their own nation, who, in later times, worked over the same ground, living among the Indians as brethren, and, by long and patient culture, enabling the germs of truth to take root and fructify in their hearts.

The Spanish commander remained in the city four or five days to recruit his fatigued and famished forces; and the modern Indians still point out, or did, at the close of the last century, a venerable cypress, under the branches of which was tied the horse of the *conquistador*—the Conqueror, as Cortés was styled, *par excellence*. Their route now opened on a broad and verdant valley, watered by a noble stream—a circumstance of not too frequent occurrence on the parched tableland of New Spain. The soil was well protected by woods, a thing still rarer at the present day; since the invaders, soon after the Conquest, swept away the magnificent growth of timber, rivalling that of our Southern and Western States in variety and beauty, which covered the plateau under the Aztecs.

All along the river, on both sides of it, an unbroken line of Indian dwellings, "so near as almost to touch one another," extended for three or four leagues; arguing a population much denser than at present. On a rough and rising ground stood a town that might contain five or six thousand inhabitants, commanded by a fortress, which, with its walls and trenches, seemed to the Spaniards quite "on a level with similar works in Europe." Here the troops again halted, and met with friendly treatment.

Cortés now determined his future line of march. At the last place he had been counselled by the natives to take the route of the ancient city of Cholula, the inhabitants of which, subjects of Montezuma, were a mild race, devoted to mechanical and other peaceful arts, and would be likely to entertain him kindly. Their Cempoalla allies, however, advised the Spaniards not to trust the Cholulans, "a false and perfidious people," but to take the road to Tlascala, that valiant little republic which had so long maintained its independence against the arms of Mexico. The people were frank as they were fearless, and fair in their dealings. They had always been on terms of amity with the Totonacs, which afforded a strong guarantee for their amicable disposition on the present occasion.

The arguments of his Indian allies prevailed with the Spanish commander, who resolved to propitiate the good will of the Tlascalans by an embassy. He selected four of the principal Cempoallans for this, and sent by them a martial gift—a cap of crimson cloth, together with a sword and a crossbow, weapons which, it was observed, excited general admiration among the natives. He added a letter, in which he asked permission to pass through their country. He expressed his admiration of the valour of the Tlascalans, and of their long resistance to the Aztecs, whose proud empire he designed to humble. It was not to be expected that this epistle, indited in good Castilian, would be very intelligible to the Tlascalans. But Cortés communicated its import to the ambassadors. Its mysterious characters might impress the natives with an idea of superior intelligence, and the letters serve instead of those hieroglyphical missives which formed the usual credentials of an Indian ambassador.

The Spaniards remained three days in this hospitable place, after the departure of the envoys, when they resumed their progress. Although in a friendly country, they marched always as if in a land of enemies, the horse and light troops in the van, with the heavy-armed and baggage in the rear, all in battle array. They were never without their armour, waking or sleeping, lying down with their weapons by their sides. This unintermitting and restless vigilance was, perhaps, more oppressive to the spirits than even bodily fatigue. But they were confident in their superiority in a fair field, and felt that the most serious danger they had to fear from Indian warfare was surprise. "We are few against many, brave companions," Cortés would say to them; "be prepared, then, not as if you were going to battle, but as if actually in the midst of it."

The road taken by the Spaniards was the same which at present leads to Tlascala; not that, however, usually followed in passing from Vera Cruz to the capital, which makes a circuit considerably to the south, towards Puebla, in the neighbourhood of the ancient Cholula. They more than once forded the stream that rolls through this beautiful plain, lingering several days on the way, in hopes of receiving an answer from the Indian republic. The unexpected delay of the messengers could not be explained and occasioned some uneasiness.

As they advanced into a country of rougher and bolder features, their progress was suddenly arrested by a remarkable fortification. It was a stone wall nine feet in height, and twenty in thickness, with a parapet a foot and a half broad, raised on the summit for the protection of those who defended it. It had only one opening, in the centre, made by two semicircular lines of wall, overlapping each other for the space of forty paces, and affording a passage-way between, ten paces wide, so contrived, therefore, as to be perfectly commanded by the inner wall. This fortification, which extended more than two leagues, rested at either end on the bold natural buttresses formed by the sierra. The work was built of immense blocks of stones nicely laid together without cement; and the remains still existing, among which are rocks of the whole breadth of the rampart, fully attest its solidity and size.

This singular structure marked the limits of Tlascala, and was intended, as the natives told the Spaniards, as a barrier against the Mexican invasions. The army paused, filled with amazement at the contemplation of this Cyclopean monument, which naturally suggested reflections on the strength and resources of the people who had raised it. It caused them, too, some painful solicitude as to the probable result of their mission to Tlascala, and their own consequent reception there. But they were too sanguine to allow such uncomfortable surmises long to dwell in their minds. Cortés put himself at the head of his cavalry, and calling out, "Forward, soldiers, the Holy Cross is our banner, and under that we shall conquer," led his little army through the undefended passage, and in a few moments they trod the soil of the free republic of Tlascala.

CHAPTER II

Republic of Tlascala—Its Institutions—Early History—
Discussions in the Senate—Desperate Battles

1519

BEFORE ADVANCING FURTHER with the Spaniards into the territory of
Tlascala, it will be well to notice some traits in the character and institutions of the nation, in many respects the most remarkable in Anahuac.
The Tlascalans belonged to the same great family with the Aztecs. They
came on the grand plateau about the same time with the kindred races,
at the close of the twelfth century, and planted themselves on the western
borders of the Lake of Tezcuco. Here they remained many years engaged
in the usual pursuits of a bold and partially civilised people. From some
cause or other, perhaps their turbulent temper, they incurred the enmity
of surrounding tribes. A coalition was formed against them; and a bloody
battle was fought on the plains of Poyauhtlan, in which the Tlascalans
were completely victorious.

Disgusted, however, with their residence among nations with whom
they found so little favour, the conquering people resolved to migrate.
They separated into three divisions, the largest of which, taking a southern course by the great *volcan* of Mexico, wound round the ancient city
of Cholula, and finally settled in the district of country overshadowed by
the *sierra* of Tlascala. The warm and fruitful valleys locked up in the
embraces of this rugged brotherhood of mountains afforded means of
subsistence for an agricultural people, while the bold eminences of the
sierra presented secure positions for their towns.

After the lapse of years, the institutions of the nation underwent an
important change. The monarchy was divided first into two, afterwards
into four separate states, bound together by a sort of federal compact,
probably not very nicely defined. Each state, however, had its lord or
supreme chief, independent in his own territories, and possessed of co-
ordinate authority with the others in all matters concerning the whole

103

republic. The affairs of government, especially all those relating to peace and war, were settled in a senate or council, consisting of the four lords with their inferior nobles.

The lower dignitaries held of the superior, each in his own district, by a kind of feudal tenure, being bound to supply his table, and enable him to maintain his state in peace, as well as to serve him in war. In return he experienced the aid and protection of his suzerain. The same mutual obligations existed between him and the followers among whom his own territories were distributed. Thus a chain of feudal dependencies was established, which, if not contrived with all the art and legal refinements of analogous institutions in the Old World, displayed their most prominent characteristics in its personal relations, the obligations of military service on the one hand, and protection on the other. This form of government, so different from that of the surrounding nations, subsisted till the arrival of the Spaniards. And it is certainly evidence of considerable civilisation, that so complex a polity should have so long continued undisturbed by violence or faction in the confederate states, and should have been found competent to protect the people in their rights, and the country from foreign invasion.

The lowest order of the people, however, do not seem to have enjoyed higher immunities than under the monarchical governments; and their rank was carefully defined by an appropriate dress, and by their exclusion from the insignia of the aristocratic orders.

The nation, agricultural in its habits, reserved its highest honours, like most other rude—unhappily also, civilised—nations, for military prowess. Public games were instituted, and prizes decreed to those who excelled in such manly and athletic exercises as might train them for the fatigues of war. Triumphs were granted to the victorious general, who entered the city, leading his spoils and captives in long procession, while his achievements were commemorated in national songs, and his effigy, whether in wood or stone, was erected in the temples. It was truly in the martial spirit of republican Rome.

An institution not unlike knighthood was introduced, very similar to one existing also among the Aztecs. The aspirant to the honours of this barbaric chivalry watched his arms and fasted fifty or sixty days in the temple, then listened to a grave discourse on the duties of his new profession. Various whimsical ceremonies followed, when his arms were restored to him; he was led in solemn procession through the public streets, and the inauguration was concluded by banquets and public rejoicings. The new knight was distinguished henceforth by certain peculiar privileges, as well as by a badge intimating his rank. It is worthy of remark, that this honour was not reserved exclusively for military merit; but was the recompense, also, of public services of other kinds, as wisdom in council, or sagacity and success in trade. For trade was held in as high estimation by the Tlascalans as by the other people of Anahuac.

The temperate climate of the tableland furnished the ready means for distant traffic. The fruitfulness of the soil was indicated by the name of the country—*Tlascala* signifying the "land of bread." Its wide plains to the slopes of its rocky hills, waved with yellow harvests of maize, and with the bountiful maguey, a plant which, as we have seen, supplied the materials for some important fabrics. With these, as well as the products of agricultural industry, the merchant found his way down the sides of the Cordilleras, wandered over the sunny regions at their base, and brought back the luxuries which nature had denied to his own.

The various arts of civilisation kept pace with increasing wealth and public prosperity; at least these arts were cultivated to the same limited extent, apparently, as among the other people of Anahuac. The Tlascalan tongue, says the national historian, simple as beseemed that of a mountain region, was rough compared with the polished Tezcucan, or the popular Aztec dialect, and, therefore, not so well fitted for composition. But they made like proficiency with the kindred nations in the rudiments of science. Their calendar was formed on the same plan. Their religion, their architecture, many of their laws and social usages were the same, arguing a common origin for all. Their tutelary deity was the same ferocious war-god as that of the Aztecs, though with a different name; their temples, in like manner, were drenched with the blood of human victims, and their boards groaned with the same cannibal repasts.

Though not ambitious of foreign conquest, the prosperity of the Tlascalans, in time, excited the jealousy of their neighbours, and especially of the opulent state of Cholula. Frequent hostilities arose between them, in which the advantage was almost always on the side of the former. A still more formidable foe appeared in later days in the Aztecs; who could ill brook the independence of Tlascala, when the surrounding nations had acknowledged, one after another, their influence or their empire. Under the ambitious Axayacatl, they demanded of the Tlascalans the same tribute and obedience rendered by other people of the country. If it were refused, the Aztecs would raze their cities to their foundations, and deliver the land to their enemies.

To this imperious summons, the little republic proudly replied, "Neither they nor their ancestors had ever paid tribute or homage to a foreign power, and never would pay it. If their country was invaded, they knew how to defend it, and would pour out their blood as freely in defence of their freedom now, as their fathers did of yore, when they routed the Aztecs on the plains of Poyauhtlan!"

This resolute answer brought on them the forces of the monarchy. A pitched battle followed, and the sturdy republicans were victorious. From this period hostilities between the two nations continued with more or less activity, but with unsparing ferocity. Every captive was mercilessly sacrificed. The children were trained from the cradle to deadly hatred against the Mexicans; and, even in the brief intervals of war, none of those intermarriages took place between the people of the respective countries which knit together in social bonds most of the other kindred races of Anahuac.

In this struggle, the Tlascalans received an important support in the accession of the Othomis, or Otomies—as usually spelt by Castilian writers—a wild and warlike race originally spread over the tableland north of the Mexican valley. A portion of them obtained a settlement in the republic, and were speedily incorporated in its armies. Their courage and fidelity to the nation of their adoption showed them worthy of trust, and the frontier places were consigned to their keeping. The mountain barriers, by which Tlascala is encompassed, afforded many strong natural positions for defence against invasion. The country was open towards the east, where a valley, of some six miles in breadth, invited the approach of an enemy. But here it was that the jealous Tlascalans erected the formidable rampart which had excited the admiration of the Spaniards, and which they manned with a garrison of Otomies.

Efforts for their subjugation were renewed on a greater scale, after the accession of Montezuma. His victorious arms had spread down the declivities of the Andes to the distant provinces of Vera Paz and Nicaragua, and his haughty spirit was chafed by the opposition of a petty state, whose territorial extent did not exceed ten leagues in breadth by fifteen in length. He sent an army against them under the command of a favourite son. His troops were beaten and his son was slain. The enraged and mortified monarch was roused to still greater preparations. He enlisted the forces of the cities bordering on his enemy, together with those of the empire, and with this formidable army swept over the devoted valleys of Tlascala. But the bold mountaineers withdrew into the recesses of their hills, and, coolly awaiting their opportunity, rushed like a torrent on the invaders, and drove them back, with dreadful slaughter, from their territories.

Still, notwithstanding the advantages gained over the enemy in the field, the Tlascalans were sorely pressed by their long hostilities with a foe so far superior to themselves in numbers and resources. The Aztec armies lay between them and the coast, cutting off all communication with that prolific region, and thus limited their supplies to the products of their own soil and manufacture. For more than half a century they had neither cotton, nor cacao, nor salt. Indeed, their taste had been so far affected by long abstinence from these articles, that it required the lapse of several generations after the Conquest to reconcile them to the use of salt at their meals. During the short intervals of war, it is said, the Aztec nobles, in the true spirit of chivalry, sent supplies of these commodities as presents, with many courteous expressions of respect, to the Tlascalan chiefs. This intercourse, we are assured by the Indian chronicler, was unsuspected by the people. Nor did it lead to any further correspondence, he adds, between the parties, prejudicial to the liberties of the republic, "which maintained its customs and good government inviolate, and the worship of its gods."

Such was the condition of Tlascala, at the coming of the Spaniards; holding, it might seem, a precarious existence under the shadow of the formidable power which seemed suspended like an avalanche over her head, but still strong in her own resources, stronger in the indomitable temper of her people; with a reputation established throughout the land for good faith and moderation in peace, for valour in war, while her uncompromising spirit of independence secured the respect even of her enemies. With such qualities of character, and with an animosity sharpened by long, deadly hostility with Mexico, her alliance was obviously of the last importance to the Spaniards, in their present enterprise. It was not easy to secure it.

The Tlascalans had been made acquainted with the advance and victorious career of the Christians, the intelligence of which had spread far and wide over the plateau. But they do not seem to have anticipated the approach of the strangers to their own borders. They were now much embarrassed by the embassy demanding a passage through their territories. The great council was convened, and a considerable difference of opinion prevailed in its members. Some, adopting the popular superstition, supposed the Spaniards might be the white and bearded men foretold by the oracles. At all events, they were the enemies of Mexico, and as such might co-operate with them in their struggle with the empire. Others argued that the strangers could have nothing in common with them. Their march throughout the land might be tracked by the broken images of the Indian gods, and desecrated temples. How did the Tlascalans even know that they were foes to Montezuma? They had received his embassies, accepted his presents, and were now in the company of his vassals on the way to his capital.

These last were the reflections of an aged chief, one of the four who presided over the republic. His name was Xicotencatl. He was nearly blind, having lived, as is said, far beyond the limits of a century. His son, an impetuous young man of the same name with himself, commanded a powerful army of Tlascalan and Otomie warriors, near the eastern frontier. It would be best, the old man said, to fall with this force at once on the Spaniards. If victorious, the latter would then be in their power. If defeated, the senate could disown the act as that of the general, not of the republic. The cunning counsel of the chief found favour with his hearers, though assuredly not in the spirit of chivalry, nor of the good faith for which his countrymen were celebrated. But with an Indian, force and stratagem, courage and deceit, were equally admissible in war, as they were among the barbarians of ancient Rome. The Cempoallan envoys were to be detained under pretence of assisting at a religious sacrifice.

Meanwhile, Cortés and his gallant band, as stated in the preceding chapter, had arrived before the rocky rampart on the eastern confines of Tlascala. From some cause or other, it was not manned by its Otomie garrison, and the Spaniards passed in, as we have seen, without resistance. Cortés rode at the head of his body of horse, and, ordering the infantry to come on at a quick pace, went forward to reconnoitre. After advancing three or four leagues, he descried a small party of Indians, armed with sword and buckler, in the fashion of the country. They fled at his approach. He made signs for them to halt, but, seeing that they only fled the faster, he and his companions put spurs to their horses, and soon came up with them. The Indians, finding escape impossible, faced round, and, instead of showing the accustomed terror of the natives at the strange and appalling aspect of a mounted trooper, they commenced a furious assault on the cavaliers. The latter, however, were too strong for them, and would have cut their enemy to pieces without much difficulty, when a body of several thousand Indians appeared in sight, and coming briskly on to the support of their countrymen.

Cortés, seeing them, despatched one of his party, in all haste, to accelerate the march of his infantry. The Indians, after discharging their missiles, fell furiously on the little band of Spaniards. They strove to tear the lances from their grasp, and to drag the riders from the horses. They brought one cavalier to the ground, who afterwards died of his wounds, and they killed two of the horses, cutting through their necks with their stout broadswords—if we may believe the chronicler—at a blow. In the narrative of these campaigns, there is sometimes but one step—and that a short one—from history to romance. The loss of the horses, so important and so few in number, was seriously felt by Cortés, who could have better spared the life of the best rider in the troop.

The struggle was a hard one. But the odds were as overwhelming as any recorded by the Spaniards in their own romances, where a handful of knights is arrayed against legions of enemies. The lances of the Christians did terrible execution here also; but they had need of the magic lance of Astolpho, that overturned myriads with a touch, to carry them safe through so unequal a contest. It was with no little satisfaction, therefore, that they beheld their comrades rapidly advancing to their support.

No sooner had the main body reached the field of battle, than, hastily forming, they poured such a volley from their muskets and crossbows as staggered the enemy. Astounded, rather than intimidated, by the terrible report of the firearms, now heard for the first time in these regions, the Indians made no further effort to continue the fight, but drew off in good order, leaving the road open to the Spaniards. The latter, too well satisfied to be rid of the annoyance, to care to follow the retreating foe, again held on their way.

Their route took them through a country sprinkled over with Indian cottages, amidst flourishing fields of maize and maguey, indicating an industrious and thriving peasantry. They were met here by two Tlascalan envoys, accompanied by two of the Cempoallans. The former, presenting themselves before the general, disavowed the assault on his troops as an unauthorised act, and assured him of a friendly reception at their capital. Cortés received the communication in a courteous manner, affecting to place more confidence in its good faith than he probably felt.

It was now growing late, and the Spaniards quickened their march, anxious to reach a favourable ground for encampment before nightfall. They found such a spot on the borders of a stream that rolled sluggishly across the plain. A few deserted cottages stood along the banks, and the fatigued and famished soldiers ransacked them in quest of food; all they could find was some tame animals resembling dogs. These they killed and dressed without ceremony, and, garnishing their unsavoury repast with the fruit of the *tuna,* the Indian fig, which grew wild in the neighbourhood, they contrived to satisfy the cravings of appetite. A careful watch was maintained by Cortés, and companies of a hundred men each relieved each other in mounting guard through the night. But no attack was made. Hostilities by night were contrary to the system of Indian tactics.

By break of day on the following morning, it being September 2, the troops were under arms. Besides the Spaniards, the whole number of Indian auxiliaries might now amount to three thousand; for Cortés had gathered recruits from the friendly places on his route; three hundred from the last. After hearing Mass, they resumed their march. They moved in close array; the general had previously admonished the men not to lag behind, or wander from the ranks a moment, as stragglers would be sure to be cut off by their stealthy and vigilant enemy. The horsemen rode three abreast, the better to give one another support; and Cortés instructed them in the heat of fight to keep together, and never to charge singly. He taught them how to carry their lances, that they might not be wrested from their hands by the Indians, who constantly attempted it. For the same reason they should avoid giving thrusts, but aim their weapons steadily at the faces of their foes.

They had not proceeded far, when they were met by the two remaining Cempoallan envoys, who with looks of terror informed the general that they had been treacherously seized and confined, in order to be sacrificed at an approaching festival of the Tlascalans, but in the night had succeeded in making their escape. They gave the unwelcome tidings, also, that a large force of the natives was already assembled to oppose the progress of the Spaniards.

Soon after, they came in sight of a body of Indians, about a thousand, apparently all armed and brandishing their weapons, as the Christians approached, in token of defiance. Cortés, when he had come within hearing, ordered the interpreters to proclaim that he had no hostile intentions; but wished only to be allowed a passage through their country, which he had entered as a friend. This declaration he commanded the royal notary, Godoy, to record on the spot, that, if blood were shed, it might not be charged on the Spaniards. This pacific proclamation was met, as usual on such occasions, by a shower of darts, stones, and arrows, which fell like rain on the Spaniards, rattling on their stout harness, and in some instances penetrating to the skin. Galled by the smart of their wounds, they called on the general to lead them on, till he sounded the well-known battle-cry, "St. Jago, and at them!"

The Indians maintained their ground for a while with spirit, when they retreated with precipitation, but not in disorder. The Spaniards, whose blood was heated by the encounter, followed up their advantage with more zeal than prudence, suffering the wily enemy to draw them into a narrow glen or defile, intersected by a little stream of water, where the broken ground was impracticable for artillery, as well as for the movements of cavalry. Pressing forward with eagerness, to extricate themselves from their perilous position, to their great dismay, on turning an abrupt angle of the pass, they came in presence of a numerous army choking up the gorge of the valley and stretching far over the plains beyond. To the astonished eyes of Cortés, they appeared a hundred thousand men, while no account estimates them at less than thirty thousand.

They presented a confused assemblage of helmets, weapons, and many-coloured plumes, glancing bright in the morning sun, and mingled with banners, above which proudly floated one that bore as a device the heron on a rock. It was the well-known ensign of the house of Titcala, and, as well as the white and yellow stripes on the bodies, and the like colours on the feather-mail of the Indians, showed that they were the warriors of Xicotencatl.

As the Spaniards came in sight, the Tlascalans set up a hideous war-cry, or rather whistle, piercing the ear with its shrillness, and which, with the beat of their melancholy drums that could be heard for half a league or more, might well have filled the stoutest heart with dismay. This formidable host came rolling on towards the Christians, as if to overwhelm them by their very numbers. But the courageous band of warriors, closely serried together and sheltered under their strong panoplies, received the shock unshaken, while the broken masses of the enemy, chafing and heaving tumultuously around them, seemed to recede only to return with new and accumulated force.

Cortés, as usual, in the front of danger, in vain endeavoured, at the head of the horse, to open a passage for the infantry. Still his men, both cavalry and foot, kept their array unbroken, offering no assailable point to their foe. A body of the Tlascalans, however, acting in concert, assaulted a soldier named Moran, one of the best riders in the troop. They succeeded in dragging him from his horse, which they despatched with a thousand blows. The Spaniards, on foot, made a desperate effort to rescue their comrade from the hands of the enemy—and from the horrible doom of the captive. A fierce struggle now began over the body of the prostrate horse. Ten of the Spaniards were wounded, when they succeeded in retrieving the unfortunate cavalier from his assailants, but in so disastrous a plight that he died on the following day. The horse was borne off in triumph by the Indians, and his mangled remains were sent, a strange trophy, to the different towns of Tlascala. The circumstance troubled the Spanish commander, as it divested the animal of the supernatural terrors with which the superstition of the natives had usually surrounded it. To prevent such a consequence, he had caused the two horses, killed on the preceding day, to be secretly buried on the spot.

The enemy now began to give ground gradually, borne down by the riders, and trampled under the hoofs of their horses. Through the whole of this sharp encounter, the Indian allies were of great service to the Spaniards. They rushed into the water, and grappled their enemies, with the desperation of men who felt that "their only safety was in the despair of safety." "I see nothing but death for us," exclaimed a Cempoallan chief to Marina; "we shall never get through the pass alive." "The God of the Christians is with us," answered the intrepid woman: "and He will carry us safely through."

Amidst the din of battle the voice of Cortés was heard, cheering on his soldiers. "If we fail now," he cried, "the cross of Christ can never be planted in the land. Forward, comrades! When was it ever known that a Castilian turned his back on a foe?" Animated by the words and heroic bearing of their general, the soldiers, with desperate efforts, at length succeeded in forcing a passage through the dark columns of the enemy, and emerged from the defile on the open plain beyond.

Here they quickly recovered their confidence with their superiority. The horse soon opened a space for the manœuvres of the artillery. The close files of their antagonists presented a sure mark; and the thunders of the ordnance vomiting forth torrents of fire and sulphurous smoke, the wide desolation caused in their ranks, and the strangely mangled carcasses of the slain, filled the barbarians with consternation and horror. They had no weapons to cope with these terrible engines, and their clumsy missiles, discharged from uncertain hands, seemed to fall ineffectual on the charmed heads of the Christians. What added to their embarrassment was the desire to carry off the dead and wounded from the field, a general practice among the people of Anahuac, but which necessarily exposed them, while thus employed, to still greater loss.

Eight of their principal chiefs had now fallen; and Xicotencatl, finding himself wholly unable to make head against the Spaniards in the open field, ordered a retreat. Far from the confusion of a panic-struck mob, so common among barbarians, the Tlascalan force moved off the ground with all the order of a well-disciplined army. Cortés, as on the preceding day, was too well satisfied with his present advantage to desire to follow it up. It was within an hour of sunset, and he was anxious before night-fall to secure a good position, where he might refresh his wounded troops, and bivouac for the night.

Gathering up his wounded, he held on his way, without loss of time; and before dusk reached a rocky eminence, called *Tzompachtepetl,* or "the hill of Tzompach." It was crowned by a sort of tower or temple, the remains of which are still visible. His first care was given to the wounded, both men and horses. Fortunately, an abundance of provisions was found in some neighbouring cottages; and the soldiers, at least all who were not disabled by their injuries, celebrated the victory of the day with feasting and rejoicing.

As to the number of killed or wounded on either side, it is matter of loosest conjecture. The Indians must have suffered severely, but the prac-tice of carrying off the dead from the field made it impossible to know to what extent. The injury sustained by the Spaniards appears to have been principally in the number of their wounded. The great object of the natives of Anahuac in their battles was to make prisoners, who might grace their triumphs, and supply victims for sacrifice. To this brutal superstition the Christians were indebted, in no slight degree, for their personal preservation. To take the reports of the Conquerors, their own losses in action were always inconsiderable. But whoever has had occa-sion to consult the ancient chroniclers of Spain in relation to its wars with the infidel, whether Arab or American, will place little confidence in numbers.

The events of the day had suggested many topics for painful reflection to Cortés. He had nowhere met with so determined a resistance within the borders of Anahuac; nowhere had he encountered native troops so formidable for their weapons, their discipline, and their valour. Far from manifesting the superstitious terrors felt by the other Indians at the strange arms and aspect of the Spaniards the Tlascalans had boldly grap-pled with their enemy, and only yielded to the inevitable superiority of his military science. How important would the alliance of such a nation be in a struggle with those of their own race—for example, with the Aztecs! But how was he to secure this alliance? Hitherto, all overtures had been rejected with disdain; and it seemed probable that every step of his progress in this populous land was to be fiercely contested. His army, especially the Indians, celebrated the events of the day with feasting and dancing, songs of merriment, and shouts of triumph. Cortés encouraged it, well knowing how important it was to keep up the spirits of his soldiers. But the sounds of revelry at length died away; and in the still watches of the night, many an anxious thought must have crowded on the mind of the general, while his little army lay buried in slumber in its encampment around the Indian hill.

CHAPTER III

Decisive Victory—Indian Council—Night Attack—Negotiations with the Enemy—Tlascalan Hero

1519

THE SPANIARDS were allowed to repose undisturbed the following day, and to recruit their strength after the fatigue and hard fighting of the preceding. They found sufficient employment, however, in repairing and cleaning their weapons, replenishing their diminished stock of arrows, and getting everything in order for further hostilities, should the severe lesson they had inflicted on the enemy prove insufficient to discourage him. On the second day, as Cortés received no overtures from the Tlascalans, he determined to send an embassy to their camp, proposing a cessation of hostilities, and expressing his intention to visit their capital as a friend. He selected two of the principal chiefs taken in the late engagement as the bearers of the message.

Meanwhile, averse to leaving his men longer in a dangerous state of inaction, which the enemy might interpret as the result of timidity or exhaustion, he put himself at the head of the cavalry and such light troops as were most fit for service, and made a foray into the neighbouring country. It was a mountainous region, formed by a ramification of the great sierra of Tlascala, with verdant slopes and valleys teeming with maize and plantations of maguey, while the eminences were crowned with populous towns and villages. In one of these, he tells us, he found three thousand dwellings. In some places he met with a resolute resistance, and on these occasions took ample vengeance by laying the country waste with fire and sword. After a successful inroad he returned laden with forage and provisions, and driving before him several hundred Indian captives. He treated them kindly, however, when arrived in camp, endeavouring to make them understand that these acts of violence were not dictated by his own wishes, but by the unfriendly policy of their countrymen. In this way he hoped to impress the nation with the conviction of his power on

115

the one hand, and of his amicable intentions, if met by them in the like spirit, on the other.

On reaching his quarters, he found the two envoys returned from the Tlascalan camp. They had fallen in with Xicotencatl at about two leagues' distance, where he lay encamped with a powerful force. The cacique gave them audience at the head of his troops. He told them to return with the answer, "That the Spaniards might pass on as soon as they chose to Tlascala; and, when they reached it, their flesh would be hewn from their bodies, for sacrifice to the gods! If they preferred to remain in their own quarters, he would pay them a visit there the next day." The ambassadors added that the chief had an immense force with him, consisting of five battalions of ten thousand men each. They were the flower of the Tlascalan and Otomie warriors, assembled under the banners of their respective leaders, by command of the senate, who were resolved to try the fortunes of the state in a pitched battle, and strike one decisive blow for the extermination of the invaders.

This bold defiance fell heavily on the ears of the Spaniards, not prepared for so pertinacious a spirit in their enemy. They had had ample proof of his courage and formidable prowess. They were now, in their crippled condition, to encounter him with a still more terrible array of numbers. The war, too, from the horrible fate with which it menaced the vanquished, wore a peculiarly gloomy aspect that pressed heavily on their spirits. "We feared death," says the lion-hearted Diaz, with his usual simplicity, "for we were men." There was scarcely one in the army that did not confess himself that night to the reverend Father Olmedo, who was occupied nearly the whole of it with administering absolution, and with the other solemn offices of the Church. Armed with the blessed sacraments, the Catholic soldier lay tranquilly down to rest, prepared for any fate that might betide him under the banner of the Cross.

As a battle was now inevitable, Cortés resolved to march out and meet the enemy in the field. This would have a show of confidence that might serve the double purpose of intimidating the Tlascalans, and inspiriting his own men, whose enthusiasm might lose somewhat of its heat, if compelled to await the assault of their antagonists, inactive in their own intrenchments. The sun rose bright on the following morning, September 5, 1519, an eventful day in the history of the Spanish Conquest. The general reviewed his army, and gave them, preparatory to marching, a few words of encouragement and advice. The infantry he instructed to rely on the point rather than the edge of their swords, and to endeavour to thrust their opponents through the body. The horsemen were to charge at half speed, with their lances aimed at the eyes of the Indians. The artillery, the arquebusiers, and crossbow-men were to support one another, some loading while others discharged their pieces, that there should be an unintermitted firing kept up through the action. Above all, they were to maintain their ranks close and unbroken, as on this depended their preservation.

They had not advanced a quarter of a league, when they came in sight of the Tlascalan army. Its dense array stretched far and wide over a vast plain or meadow ground, about six miles square. Its appearance justified the report which had been given of its numbers. Nothing could be more picturesque than the aspect of these Indian battalions, with the naked bodies of the common soldiers gaudily painted, the fantastic helmets of the chiefs glittering with gold and precious stones, and the glowing panoplies of featherwork which decorated their persons. Innumerable spears and darts tipped with points of transparent *itztli,* or fiery copper, sparkled bright in the morning sun, like the phosphoric gleams playing on the surface of a troubled sea, while the rear of the mighty host was dark with the shadows of banners, on which were emblazoned the armorial bearings of the great Tlascalan and Otomie chieftains. Among these, the white heron on the rock, the cognisance of the house of Xicotencatl, was conspicuous, and, still more, the golden eagle with outspread wings, in the fashion of a Roman *signum,* richly ornamented with emeralds and silver work, the great standard of the republic of Tlascala.

The common file wore no covering except a girdle round the loins. Their bodies were painted with the appropriate colours of the chieftain whose banner they followed. The feather-mail of the higher class of warriors exhibited, also, a similar selection of colours for the like object, in the same manner as the colour of the tartan indicates the peculiar clan of the Highlander. The caciques and principal warriors were clothed in a quilted cotton tunic, two inches thick, which, fitting close to the body, protected also the thighs and the shoulders. Over this the wealthier Indians wore cuirasses of thin gold plate, or silver. Their legs were defended by leathern boots or sandals, trimmed with gold. But the most brilliant part of their costume was a rich mantle of the *plumaje* or featherwork, embroidered with curious art, and furnishing some resemblance to the gorgeous surcoat worn by the European knight over his armour in the Middle Ages. This graceful and picturesque dress was surmounted by a fantastic head-piece made of wood or leather, representing the head of some wild animal, and frequently displaying a formidable array of teeth. With this covering the warrior's head was enveloped, producing a most grotesque and hideous effect. From the crown floated a splendid panache of the richly variegated plumage of the Tropics, indicating, by its form and colours, the rank and family of the wearer. To complete their defensive armour, they carried shields or targets, made sometimes of wood covered with leather, but more usually of a light frame of reeds quilted with cotton, which were preferred as tougher and less liable to fracture than the former. They had other bucklers, in which the cotton was covered with an elastic substance, enabling them to be shut up in a more compact form, like a fan or umbrella. These shields were decorated with showy ornaments, according to the taste or wealth of the wearer, and fringed with a beautiful pendant of featherwork.

Their weapons were slings, bows and arrows, javelins, and darts. They were accomplished archers, and would discharge two or even three arrows at a time. But they most excelled in throwing the javelin. One species of this, with a thong attached to it, which remained in the slinger's hand, that he might recall the weapon, was especially dreaded by the Spaniards. These various weapons were pointed with bone, or the mineral *itztli* (obsidian), the hard vitreous substance already noticed, as capable of taking an edge like a razor, though easily blunted. Their spears and arrows were also frequently headed with copper. Instead of a sword, they bore a two-handed staff, about three feet and a half long, in which, at regular distances, were inserted, transversely, sharp blades of *itztli*—a formidable weapon, which, an eye-witness assures us, he had seen fell a horse at a blow.

Such was the costume of the Tlascalan warrior, and, indeed, of that great family of nations generally, who occupied the plateau of Anahuac. Some parts of it, as the targets and the cotton mail or *escaupil,* as it was called in Castilian, were so excellent, that they were subsequently adopted by the Spaniards, as equally effectual in the way of protection, and superior, on the score of lightness and convenience, to their own. They were of sufficient strength to turn an arrow, or the stroke of a javelin, although impotent as a defence against firearms. But what armour is not? Yet it is probably no exaggeration to say that, in convenience, gracefulness, and strength, the arms of the Indian warrior were not very inferior to those of the polished nations of antiquity.

As soon as the Castilians came in sight, the Tlascalans set up their yell of defiance, rising high above the wild barbaric minstrelsy of shell, atabal, and trumpet, with which they proclaimed their triumphant anticipations of victory over the paltry forces of the invaders. When the latter had come within bowshot, the Indians hurled a tempest of missiles that darkened the sun for a moment as with a passing cloud, strewing the earth around with heaps of stones and arrows. Slowly and steadily the little band of Spaniards held on its way amidst this arrowy shower, until it had reached what appeared the proper distance for delivering its fire with full effect. Cortés then halted, and, hastily forming his troops, opened a general well-directed fire along the whole line. Every shot bore its errand of death; and the ranks of the Indians were mowed down faster than their comrades in the rear could carry off their bodies, according to custom, from the field. The balls in their passage through the crowded files, bearing splinters of the broken harness and mangled limbs of the warriors, scattered havoc and desolation in their path. The mob of barbarians stood petrified with dismay, till, at length, galled to desperation by their intolerable suffering, they poured forth simultaneously their hideous war-shriek, and rushed impetuously on the Christians.

On they came like an avalanche, or mountain torrent, shaking the solid earth, and sweeping away every obstacle in its path. The little army of Spaniards opposed a bold front to the overwhelming mass. But no strength could withstand it. They faltered, gave way, were borne along before it, and their ranks were broken and thrown into disorder. It was in vain the general called on them to close again and rally. His voice was drowned by the din of fight and the fierce cries of the assailants. For a moment, it seemed that all was lost. The tide of battle had turned against them, and the fate of the Christians was sealed.

But every man had that within his bosom which spoke louder than the voice of the general. Despair gave unnatural energy to his arm. The naked body of the Indian afforded no resistance to the sharp Toledo steel; and with their good swords, the Spanish infantry at length succeeded in staying the human torrent. The heavy guns from a distance thundered on the flank of the assailants, which, shaken by the iron tempest, was thrown into disorder. Their very numbers increased the confusion, as they were precipitated on the masses in front. The horse at the same moment, charging gallantly under Cortés, followed up the advantage, and at length compelled the tumultuous throng to fall back with greater precipitation and disorder than that with which they had advanced.

More than once in the course of the action, a similar assault was attempted by the Tlascalans, but each time with less spirit, and greater loss. They were too deficient in military science to profit by their vast superiority in numbers. They were distributed into companies, it is true, each serving under its own chieftain and banner. But they were not arranged by rank and file, and moved in a confused mass, promiscuously heaped together. They knew not how to concentrate numbers on a given point, or even how to sustain an assault, by employing successive detachments to support and relieve one another. A very small part only of their array could be brought into contact with an enemy inferior to them in amount of forces. The remainder of the army, inactive and worse than useless in the rear, served only to press tumultuously on the advance, and embarrass its movements by mere weight of numbers, while, on the least alarm, they were seized with a panic and threw the whole body into inextricable confusion. It was, in short, the combat of the ancient Greeks and Persians over again.

Still, the great numerical superiority of the Indians might have enabled them, at a severe cost of their own lives, indeed, to wear out, in time, the constancy of the Spaniards, disabled by wounds and incessant fatigue. But, fortunately for the latter, dissensions arose among their enemies. A Tlascalan chieftain, commanding one of the great divisions, had taken umbrage at the haughty demeanour of Xicotencatl, who had charged him with misconduct or cowardice in the late action. The injured cacique challenged his rival to single combat. This did not take place. But, burning with resentment, he chose the present occasion to indulge it, by drawing off his forces, amounting to ten thousand men, from the field. He also persuaded another of the commanders to follow his example.

Thus reduced to about half his original strength, and that greatly crippled by the losses of the day, Xicotencatl could no longer maintain his ground against the Spaniards. After disputing the field with admirable courage for four hours, he retreated and resigned it to the enemy. The Spaniards were too much jaded, and too many were disabled by wounds, to allow them to pursue; and Cortés, satisfied with the decisive victory he had gained, returned in triumph to his position on the hill of Tzompach.

The number of killed in his own ranks had been very small, notwith-

standing the severe loss inflicted on the enemy. These few he was careful
to bury where they could not be discovered, anxious to conceal not only
the amount of the slain, but the fact that the whites were mortal. But
very many of the men were wounded, and all the horses. The trouble of
the Spaniards was much enhanced by the want of many articles important
to them in their present exigency. They had neither oil, nor salt, which,
as before noticed, was not to be obtained in Tlascala. Their clothing, accommodated to a softer climate, was ill adapted to the rude air of the
mountains; and bows and arrows, as Bernal Diaz sarcastically remarks,
formed an indifferent protection against the inclemency of the weather.

Still, they had much to cheer them in the events of the day; and they
might draw from them a reasonable ground for confidence in their own
resources, such as no other experience could have supplied. Not that the
results could authorise anything like contempt for their Indian foe. Singly
and with the same weapons, he might have stood his ground against the
Spaniards. But the success of the day established the superiority of science
and discipline over mere physical courage and numbers. It was fighting
over again, as we have said, the old battle of the European and the
Asiatic. But the handful of Greeks who routed the hosts of Xerxes and
Darius, it must be remembered, had not so obvious an advantage on the
score of weapons, as was enjoyed by the Spaniards in these wars. The
use of firearms gave an ascendency which cannot easily be estimated; one
so great, that a contest between nations equally civilised, which should be
similar in all other respects to that between the Spaniards and the Tlascalans, would probably be attended with a similar issue. To all this must
be added the effect produced by the cavalry. The nations of Anahuac had
no large domesticated animals, and were unacquainted with any beast of
burden. Their imaginations were bewildered when they beheld the strange
apparition of the horse and his rider moving in unison and obedient to one
impulse, as if possessed of a common nature; and as they saw the terrible
animal, with his "neck clothed in thunder," bearing down their squadrons
and trampling them in the dust, no wonder they should have regarded
him with the mysterious terror felt for a supernatural being. A very little
reflection on the manifold grounds of superiority, both moral and physical, possessed by the Spaniards in this contest, will surely explain the
issue, without any disparagement to the courage or capacity of their
opponents.

Cortés, thinking the occasion favourable, followed up the important
blow he had struck by a new mission to the capital, bearing a message

of similar import with that recently sent to the camp. But the senate was
not yet sufficiently humbled. The late defeat caused, indeed, general consternation. Maxixcatzin, one of the four great lords who presided over
the republic, reiterated with greater force the arguments before urged
by him for embracing the proffered alliance of the strangers. The armies
of the state had been beaten too often to allow any reasonable hope of
successful resistance; and he enlarged on the generosity shown by the
politic Conqueror to his prisoners—so unusual in Anahuac—as an additional motive for an alliance with men who knew how to be friends as
well as foes.

But in these views he was overruled by the war-party, whose animosity
was sharpened, rather than subdued, by the late discomfiture. Their
hostile feelings were further exasperated by the younger Xicotencatl,
who burned for an opportunity to retrieve his disgrace, and to wipe away
the stain which had fallen for the first time on the arms of the republic.

In their perplexity they called in the assistance of the priests, whose
authority was frequently invoked in the deliberations of the American
chiefs. The latter inquired, with some simplicity, of these interpreters of
fate, whether the strangers were supernatural beings, or men of flesh and
blood like themselves. The priests, after some consultation, are said to
have made the strange answer that the Spaniards, though not gods, were
children of the sun; that they derived their strength from that luminary,
and, when his beams were withdrawn, their powers would also fail. They
recommended a night attack, therefore, as one which afforded the best
chance of success. This apparently childish response may have had in it
more of cunning than credulity. It was not improbably suggested by
Xicotencatl himself, or by the caciques in his interest, to reconcile the
people to a measure which was contrary to the military usages—indeed,
it may be said, to the public law of Anahuac. Whether the fruit of artifice
or superstition, it prevailed; and the Tlascalan general was empowered,
at the head of a detachment of ten thousand warriors, to try the effect of
an assault by night on the Christian camp.

The affair was conducted with such secrecy that it did not reach the
ears of the Spaniards. But their general was not one who allowed himself,
sleeping or waking, to be surprised on his post. Fortunately the night
appointed was illumined by the full beams of an autumnal moon; and
one of the videttes perceived by its light, at a considerable distance, a
large body of Indians moving towards the Christian lines. He was not
slow in giving the alarm to the garrison.

The Spaniards slept, as has been said, with their arms by their sides; while their horses, picketed near them, stood ready saddled, with the bridle hanging at the bow. In five minutes the whole camp was under arms, when they beheld the dusky columns of the Indians cautiously advancing over the plain, their heads just peering above the tall maize with which the land was partially covered. Cortés determined not to abide the assault in his intrenchments, but to sally out and pounce on the enemy when he had reached the bottom of the hill.

Slowly and stealthily the Indians advanced, while the Christian camp, hushed in profound silence, seemed to them buried in slumber. But no sooner had they reached the slope of the rising ground, than they were astounded by the deep battle-cry of the Spaniards, followed by the instantaneous apparition of the whole army, as they sallied forth from the works, and poured down the sides of the hill. Brandishing aloft their weapons, they seemed to the troubled fancies of the Tlascalans like so many spectres or demons hurrying to and fro in mid air, while the uncertain light magnified their numbers, and expanded the horse and his rider into gigantic and unearthly dimensions.

Scarcely waiting the shock of their enemy, the panic-struck barbarians let off a feeble volley of arrows, and, offering no other resistance, fled rapidly and tumultuously across the plain. The horse easily overtook the fugitives, riding them down and cutting them to pieces without mercy, until Cortés, weary with slaughter, called off his men, leaving the field loaded with the bloody trophies of victory.

The next day, the Spanish commander, with his usual policy after a decisive blow had been struck, sent a new embassy to the Tlascalan capital. The envoys received their instructions through the interpreter, Marina. That remarkable woman had attracted general admiration by the constancy and cheerfulness with which she endured all the privations of the camp. Far from betraying the natural weakness and timidity of her sex, she had shrunk from no hardship herself, and had done much to fortify the drooping spirits of the soldiers; while her sympathies, whenever occasion offered, had been actively exerted in mitigating the calamities of her Indian countrymen.

Through his faithful interpreter, Cortés communicated the terms of his message to the Tlascalan envoys. He made the same professions of amity as before, promising oblivion of all past injuries; but, if this proffer were rejected, he would visit their capital as a conqueror, raze every house in it to the ground, and put every inhabitant to the sword! He then dismissed the ambassadors with the symbolical presents of a letter in one hand, and an arrow in the other.

The envoys obtained respectful audience from the council of Tlascala, whom they found plunged in deep dejection by their recent reverses. The failure of the night attack had extinguished every spark of hope in their bosoms. Their armies had been beaten again and again, in the open field and in secret ambush. Stratagem and courage, all their resources, had alike proved ineffectual against a foe whose hand was never weary, and whose eye was never closed. Nothing remained but to submit. They selected four principal caciques, whom they intrusted with a mission to the Christian camp. They were to assure the strangers of a free passage through the country, and a friendly reception in the capital. The proffered friendship of the Spaniards was cordially embraced, with many awkward excuses for the past. The envoys were to touch at the Tlascalan camp on their way, and inform Xicotencatl of their proceedings. They were to require him, at the same time, to abstain from all further hostilities, and to furnish the white men with an ample supply of provisions.

But the Tlascalan deputies, on arriving at the quarters of that chief, did not find him in the humour to comply with these instructions. His repeated collisions with the Spaniards, or, it may be, his constitutional courage, left him inaccessible to the vulgar terrors of his countrymen. He regarded the strangers not as supernatural beings, but as men like himself. The animosity of a warrior had rankled into a deadly hatred from the mortifications he had endured at their hands, and his head teemed with plans for recovering his fallen honours, and for taking vengeance on the invaders of his country. He refused to disband any of the force, still formidable, under his command; or to send supplies to the enemy's camp. He further induced the ambassadors to remain in his quarters, and relinquish their visit to the Spaniards. The latter, in consequence, were kept in ignorance of the movements in their favour which had taken place in the Tlascalan capital.

The conduct of Xicotencatl is condemned by Castilian writers as that of a ferocious and sanguinary barbarian. It is natural they should so regard it. But those who have no national prejudice to warp their judgments may come to a different conclusion. They may find much to admire in that high, unconquerable spirit, like some proud column, standing alone in its majesty amidst the fragments and ruins around it. They may see evidences of a clear-sighted sagacity, which, piercing the thin veil of insidious friendship proffered by the Spaniards, and penetrating the future, discerned the coming miseries of his country; the noble patriotism of one who would rescue that country at any cost, and, amidst the gathering darkness, would infuse his own intrepid spirit into the hearts of his nation, to animate them to a last struggle for independence.

CHAPTER IV

Discontents in the Army—Tlascalan Spies—Peace with the Republic—Embassy from Montezuma

1519

DESIROUS to keep up the terror of the Castilian name, by leaving the enemy no respite, Cortés on the same day that he despatched the embassy to Tlascala, put himself at the head of a small corps of cavalry and light troops to scour the neighbouring country. He was at that time so ill from fever, aided by medical treatment, that he could hardly keep his seat in the saddle. It was a rough country, and the sharp winds from the frosty summits of the mountains pierced the scanty covering of the troops, and chilled both men and horses. Four or five of the animals gave out, and the general, alarmed for their safety, sent them back to the camp. The soldiers, discouraged by this ill omen, would have persuaded him to return. But he made answer, "We fight under the banner of the Cross; God is stronger than nature," and continued his march.

It led through the same kind of chequered scenery of rugged hill and cultivated plain as that already described, well covered with towns and villages, some of them the frontier posts occupied by the Otomies. Practising the Roman maxim of lenity to the submissive foe, he took full vengeance on those who resisted, and, as resistance too often occurred, marked his path with fire and desolation. After a short absence, he returned in safety, laden with the plunder of a successful foray. It would have been more honourable to him had it been conducted with less rigour. The excesses are imputed by Bernal Diaz to the Indian allies, whom in the heat of victory it was found impossible to restrain. On whose head soever they fall, they seem to have given little uneasiness to the general, who declares in his letter to the Emperor Charles the Fifth, "As we fought under the standard of the Cross, for the true Faith, and the service of your Highness, Heaven crowned our arms with such success, that, while multitudes of the infidel were slain, little loss was suffered by the Castilians." The Spanish Conquerors, to judge from their writings, unconscious of any worldly motive lurking in the bottom of their hearts, regarded themselves as soldiers of the Church, fighting the great battle of Christianity; and in the same edifying and comfortable light are regarded by most of the national historians of a later day.

On his return to the camp, Cortés found a new cause of disquietude in the discontents which had broken out among the soldiery. Their patience was exhausted by a life of fatigue and peril, to which there seemed to be no end. The battles they had won against such tremendous odds had not advanced them a jot. The idea of their reaching Mexico, says the old soldier so often quoted, "was treated as a jest by the whole army"; and the indefinite prospect of hostilities with the ferocious people among whom they were now cast, threw a deep gloom over their spirits.

Among the malcontents were a number of noisy, vapouring persons, such as are found in every camp, who, like empty bubbles, are sure to rise to the surface and make themselves seen in seasons of agitation. They were, for the most part, of the old faction of Velasquez, and had estates in Cuba, to which they turned many a wistful glance as they receded more and more from the coast. They now waited on the general, not in a mutinous spirit of resistance—for they remembered the lesson in Villa Rica—but with the design of frank expostulation, as with a brother adventurer in a common cause. The tone of familiarity thus assumed was eminently characteristic of the footing of equality on which the parties in the expedition stood with one another.

Their sufferings, they told him, were too great to be endured. All the men had received one, most of them two or three wounds. More than fifty had perished, in one way or another, since leaving Vera Cruz. There was no beast of burden but led a life preferable to theirs. For when the night came, the former could rest from his labours; but they, fighting or watching, had no rest, day or night. As to conquering Mexico, the very thought of it was madness. If they had encountered such opposition from the petty republic of Tlascala, what might they not expect from the great Mexican empire? There was now a temporary suspension of hostilities. They should avail themselves of it to retrace their steps to Vera Cruz. It is true, the fleet there was destroyed; and by this act, unparalleled for rashness even in Roman annals, the general had become responsible for the fate of the whole army. Still there was one vessel left. That might be despatched to Cuba, for reinforcements and supplies;

and, when these arrived, they would be enabled to resume operations with some prospect of success.

Cortés listened to this singular expostulation with perfect composure. He knew his men, and, instead of rebuke or harsher measures, replied in the same frank and soldier-like vein which they had affected.

There was much truth, he allowed, in what they said. The sufferings of the Spaniards had been great; greater than those recorded of any heroes in Greek or Roman story. So much the greater would be their glory. He had often been filled with admiration as he had seen his little host encircled by myriads of barbarians, and felt that no people but Spaniards could have triumphed over such formidable odds. Nor could they, unless the arm of the Almighty had been over them. And they might reasonably look for His protection hereafter; for was it not in His cause they were fighting? They had encountered dangers and difficulties, it was true; but they had not come here expecting a life of idle dalliance and pleasure. Glory, as he had told them at the outset, was to be won only by toil and danger. They would do him the justice to acknowledge that he had never shrunk from his share of both. This was a truth—adds the honest chronicler, who heard and reports the dialogue—which no one could deny. But, if they had met with hardships, he continued, they had been everywhere victorious. Even now they were enjoying the fruits of this, in the plenty which reigned in the camp. And they would soon see the Tlascalans, humbled by their late reverses, suing for peace on any terms. To go back now was impossible. The very stones would rise up against them. The Tlascalans would hunt them in triumph down to the water's edge. And how would the Mexicans exult at this miserable issue of their vainglorious vaunts! Their former friends would become their enemies; and the Totonacs, to avert the vengeance of the Aztecs, from which the Spaniards could no longer shield them, would join in the general cry. There was no alternative, then, but to go forward in their career. And he besought them to silence their pusillanimous scruples, and, instead of turning their eyes towards Cuba, to fix them on Mexico, the great object of their enterprise.

While this singular conference was going on, many other soldiers had gathered round the spot; and the discontented party, emboldened by the presence of their comrades, as well as by the general's forbearance, replied that they were far from being convinced. Another such victory as the last would be their ruin. They were going to Mexico only to be slaughtered. Until, at length, the general's patience being exhausted, he cut the argument short by quoting a verse from an old song, implying that it was better to die with honour, than to live disgraced; a sentiment which was loudly echoed by the greater part of his audience, who, notwithstanding their occasional murmurs, had no design to abandon the expedition, still less the commander, to whom they were passionately devoted. The malcontents, disconcerted by this rebuke, slunk back to their own quarters, muttering half-smothered execrations on the leader who had projected the enterprise, the Indians who had guided him, and their own countrymen who supported him in it.

Such were the difficulties that lay in the path of Cortés: a wily and ferocious enemy; a climate uncertain, often unhealthy; illness in his own person, much aggravated by anxiety as to the manner in which his conduct would be received by his sovereign; last, not least, disaffection among his soldiers, on whose constancy and union he rested for the success of his operations—the great lever by which he was to overturn the empire of Montezuma.

On the morning following this event, the camp was surprised by the appearance of a small body of Tlascalans, decorated with badges, the white colour of which intimated peace. They brought a quantity of provisions, and some trifling ornaments, which, they said, were sent by the Tlascalan general, who was weary of the war, and desired an accommodation with the Spaniards. He would soon present himself to arrange this in person. The intelligence diffused general joy, and the emissaries received a friendly welcome.

A day or two elapsed, and while a few of the party left the Spanish quarters, the others, about fifty in number, who remained, excited some distrust in the bosom of Marina. She communicated her suspicions to Cortés that they were spies. He caused several of them, in consequence, to be arrested, examined them separately, and ascertained that they were employed by Xicotencatl to inform him of the state of the Christian camp, preparatory to a meditated assault, for which he was mustering his forces. Cortés, satisfied of the truth of this, determined to make such an example of the delinquents as should intimidate his enemy from repeating the attempt. He ordered their hands to be cut off, and in that condition sent them back to their countrymen, with the message, "that the Tlascalans might come by day or night; they would find the Spaniards ready for them."

The doleful spectacle of their comrades returning in this mutilated state filled the Indian camp with horror and consternation. The haughty crest of their chief was humbled. From that moment, he lost his wonted buoyancy and confidence. His soldiers, filled with superstitious fear, refused to serve longer against a foe who could read their very thoughts, and divine their plans before they were ripe for execution.

The punishment inflicted by Cortés may well shock the reader by its brutality. But it should be considered in mitigation that the victims of it were spies, and, as such, by the laws of war, whether among civilised or savage nations, had incurred the penalty of death. The amputation of the limbs was a milder punishment, and reserved for inferior offences. If we revolt at the barbarous nature of the sentence, we should reflect that it was no uncommon one at that day; not more uncommon, indeed, than whipping and branding with a hot iron were in our own country at the beginning of the present century, or than cropping the ears was in the preceding one. A higher civilisation, indeed, rejects such punishments as pernicious in themselves, and degrading to humanity. But in the sixteenth century, they were openly recognised by the laws of the most polished nations in Europe. And it is too much to ask of any man, still less one bred to the iron trade of war, to be in advance of the refinement of his age. We may be content, if, in circumstances so unfavourable to humanity, he does not fall below it.

All thoughts of further resistance being abandoned, the four delegates of the Tlascalan republic were now allowed to proceed on their mission. They were speedily followed by Xicotencatl himself, attended by a numerous train of military retainers. As they drew near the Spanish lines, they were easily recognised by the white and yellow colours of their uniforms, the livery of the house of Titcala. The joy of the army was great at this sure intimation of the close of hostilities; and it was with difficulty that Cortés was enabled to restore the men to tranquillity, and the assumed indifference which it was proper to maintain in presence of an enemy.

The Spaniards gazed with curious eyes on the valiant chief who had so long kept his enemies at bay, and who now advanced with the firm and fearless step of one who was coming rather to bid defiance than to sue for peace. He was rather above the middle size, with broad shoulders, and a muscular frame intimating great activity and strength. His head was large, and his countenance marked with the lines of hard service rather than of age, for he was but thirty-five. When he entered the presence of Cortés, he made the usual salutation, by touching the ground with his hand, and carrying it to his head; while the sweet incense of aromatic gums rolled up in clouds from the censers carried by his slaves.

Far from a pusillanimous attempt to throw the blame on the senate, he assumed the whole responsibility of the war. He had considered the white men, he said, as enemies, for they came with the allies and vassals of Montezuma. He loved his country, and wished to preserve the independence which she had maintained through her long wars with the Aztecs. He had been beaten. They might be the strangers who, it had been so long predicted, would come from the east, to take possession of the country. He hoped they would use their victory with moderation, and not trample on the liberties of the republic. He came now in the name of his nation, to tender their obedience to the Spaniards, assuring them they would find his countrymen as faithful in peace as they had been firm in war.

Cortés, far from taking umbrage, was filled with admiration at the lofty spirit which thus disdained to stoop beneath misfortunes. The brave man knows how to respect bravery in another. He assumed, however, a severe aspect, as he rebuked the chief for having so long persisted in hostilities. Had Xicotencatl believed the word of the Spaniards, and accepted their proffered friendship sooner, he would have spared his people much suffering, which they well merited by their obstinacy. But it was impossible, continued the general, to retrieve the past. He was willing to bury it in oblivion, and to receive the Tlascalans as vassals to the emperor, his master. If they proved true, they should find him a sure column of support; if false, he would take such vengeance on them as he had intended to take on their capital, had they not speedily given in their submission. It proved an ominous menace for the chief to whom it was addressed.

The cacique then ordered his slaves to bring forward some trifling ornaments of gold and feather embroidery, designed as presents. They were of little value, he said, with a smile, for the Tlascalans were poor. They had little gold, not even cotton, nor salt; the Aztec emperor had left them nothing but their freedom and their arms. He offered this gift only as a token of his good will. "As such I receive it," answered Cortés, "and coming from the Tlascalans, set more value on it than I should from any other source, though it were a house full of gold"; a politic, as well as magnanimous reply, for it was by the aid of this good will that he was to win the gold of Mexico.

Thus ended the bloody war with the fierce republic of Tlascala, during the course of which the fortunes of the Spaniards, more than once, had trembled in the balance. Had it been persevered in but a little longer, it must have ended in their confusion and ruin, exhausted as they were by wounds, watching, and fatigues, with the seeds of disaffection rankling among themselves. As it was, they came out of the fearful contest with untarnished glory. To the enemy, they seemed invulnerable, bearing charmed lives, proof alike against the accidents of fortune and the assaults of man. No wonder that they indulged a similar conceit in their own bosoms, and that the humblest Spaniard should have fancied himself the subject of a special interposition of providence, which shielded him in the hour of battle, and reserved him for a higher destiny.

While the Tlascalans were still in the camp, an embassy was announced from Montezuma. Tidings of the exploits of the Spaniards had spread far and wide over the plateau. The emperor, in particular, had watched every step of their progress, as they climbed the steeps of the Cordilleras, and advanced over the broad tableland on their summit. He had seen them, with great satisfaction, take the road to Tlascala, trusting that, if they were mortal men, they would find their graves there. Great was his dismay, when courier after courier brought him intelligence of their successes, and that the most redoubtable warriors on the plateau had been scattered like chaff by the swords of this handful of strangers.

His superstitious fears returned in full force. He saw in the Spaniards "the men of destiny" who were to take possession of his sceptre. In his alarm and uncertainty, he sent a new embassy to the Christian camp. It consisted of five great nobles of his court, attended by a train of two hundred slaves. They brought with them a present, as usual, dictated partly by fear, and, in part, by the natural munificence of his disposition. It consisted of three thousand ounces of gold, in grains, or in various manufactured articles, with several hundred mantles and dresses of embroidered cotton, and the picturesque featherwork. As they laid these at the feet of Cortés, they told him they had come to offer the congratulations of their master on the late victories of the white men. The emperor only regretted that it would not be in his power to receive them in his capital, where the numerous population was so unruly, that their safety would be placed in jeopardy. The mere intimation of the Aztec emperor's wishes, in the most distant way, would have sufficed with the Indian nations. It had very little weight with the Spaniards; and the envoys, finding this puerile expression of them ineffectual, resorted to another argument, offering a tribute in their master's name to the Castilian sovereign, provided the Spaniards would relinquish their visit to his capital. This was a greater error; it was displaying the rich casket with one hand, which he was unable to defend with the other. Yet the author of this pusillanimous policy, the unhappy victim of superstition, was a monarch renowned among the Indian nations for his intrepidity and enterprise—the terror of Anahuac!

Cortés, while he urged his own sovereign's commands as a reason for disregarding the wishes of Montezuma, uttered expressions of the most profound respect for the Aztec prince, and declared that if he had not the means of requiting his munificence, as he could wish, at present, he trusted *to repay him, at some future day, with good works!*

The Mexican ambassadors were not much gratified with finding the war at an end, and a reconciliation established between their mortal enemies and the Spaniards. The mutual disgust of the two parties with each other was too strong to be repressed even in the presence of the general, who saw with satisfaction the evidences of a jealousy, which, undermining the strength of the Indian emperor, was to prove the surest source of his own success.

Two of the Aztec mission returned to Mexico, to acquaint their sovereign with the state of affairs in the Spanish camp. The others remained with the army, Cortés being willing that they should be personal spectators of the deference shown him by the Tlascalans. Still he did not hasten his departure for their capital. Not that he placed reliance on the injurious intimations of the Mexicans respecting their good faith. Yet he was willing to put this to some longer trial, and, at the same time, to re-establish his own health more thoroughly, before his visit. Meanwhile, messengers daily arrived from the city, pressing his journey, and were finally followed by some of the aged rulers of the republic, attended by a numerous retinue, impatient of his long delay. They brought with them a body of five hundred *tamanes,* or *men of burden,* to drag his cannon, and relieve his own forces from this fatiguing part of their duty. It was impossible to defer his departure longer; and after Mass, and a solemn thanksgiving to the great Being who had crowned their arms with triumph, the Spaniards bade adieu to the quarters which they had occupied for nearly three weeks on the hill of Tzompach. The strong tower, or *teocalli,* which commanded it, was called, in commemoration of their residence, "The Tower of Victory"; and a few stones which still survive of its ruins point out to the eye of the traveller a spot ever memorable in history for the courage and constancy of the early Conquerors.

CHAPTER V

Spaniards Enter Tlascala—Description of the Capital—Attempted Conversion—Aztec Embassy—Invited to Cholula

1519

THE CITY OF TLASCALA, the capital of the republic of the same name, lay at the distance of about six leagues from the Spanish camp. The road led into a hilly region, exhibiting in every arable patch of ground the evidence of laborious cultivation. Over a deep *barranca,* or ravine, they crossed on a bridge of stone, which, according to tradition—a slippery authority—is the same still standing, and was constructed originally for the passage of the army. They passed some considerable towns on their route, where they experienced a full measure of Indian hospitality. As they advanced, the approach to a populous city was intimated by the crowds who flocked out to see and welcome the strangers; men and women in their picturesque dresses, with bunches and wreaths of roses, which they gave to the Spaniards, or fastened to the necks and caparisons of their horses, in the same manner as at Cempoalla. Priests, with their white robes, and long matted tresses floating over them, mingled in the crowd, scattering volumes of incense from their burning censers. In this way, the multitudinous and motley procession defiled through the gates of the ancient capital of Tlascala. It was September 23, 1519, the anniversary of which is still celebrated by the inhabitants as a day of jubilee.

The press was now so great, that it was with difficulty the police of the city could clear a passage for the army; while the *azoteas,* or flat-terraced roofs of the buildings, were covered with spectators, eager to catch a glimpse of the wonderful strangers. The houses were hung with festoons of flowers, and arches of verdant boughs, intertwined with roses and honeysuckle, were thrown across the streets. The whole population abandoned itself to rejoicing; and the air was rent with songs and shouts of triumph mingled with the wild music of the national instruments, that might have excited apprehensions in the breasts of the soldiery, had they not gathered their peaceful import from the assurance of Marina, and the joyous countenances of the natives.

With these accompaniments, the procession moved along the principal streets to the mansion of Xicotencatl, the aged father of the Tlascalan general, and one of the four rulers of the republic. Cortés dismounted from his horse, to receive the old chieftain's embrace. He was nearly blind; and satisfied, as far as he could, a natural curiosity respecting the person of the Spanish general, by passing his hand over his features. He then led the way to a spacious hall in his palace, where a banquet was served to the army. In the evening, they were shown to their quarters, in the buildings and open ground surrounding one of the principal *teocallis;* while the Mexican ambassadors, at the desire of Cortés, had apartments assigned them next to his own, that he might the better watch over their safety, in this city of their enemies.

Tlascala was one of the most important and populous towns on the tableland. Cortés, in his letter to the emperor, compares it to Granada, affirming that it was larger, stronger, and more populous than the Moorish capital, at the time of the conquest, and quite as well built. But notwithstanding we are assured by a most respectable writer at the close of the last century that its remains justify the assertion, we shall be slow to believe that its edifices could have rivalled those monuments of Oriental magnificence, whose light, aerial forms still survive, after the lapse of ages, the admiration of every traveller of sensibility and taste. The truth is, that Cortés, like Columbus, saw objects through the warm medium of his own fond imagination, giving them a higher tone of colouring and larger dimensions than were strictly warranted by the fact. It was natural that the man who had made such rare discoveries should unconsciously magnify their merits to his own eyes and to those of others.

The houses were built, for the most part, of mud or earth; the better sort of stone and lime, or bricks dried in the sun. They were unprovided with doors or windows, but in the apertures for the former hung mats fringed with pieces of copper or something which, by its tingling sound, would give notice of any one's entrance. The streets were narrow and dark. The population must have been considerable if, as Cortés asserts, thirty thousand souls were often gathered in the market on a public day. These meetings were a sort of fair, held, as usual in all the great towns, every fifth day, and attended by the inhabitants of the adjacent country, who brought there for sale every description of domestic produce and manufacture with which they were acquainted. They peculiarly excelled in pottery, which was considered as equal to the best in Europe. It is a further proof of civilised habits, that the Spaniards found barbers' shops, and baths, both of vapour and hot water, familiarly used by the inhabitants. A still higher proof of refinement may be discerned in a vigilant police which repressed everything like disorder among the people.

The city was divided into four quarters, which might rather be called so many separate towns, since they were built at different times, and separated from each other by high stone walls, defining their respective limits. Over each of these districts ruled one of the four great chiefs of the republic, occupying his own spacious mansion, and surrounded by his own immediate vassals. Strange arrangement—and more strange that it should have been compatible with social order and tranquillity! The ancient capital, through one quarter of which flowed the rapid current of the Zahuatl, stretched along the summits and sides of hills, at whose base are now gathered the miserable remains of its once flourishing population. Far beyond, to the south-west, extended the bold sierra of Tlascala, and the huge Malinche, crowned with the usual silver diadem of the highest Andes, having its shaggy sides clothed with dark green forests of firs, gigantic sycamores, and oaks whose towering stems rose to the height of forty or fifty feet, unencumbered by a branch. The clouds, which sailed over from the distant Atlantic, gathered round the lofty peaks of the sierra, and, settling into torrents, poured over the plains in the neighbourhood of the city, converting them, at such seasons, into swamps. Thunderstorms, more frequent and terrible here than in other parts of the tableland, swept down the sides of the mountains, and shook the frail tenements of the capital to their foundations. But, although the bleak winds of the sierra gave an austerity to the climate, unlike the sunny skies and genial temperature of the lower regions, it was far more favourable to the development of both the physical and moral energies. A bold and hardy peasantry was nurtured among the recesses of the hills, fit equally to cultivate the land in peace and to defend it in war. Unlike the spoiled child of nature, who derives such facilities of subsistence from her too prodigal hand, as supersede the necessity of exertion on his own part, the Tlascalan earned his bread—from a soil not ungrateful, it is true—by the sweat of his brow. He led a life of temperance and toil.

Cut off by his long wars with the Aztecs from commercial intercourse, he was driven chiefly to agricultural labour, the occupation most propitious to purity of morals and sinewy strength of constitution. His honest breast glowed with the patriotism—or local attachment to the soil, which is the fruit of its diligent culture; while he was elevated by a proud consciousness of independence, the natural birthright of the child of the mountains. Such was the race with whom Cortés was now associated for the achievement of his great work.

Some days were given by the Spaniards to festivity, in which they were successively entertained at the hospitable boards of the four great nobles, in their several quarters of the city. Amidst these friendly demonstrations, however, the general never relaxed for a moment his habitual vigilance, or the strict discipline of the camp; and he was careful to provide for the security of the citizens by prohibiting, under severe penalties, any soldier from leaving his quarters without express permission. Indeed, the severity of his discipline provoked the remonstrance of more than one of his officers, as a superfluous caution; and the Tlascalan chiefs took some exception at it, as inferring an unreasonable distrust of them. But, when Cortés explained it as in obedience to an established military system, they testified their admiration, and the ambitious young general of the republic proposed to introduce it, if possible, into his own ranks.

The Spanish commander, having assured himself of the loyalty of his new allies, next proposed to accomplish one of the great objects of his mission—their conversion to Christianity. By the advice of Father Olmedo, always opposed to precipitate measures, he had deferred this till a suitable opportunity presented itself for opening the subject. Such a one occurred when the chiefs of the state proposed to strengthen the alliance with the Spaniards, by the intermarriage of their daughters with Cortés and his officers. He told them this could not be, while they continued in the darkness of infidelity. Then, with the aid of the good friar, he expounded as well as he could the doctrines of the Faith; and, exhibiting the image of the Virgin with the infant Redeemer, told them that there was the God, in whose worship alone they would find salvation, while that of their own false idols would sink them in eternal perdition.

It is unnecessary to burden the reader with a recapitulation of his homily, which contained, probably, dogmas quite as incomprehensible to the untutored Indian as any to be found in his own rude mythology. But, though it failed to convince his audience, they listened with a deferential awe. When he had finished, they replied they had no doubt that the God of the Christians must be a good and a great God, and as such they were willing to give him a place among the divinities of Tlascala. The polytheistic system of the Indians, like that of the ancient Greeks, was of that accommodating kind which could admit within its elastic folds the deities of any other religion, without violence to itself. But every nation, they continued, must have its own appropriate and tutelary deities. Nor could they, in their old age, abjure the service of those who had watched over them from youth. It would bring down the vengeance of their gods, and of their own nation, who were as warmly attached to their religion as their liberties, and would defend both with the last drop of their blood!

It was clearly inexpedient to press the matter further, at present. But the zeal of Cortés, as usual, waxing warm by opposition, had now mounted too high for him to calculate obstacles; nor would he have shrunk, probably, from the crown of martyrdom in so good a cause. But fortunately, at least for the success of his temporal cause, this crown was not reserved for him.

The good monk, his ghostly adviser, seeing the course things were likely to take, with better judgment interposed to prevent it. He had no desire, he said, to see the same scenes acted over again as at Cempoalla. He had no relish for forced conversions. They could hardly be lasting. The growth of an hour might well die with the hour. Of what use was it to overturn the altar, if the idol remained enthroned in the heart? or to destroy the idol itself, if it were only to make room for another? Better to wait patiently the effect of time and teaching to soften the heart and open the understanding, without which there could be no assurance of a sound and permanent conviction. These rational views were enforced by the remonstrances of Alvarado, Velasquez de Leon, and those in whom Cortés placed most confidence; till, driven from his original purpose, the military polemic consented to relinquish the attempt at conversion, for the present, and to refrain from a repetition of the scenes, which, considering the different mettle of the population, might have been attended with very different results from those at Cozumel and Cempoalla.

In the course of our narrative, we have had occasion to witness more than once the good effects of the interposition of Father Olmedo. Indeed, it is scarcely too much to say that his discretion in spiritual matters contributed as essentially to the success of the expedition, as did the sagacity and courage of Cortés in temporal. He was a true disciple in the school of Las Casas. His heart was unscathed by that fiery fanaticism which sears and hardens whatever it touches. It melted with the warm glow of Christian charity. He had come out to the New World as a missionary among the heathen, and he shrank from no sacrifice but that of the welfare of the poor benighted flock to whom he had consecrated his days. If he followed the banners of the warrior, it was to mitigate the ferocity of war, and to turn the triumphs of the Cross to a good account for the natives themselves, by the spiritual labours of conversion. He afforded the uncommon example—not to have been looked for, certainly, in a Spanish monk of the sixteenth century—of enthusiasm controlled by reason, a quickening zeal tempered by the mild spirit of toleration.

But though Cortés abandoned the ground of conversion for the present, he compelled the Tlascalans to break the fetters of the unfortunate victims reserved for sacrifice; an act of humanity unhappily only transient in its effects, since the prisons were filled with fresh victims on his departure.

He also obtained permission for the Spaniards to perform the services of their own religion unmolested. A large cross was erected in one of the great courts or squares. Mass was celebrated every day in the presence of the army and of crowds of natives, who, if they did not comprehend its full import, were so far edified that they learned to reverence the religion of their conquerors. The direct interposition of Heaven, however, wrought more for their conversion than the best homily of priest or soldier. Scarcely had the Spaniards left the city—the tale is told on very respectable authority—when a thin, transparent cloud descended and settled like a column on the cross, and, wrapping it round in its luminous folds, continued to emit a soft, celestial radiance through the night, thus proclaiming the sacred character of the symbol, on which was shed the halo of divinity!

The principle of toleration in religious matters being established, the Spanish general consented to receive the daughters of the caciques. Five or six of the most beautiful Indian maidens were assigned to as many of his principal officers, after they had been cleansed from the stains of infidelity by the waters of baptism. They received, as usual, on this occasion, good Castilian names, in exchange for the barbarous nomenclature of their own vernacular.

Among them, Xicotencatl's daughter, Doña Louisa, as she was called after her baptism, was a princess of the highest estimation and authority in Tlascala. She was given by her father to Alvarado, and their posterity intermarried with the noblest families of Castile. The frank and joyous manners of this cavalier made him a great favourite with the Tlascalans; and his bright open countenance, fair complexion, and golden locks, gave him the name of *Tonatiuh,* the "Sun." The Indians often pleased their fancies by fastening a *sobriquet,* or some characteristic epithet, on the Spaniards. As Cortés was always attended, on public occasions, by Doña Marina or Malinche, as she was called by the natives, they distinguished him by the same name. By these epithets, originally bestowed in Tlascala, the two Spanish captains were popularly designated among the Indian nations.

While these events were passing, another embassy arrived from the court of Mexico. It was charged, as usual, with a costly donative of embossed gold plate, and rich embroidered stuffs of cotton and feather-work. The terms of the message might well argue a vacillating and timid temper in the monarch, did they not mask a deeper policy. He now invited the Spaniards to his capital, with the assurance of a cordial welcome. He besought them to enter into no alliance with the base and barbarous Tlascalans; and he invited them to take the route of the friendly city of Cholula, where arrangements, according to his orders, were made for their reception.

The Tlascalans viewed with deep regret the general's proposed visit to Mexico. Their reports fully confirmed all he had before heard of the power and ambition of Montezuma. His armies, they said, were spread over every part of the continent. His capital was a place of great strength, and as, from its insular position, all communication could be easily cut off with the adjacent country, the Spaniards, once entrapped there, would be at his mercy. His policy, they represented, was as insidious as his ambition was boundless. "Trust not his fair words," they said, "his courtesies, and his gifts. His professions are hollow, and his friendships are false." When Cortés remarked that he hoped to bring about a better understanding between the emperor and them, they replied it would be impossible; however smooth his words, he would hate them at heart.

They warmly protested, also, against the general's taking the route of Cholula. The inhabitants, not brave in the open field, were more danger-ous from their perfidy and craft. They were Montezuma's tools, and would do his bidding. The Tlascalans seemed to combine with this dis-trust a superstitious dread of the ancient city, the headquarters of the religion of Anahuac. It was here that the god Quetzalcoatl held the pristine seat of his empire. His temple was celebrated throughout the land, and the priests were confidently believed to have the power, as they themselves boasted, of opening an inundation from the foundations of his shrine, which should bury their enemies in the deluge. The Tlascalans further reminded Cortés that while so many other and distant places had sent to him at Tlascala, to testify their good will, and offer their allegiance to his sovereign, Cholula, only six leagues distant, had done neither. The last suggestion struck the general more forcibly than any of the preceding. He instantly despatched a summons to the city requiring a formal tender of its submission.

Among the embassies from different quarters which had waited on the Spanish commander, while at Tlascala, was one from Ixtlilxochitl, son of the great Nezahualpilli, and an unsuccessful competitor with his elder brother—as noticed in a former part of our narrative—for the crown of Tezcuco. Though defeated in his pretensions, he had obtained a part of the kingdom, over which he ruled with a deadly feeling of animosity towards his rival, and to Montezuma, who had sustained him. He now offered his services to Cortés, asking his aid, in return, to place him on the throne of his ancestors. The politic general returned such an answer to the aspiring young prince, as might encourage his expectations, and attach him to his interests. It was his aim to strengthen his cause by attracting to himself every particle of disaffection that was floating through the land.

It was not long before deputies arrived from Cholula, profuse in their expressions of good will, and inviting the presence of the Spaniards in their capital. The messengers were of low degree, far beneath the usual rank of ambassadors. This was pointed out by the Tlascalans; and Cortés regarded it as a fresh indignity. He sent in consequence a new summons, declaring, if they did not instantly send him a deputation of their principal men, he would deal with them as *rebels* to his own sovereign, the rightful lord of these realms! The menace had the desired effect. The Cholulans were not inclined to contest, at least for the present, his magnificent pretensions. Another embassy appeared in the camp, consisting of some of the highest nobles; who repeated the invitation for the Spaniards to visit their city, and excused their own tardy appearance by apprehensions for their personal safety in the capital of their enemies. The explanation was plausible, and was admitted by Cortés.

The Tlascalans were now more than ever opposed to his projected visit. A strong Aztec force, they had ascertained, lay in the neighbourhood of Cholula, and the people were actively placing their city in a posture of defence. They suspected some insidious scheme concerted by Montezuma to destroy the Spaniards.

These suggestions disturbed the mind of Cortés, but did not turn him from his purpose. He felt a natural curiosity to see the venerable city so celebrated in the history of the Indian nations. He had, besides, gone too far to recede—too far, at least, to do so without a show of apprehension, implying a distrust in his own resources, which could not fail to have a bad effect on his enemies, his allies, and his own men. After a brief consultation with his officers, he decided on the route to Cholula.

It was now three weeks since the Spaniards had taken up their residence within the hospitable walls of Tlascala; and nearly six since they entered her territory. They had been met on the threshold as an enemy, with the most determined hostility. They were now to part with the same people, as friends and allies; fast friends, who were to stand by them, side by side, through the whole of their arduous struggle. The result of their visit, therefore, was of the last importance, since on the co-operation of these brave and warlike republicans greatly depended the ultimate success of the expedition.

CHAPTER VI

City of Cholula—Great Temple—March to Cholula—Reception of the Spaniards—Conspiracy Detected

1519

THE ANCIENT CITY OF CHOLULA, capital of the republic of that name, lay nearly six leagues south of Tlascala, and about twenty east, or rather south-east, of Mexico. It was said by Cortés to contain twenty thousand houses within the walls, and as many more in the environs; though now dwindled to a population of less than sixteen thousand souls. Whatever was its real number of inhabitants, it was unquestionably, at the time of the Conquest, one of the most populous and flourishing cities in New Spain.

It was of great antiquity, and was founded by the primitive races who overspread the land before the Aztecs. We have few particulars of its form of government, which seems to have been cast on a republican model similar to that of Tlascala. This answered so well, that the state maintained its independence down to a very late period, when, if not reduced to vassalage by the Aztecs, it was so far under their control as to enjoy few of the benefits of a separate political existence. Their connection with Mexico brought the Cholulans into frequent collision with their neighbours and kindred, the Tlascalans. But, although far superior to them in refinement and the various arts of civilisation, they were no match in war for the bold mountaineers, the Swiss of Anahuac. The Cholulan capital was the great commercial emporium of the plateau. The inhabitants excelled in various mechanical arts, especially that of working in metals, the manufacture of cotton and agave cloths, and of a delicate kind of pottery, rivalling, it was said, that of Florence in beauty. But such attention to the arts of a polished and peaceful community naturally indisposed them to war, and disqualified them for coping with those who made war the great business of life. The Cholulans were accused of effeminacy, and were less distinguished—it is the charge of their rivals—by their courage than their cunning.

But the capital, so conspicuous for its refinement and its great antiquity, was even more venerable for the religious traditions which invested it. It was here that the god Quetzalcoatl paused in his passage to the coast, and passed twenty years in teaching the Toltec inhabitants the arts of civilisation. He made them acquainted with better forms of government, and a more spiritualised religion, in which the only sacrifices were the fruits and flowers of the season. It is not easy to determine what he taught, since his lessons have been so mingled with the licentious dogmas of his own priests, and the mystic commentaries of the Christian missionary. It is probable that he was one of those rare and gifted beings, who, dissipating the darkness of the age by the illumination of their own genius, are deified by a grateful posterity, and placed among the lights of Heaven.

It was in honour of this benevolent deity, that the stupendous mound was erected on which the traveller still gazes with admiration as the most colossal fabric in New Spain, rivalling in dimensions, and somewhat resembling in form, the pyramidal structures of ancient Egypt. The date of its erection is unknown, for it was found there when the Aztecs entered on the plateau. It had the form common to the Mexican *teocallis,* that of a truncated pyramid, facing with its four sides the cardinal points, and divided into the same number of terraces. Its original outlines, however, have been effaced by the action of time and of the elements, while the exuberant growth of shrubs and wild flowers, which have mantled over its surface, give it the appearance of one of those symmetrical elevations thrown up by the caprice of nature, rather than by the industry of man. It is doubtful, indeed, whether the interior be not a natural hill, though it seems not improbable that it is an artificial composition of stone and earth, deeply incrusted, as is certain, in every part, with alternate strata of brick and clay.

The perpendicular height of the pyramid is one hundred and seventy-seven feet. Its base is one thousand four hundred and twenty-three feet long, twice as long as that of the great pyramid of Cheops. It may give some idea of its dimensions to state that its base, which is square, covers about forty-four acres, and the platform on its truncated summit embraces more than one. It reminds us of those colossal monuments of brickwork, which are still seen in ruins on the banks of the Euphrates, and, in much higher preservation, on those of the Nile.

On the summit stood a sumptuous temple, in which was the image of the mystic deity, "god of the air," with ebon features, unlike the fair complexion which he bore upon earth, wearing a mitre on his head waving with *plumes of fire,* with a resplendent collar of gold round his neck, pendants of mosaic turquoise in his ears, a jewelled sceptre in one hand, and a shield curiously painted, the emblem of his rule over the winds, in the other. The sanctity of the place, hallowed by hoary tradition, and the magnificence of the temple and its services, made it an object of veneration throughout the land, and pilgrims from the furthest corners of Anahuac came to offer up their devotions at the shrine of Quetzalcoatl. The number of these was so great as to give an air of mendicity to the motley population of the city; and Cortés, struck with the novelty, tells us that he saw multitudes of beggars such as are to be found in the enlightened capitals of Europe; a whimsical criterion of civilisation which must place our own prosperous land somewhat low in the scale.

Cholula was not the resort only of the indigent devotee. Many of the kindred races had temples of their own in the city, in the same manner as some Christian nations have in Rome, and each temple was provided with its own peculiar ministers for the service of the deity to whom it was consecrated. In no city was there seen such a concourse of priests, so many processions, such pomp of ceremonial sacrifice, and religious festivals. Cholula was, in short, what Mecca is among Mahometans, or Jerusalem among Christians; it was the Holy City of Anahuac.

The religious rites were not performed, however, in the pure spirit originally prescribed by its tutelary deity. His altars, as well as those of the numerous Aztec gods, were stained with human blood; and six thousand victims *are said* to have been annually offered up at their sanguinary shrines. The great number of these may be estimated from the declaration of Cortés that he counted four hundred towers in the city; yet no temple had more than two, many only one. High above the rest rose the great "pyramid of Cholula," with its undying fires flinging their radiance far and wide over the capital, and proclaiming to the nations that there was the mystic worship—alas!—how corrupted by cruelty and superstition—of the good deity who was one day to return and resume his empire over the land.

Nothing could be more grand than the view which met the eye from the area on the truncated summit of the pyramid. Toward the north stretched that bold barrier of porphyritic rock which nature has reared round the Valley of Mexico, with the huge Popocatepetl and Iztaccihuatl

standing like two colossal sentinels to guard the entrance to the enchanted region. Far away to the south was seen the conical head of
Orizaba soaring high into the clouds, and nearer, the barren, though
beautifully shaped, Sierra de Malinche, throwing its broad shadows over
the plains of Tlascala. Three of these are volcanoes, higher than the
highest mountain-peak in Europe, and shrouded in snows which never
melt under the fierce sun of the tropics. At the foot of the spectator lay
the sacred city of Cholula, with its bright towers and pinnacles sparkling
in the sun, reposing amidst gardens and verdant groves, which then
thickly studded the cultivated environs of the capital. Such was the magnificent prospect which met the gaze of the Conquerors, and may still,
with slight change, meet that of the modern traveller, as from the platform of the great pyramid his eye wanders over the fairest portion of the
beautiful plateau of Puebla.

But it is time to return to Tlascala. On the appointed morning the
Spanish army took up its march to Mexico by the way of Cholula. It was
followed by crowds of the citizens, filled with admiration at the intrepidity of men who, so few in number, would venture to brave the
great Montezuma in his capital. Yet an immense body of warriors
offered to share the dangers of the expedition; but Cortés, while he
showed his gratitude for their good will, selected only six thousand of
the volunteers to bear him company. He was unwilling to encumber
himself with an unwieldy force that might impede his movements; and
probably did not care to put himself so far in the power of allies whose
attachment was too recent to afford sufficient guaranty for their fidelity.

After crossing some rough and hilly ground, the army entered on the
wide plain which spreads out for miles around Cholula. At the elevation
of more than six thousand feet above the sea they beheld the rich products
of various climes growing side by side, fields of towering maize, the juicy
aloe, the *chilli* or Aztec pepper, and large plantations of the cactus, on
which the brilliant cochineal is nourished. Not a rood of land but was
under cultivation; and the soil—a common thing on the tableland—was
irrigated by numerous streams and canals, and well shaded by woods
that have disappeared before the rude axe of the Spaniards. Towards evening they reached a small stream, on the banks of which Cortés determined to take up his quarters for the night, being unwilling to disturb
the tranquillity of the city by introducing so large a force into it at an
unseasonable hour.

Here he was soon joined by a number of Cholulan caciques and their

attendants, who came to view and welcome the strangers. When they saw
their Tlascalan enemies in the camp, however, they exhibited signs of
displeasure, and intimated an apprehension that their presence in the
town might occasion disorder. The remonstrance seemed reasonable to
Cortés, and he accordingly commanded his allies to remain in their
present quarters, and to join him as he left the city on the way to Mexico.

On the following morning he made his entrance at the head of his
army into Cholula, attended by no other Indians than those from Cempoalla, and a handful of Tlascalans to take charge of the baggage. His
allies, at parting, gave him many cautions respecting the people he was
to visit, who, while they affected to despise them as a nation of traders,
employed the dangerous arms of perfidy and cunning. As the troops
drew near the city, the road was lined with swarms of people of both
sexes and every age—old men tottering with infirmity, women with children in their arms—all eager to catch a glimpse of the strangers, whose
persons, weapons, and horses were objects of intense curiosity to eyes
which had not hitherto ever encountered them in battle. The Spaniards,
in turn, were filled with admiration at the aspect of the Cholulans,
much superior in dress and general appearance to the nations they had
hitherto seen. They were particularly struck with the costume of the
higher classes, who wore fine embroidered mantles, resembling the graceful *albornoz,* or Moorish cloak, in their texture and fashion. They
showed the same delicate taste for flowers as the other tribes of the
plateau, decorating their persons with them, and tossing garlands and
bunches among the soldiers. An immense number of priests mingled
with the crowd, swinging their aromatic censers, while music from
various kinds of instruments gave a lively welcome to the visitors, and
made the whole scene one of gay, bewildering enchantment. If it did not
have the air of a triumphal procession so much as at Tlascala, where
the melody of instruments was drowned by the shouts of the multitude,
it gave a quiet assurance of hospitality and friendly feeling not less
grateful.

The Spaniards were also struck with the cleanliness of the city, the
width and great regularity of the streets, which seemed to have been
laid out on a settled plan, with the solidity of the houses, and the
number and size of the pyramidal temples. In the court of one of these,
and its surrounding buildings, they were quartered.

They were soon visited by the principal lords of the place, who seemed
solicitous to provide them with accommodations. Their table was plen-

tifully supplied, and, in short, they experienced such attentions as were calculated to dissipate their suspicions, and made them impute those of their Tlascalan friends to prejudice and old national hostility.

In a few days the scene changed. Messengers arrived from Montezuma, who, after a short and unpleasant intimation to Cortés that his approach occasioned such disquietude to their master, conferred separately with the Mexican ambassadors still in the Castilian camp, and then departed, taking one of the latter along with them. From this time, the deportment of their Cholulan hosts underwent a visible alteration. They did not visit the quarters as before, and, when invited to do so, excused themselves on pretence of illness. The supply of provisions was stinted, on the ground that they were short of maize. These symptoms of alienation, independently of temporary embarrassment, caused serious alarm in the breast of Cortés, for the future. His apprehensions were not allayed by the reports of the Cempoallans, who told him that in wandering round the city they had seen several streets barricaded; the *azoteas,* or flat roofs of the houses, loaded with huge stones and other missiles, as if preparatory to an assault; and in some places they had found holes covered over with branches, and upright stakes planted within, as if to embarrass the movements of the cavalry. Some Tlascalans coming in also from their camp informed the general that a great sacrifice, mostly of children, had been offered up in a distant quarter of the town, to propitiate the favour of the gods, apparently for some intended enterprise. They added that they had seen numbers of the citizens leaving the city with their women and children, as if to remove them to a place of safety. These tidings confirmed the worst suspicions of Cortés, who had no doubt that some hostile scheme was in agitation. If he had felt any, a discovery by Marina, the good angel of the expedition, would have turned these doubts into certainty.

The amiable manners of the Indian girl had won her the regard of the wife of one of the caciques, who repeatedly urged Marina to visit her house, darkly intimating that in this way she would escape the fate that awaited the Spaniards. The interpreter, seeing the importance of obtaining further intelligence, at once pretended to be pleased with the proposal, and affected, at the same time, great discontent with the white men, by whom she was detained in captivity. Thus throwing the credulous Cholulan off her guard, Marina gradually insinuated herself into her confidence, so far as to draw from her a full account of the conspiracy.

It originated, she said, with the Aztec emperor, who had sent rich bribes to the great caciques, and to her husband among others, to secure them in his views. The Spaniards were to be assaulted as they marched out of the capital, when entangled in its streets, in which numerous impediments had been placed to throw the cavalry into disorder. A force of twenty thousand Mexicans was already quartered at no great distance from the city, to support the Cholulans in the assault. It was confidently expected that the Spaniards, thus embarrassed in their movements, would fall an easy prey to the superior strength of their enemy. A sufficient number of prisoners was to be reserved to grace the sacrifices of Cholula; the rest were to be led in fetters to the capital of Montezuma.

While this conversation was going on, Marina occupied herself with putting up such articles of value and wearing apparel as she proposed to take with her in the evening, when she could escape unnoticed from the Spanish quarters to the house of her Cholulan friend, who assisted her in the operation. Leaving her visitor thus employed, Marina found an opportunity to steal away for a few moments, and, going to the general's apartment, disclosed to him her discoveries. He immediately caused the cacique's wife to be seized, and on examination she fully confirmed the statement of his Indian mistress.

The intelligence thus gathered by Cortés filled him with the deepest alarm. He was fairly taken in the snare. To fight or to fly seemed equally difficult. He was in a city of enemies, where every house might be converted into a fortress, and where such embarrassments were thrown in the way as might render the manœuvres of his artillery and horse nearly impracticable. In addition to the wily Cholulans, he must cope, under all these disadvantages, with the redoubtable warriors of Mexico. He was like a traveller who has lost his way in the darkness among precipices, where any step may dash him to pieces, and where to retreat or to advance is equally perilous.

He was desirous to obtain still further confirmation and particulars of the conspiracy. He accordingly induced two of the priests in the neighbourhood, one of them a person of much influence in the place, to visit his quarters. By courteous treatment, and liberal largesses of the rich presents he had received from Montezuma—thus turning his own gifts against the giver—he drew from them a full confirmation of the previous report. The emperor had been in a state of pitiable vacillation since the arrival of the Spaniards. His first orders to the Cholulans were to receive the strangers kindly. He had recently consulted his oracles anew, and obtained for answer that Cholula would be the grave of his enemies; for the gods would be sure to support him in avenging the sacrilege offered to the Holy City. So confident were the Aztecs of success that numerous manacles, or poles with thongs which served as such, were already in the place to secure the prisoners.

Cortés, now feeling himself fully possessed of the facts, dismissed the priests with injunctions of secrecy scarcely necessary. He told them it was his purpose to leave the city on the following morning, and requested that they would induce some of the principal caciques to grant him an interview in his quarters. He then summoned a council of his officers, though, as it seems, already determined as to the course he was to take.

The members of the council were differently affected by the startling intelligence, according to their different characters. The more timid, disheartened by the prospect of obstacles which seemed to multiply as they drew nearer the Mexican capital, were for retracing their steps, and seeking shelter in the friendly city of Tlascala. Others, more persevering, but prudent, were for taking the more northerly route originally recommended by their allies. The greater part supported the general, who was ever of opinion that they had no alternative but to advance. Retreat would be ruin. Half-way measures were scarcely better; and would infer a timidity which must discredit them with both friend and foe. Their true policy was to rely on themselves; to strike such a blow as should intimidate their enemies, and show them that the Spaniards were as incapable of being circumvented by artifice, as of being crushed by weight of numbers and courage in the open field.

When the caciques, persuaded by the priests, appeared before Cortés, he contented himself with gently rebuking their want of hospitality, and assured them the Spaniards would be no longer a burden to their city, as he proposed to leave it early on the following morning. He requested, moreover, that they would furnish a reinforcement of two thousand men to transport his artillery and baggage. The chiefs, after some consultation, acquiesced in a demand which might in some measure favour their own designs.

On their departure, the general summoned the Aztec ambassadors before him. He briefly acquainted them with his detection of the treacherous plot to destroy his army, the contrivance of which, he said, was imputed to their master, Montezuma. It grieved him much, he added, to find the emperor implicated in so nefarious a scheme, and that the

Spaniards must now march as enemies against the prince, whom they had hoped to visit as a friend.

The ambassadors, with earnest protestations, asserted their entire ignorance of the conspiracy; and their belief that Montezuma was equally innocent of a crime, which they charged wholly on the Cholulans. It was clearly the policy of Cortés to keep on good terms with the Indian monarch; to profit as long as possible by his good offices; and to avail himself of his fancied security—such feelings of security as the general could inspire him with—to cover his own future operations. He affected to give credit, therefore, to the assertion of the envoys, and declared his unwillingness to believe that a monarch, who had rendered the Spaniards so many friendly offices, would now consummate the whole by a deed of such unparalleled baseness. The discovery of their twofold duplicity, he added, sharpened his resentment against the Cholulans, on whom he would take such vengeance as should amply requite the injuries done both to Montezuma and the Spaniards. He then dismissed the ambassadors, taking care, notwithstanding this show of confidence, to place a strong guard over them to prevent communication with the citizens.

That night was one of deep anxiety to the army. The ground they stood on seemed loosening beneath their feet, and any moment might be the one marked for their destruction. Their vigilant general took all possible precautions for their safety, increasing the number of the sentinels, and posting his guns in such a manner as to protect the approaches to the camp. His eyes, it may well be believed, did not close during the night. Indeed every Spaniard lay down in his arms, and every horse stood saddled and bridled, ready for instant service. But no assault was meditated by the Indians, and the stillness of the hour was undisturbed except by the occasional sounds heard in a populous city, even when buried in slumber, and by the hoarse cries of the priests from the turrets of the *teocallis,* proclaiming through their trumpets the watches of the night.

CHAPTER VII

*Terrible Massacre—Tranquillity Restored—Reflections on
the Massacre—Further Proceedings—Envoys from
Montezuma*

1519

WITH the first streak of morning light, Cortés was seen on horseback, directing the movements of his little band. The strength of his forces he drew up in the great square or court, surrounded partly by buildings, as before noticed, and in part by a high wall. There were three gates of entrance, at each of which he placed a strong guard. The rest of his troops, with his great guns, he posted without the enclosure, in such a manner as to command the avenues, and secure those within from interruption in their bloody work. Orders had been sent the night before to the Tlascalan chiefs to hold themselves ready, at a concerted signal, to march into the city and join the Spaniards.

The arrangements were hardly completed, before the Cholulan caciques appeared, leading a body of levies, *tamanes,* even more numerous than had been demanded. They were marched at once into the square, commanded, as we have seen, by the Spanish infantry, which was drawn up under the walls. Cortés then took some of the caciques aside. With a stern air, he bluntly charged them with the conspiracy, showing that he was well acquainted with all the particulars. He had visited their city, he said, at the invitation of their emperor; had come as a friend; had respected the inhabitants and their property; and, to avoid all cause of umbrage, had left a great part of his forces without the walls. They had received him with a show of kindness and hospitality, and, reposing on this, he had been decoyed into the snare, and found this kindness only a mask to cover the blackest perfidy.

The Cholulans were thunderstruck at the accusation. An undefined awe crept over them as they gazed on the mysterious strangers, and felt themselves in the presence of beings who seemed to have the power of reading the thoughts scarcely formed in their bosoms. There was no use in prevarication or denial before such judges. They confessed the whole, and endeavoured to excuse themselves by throwing the blame on Montezuma. Cortés, assuming an air of higher indignation at this, assured them that the pretence should not serve, since, even if well founded, it would be no justification; and he would now make such an example of them for their treachery that the report of it should ring throughout the wide borders of Anahuac.

The fatal signal, the discharge of an arquebuse, was then given. In an instant every musket and crossbow was levelled at the unfortunate Cholulans in the courtyard, and a frightful volley poured into them as they stood crowded together like a herd of deer in the centre. They were taken by surprise, for they had not heard the preceding dialogue with the chiefs. They made scarcely any resistance to the Spaniards, who followed up the discharge of their pieces by rushing on them with their swords; and, as the half-naked bodies of the natives afforded no protection, they hewed them down with as much ease as the reaper mows down the ripe corn in harvest time. Some endeavoured to scale the walls, but only afforded a surer mark to the arquebusiers and archers. Others threw themselves into the gateways, but were received on the long pikes of the soldiers who guarded them. Some few had better luck in hiding themselves under the heaps of slain with which the ground was soon loaded.

While this work of death was going on, the countrymen of the slaughtered Indians, drawn together by the noise of the massacre, had commenced a furious assault on the Spaniards from without. But Cortés had placed his battery of heavy guns in a position that commanded the avenues, and swept off the files of the assailants as they rushed on. In the intervals between the discharges, which, in the imperfect state of the science in that day, were much longer than in ours, he forced back the press by charging with the horse into the midst. The steeds, the guns, the weapons of the Spaniards, were all new to the Cholulans. Notwithstanding the novelty of the terrific spectacle, the flash of firearms, mingling with the deafening roar of the artillery, as its thunders reverberated among the buildings, the despairing Indians pushed on to take the places of their fallen comrades.

While this fierce struggle was going forward, the Tlascalans, hearing the concerted signal, had advanced with quick pace into the city.

They had bound, by order of Cortés, wreaths of sedge round their heads, that they might the more surely be distinguished from the Cholulans. Coming up in the very heat of the engagement, they fell on the defenceless rear of the townsmen, who, trampled down under the heels of the Castilian cavalry on one side, and galled by their vindictive enemies on the other, could no longer maintain their ground. They gave way, some taking refuge in the nearest buildings, which, being partly of wood, were speedily set on fire. Others fled to the temples. One strong party, with a number of priests at its head, got possession of the great *teocalli.* There was a vulgar tradition, already alluded to, that, on removal of part of the walls, the god would send forth an inundation to overwhelm his enemies. The superstitious Cholulans with great difficulty succeeded in wrenching away some of the stones in the walls of the edifice. But dust, not water, followed. Their false gods deserted them in the hour of need. In despair they flung themselves into the wooden turrets that crowned the temple, and poured down stones, javelins, and burning arrows on the Spaniards, as they climbed the great staircase, which, by a flight of one hundred and twenty steps, scaled the face of the pyramid. But the fiery shower fell harmless on the steel bonnets of the Christians, while they availed themselves of the burning shafts to set fire to the wooden citadel, which was speedily wrapt in flames. Still the garrison held out, and though quarter, *it is said,* was offered, only one Cholulan availed himself of it. The rest threw themselves headlong from the parapet, or perished miserably in the flames.

All was now confusion and uproar in the fair city which had so lately reposed in security and peace. The groans of the dying, the frantic supplications of the vanquished for mercy, were mingled with the loud battle-cries of the Spaniards, as they rode down their enemy, and with the shrill whistle of the Tlascalans, who gave full scope to the long-cherished rancour of ancient rivalry. The tumult was still further swelled by the incessant rattle of musketry, and the crash of falling timbers, which sent up a volume of flame that outshone the ruddy light of morning, making altogether a hideous confusion of sights and sounds, that converted the Holy City into a Pandemonium. As resistance slackened, the victors broke into the houses and sacred places, plundering them of whatever valuables they contained, plate, jewels, which were found in some quantity, wearing apparel and provisions, the two last coveted even more than the former by the simple Tlascalans, thus facilitating a division of the spoil, much to the satisfaction of their Christian confederates. Amidst this universal licence, it is worthy of remark, the commands of Cortés were so far respected that no violence was offered to women or children, though these, as well as numbers of the men, were made prisoners, to be swept into slavery by the Tlascalans. These scenes of violence had lasted some hours, when Cortés, moved by the entreaties of some Cholulan chiefs, who had been reserved from the massacre, backed by the prayers of the Mexican envoys, consented, out of regard, as he said, to the latter, the representatives of Montezuma, to call off the soldiers, and put a stop, as well as he could, to further outrage. Two of the caciques were also permitted to go to their countrymen with assurances of pardon and protection to all who would return to their obedience.

These measures had their effect. By the joint efforts of Cortés and the caciques the tumult was with much difficulty appeased. The assailants, Spaniards and Indians, gathered under their respective banners, and the Cholulans, relying on the assurance of their chiefs, gradually returned to their homes.

The first act of Cortés was to prevail on the Tlascalan chiefs to liberate their captives. Such was their deference to the Spanish commander that they acquiesced, though not without murmurs, contenting themselves as they best could with the rich spoil rifled from the Cholulans, consisting of various luxuries long since unknown in Tlascala. His next care was to cleanse the city from its loathsome impurities, particularly from the dead bodies which lay festering in heaps in the streets and great square. The general, in his letter to Charles the Fifth, admits three thousand slain; most accounts say six, and some swell the amount yet higher. As the eldest and principal cacique was among the number, Cortés assisted the Cholulans in installing a successor in his place. By these pacific measures confidence was gradually restored. The people in the environs, reassured, flocked into the capital to supply the place of the diminished population. The markets were again opened; and the usual avocations of an orderly, industrious community were resumed. Still, the long piles of black and smouldering ruins proclaimed the hurricane which had so lately swept over the city, and the walls surrounding the scene of slaughter in the great square, which were standing more than fifty years after the event, told the sad tale of the Massacre of Cholula.

This passage in their history is one of those that have left a dark stain on the memory of the Conquerors. Nor can we contemplate at this day, without a shudder, the condition of this fair and flourishing capital thus invaded in its privacy, and delivered over to the excesses of a rude and ruthless soldiery. But, to judge the action fairly, we must transport ourselves to the age when it happened. The difficulty that meets us in the outset is to find a justification of the right of conquest at all. But it should be remembered that religious infidelity, at this period, and till a much later, was regarded—no matter whether founded on ignorance or education, whether hereditary or acquired, heretical or pagan—as a sin to be punished with fire and faggot in this world, and eternal suffering in the next. This doctrine, monstrous as it is, was the creed of the Romish, in other words, of the Christian Church—the basis of the Inquisition, and of those other species of religious persecutions, which have stained the annals, at some time or other, of nearly every nation in Christendom. Under this code the territory of the heathen, wherever found, was regarded as a sort of religious waif, which, in default of a legal proprietor, was claimed and taken possession of by the Holy See, and as such was freely given away, by the head of the Church, to any temporal potentate whom he pleased that would assume the burden of conquest. Thus, Alexander the Sixth generously granted a large portion of the Western Hemisphere to the Spaniards, and of the Eastern to the Portuguese. These lofty pretensions of the successors of the humble fisherman of Galilee, far from being nominal, were acknowledged and appealed to as conclusive in controversies between nations.

With the right of conquest, thus conferred, came also the obligation, on which it may be said to have been founded, to retrieve the nations sitting in darkness from eternal perdition. This obligation was acknowledged by the best and the bravest, the gownsman in his closet, the missionary, and the warrior in the crusade. However much it may have been debased by temporal motives and mixed up with worldly considerations of ambition and avarice, it was still active in the mind of the Christian Conqueror. We have seen how far paramount it was to every calculation of personal interest in the breast of Cortés. The concession of the Pope then, founded on and enforcing the imperative duty of conversion, was the assumed basis—and, in the apprehension of that age, a sound one—of the right of conquest.

The right could not, indeed, be construed to authorise any unnecessary act of violence to the natives. The present expedition, up to the period of its history at which we are now arrived, had probably been stained with fewer of such acts than almost any similar enterprise of the Spanish discoverers in the New World. Throughout the campaign, Cortés had prohibited all wanton injuries to the natives, in person or property, and had punished the perpetrators of them with exemplary severity. He had been faithful to his friends, and, with perhaps a single exception, not unmerciful to his foes. Whether from policy or principle, it should be recorded to his credit; though, like every sagacious mind, he may have felt that principle and policy go together.

He had entered Cholula as a friend, at the invitation of the Indian emperor, who had a real, if not avowed, control over the state. He had been received as a friend, with every demonstration of good will; when, without any offence of his own or his followers, he found they were to be the victims of an insidious plot—that they were standing on a mine which might be sprung at any moment, and bury them all in its ruins. His safety, as he truly considered, left no alternative but to anticipate the blow of his enemies. Yet who can doubt that the punishment thus inflicted was excessive—that the same end might have been attained by directing the blow against the guilty chiefs, instead of letting it fall on the ignorant rabble, who but obeyed the commands of their masters? But when was it ever seen that fear, armed with power, was scrupulous in the exercise of it? or that the passions of a fierce soldiery, inflamed by conscious injuries, could be regulated in the moment of explosion?

We shall, perhaps, pronounce more impartially on the conduct of the Conquerors, if we compare it with that of our own contemporaries under somewhat similar circumstances. The atrocities at Cholula were not so bad as those inflicted on the descendants of these very Spaniards, in the late war of the Peninsula, by the most polished nations of our time; by the British at Badajoz, for example—at Taragona, and a hundred other places, by the French. The wanton butchery, the ruin of property, and, above all, those outrages worse than death, from which the female part of the population were protected at Cholula, show a catalogue of enormities quite as black as those imputed to the Spaniards, and without the same apology for resentment—with no apology indeed, but that afforded by a brave and patriotic resistance. The consideration of these events, which, from their familiarity, make little impression on our senses, should render us more lenient in our judgments of the past, showing, as they do, that man in a state of excitement, savage or civilised, is much the same in every age. It may teach us—it is one of the best lessons of history—that, since such are the *inevitable* evils of war, even among the most polished people, those who hold the destinies of nations in their hands, whether rulers or legislators, should submit to every sacrifice, save that of honour, before authorising an appeal to arms. The extreme solicitude to avoid these calamities, by the aid of peaceful congresses and impartial mediation, is, on the whole, the strongest evidence, stronger than that afforded by the progress of science and art, of our boasted advance in civilisation.

It is far from my intention to vindicate the cruel deeds of the old Conquerors. Let them lie heavy on their heads. They were an iron race, who perilled life and fortune in the cause; and, as they made little account of danger and suffering for themselves, they had little sympathy to spare for their unfortunate enemies. But, to judge them fairly, we must not do it by the lights of our own age. We must carry ourselves back to theirs, and take the point of view afforded by the civilisation of their time. Thus only can we arrive at impartial criticism in reviewing the generations that are past. We must extend to them the same justice which we shall have occasion to ask from posterity, when, by the light of a higher civilisation, it surveys the dark or doubtful passages in our own history, which hardly arrest the eye of the contemporary.

But whatever be thought of this transaction in a moral view, as a stroke of policy it was unquestionable. The nations of Anahuac had beheld, with admiration mingled with awe, the little band of Christian warriors steadily advancing along the plateau in face of every obstacle, overturning army after army with as much ease, apparently, as the good ship throws off the angry billows from her bows; or rather like the lava, which, rolling from their own volcanoes, holds on its course unchecked by obstacles, rock, tree, or building, bearing them along, or crushing and consuming them in its fiery path. The prowess of the Spaniards—"the white gods," as they were often called—made them to be thought invincible. But it was not till their arrival at Cholula that the natives learned how terrible was their vengeance—and they trembled!

None trembled more than the Aztec emperor on his throne among the mountains. He read in these events the dark character traced by the finger of Destiny. He felt his empire melting away like a morning mist. He might well feel so. Some of the most important cities in the neighbourhood of Cholula, intimidated by the fate of that capital, now sent their envoys to the Castilian camp, tendering their allegiance, and propitiating the favour of the strangers by rich presents of gold and slaves. Montezuma, alarmed at these signs of defection, took counsel again of his impotent deities; but, although the altars smoked with fresh hecatombs of human victims, he obtained no cheering response. He determined, therefore, to send another embassy to the Spaniards, disavowing any participation in the conspiracy of Cholula.

Meanwhile Cortés was passing his time in that capital. He thought that the impression produced by the late scenes, and by the present restoration of tranquillity, offered a fair opportunity for the good work of conversion. He accordingly urged the citizens to embrace the Cross, and abandon the false guardians who had abandoned them in their extremity. But the traditions of centuries rested on the Holy City, shedding a halo of glory around it as "the sanctuary of the gods," the religious capital of Anahuac. It was too much to expect that the people would willingly resign this pre-eminence, and descend to the level of an ordinary community. Still Cortés might have pressed the matter, however unpalatable, but for the renewed interposition of the wise Olmedo, who persuaded him to postpone it till after the reduction of the whole country.

The Spanish general, however, had the satisfaction to break open the cages in which the victims for sacrifice were confined, and to dismiss the trembling inmates to liberty and life. He also seized upon the great *teocalli,* and devoted that portion of the building, which, being of stone, had escaped the fury of the flames, to the purposes of a Christian church; while a crucifix of stone and lime, of gigantic dimensions, spreading out its arms above the city, proclaimed that the population below was under the protection of the Cross. On the same spot now stands a temple, overshadowed by dark cypresses of unknown antiquity, and dedicated to Our Lady *de los Remedios.* An image of the Virgin presides over it, *said* to have been left by the Conqueror himself; and an Indian ecclesiastic, a descendant of the ancient Cholulans, performs the peaceful services of the Roman Catholic communion, on the spot where his ancestors celebrated the sanguinary rites of the mystic Quetzalcoatl.

During the occurrence of these events, envoys arrived from Mexico. They were charged, as usual, with a rich present of plate and ornaments of gold; among others, artificial birds in imitation of turkeys, with plumes of the same precious metal. To these were added fifteen hundred cotton dresses of delicate fabric. The emperor even expressed his regret at the catastrophe of Cholula, vindicated himself from any share in the conspiracy, which, he said, had brought deserved retribution on the heads of its authors, and explained the existence of an Aztec force in the neighbourhood, by the necessity of repressing some disorders there.

One cannot contemplate this pusillanimous conduct of Montezuma without mingled feelings of pity and contempt. It is not easy to reconcile his assumed innocence of the plot with many circumstances connected with it. But it must be remembered, here and always, that his history is to be collected solely from Spanish writers, and such of the natives as flourished after the Conquest, when the country had become a colony of Spain. Not an Aztec record of the primitive age survives, in a form capable of interpretation. It is the hard fate of this unfortunate monarch to be wholly indebted for his portraiture to the pencil of his enemies.

More than a fortnight had elapsed since the entrance of the Spaniards into Cholula, and Cortés now resolved, without loss of time, to resume his march towards the capital. His rigorous reprisals had so far intimidated the Cholulans, that he felt assured he should no longer leave an active enemy in his rear, to annoy him in case of retreat. He had the satisfaction, before his departure, to heal the feud—in outward appearance, at least—that had so long subsisted between the Holy City and Tlascala, and which, under the revolution which so soon changed the destinies of the country, never revived.

It was with some disquietude that he now received an application from his Cempoallan allies to be allowed to withdraw from the expedition, and return to their own homes. They had incurred too deeply the resentment of the Aztec emperor, by their insults to his collectors, and by their co-operation with the Spaniards, to care to trust themselves in his capital. It was in vain Cortés endeavoured to reassure them by promises of his protection. Their habitual distrust and dread of "the great Montezuma" were not to be overcome. The general learned their determination with regret, for they had been of infinite service to the cause by their staunch fidelity and courage. All this made it the more difficult for him to resist their reasonable demand. Liberally recompensing their services, therefore, from the rich wardrobe and treasures of the emperor, he took leave of his faithful followers, before his own departure from Cholula. He availed himself of their return to send letters to Juan de Escalante, his lieutenant at Vera Cruz, acquainting him with the successful progress of the expedition. He enjoined on that officer to strengthen the fortifications of the place, so as the better to resist any hostile interference from Cuba—an event for which Cortés was ever on the watch—and to keep down revolt among the natives. He especially commended the Totonacs to his protection, as allies whose fidelity to the Spaniards exposed them, in no slight degree, to the vengeance of the Aztecs.

CHAPTER VIII

March Resumed—Ascent of the Great Volcano—Valley of Mexico—Impression on the Spaniards—Conduct of Montezuma—They Descend into the Valley

1519

EVERYTHING being now restored to quiet in Cholula, the allied army of Spaniards and Tlascalans set forward in high spirits, and resumed the march on Mexico. The road lay through the beautiful savannas and luxuriant plantations that spread out for several leagues in every direction. On the march they were met occasionally by embassies from the neighbouring places, anxious to claim the protection of the white men, and to propitiate them by gifts, especially of gold, for which their appetite was generally known throughout the country.

Some of these places were allies of the Tlascalans, and all showed much discontent with the oppressive rule of Montezuma. The natives cautioned the Spaniards against putting themselves in his power by entering his capital; and they stated, as evidence of his hostile disposition, that he had caused the direct road to it to be blocked up, that the strangers might be compelled to choose another, which, from its narrow passes and strong positions, would enable him to take them at great disadvantage.

The information was not lost on Cortés, who kept a strict eye on the movements of the Mexican envoys, and redoubled his own precautions against surprise. Cheerful and active, he was ever where his presence was needed, sometimes in the van, at others in the rear, encouraging the weak, stimulating the sluggish, and striving to kindle in the breasts of others the same courageous spirit which glowed in his own. At night he never omitted to go the rounds to see that every man was at his post. On one occasion his vigilance had well-nigh proved fatal to him. He approached so near a sentinel that the man, unable to distinguish his person in the dark, levelled his crossbow at him, when, fortunately, an exclamation of the general, who gave the watchword of the night, arrested a movement which might else have brought the campaign to a close, and given a respite for some time longer to the empire of Montezuma.

The army came at length to the place mentioned by the friendly Indians, where the road forked, and one arm of it was found, as they had foretold, obstructed with large trunks of trees and huge stones which had been strewn across it. Cortés inquired the meaning of this from the Mexican ambassadors. They said it was done by the emperor's orders, to prevent their taking a route which, after some distance, they would find nearly impracticable for the cavalry. They acknowledged, however, that it was the most direct road; and Cortés, declaring that this was enough to decide him in favour of it, as the Spaniards made no account of obstacles, commanded the rubbish to be cleared away. Some of the timber might still be seen by the roadside, as Bernal Diaz tells us, many years after. The event left little doubt in the general's mind of the meditated treachery of the Mexicans. But he was too politic to betray his suspicions.

They were now leaving the pleasant champaign country, as the road wound up the bold sierra which separates the great plateaux of Mexico and Puebla. The air, as they ascended, became keen and piercing; and the blasts, sweeping down the frozen sides of the mountains, made the soldiers shiver in their thick harness of cotton, and benumbed the limbs of both men and horses.

They were passing between two of the highest mountains on the North American continent, Popocatepetl, "the hill that smokes," and Iztacci-huatl, or "white woman"—a name suggested, doubtless, by the bright robe of snow spread over its broad and broken surface. A puerile super-stition of the Indians regarded these celebrated mountains as gods, and Iztaccihuatl as the wife of her more formidable neighbour. A tradition of a higher character described the northern volcano as the abode of the departed spirits of wicked rulers, whose fiery agonies in their prison-house caused the fearful bellowings and convulsions in times of eruption. It was the classic fable of antiquity. These superstitious legends had invested the mountain with a mysterious horror that made the natives shrink from attempting its ascent, which indeed was, from natural causes, a work of incredible difficulty.

The great *volcan,* as Popocatepetl was called, rose to the enormous height of 17,852 feet above the level of the sea; more than 2000 feet above the "monarch of mountains"—the highest elevation in Europe. During the present century it has rarely given evidence of its volcanic origin, and "the hill that smokes" has almost forfeited its claim to the appellation. But at the time of the Conquest it was frequently in a state of activity, and raged with uncommon fury while the Spaniards were at Tlascala; an evil omen, it was thought, for the natives of Anahuac. Its head, gathered into a regular cone by the deposit of successive eruptions, wore the usual form of volcanic mountains, when not disturbed by the falling in of the crater. Soaring towards the skies, with its silver sheet of everlasting snow, it was seen far and wide over the broad plains of Mexico and Puebla, the first object which the morning sun greeted in his rising, the last where his evening rays were seen to linger, shedding a glorious effulgence over its head, that contrasted strikingly with the ruinous waste of sand and lava immediately below, and the deep fringe of funereal pines that shrouded its base.

The mysterious terrors which hung over the spot, and the wild love of adventure, made some of the Spanish cavaliers desirous to attempt the ascent, which the natives declared no man could accomplish and live. Cortés encouraged them in the enterprise, willing to show the Indians that no achievement was above the dauntless daring of his followers. One of his captains, accordingly, Diego Ordaz, with nine Spaniards, and several Tlascalans, encouraged by their example, undertook the ascent. It was attended with more difficulty than had been anticipated.

The lower region was clothed with a dense forest, so thickly matted that in some places it was scarcely possible to penetrate it. It grew thinner, however, as they advanced, dwindling by degrees into a straggling, stunted vegetation, till at the height of somewhat more than thirteen thousand feet it faded away altogether. The Indians who had held on thus far, intimidated by the strange subterranean sounds of the volcano, even then in a state of combustion, now left them. The track opened on a black surface of glazed volcanic sand and of lava, the broken fragments of which, arrested in its boiling progress in a thousand fantastic forms, opposed continual impediments to their advance. Amidst these, one huge rock, the *Pico del Fraile*, a conspicuous object from below, rose to the perpendicular height of a hundred and fifty feet, compelling them to take a wide circuit. They soon came to the limits of perpetual snow, where new difficulties presented themselves, as the treacherous ice gave an imperfect footing, and a false step might precipitate them into the frozen chasms that yawned around. To increase their distress, respiration in these aerial regions became so difficult that every effort was attended with sharp pains in the head and limbs. Still they pressed on till, drawing nearer the crater, such volumes of smoke, sparks, and cinders were belched forth from its burning entrails, and driven down the sides of the mountain, as nearly suffocated and blinded them. It was too much even for their hardy frames to endure, and however reluctantly, they were compelled to abandon the attempt on the eve of its completion. They brought back some huge icicles—a curious sight in these tropical regions —as a trophy of their achievement, which, however imperfect, was sufficient to strike the minds of the natives with wonder, by showing that with the Spaniards the most appalling and mysterious perils were only as pastimes. The undertaking was eminently characteristic of the bold spirit of the cavalier of that day, who, not content with the dangers that lay in his path, seemed to court them from the mere Quixotic love of adventure. A report of the affair was transmitted to the Emperor Charles the Fifth, and the family of Ordaz was allowed to commemorate the exploit by assuming a burning mountain on their escutcheon.

The general was not satisfied with the result. Two years after he sent up another party, under Francisco Montaño, a cavalier of determined resolution. The object was to obtain sulphur to assist in making gunpowder for the army. The mountain was quiet at this time, and the expedition was attended with better success. The Spaniards, five in number, climbed to the very edge of the crater, which presented an irregular ellipse at its mouth, more than a league in circumference. Its depth might be from eight hundred to a thousand feet. A lurid flame burned gloomily at the bottom, sending up a sulphureous steam, which, cooling as it rose, was precipitated on the sides of the cavity. The party cast lots, and it fell on Montaño himself to descend in a basket into this hideous abyss, into which he was lowered by his companions to the depth of four hundred feet. This was repeated several times, till the adventurous cavalier had collected a sufficient quantity of sulphur for the wants of the army. This doughty enterprise excited general admiration at the time. Cortés concludes his report of it, to the emperor, with the judicious reflection that it would be less inconvenient, on the whole, to import their powder from Spain.

But it is time to return from our digression, which may, perhaps, be excused as illustrating, in a remarkable manner, the chimerical spirit of enterprise—not inferior to that in his own romances of chivalry—which glowed in the breast of the Spanish cavalier in the sixteenth century.

The army held on its march through the intricate gorges of the sierra. The route was nearly the same as that pursued at the present day by the courier from the capital to Puebla, by the way of Mecameca. It was not that usually taken by travellers from Vera Cruz, who follow the more circuitous road round the northern base of Iztaccihuatl, as less fatiguing than the other, though inferior in picturesque scenery and romantic points of view. The icy winds that now swept down the sides of the mountains brought with them a tempest of arrowy sleet and snow, from which the Christians suffered even more than the Tlascalans, reared from infancy among the wild solitudes of their own native hills. As night came on, their sufferings would have been intolerable, but they luckily found a shelter in the commodious stone buildings which the Mexican government had placed at stated intervals along the roads for the accommodation of the traveller and their own couriers. It little dreamed it was providing a protection for its enemies.

The troops, refreshed by a night's rest, succeeded, early on the following day, in gaining the crest of the sierra of Ahualco, which stretches like a curtain between the two great mountains on the north and south. Their progress was now comparatively easy, and they marched forward with a buoyant step, as they felt they were treading the soil of Montezuma.

They had not advanced far, when, turning an angle of the sierra, they suddenly came on a view which more than compensated the toils of the preceding day. It was that of the Valley of Mexico, or Tenochtitlan, as more commonly called by the natives; which, with its picturesque assemblage of water, woodland, and cultivated plains, its shining cities and shadowy hills, was spread out like some gay and gorgeous panorama before them. In the highly rarefied atmosphere of these upper regions, even remote objects have a brilliancy of colouring and a distinctness of outline which seem to annihilate distance. Stretching far away at their feet were seen noble forests of oak, sycamore, and cedar, and beyond, yellow fields of maize and the towering maguey, intermingled with orchards and blooming gardens; for flowers, in such demand for their religious festivals, were even more abundant in this populous valley than in other parts of Anahuac. In the centre of the great basin were beheld the lakes, occupying then a much larger portion of its surface than at present; their borders thickly studded with towns and hamlets, and, in the midst—like some Indian empress with her coronal of pearls—the fair city of Mexico, with her white towers and pyramidal temples, reposing, as it were, on the bosom of the waters—the far-famed "Venice of the Aztecs." High over all rose the royal hill of Chapultepec, the residence of the Mexican monarchs, crowned with the same grove of gigantic cypresses which at this day fling their broad shadows over the land. In the distance beyond the blue waters of the lake, and nearly screened by inter-vening foliage, was seen a shining speck, the rival capital of Tezcuco, and, still further on, the dark belt of porphyry, girding the valley around, like a rich setting which nature had devised for the fairest of her jewels.

Such was the beautiful vision which broke on the eyes of the Con-querors. And even now, when so sad a change has come over the scene; when the stately forests have been laid low, and the soil, unsheltered from the fierce radiance of a tropical sun, is in many places abandoned to sterility; when the waters have retired, leaving a broad and ghastly margin white with the incrustation of salts, while the cities and hamlets on their borders have mouldered into ruins—even now that desolation broods over the landscape, so indestructible are the lines of beauty which nature has traced on its features, that no traveller, however cold, can gaze on them with any other emotions than those of astonishment and rapture.

What, then, must have been the emotions of the Spaniards, when, after working their toilsome way into the upper air, the cloudy tabernacle parted before their eyes, and they beheld these fair scenes in all their pristine magnificence and beauty! It was like the spectacle which greeted the eyes of Moses from the summit of Pisgah, and, in the warm glow of their feelings, they cried out, "It is the promised land!"

But these feelings of admiration were soon followed by others of a very different complexion; as they saw in all this the evidences of a civilisation and power far superior to anything they had yet encountered. The more timid, disheartened by the prospect, shrank from a contest so unequal, and demanded, as they had done on some former occasions, to be led back again to Vera Cruz. Such was not the effect produced on the sanguine spirit of the general. His avarice was sharpened by the display of the dazzling spoil at his feet; and, if he felt a natural anxiety at the formidable odds, his confidence was renewed, as he gazed on the lines of his veterans, whose weather-beaten visages and battered armour told of battles won and difficulties surmounted, while his bold barbarians, with appetites whetted by the view of their enemy's country, seemed like eagles on the mountains, ready to pounce upon their prey. By argument, en-treaty, and menace, he endeavoured to restore the faltering courage of the soldiers, urging them not to think of retreat, now that they had reached the goal for which they had panted, and the golden gates were open to receive them. In these efforts he was well seconded by the brave cavaliers, who held honour as dear to them as fortune; until the dullest spirits caught somewhat of the enthusiasm of their leaders, and the general had the satisfaction to see his hesitating columns, with their usual buoyant step, once more on their march down the slopes of the sierra.

With every step of their progress, the woods became thinner; patches of cultivated land more frequent; and hamlets were seen in the green and sheltered nooks, the inhabitants of which, coming out to meet them, gave the troops a kind reception. Everywhere they heard complaints of Montezuma, especially of the unfeeling manner in which he carried off their young men to recruit his armies, and their maidens for his harem. These symptoms of discontent were noticed with satisfaction by Cortés, who saw that Montezuma's "mountain throne," as it was called, was indeed seated on a volcano, with the elements of combustion so active within, that it seemed as if any hour might witness an explosion. He encouraged the disaffected natives to rely on his protection, as he had come to redress their wrongs. He took advantage, moreover, of their favourable dispositions to scatter among them such gleams of spiritual light as time and the preaching of Father Olmedo could afford.

He advanced by easy stages, somewhat retarded by the crowd of curious inhabitants gathered on the highways to see the strangers, and halting at every spot of interest or importance. On the road he was met by another embassy from the capital. It consisted of several Aztec lords, freighted, as usual, with a rich largess of gold, and robes of delicate furs and feathers. The message of the emperor was couched in the same deprecatory terms as before. He even condescended to bribe the return of the Spaniards, by promising, in that event, four loads of gold to the general, and one to each of the captains, with a yearly tribute to their sovereign. So effectually had the lofty and naturally courageous spirit of the barbarian monarch been subdued by the influence of superstition!

But the man whom the hostile array of armies could not daunt, was not to be turned from his purpose by a woman's prayers. He received the embassy with his usual courtesy, declaring, as before, that he could not answer it to his own sovereign, if he were now to return without visiting the emperor in his capital. It would be much easier to arrange matters by a personal interview than by distant negotiation. The Spaniards came in the spirit of peace. Montezuma would so find it, but, should their presence prove burdensome to him, it would be easy for them to relieve him of it.

The Aztec monarch, meanwhile, was a prey to the most dismal apprehensions. It was intended that the embassy above noticed should reach the Spaniards before they crossed the mountains. When he learned that this was accomplished, and that the dread strangers were on their march across the valley, the very threshold of his capital, the last spark of hope died away in his bosom. Like one who suddenly finds himself on the brink of some dark and yawning gulf, he was too much bewildered to be able to rally his thoughts, or even to comprehend his situation. He was the victim of an absolute destiny, against which no foresight or precautions could have availed. It was as if the strange beings, who had thus invaded his shores, had dropped from some distant planet, so different were they from all he had ever seen, in appearance and manners; so superior—though a mere handful in numbers—to the banded nations of Anahuac in strength and science, and all the fearful accompaniments of war! They were now in the valley. The huge mountain-screen, which nature had so kindly drawn around it for its defence, had been overleaped. The golden visions of security and repose, in which he had so long indulged, the lordly sway descended from his ancestors, his broad imperial domain, were all to pass away. It seemed like some terrible dream—from which he was now, alas! to awake to a still more terrible reality.

In a paroxysm of despair he shut himself up in his palace, refused food, and sought relief in prayer and in sacrifice. But the oracles were dumb. He then adopted the more sensible expedient of calling a council of his principal and oldest nobles. Here was the same division of opinion which had before prevailed. Cacama, the young King of Tezcuco, his nephew, counselled him to receive the Spaniards courteously, as ambassadors, so styled by themselves, of a foreign prince. Cuitlahua, Montezuma's more warlike brother, urged him to muster his forces on the instant, and drive back the invaders from his capital, or die in its defence. But the monarch found it difficult to rally his spirits for this final struggle. With downcast eye and dejected mien he exclaimed, "Of what avail is resistance when the gods have declared themselves against us! Yet I mourn most for the old and infirm, the women and children, too feeble to fight or to fly. For myself and the brave men around me, we must bare our breasts to the storm, and meet it as we may!" Such are the sorrowful and sympathetic tones in which the Aztec emperor is said to have uttered the bitterness of his grief. He would have acted a more glorious part had he put his capital in a posture of defence, and prepared, like the last of the Palæologi, to bury himself under its ruins.

He straightway prepared to send a last embassy to the Spaniards, with his nephew, the lord of Tezcuco, at its head, to welcome them to Mexico. The Christian army, meanwhile, had advanced as far as Amaquemecan, a well-built town of several thousand inhabitants. They were kindly received by the cacique, lodged in large commodious stone buildings, and at their departure presented, among other things, with gold to the amount of three thousand *castellanos*. Having halted there a couple of days, they descended among flourishing plantations of maize and of maguey, the latter of which might be called the Aztec vineyards, towards the lake of Chalco. Their first resting-place was Ajotzinco, a town of considerable size, with a great part of it then standing on piles in the water. It was the first specimen which the Spaniards had seen of this maritime architecture. The canals, which intersected the city instead of streets, presented an animated scene from the number of barks which glided up and down, freighted with provisions and other articles for the inhabitants. The Spaniards were particularly struck with the style and commodious structure of the houses, built chiefly of stone, and with the general aspect of wealth, and even elegance which prevailed there.

Though received with the greatest show of hospitality, Cortés found some occasion for distrust in the eagerness manifested by the people to see and approach the Spaniards. Not content with gazing at them in the roads, some even made their way stealthily into their quarters, and fifteen or twenty unhappy Indians were shot down by the sentinels as spies. Yet there appears, as well as we can judge at this distance of time, to have been no real ground for such suspicion. The undisguised jealousy of the court, and the cautions he had received from his allies, while they very properly put the general on his guard, seem to have given an unnatural acuteness, at least in the present instance, to his perceptions of danger.

Early on the following morning, as the army was preparing to leave the place, a courier came, requesting the general to postpone his departure till after the arrival of the King of Tezcuco, who was advancing to meet him. It was not long before he appeared, borne in a palanquin or litter, richly decorated with plates of gold and precious stones, having pillars curiously wrought, supporting a canopy of green plumes, a favourite colour with the Aztec princes. He was accompanied by a numerous suite of nobles and inferior attendants. As he came into the presence of Cortés, the lord of Tezcuco descended from his palanquin, and the obsequious officers swept the ground before him as he advanced. He appeared to be a young man of about twenty-five years of age, with a comely presence, erect and stately in his deportment. He made the Mexican salutation usually addressed to persons of high rank, touching the earth with his right hand, and raising it to his head. Cortés embraced him as he rose, when the young prince informed him that he came as the representative of Montezuma, to bid the Spaniards welcome to his capital. He then presented the general with three pearls of uncommon size and lustre. Cortés, in return, threw over Cacama's neck a chain of cut glass, which, where glass was as rare as diamonds, might be admitted to have a value as real as the latter. After this interchange of courtesies, and the most friendly and respectful assurances on the part of Cortés, the Indian prince withdrew, leaving the Spaniards strongly impressed with the superiority of his state and bearing over anything they had hitherto seen in the country.

Resuming its march, the army kept along the southern borders of the lake of Chalco, overshadowed at that time by noble woods, and by orchards glowing with autumnal fruits, of unknown names, but rich and tempting hues. More frequently it passed through cultivated fields waving with the yellow harvest, and irrigated by canals introduced from the neighbouring lake; the whole showing a careful and economical husbandry, essential to the maintenance of a crowded population.

Leaving the main land, the Spaniards came on the great dike or causeway, which stretches some four or five miles in length, and divides Lake Chalco from Xochicalco on the west. It was a lance in breadth in the narrowest part, and in some places wide enough for eight horsemen to ride abreast. It was a solid structure of stone and lime, running directly through the lake, and struck the Spaniards as one of the most remarkable works which they had seen in the country.

At they passed along, they beheld the gay spectacle of multitudes of Indians darting up and down in their light pirogues, eager to catch a glimpse of the strangers, or bearing the products of the country to the neighbouring cities. They were amazed, also, by the sight of the *chinampas,* or floating gardens—those wandering islands of verdure, to which we shall have occasion to return hereafter—teeming with flowers and vegetables, and moving like rafts over the waters. All round the margin, and occasionally far in the lake, they beheld little towns and villages, which, half concealed by the foliage, and gathered in white clusters round the shore, looked in the distance like companies of wild swans riding quietly on the waves. A scene so new and wonderful filled their rude hearts with amazement. It seemed like enchantment; and they could find nothing to compare it with, but the magical pictures in the *Adamis de Gaula*. Few pictures, indeed, in that or any other legend of chivalry, could surpass the realities of their own experience. The life of the adventurer in the New World was romance put into action. What wonder, then, if the Spaniard of that day, feeding his imagination with dreams of enchantment at home, and with its realities abroad, should have displayed a Quixotic enthusiasm—a romantic exaltation of character, not to be comprehended by the colder spirits of other lands!

Midway across the lake the army halted at the town of Cuitlahuac, a place of moderate size, but distinguished by the beauty of the buildings—the most beautiful, according to Cortés, that he had yet seen in the country. After taking some refreshment at this place, they continued their march along the dike. Though broader in this northern section, the troops found themselves much embarrassed by the throng of Indians, who, not content with gazing on them from the boats, climbed up the causeway, and lined the sides of the roads. The general, afraid that his ranks might be disordered, and that too great familiarity might diminish a salutary awe in the natives, was obliged to resort not merely to command but menace, to clear a passage. He now found, as he advanced, a considerable change in the feelings shown towards the government. He heard only of the pomp and magnificence, nothing of the oppressions of Montezuma. Contrary to the usual fact, it seemed that the respect for the court was greatest in its immediate neighbourhood.

From the causeway, the army descended on that narrow point of land which divides the waters of the Chalco from the Tezcucan lake, but which in those days was overflowed for many a mile, now laid bare. Traversing this peninsula, they entered the royal residence of Iztapalapan, a place containing twelve or fifteen thousand houses, according to Cortés. It was governed by Cuitlahuac, the emperor's brother, who, to do greater honour to the general, had invited the lords of some neighbouring cities, of the royal house of Mexico, like himself, to be present at the interview. This was conducted with much ceremony, and, after the usual presents of gold and delicate stuffs, a collation was served to the Spaniards in one of the great halls of the palace. The excellence of the architecture here, also, excited the admiration of the general, who does not hesitate, in the glow of his enthusiasm, to pronounce some of the buildings equal to the best in Spain. They were of stone, and the spacious apartments had roofs of odorous cedar-wood, while the walls were tapestried with fine cottons stained with brilliant colours.

But the pride of Iztapalapan, on which its lord had freely lavished his care and his revenues, was its celebrated gardens. They covered an immense tract of land; were laid out in regular squares, and the paths intersecting them were bordered with trellises, supporting creepers and aromatic shrubs, that loaded the air with their perfumes. The gardens were stocked with fruit trees, imported from distant places, and with the gaudy family of flowers which belong to the Mexican flora, scientifically arranged, and growing luxuriant in the equable temperature of the tableland. The natural dryness of the atmosphere was counteracted by means of aqueducts and canals, that carried water into all parts of the grounds.

In one quarter was an aviary, filled with numerous kinds of birds, remarkable in this region both for brilliancy of plumage and of song. The gardens were intersected by a canal communicating with the lake of Tezcuco, and of sufficient size for barges to enter from the latter. But the most elaborate piece of work was a huge reservoir of stone, filled to a considerable height with water, well supplied with different sorts of fish. This basin was sixteen hundred paces in circumference, and was surrounded by a walk, made also of stone, wide enough for four persons to go abreast. The sides were curiously sculptured, and a flight of steps led to the water below, which fed the aqueducts above noticed, or, collected into fountains, diffused a perpetual moisture.

Such are the accounts transmitted of these celebrated gardens, at a period when similar horticultural establishments were unknown in Europe; and we might well doubt their existence in this semi-civilised land, were it not a matter of such notoriety at the time, and so explicitly attested by the invaders. But a generation had scarcely passed after the Conquest before a sad change came over these scenes so beautiful. The town itself was deserted, and the shore of the lake was strewed with the wreck of buildings which once were its ornament and its glory. The gardens shared the fate of the city. The retreating waters withdrew the means of nourishment, converting the flourishing plains into a foul and unsightly morass, the haunt of loathsome reptiles; and the water-fowl built her nest in what had once been the palaces of princes!

In the city of Iztapalapan, Cortés took up his quarters for the night. We may imagine what a crowd of ideas must have pressed on the mind of the Conqueror, as, surrounded by these evidences of civilisation, he prepared, with his handful of followers, to enter the capital of a monarch, who, as he had abundant reason to know, regarded him with distrust and aversion. This capital was now but a few miles distant, distinctly visible from Iztapalapan. And as its long lines of glittering edifices, struck by the rays of the evening sun, trembled on the dark blue waters of the lake, it looked like a thing of fairy creation, rather than the work of mortal hands. Into this city of enchantment Cortés prepared to make his entry on the following morning.

CHAPTER IX

Environs of Mexico—Interview with Montezuma—Entrance into the Capital—Hospitable Reception—Visit to the Emperor

1519

WITH the first faint streak of dawn, the Spanish general was up, mustering his followers. They gathered, with beating hearts, under their respective banners as the trumpet sent forth its spirit-stirring sounds across water and woodland, till they died away in distant echoes among the mountains. The sacred flames on the altars of numberless *teocallis,* dimly seen through the grey mists of morning, indicated the site of the capital, till temple, tower, and palace were fully revealed in the glorious illumination which the sun, as he rose above the eastern barrier, poured over the beautiful valley. It was November 8, 1519; a conspicuous day in history, as that on which the Europeans first set foot in the capital of the Western World.

Cortés with his little body of horse formed a sort of advance guard to the army. Then came the Spanish infantry, who in a summer's campaign had acquired the discipline and the weather-beaten aspect of veterans. The baggage occupied the centre; and the rear was closed by the dark files of Tlascalan warriors. The whole number must have fallen short of seven thousand; of which less than four hundred were Spaniards.

For a short distance, the army kept along the narrow tongue of land that divides the Tezcucan from the Chalcan waters, when it entered on the great dike which, with the exception of an angle near the commencement, stretches in a perfectly straight line across the salt floods of Tezcuco to the gates of the capital. It was the same causeway, or rather the basis of that which still forms the great southern avenue of Mexico. The Spaniards had occasion more than ever to admire the mechanical science of the Aztecs in the geometrical precision with which the work was executed, as well as the solidity of its construction. It was composed

179

of huge stones well laid in cement; and wide enough, throughout its whole extent, for ten horsemen to ride abreast.

They saw, as they passed along, several large towns, resting on piles, and reaching far into the water—a kind of architecture which found great favour with the Aztecs, being in imitation of that of their metropolis. The busy population obtained a good subsistence from the manufacture of salt, which they extracted from the waters of the great lake. The duties on the traffic in this article were a considerable source of revenue to the crown.

Everywhere the Conquerors beheld the evidence of a crowded and thriving population, exceeding all they had yet seen. The temples and principal buildings of the cities were covered with a hard white stucco, which glistened like enamel in the level beams of the morning. The margin of the great basin was more thickly gemmed than that of Chalco, with towns and hamlets. The water was darkened by swarms of canoes filled with Indians, who clambered up the sides of the causeway, and gazed with curious astonishment on the strangers. And here, also, they beheld those fairy islands of flowers, overshadowed occasionally by trees of considerable size, rising and falling with the gentle undulation of the billows. At the distance of half a league from the capital, they encountered a solid work, or curtain of stone, which traversed the dike. It was twelve feet high, was strengthened by towers at the extremities, and in the centre was a battlemented gateway, which opened a passage to the troops. It was called the Fort of Xoloc, and became memorable in after times as the position occupied by Cortés in the famous siege of Mexico.

Here they were met by several hundred Aztec chiefs, who came out to announce the approach of Montezuma, and to welcome the Spaniards to his capital. They were dressed in the fanciful gala costume of the country, with the *maxtlatl,* or cotton sash, around their loins, and a broad mantle of the same material, or of the brilliant feather-embroidery, flowing gracefully down their shoulders. On their necks and arms they displayed collars and bracelets of turquoise mosaic, with which delicate plumage was curiously mingled, while their ears, under-lips, and occasionally their noses, were garnished with pendants formed of precious stones, or crescents of fine gold. As each cacique made the usual formal salutation of the country separately to the general, the tedious ceremony delayed the march more than an hour. After this the army experienced no further interruption till it reached a bridge near the gates of the city. It was built of wood, since replaced by one of stone, and was thrown across an opening of the dike, which furnished an outlet to the waters, when agitated by the winds, or swollen by a sudden influx in the rainy season. It was a drawbridge; and the Spaniards, as they crossed it, felt how truly they were committing themselves to the mercy of Montezuma, who, by thus cutting off their communications with the country, might hold them prisoners in his capital.

In the midst of these unpleasant reflections, they beheld the glittering retinue of the emperor emerging from the great street which led then, as it still does, through the heart of the city. Amidst a crowd of Indian nobles, preceded by three officers of state, bearing golden wands, they saw the royal palanquin blazing with burnished gold. It was borne on the shoulders of nobles, and over it a canopy of gaudy featherwork, pow-dered with jewels, and fringed with silver, was supported by four attendants of the same rank. They were barefooted, and walked with a slow, measured pace, and with eyes bent on the ground. When the train had come within a convenient distance it halted, and Montezuma, descending from his litter, came forward leaning on the arms of the lords of Tezcuco and Iztapalapan, his nephew and brother, both of whom, as we have seen, had already been made known to the Spaniards. As the monarch advanced under the canopy, the obsequious attendants strewed the ground with cotton tapestry, that his imperial feet might not be contaminated by the rude soil. His subjects of high and low degree, who lined the sides of the causeway, bent forward with their eyes fastened on the ground as he passed, and some of the humbler class prostrated them-selves before him. Such was the homage paid to the Indian despot, show-ing that the slavish forms of Oriental adulation were to be found among the rude inhabitants of the Western World.

Montezuma wore the girdle and ample square cloak, *tilmatli,* of his nation. It was made of the finest cotton, with the embroidered ends gathered in a knot round his neck. His feet were defended by sandals having soles of gold, and the leathern thongs which bound them to his ankles were embossed with the same metal. Both the cloak and sandals were sprinkled with pearls and precious stones, among which the emerald and the *chalchivitl*—a green stone of higher estimation than any other among the Aztecs—were conspicuous. On his head he wore no other ornament than a *panache* of plumes of the royal green, which floated down his back, the badge of military rather than of regal rank.

He was at this time about forty years of age. His person was tall and thin, but not ill made. His hair, which was black and straight, was not very long; to wear it short was considered unbecoming persons of rank. His beard was thin; his complexion somewhat paler than is often found in his dusky, or rather copper-coloured race. His features, though serious in their expression, did not wear the look of melancholy, indeed, of dejection, which characterises his portrait, and which may well have settled on them at a later period. He moved with dignity, and his whole demeanour, tempered by an expression of benignity not to have been anticipated from the reports circulated of his character, was worthy of a great prince. Such is the portrait left to us of the celebrated Indian emperor, in this his first interview with the white men.

The army halted as he drew near. Cortés, dismounting, threw his reins to a page, and, supported by a few of the principal cavaliers, advanced to meet him. The interview must have been one of uncommon interest to both. In Montezuma Cortés beheld the lord of the broad realms he had traversed, whose magnificence and power had been the burden of every tongue. In the Spaniard, on the other hand, the Aztec prince saw the strange being whose history seemed to be so mysteriously connected with his own; the predicted one of his oracles; whose achievements proclaimed him something more than human. But, whatever may have been the monarch's feelings, he so far suppressed them as to receive his guest with princely courtesy, and to express his satisfaction at personally seeing him in his capital. Cortés responded by the most profound expressions of respect, while he made ample acknowledgments for the substantial proofs which the emperor had given the Spaniards of his munificence. He then hung round Montezuma's neck a sparkling chain of coloured crystal, accompanying this with a movement as if to embrace him, when he was restrained by the two Aztec lords, shocked at the menaced profanation of the sacred person of their master. After the interchange of these civilities, Montezuma appointed his brother to conduct the Spaniards to their residence in the capital, and again entering his litter, was borne off amidst prostrate crowds in the same state in which he had come. The Spaniards quickly followed and, with colours flying and music playing, soon made their entrance into the southern quarter of Tenochtitlan.

Here, again, they found fresh cause for admiration in the grandeur of the city, and the superior style of its architecture. The dwellings of the poorer class were, indeed, chiefly of reeds and mud. But the great avenue through which they were now marching was lined with the houses of the nobles, who were encouraged by the emperor to make the capital their residence. They were built of a red porous stone drawn from quarries in the neighbourhood, and, though they rarely rose to a second story, often covered a large space of ground. The flat roofs, *azoteas,* were protected by stone parapets, so that every house was a fortress. Sometimes these roofs resembled parterres of flowers, so thickly were they covered with them, but more frequently these were cultivated in broad terraced gardens, laid out between the edifices. Occasionally a great square or market-place intervened, surrounded by its porticoes of stone and stucco; or a pyramidal temple reared its colossal bulk, crowned with its tapering sanctuaries, and altars blazing with inextinguishable fires. The great street facing the southern causeway, unlike most others in the place, was wide, and extended some miles in nearly a straight line, as before noticed, through the centre of the city. A spectator standing at one end of it, as his eye ranged along the deep vista of temples, terraces, and gardens, might clearly discern the other, with the blue mountains in the distance, which, in the transparent atmosphere of the tableland, seemed almost in contact with the buildings.

But what most impressed the Spaniards were the throngs of people who swarmed through the streets and on the canals, filling every doorway and window, and clustering on the roofs of the buildings. "I well remember the spectacle," exclaims Bernal Diaz; "it seems now, after so many years, as present to my mind as if it were but yesterday." But what must have been the sensations of the Aztecs themselves, as they looked on the portentous pageant! as they heard, now for the first time, the well-cemented pavement ring under the iron tramp of the horses—the strange animals which fear had clothed in such supernatural terrors; as they gazed on the children of the East, revealing their celestial origin in their fair complexions; saw the bright falchions and bonnets of steel, a metal to them unknown, glancing like meteors in the sun, while sounds of unearthly music—at least, such as their rude instruments had never wakened—floated in the air! But every other emotion was lost in that of deadly hatred, when they beheld their detested enemy, the Tlascalan, stalking in defiance as it were through their streets, and staring around with looks of ferocity and wonder, like some wild animal of the forest, who had strayed by chance from his native fastnesses into the haunts of civilisation.

As they passed down the spacious street, the troops repeatedly traversed bridges suspended above canals, along which they saw the Indian barks gliding swiftly with their little cargoes of fruits and vegetables for the markets of Tenochtitlan. At length they halted before a broad area near the centre of the city, where rose the huge pyramidal pile dedicated to the patron war-god of the Aztecs, second only in size, as well as sanctity, to the temple of Cholula, and covering the same ground now in part occupied by the great cathedral of Mexico.

Facing the western gate of the inclosure of the temple stood a low range of stone buildings, spreading over a wide extent of ground, the palace of Axayacatl, Montezuma's father, built by that monarch about fifty years before. It was appropriated as the barracks of the Spaniards. The emperor himself was in the courtyard waiting to receive them. Approaching Cortés, he took from a vase of flowers, borne by one of his slaves, a massy collar, in which the shell of a species of craw-fish, much prized by the Indians, was set in gold, and connected by heavy links of the same metal. From this chain depended eight ornaments, also of gold, made in resemblance of the same shell-fish, a span in length each, and of delicate workmanship; for the Aztec goldsmiths were confessed to have shown skill in their craft, not inferior to their brethren of Europe. Montezuma, as he hung the gorgeous collar round the general's neck, said, "This palace belongs to you, Malinche" (the epithet by which he always addressed him), "and your brethren. Rest after your fatigues, for you have much need to do so, and in a little while I will visit you again." So saying, he withdrew with his attendants, evincing, in this act, a delicate consideration not to have been expected in a barbarian.

Cortés' first care was to inspect his new quarters. The building, though spacious, was low, consisting of one floor, except indeed in the centre, where it rose to an additional story. The apartments were of great size, and afforded accommodations, according to the testimony of the Conquerors themselves, for the whole army! The hardy mountaineers of Tlascala were, probably, not very fastidious, and might easily find a shelter in the outbuildings, or under temporary awnings in the ample courtyards. The best apartments were hung with gay cotton draperies, the floors covered with mats or rushes. There were, also, low stools made of single pieces of wood elaborately carved, and in most of the apartments beds made of the palm-leaf, woven into a thick mat, with coverlets, and sometimes canopies of cotton. These mats were the only beds used by the natives, whether of high or low degree.

After a rapid survey of this gigantic pile, the general assigned to his troops their respective quarters, and took as vigilant precautions for security, as if he had anticipated a siege, instead of a friendly entertainment. The place was encompassed by a stone wall of considerable thickness, with towers or heavy buttresses at intervals, affording a good means of defence. He planted his cannon so as to command the approaches, stationed his sentinels along the works, and, in short, enforced in every respect as strict military discipline as had been observed in any part of the march. He well knew the importance to his little band, at least for the present, of conciliating the good will of the citizens; and to avoid all possibility of collision he prohibited any soldier from leaving his quarters without orders, under pain of death. Having taken these precautions, he allowed his men to partake of the bountiful collation which had been prepared for them.

They had been long enough in the country to become reconciled to, if not to relish, the peculiar cooking of the Aztecs. The appetite of the soldier is not often dainty, and on the present occasion it cannot be doubted that the Spaniards did full justice to the savoury productions of the royal kitchen. During the meal they were served by numerous Mexican slaves, who were indeed, distributed through the palace, anxious to do the bidding of the strangers. After the repast was concluded, and they had taken their *siesta,* not less important to a Spaniard than food itself, the presence of the emperor was again announced.

Montezuma was attended by a few of his principal nobles. He was received with much deference by Cortés; and, after the parties had taken their seats, a conversation commenced between them through the aid of Doña Marina, while the cavaliers and Aztec chieftains stood around in respectful silence.

Montezuma made many inquiries concerning the country of the Spaniards, their sovereign, the nature of his government, and especially their own motives in visiting Anahuac. Cortés explained these motives by the desire to see so distinguished a monarch, and to declare to him the true Faith professed by the Christians. With rare discretion he contented himself with dropping this hint for the present, allowing it to ripen in the mind of the emperor till a future conference. The latter asked whether those white men, who in the preceding year had landed on the eastern shores of his empire, were their countrymen. He showed himself well informed of the proceedings of the Spaniards from their arrival in Tabasco to the present time, information of which had been regularly transmitted in the hieroglyphical paintings. He was curious, also, in regard to the rank of his visitors in their own country; inquiring if they were the kinsmen of the sovereign. Cortés replied they were kinsmen of

one another, and subjects of their great monarch, who held them all in
peculiar estimation. Before his departure Montezuma made himself
acquainted with the names of the principal cavaliers, and the position
they occupied in the army.

At the conclusion of the interview the Aztec prince commanded his
attendants to bring forward the presents prepared for his guests. They
consisted of cotton dresses, enough to supply every man, it is said, including the allies, with a suit! And he did not fail to add the usual accom-
paniment of gold chains and other ornaments, which he distributed in
profusion among the Spaniards. He then withdrew with the same ceremony with which he had entered, leaving every one deeply impressed with
his munificence and his affability, so unlike what they had been taught to
expect by what they now considered an invention of the enemy.

That evening the Spaniards celebrated their arrival in the Mexican
capital by a general discharge of artillery. The thunders of the ordnance
reverberating among the buildings and shaking them to their foundations,
the stench of the sulphureous vapour that rolled in volumes above the
walls of the encampment, reminding the inhabitants of the explosions of
the great *volcan,* filled the hearts of the superstitious Aztecs with dismay.
It proclaimed to them that their city held in its bosom those dread beings
whose path had been marked with desolation, and who could call down
the thunderbolts to consume their enemies! It was doubtless the policy of
Cortés to strengthen this superstitious feeling as far as possible, and to
impress the natives, at the outset, with a salutary awe of the supernatural
powers of the Spaniards.

On the following morning the general requested permission to return
the emperor's visit by waiting on him in his palace. This was readily
granted, and Montezuma sent his officers to conduct the Spaniards to his
presence. Cortés dressed himself in his richest habit, and left the quarters
attended by Alvarado, Sandoval, Velasquez, and Ordaz, together with
five or six of the common file.

The royal habitation was at no great distance. It stood on the ground,
to the south-west of the cathedral, since covered in part by the *casa del
Estado,* the palace of the Dukes of Monteleone, the descendants of
Cortés. It was a vast, irregular pile of low stone buildings, like that
garrisoned by the Spaniards. So spacious was it indeed, that, as one of the
Conquerors assures us, although he had visited it more than once, for
the express purpose, he had been too much fatigued each time by wandering through the apartments ever to see the whole of it. It was built of the

red porous stone of the country, *tetzontli,* was ornamented with marble, and on the façade over the principal entrance were sculptured the arms or device of Montezuma, an eagle bearing an ocelot in his talons.

In the courts through which the Spaniards passed fountains of crystal water were playing, fed from the copious reservoir on the distant hill of Chapultepec, and supplying in their turn more than a hundred baths in the interior of the palace. Crowds of Aztec nobles were sauntering up and down in these squares, and in the outer halls, loitering away their hours in attendance on the court. The apartments were of immense size, though not lofty. The ceilings were of various sorts of odoriferous wood ingeniously carved; the floors covered with mats of the palm-leaf. The walls were hung with cotton richly stained, with the skins of wild animals, or gorgeous draperies of featherwork wrought in imitation of birds, insects, and flowers, with the nice art and glowing radiance of colours that might compare with the tapestries of Flanders. Clouds of incense rolled up from censers, and diffused intoxicating odours through the apartments. The Spaniards might well have fancied themselves in the voluptuous precincts of an Eastern harem, instead of treading the halls of a wild barbaric chief in the Western World.

On reaching the hall of audience, the Mexican officers took off their sandals, and covered their gay attire with a mantle of *nequen,* a coarse stuff made of the fibres of the maguey, worn only by the poorest classes. This act of humiliation was imposed on all, except the members of his own family, who approached the sovereign. Thus barefooted, with downcast eyes, and formal obeisance, they ushered the Spaniards into the royal presence.

They found Montezuma seated at the further end of a spacious saloon, and surrounded by a few of his favourite chiefs. He received them kindly, and very soon Cortés, without much ceremony, entered on the subject which was uppermost in his thoughts. He was fully aware of the importance of gaining the royal convert, whose example would have such an influence on the conversion of his people. The general, therefore, prepared to display the whole store of his theological science, with the most winning arts of rhetoric he could command, while the interpretation was conveyed through the silver tones of Marina, as inseparable from him on these occasions as his shadow.

He set forth, as clearly as he could, the ideas entertained by the Church in regard to the holy mysteries of the Trinity, the Incarnation, and the Atonement. From this he ascended to the origin of things, the creation of

the world, the first pair, paradise, and the fall of man. He assured
Montezuma that the idols he worshipped were Satan under different
forms. A sufficient proof of it was the bloody sacrifices they imposed,
which he contrasted with the pure and simple rite of the Mass. Their
worship would sink him in perdition. It was to snatch his soul, and the
souls of his people, from the flames of eternal fire by opening to them a
purer faith that the Christians had come to his land. And he earnestly
besought him not to neglect the occasion, but to secure his salvation by
embracing the Cross, the great sign of human redemption.

The eloquence of the preacher was wasted on the insensible heart of
his royal auditor. It doubtless lost somewhat of its efficacy, strained
through the imperfect interpretation of so recent a neophyte as the Indian
damsel. But the doctrines were too abstruse in themselves to be comprehended at a glance by the rude intellect of a barbarian. And Montezuma
may have, perhaps, thought it was not more monstrous to feed on the
flesh of a fellow-creature than on that of the Creator himself. He was,
besides, steeped in the superstitions of his country from his cradle. He had
been educated in the straitest sect of her religion; had been himself a
priest before his election to the throne; and was now the head both of the
religion and the state. Little probability was there that such a man would
be open to argument or persuasion, even from the lips of a more practised
polemic than the Spanish commander. How could he abjure the faith
that was intertwined with the dearest affections of his heart, and the
very elements of his being? How could he be false to the gods who had
raised him to such prosperity and honours, and whose shrines were intrusted to his especial keeping?

He listened, however, with silent attention, until the general had
concluded his homily. He then replied that he knew the Spaniards had
held this discourse wherever they had been. He doubted not their God
was, as they said, a good being. His gods, also, were good to him. Yet
what his visitor said of the creation of the world was like what he had
been taught to believe. It was not worth while to discourse further of the
matter. His ancestors, he said, were not the original proprietors of the
land. They had occupied it but a few ages, and had been led there by a
great Being, who, after giving them laws and ruling over the nation for
a time, had withdrawn to the regions where the sun rises. He had declared, on his departure, that he or his descendants would again visit
them and resume his empire. The wonderful deeds of the Spaniards,
their fair complexions. and the quarter whence they came, all showed

they were his descendants. If Montezuma had resisted their visit to his capital, it was because he had heard such accounts of their cruelties— that they sent the lightning to consume his people, or crushed them to pieces under the hard feet of the ferocious animals on which they rode. He was now convinced that these were idle tales; that the Spaniards were kind and generous in their natures; they were mortals of a different race, indeed, from the Aztecs, wiser, and more valiant—and for this he honoured them.

"You, too," he added, with a smile, "have been told, perhaps, that I am a god, and dwell in palaces of gold and silver. But you see it is false. My houses, though large, are of stone and wood like those of others; and as to my body," he said, baring his tawny arm, "you see it is flesh and bone like yours. It is true I have a great empire, inherited from my ancestors; lands, and gold, and silver. But your sovereign beyond the waters is, I know, the rightful lord of all. I rule in his name. You, Malintzin, are his ambassador; you and your brethren shall share these things with me. Rest now from your labours. You are here in your own dwellings, and everything shall be provided for your subsistence. I will see that your wishes shall be obeyed in the same way as my own." As the monarch concluded these words a few natural tears suffused his eyes, while the image of ancient independence, perhaps, flitted across his mind.

Cortés, while he encouraged the idea that his own sovereign was the great Being indicated by Montezuma, endeavoured to comfort the monarch by the assurance that his master had no desire to interfere with his authority, otherwise than, out of pure concern for his welfare, to effect his conversion and that of his people to Christianity. Before the emperor dismissed his visitors he consulted his munificent spirit, as usual, by distributing rich stuffs and trinkets of gold among them, so that the poorest soldier, says Bernal Diaz, one of the party, received at least two heavy collars of the precious metal for his share. The iron hearts of the Spaniards were touched with the emotion displayed by Montezuma, as well as by his princely spirit of liberality. As they passed him, the cavaliers, with bonnets in hand, made him the most profound obeisance, and, "on the way home," continues the same chronicler, "we could discourse of nothing but the gentle breeding and courtesy of the Indian monarch, and of the respect we entertained for him."

Speculations of a graver complexion must have pressed on the mind of the general, as he saw around him the evidences of a civilisation, and consequently power, for which even the exaggerated reports of the natives

—discredited from their apparent exaggeration—had not prepared him. In the pomp and burdensome ceremonial of the court, he saw that nice system of subordination and profound reverence for the monarch which characterise the semi-civilised empires of Asia. In the appearance of the capital, its massy, yet elegant architecture, its luxurious social accommodations, its activity in trade, he recognised the proofs of the intellectual progress, mechanical skill, and enlarged resources, of an old and opulent community; while the swarms in the streets attested the existence of a population capable of turning these resources to the best account.

In the Aztec he beheld a being unlike either the rude republican Tlascalan, or the effeminate Cholulan; but combining the courage of the one with the cultivation of the other. He was in the heart of a great capital, which seemed like an extensive fortification, with its dikes and its drawbridges, where every house might be easily converted into a castle. Its insular position removed it from the continent, from which, at the mere nod of the sovereign, all communication might be cut off, and the whole warlike population be at once precipitated on him and his handful of followers. What could superior science avail against such odds?

As to the subversion of Montezuma's empire, now that he had seen him in his capital, it must have seemed a more doubtful enterprise than ever. The recognition which the Aztec prince had made of the feudal supremacy, if I may so say, of the Spanish sovereign, was not to be taken too literally. Whatever show of deference he might be disposed to pay the latter, under the influence of his present—perhaps temporary—delusion, it was not to be supposed that he would so easily relinquish his actual power and possessions, or that his people would consent to it. Indeed, his sensitive apprehensions in regard to this very subject, on the coming of the Spaniards, were sufficient proof of the tenacity with which he clung to his authority. It is true that Cortés had a strong lever for future operations in the superstitious reverence felt for himself both by prince and people. It was undoubtedly his policy to maintain this sentiment unimpaired in both as far as possible. But, before settling any plan of operations, it was necessary to make himself personally acquainted with the topography and local advantages of the capital, the character of its population, and the real nature and amount of its resources. With this view he asked the emperor's permission to visit the principal public edifices.

RESIDENCE IN MEXICO

CHAPTER I

Tezcucan Lake—Description of the Capital—Palaces and Museums—Royal Household—Montezuma's Way of Life

1519

THE ANCIENT CITY OF MEXICO covered the same spot occupied by the modern capital. The great causeways touched it in the same points; the streets ran in much the same direction, nearly from north to south, and from east to west; the cathedral in the *plaza mayor* stands on the same ground that was covered by the temple of the Aztec war-god; and the four principal quarters of the town are still known among the Indians by their ancient names. Yet an Aztec of the days of Montezuma, could he behold the modern metropolis, which has risen with such phœnix-like splendour from the ashes of the old, would not recognise its site as that of his own Tenochtitlan. For the latter was encompassed by the salt floods of Tezcuco, which flowed in ample canals through every part of the city; while the Mexico of our day stands high and dry on the main land, nearly a league distant, at its centre, from the water. The cause of this apparent change in its position is the diminution of the lake, which, from the rapidity of evaporation in these elevated regions, had become perceptible before the Conquest, but which has since been greatly accelerated by artificial causes.

The average level of the Tezcucan lake, at the present day, is but four feet lower than the great square of Mexico. It is considerably lower than the other great basins of water which are found in the valley. In the heavy swell sometimes caused by long and excessive rains, these latter reservoirs anciently overflowed into the Tezcuco, which, rising with the accumulated volume of waters, burst through the dikes, and, pouring into the streets of the capital, buried the lower parts of the buildings under a deluge. This was comparatively a light evil, when the houses stood on piles so elevated that boats might pass under them; when the streets were canals, and the ordinary mode of communication was by water. But it became more disastrous, as these canals, filled up with the rubbish of the ruined Indian city, were supplanted by streets of solid earth, and the foundations of the capital were gradually reclaimed from the watery element. To obviate this alarming evil, the famous drain of Huehuetoca was opened, at an enormous cost, in the beginning of the seventeenth century, and Mexico, after repeated inundations, has been at length placed above the reach of the flood. But what was gained to the useful, in this case, as in some others, has been purchased at the expense of the beautiful. By this shrinking of the waters, the bright towns and hamlets once washed by them have been removed some miles into the interior, while a barren strip of land, ghastly from the incrustation of salts formed on the surface, has taken the place of the glowing vegetation which once enamelled the borders of the lake, and of the dark groves of oak, cedar, and sycamore which threw their broad shadows over its bosom.

The *chinampas,* that archipelago of wandering islands, to which our attention was drawn in the last chapter, have also nearly disappeared. These had their origin in the detached masses of earth, which, loosening from the shores, were still held together by the fibrous roots with which they were penetrated. The primitive Aztecs, in their poverty of land, availed themselves of the hint thus afforded by nature. They constructed rafts of reeds, rushes, and other fibrous materials, which, tightly knit together, formed a sufficient basis for the sediment that they drew up from the bottom of the lake. Gradually islands were formed, two or three hundred feet in length, and three or four feet in depth, with a rich stimulated soil, on which the economical Indian raised his vegetables and flowers for the markets of Tenochtitlan. Some of these *chinampas* were even firm enough to allow the growth of small trees, and to sustain a hut for the residence of the person that had charge of it, who, with a long pole resting on the sides or the bottom of the shallow basin, could change the position of his little territory at pleasure, which with its rich freight of vegetable stores were seen moving like some enchanted island over the water.

The ancient dikes were three in number. That of Iztapalapan, by which the Spaniards entered, approaching the city from the south. That of Tepejacac, on the north, which, continuing the principal street, might be regarded, also, as a continuation of the first causeway. Lastly, the dike of Tlacopan, connecting the island-city with the continent on the west. This last causeway, memorable for the disastrous retreat of the Spaniards, was about two miles in length. They were all built in the same substantial manner, of lime and stone, were defended by drawbridges, and were wide enough for ten or twelve horsemen to ride abreast.

The rude founders of Tenochtitlan built their frail tenements of reeds and rushes on the group of small islands in the western part of the lake. In process of time these were supplanted by more substantial buildings. A quarry in the neighborhood, of a red porous amygdaloid, *tetzontli,* was opened, and a light, brittle stone drawn from it, and wrought with little difficulty. Of this their edifices were constructed, with some reference to architectural solidity, if not elegance. Mexico, as already noticed, was the residence of the great chiefs, whom the sovereign encouraged, or rather compelled, from obvious motives of policy, to spend part of the year in the capital. It was also the temporary abode of the great lords of Tezcuco and Tlacopan, who shared nominally, at least, the sovereignty of the empire. The mansions of these dignitaries, and of the principal nobles, were on a scale of rude magnificence corresponding with their state. They were low, indeed; seldom of more than one floor, never exceeding two. But they spread over a wide extent of ground; were arranged in a quadrangular form, with a court in the centre, and were surrounded by porticoes embellished with porphyry and jasper, easily found in the neighbourhood, while not unfrequently a fountain of crystal water in the centre shed a grateful coolness over the atmosphere. The dwellings of the common people were also placed on foundations of stone, which rose to the height of a few feet, and were then succeeded by courses of unbaked bricks, crossed occasionally by wooden rafters. Most of the streets were mean and narrow. Some few, however, were wide and of great length. The principal street, conducting from the great southern causeway, penetrated in a straight line the whole length of the city, and afforded a noble vista, in which the long lines of low stone edifices were broken occasionally by intervening gardens, rising on terraces, and displaying all the pomp of Aztec horticulture.

The great streets, which were coated with a hard cement, were intersected by numerous canals. Some of these were flanked by a solid way, which served as a foot-walk for passengers, and as a landing-place where boats might discharge their cargoes. Small buildings were erected at intervals, as stations for the revenue officers who collected the duties on different articles of merchandise. The canals were traversed by numerous bridges, many of which could be raised, affording the means of cutting off communication between different parts of the city.

From the accounts of the ancient capital, one is reminded of those aquatic cities in the Old World, the positions of which have been selected from similar motives of economy and defence; above all, of Venice—if it be not rash to compare the rude architecture of the American Indian with the marble palaces and temples—alas, how shorn of their splendour! —which crowned the once proud mistress of the Adriatic. The example of the metropolis was soon followed by the other towns in the vicinity. Instead of resting their foundations on *terra firma,* they were seen advancing far into the lake, the shallow waters of which in some parts do not exceed four feet in depth. Thus an easy means of intercommunication was opened, and the surface of this inland "sea," as Cortés styles it, was darkened by thousands of canoes—an Indian term—industriously engaged in the traffic between these little communities. How gay and picturesque must have been the aspect of the lake in those days, with its shining cities, and flowering islets rocking, as it were, at anchor on the fair bosom of its waters!

The population of Tenochtitlan, at the time of the Conquest, is variously stated. No contemporary writer estimates it at less than sixty thousand houses, which, by the ordinary rules of reckoning, would give three hundred thousand souls. If a dwelling often contained, as is asserted, several families, it would swell the amount considerably higher. Nothing is more uncertain than estimates of numbers among barbarous communities, who necessarily live in a more confused and promiscuous manner than civilised, and among whom no regular system is adopted for ascertaining the population. The concurrent testimony of the Conquerors; the extent of the city, which was said to be nearly three leagues in circumference; the immense size of its great market-place; the long lines of edifices, vestiges of whose ruins may still be found in the suburbs, miles from the modern city; the fame of the metropolis throughout Anahuac, which, however, could boast many large and populous places; lastly, the economical husbandry and the ingenious contrivances to extract aliment from the most unpromising sources—all attest a numerous population, far beyond that of the present capital.

A careful police provided for the health and cleanliness of the city. A thousand persons are said to have been daily employed in watering and sweeping the streets, so that a man—to borrow the language of an old Spaniard—"could walk through them with as little danger of soiling his feet as his hands." The water, in a city washed on all sides by the salt floods, was extremely brackish. A liberal supply of the pure element, however, was brought from Chapultepec, "the grasshopper's hill," less than a league distant. It was brought through an earthen pipe, along a dike constructed for the purpose. That there might be no failure in so essential an article, when repairs were going on, a double course of pipes was laid. In this way a column of water the size of a man's body was conducted into the heart of the capital, where it fed the fountains and reservoirs of the principal mansions. Openings were made in the aqueduct as it crossed the bridges, and thus a supply was furnished to the canoes below, by means of which it was transported to all parts of the city.

While Montezuma encouraged a taste for architectural magnificence in his nobles, he contributed his own share towards the embellishment of the city. It was in his reign that the famous calendar-stone, weighing, probably, in its primitive state, nearly fifty tons, was transported from its native quarry, many leagues distant, to the capital, where it still forms one of the most curious monuments of Aztec science. Indeed, when we reflect on the difficulty of hewing such a stupendous mass from its hard basaltic bed without the aid of iron tools, and that of transporting it such a distance across land and water without the help of animals, we may feel admiration at the mechanical ingenuity and enterprise of the people who accomplished it.

Not content with the spacious residence of his father, Montezuma erected another on a yet more magnificent scale. It occupied, as before mentioned, the ground partly covered by the private dwellings on one side of the *plaza mayor* of the modern city. This building, or, as it might more correctly be styled, pile of buildings, spread over an extent of ground so vast, that, as one of the Conquerors assures us, its terraced roof might have afforded ample room for thirty knights to run their courses in a regular tourney. I have already noticed its interior decorations, its fanciful draperies, its roofs inlaid with cedar and other odoriferous woods, held together without a nail, and probably without a knowledge of the arch, its numerous and spacious apartments, which Cortés, with enthusiastic hyperbole, does not hesitate to declare superior to anything of the kind in Spain.

Adjoining the principal edifices were others devoted to various objects. One was an armoury, filled with the weapons and military dresses worn by the Aztecs, all kept in the most perfect order, ready for instant use. The emperor was himself very expert in the management of the *maquahuitl,* or Indian sword, and took great delight in witnessing athletic exercises, and the mimic representation of war by his young nobility.

Another building was used as a granary, and others as warehouses for the different articles of food and apparel contributed by the districts charged with the maintenance of the royal household.

There were also edifices appropriated to objects of quite another kind. One of these was an immense aviary, in which birds of splendid plumage were assembled from all parts of the empire. Here was the scarlet cardinal, the golden pheasant, the endless parrot-tribe with their rainbow hues (the royal green predominant) and that miniature miracle of nature, the humming-bird, which delights to revel among the honeysuckle bowers of Mexico. Three hundred attendants had charge of this aviary, who made themselves acquainted with the appropriate food of its inmates, oftentimes procured at great cost, and in the moulting season were careful to collect the beautiful plumage, which, with its many-coloured tints, furnished the materials for the Aztec painter.

A separate building was reserved for the fierce birds of prey; the voracious vulture-tribes and eagles of enormous size, whose home was in the snowy solitudes of the Andes. No less than five hundred turkeys, the cheapest meat in Mexico, were allowed for the daily consumption of these tyrants of the feathered race.

Adjoining this aviary was a menagerie of wild animals, gathered from the mountain forests, and even from the remote swamps of the *tierra caliente.* The resemblance of the different species to those in the Old World, with which no one of them, however, was identical, led to a perpetual confusion in the nomenclature of the Spaniards, as it has since done in that of better instructed naturalists. The collection was still further swelled by a great number of reptiles and serpents, remarkable for their size and venomous qualities, among which the Spaniards beheld the fiery little animal "with the castanets in his tail," the terror of the American wilderness. The serpents were confined in long cages, lined with down or feathers, or in troughs of mud and water. The beasts and birds of prey were provided with apartments large enough to allow of their moving about, and secured by a strong lattice-work, through which light and air were freely admitted. The whole was placed under the charge of numerous keepers, who acquainted themselves with the habits of their prisoners, and provided for their comfort and cleanliness. With what deep interest would the enlightened naturalist of that day—an Oviedo, or a Martyr, for example—have surveyed this magnificent collection, in which the various tribes which roamed over the Western wilderness, the unknown races of an unknown world, were brought into one view! How would they have delighted to study the peculiarities of these new species, compared with those of their own hemisphere, and thus have risen to some comprehension of the general laws by which nature acts in all her works! The rude followers of Cortés did not trouble themselves with such refined speculations. They gazed on the spectacle with a vague curiosity, not unmixed with awe; and, as they listened to the wild cries of the ferocious animals and the hissings of the serpents, they almost fancied themselves in the infernal regions.

I must not omit to notice a strange collection of human monsters, dwarfs, and other unfortunate persons, in whose organisation nature had capriciously deviated from her regular laws. Such hideous anomalies were regarded by the Aztecs as a suitable appendage of state. It is even said they were in some cases the result of artificial means, employed by unnatural parents, desirous to secure a provision for their offspring by thus qualifying them for a place in the royal museum!

Extensive gardens were spread out around these buildings, filled with fragrant shrubs and flowers, and especially with medicinal plants. No country has afforded more numerous species of these last than New Spain; and their virtues were perfectly understood by the Aztecs, with whom medical botany may be said to have been studied as a science. Amidst this labyrinth of sweet-scented groves and shrubberies, fountains of pure water might be seen throwing up their sparkling jets, and scattering refreshing dews over the blossoms. Ten large tanks, well stocked with fish, afforded a retreat on their margins to various tribes of waterfowl, whose habits were so carefully consulted that some of these ponds were of salt water, as that which they most loved to frequent. A tessellated pavement of marble inclosed the ample basins, which were overhung by light and fanciful pavilions, that admitted the perfumed breezes of the gardens, and offered a grateful shelter to the monarch and his mistresses in the sultry heats of summer.

But the most luxurious residence of the Aztec monarch, at that season, was the royal hill of Chapultepec, a spot consecrated, moreover, by the ashes of his ancestors. It stood in a westerly direction from the capital, and its base was, in his day, washed by the waters of the Tezcuco. On its lofty crest of porphyritic rock there now stands the magnificent, though desolate, castle erected by the young viceroy Galvez, at the close of the seventeenth century. The view from its windows is one of the finest in the environs of Mexico. The landscape is not disfigured here, as in many other quarters, by the white and barren patches, so offensive to the sight; but the eye wanders over an unbroken expanse of meadows and cultivated fields, waving with rich harvests of European grain. Montezuma's gardens stretched for miles around the base of the hill. Two statues of that monarch and his father, cut in *bas-relief* in the porphyry, were spared till the middle of the last century; and the grounds are still shaded by gigantic cypresses, more than fifty feet in circumference, which were centuries old at the time of the Conquest. The place is now a tangled wilderness of wild shrubs, where the myrtle mingles its dark, glossy leaves with the red berries and delicate foliage of the pepper-tree. Surely there is no spot better suited to awaken meditation on the past; none where the traveller, as he sits under those stately cypresses grey with the moss of ages, can so fitly ponder on the sad destinies of the Indian races and the monarch who once held his courtly revels under the shadow of their branches.

The domestic establishment of Montezuma was on the same scale of barbaric splendour as everything else about him. He could boast as many wives as are found in the harem of an Eastern sultan. They were lodged in their own apartments, and provided with every accommodation, according to their ideas, for personal comfort and cleanliness. They passed their hours in the usual feminine employments of weaving and embroidery, especially in the graceful featherwork, for which such rich materials were furnished by the royal aviaries. They conducted themselves with strict decorum, under the supervision of certain aged females, who acted in the respectable capacity of duennas, in the same manner as in the religious houses attached to the *teocallis*. The palace was supplied with numerous baths, and Montezuma set the example, in his own person, of frequent ablutions. He bathed at least once, and changed his dress four times, it is said, every day. He never put on the same apparel a second time, but gave it away to his attendants. Queen Elizabeth, with a similar taste for costume, showed a less princely spirit in hoarding her discarded suits. Her wardrobe was, probably, somewhat more costly than that of the Indian emperor.

Besides his numerous female retinue, the halls and antechambers were filled with nobles in constant attendance on his person, who served also as a sort of bodyguard. It had been usual for plebeians of merit to fill certain offices in the palace. But the haughty Montezuma refused to be waited upon by any but men of noble birth. They were not unfrequently the sons of the great chiefs, and remained as hostages in the absence of their fathers; thus serving the double purpose of security and state.

His meals the emperor took alone. The well-matted floor of a large saloon was covered with hundreds of dishes. Sometimes Montezuma himself, but more frequently his steward, indicated those which he preferred, and which were kept hot by means of chafing-dishes. The royal bill of fare comprehended, besides domestic animals, game from the distant forests, and fish which, the day before, were swimming in the Gulf of Mexico! They were dressed in manifold ways, for the Aztec *artistes,* as we have already had occasion to notice, had penetrated deep into the mysteries of culinary science.

The meats were served by the attendant nobles, who then resigned the office of waiting on the monarch to maidens selected for their personal grace and beauty. A screen of richly gilt and carved wood was drawn around him, so as to conceal him from vulgar eyes during the repast. He was seated on a cushion, and the dinner was served on a low table, covered with a delicate cotton cloth. The dishes were of the finest ware of Cholula. He had a service of gold, which was reserved for religious celebrations. Indeed, it would scarcely have comported with even his princely revenues to have used it on ordinary occasions, when his table equipage was not allowed to appear a second time, but was given away to his attendants. The saloon was lighted by torches made of a resinous wood, which sent forth a sweet odour, and probably not a little smoke, as they burned. At his meal he was attended by five or six of his ancient counsellors, who stood at a respectful distance, answering his questions, and occasionally rejoiced by some of the viands with which he complimented them from his table.

This course of solid dishes was succeeded by another of sweetmeats and pastry, for which the Aztec cooks, provided with the important requisites of maize-flour, eggs, and the rich sugar of the aloe, were famous. Two girls were occupied at the further end of the apartment, during dinner, in preparing fine rolls and wafers, with which they garnished the board from time to time. The emperor took no other beverage than the *chocolatl,* a potation of chocolate, flavoured with vanilla and other spices, and so prepared as to be reduced to a froth of the consistency of honey, which gradually dissolved in the mouth. This beverage, if so it could be called, was served in golden goblets, with spoons of the same metal or of tortoise-shell finely wrought. The emperor was exceedingly fond of it, to judge from the quantity—no less than fifty jars or pitchers being prepared for his own daily consumption! Two thousand more were allowed for that of his household.

The general arrangement of the meal seems to have been not very unlike that of Europeans. But no prince in Europe could boast a dessert which could compare with that of the Aztec emperor: for it was gathered fresh from the most opposite climes; and his board displayed the products of his own temperate region, and the luscious fruits of the tropics, plucked the day previous, from the green groves of the *tierra caliente,* and transmitted with the speed of steam, by means of couriers, to the capital. It was as if some kind fairy should crown our banquets with the spicy products that but yesterday were growing in a sunny isle of the far-off Indian seas!

After the royal appetite was appeased, water was handed to him by the female attendants in a silver basin, in the same manner as had been done before commencing his meal; for the Aztecs were as constant in their ablutions, at these times, as any nation of the East. Pipes were then brought, made of a varnished and richly gilt wood, from which he inhaled, sometimes through the nose, at others through the mouth, the fumes of an intoxicating weed, "called *tobacco,*" mingled with liquid-amber. While this soothing process of fumigation was going on, the emperor enjoyed the exhibitions of his mountebanks and jugglers, of whom a regular corps was attached to the palace. No people, not even those of China or Hindostan, surpassed the Aztecs in feats of agility and legerdemain.

Sometimes he amused himself with his jester; for the Indian monarch had his jesters, as well as his more refined brethren of Europe, at that day. Indeed he used to say that more instruction was to be gathered from them than from wiser men, for they dared to tell the truth. At other times, he witnessed the graceful dances of his women, or took delight in listening to music—if the rude minstrelsy of the Mexicans deserve that name—accompanied by a chant, in slow and solemn cadence, celebrating the heroic deeds of great Aztec warriors or of his own princely line.

When he had sufficiently refreshed his spirits with these diversions, he composed himself to sleep, for in his *siesta* he was as regular as a Spaniard. On awaking, he gave audience to ambassadors from foreign states, or his own tributary cities, or to such caciques as had suits to prefer to him. They were introduced by the young nobles in attendance, and, whatever might be their rank, unless of the blood royal, they were obliged to submit to the humiliation of shrouding their rich dresses under the coarse mantle of *nequen,* and entering barefooted, with downcast eyes, into the presence. The emperor addressed few and brief remarks to the suitors, answering them generally by his secretaries; and the parties retired with the same reverential obeisance, taking care to keep their faces turned towards the monarch. Well might Cortés exclaim that no court, whether of the Grand Seignior or any other infidel, ever displayed so pompous and elaborate a ceremonial!

Besides the crowd of retainers already noticed, the royal household was not complete without a host of artisans constantly employed in the erection or repair of buildings, besides a great number of jewellers and persons skilled in working metals, who found abundant demand for their trinkets among the dark-eyed beauties of the harem. The imperial mummers and jugglers were also very numerous, and the dancers belonging to the palace occupied a particular district of the city, appropriated exclusively to them.

The maintenance of this little host, amounting to some thousands of individuals, involved a heavy expenditure, requiring accounts of a complicated, and, to a simple people, it might well be, embarrassing nature. Everything, however, was conducted with perfect order; and all the various receipts and disbursements were set down in the picture-writing of the country. The arithmetical characters were of a more refined and conventional sort than those for narrative purposes; and a separate apartment was filled with hieroglyphical ledgers, exhibiting a complete view of the economy of the palace. The care of all this was instructed to a treasurer, who acted as a sort of major-domo in the household, having a general superintendence over all its concerns. This responsible office, on the arrival of the Spaniards, was in the hands of a trusty cacique named Tapia.

Such is the picture of Montezuma's domestic establishment and way of living, as delineated by the Conquerors, and their immediate followers, who had the best means of information, too highly coloured, it may be, by the proneness to exaggerate, which was natural to those who first witnessed a spectacle so striking to the imagination, so new and unexpected. I have thought it best to present the full details, trivial though they may seem to the reader, as affording a curious picture of manners, so superior in point of refinement to those of the other aboriginal tribes on the North American continent. Nor are they, in fact, so trivial, when we reflect that in these details of private life we possess a surer measure of civilisation than in those of a public nature.

In surveying them we are strongly reminded of the civilisation of the East; not of that higher, intellectual kind which belonged to the more polished Arabs and the Persians, but that semi-civilisation which has distinguished, for example, the Tartar races, among whom art, and even science, have made, indeed, some progress in their adaptation to material wants and sensual gratification, but little in reference to the higher and more ennobling interests of humanity. It is characteristic of such a people to find a puerile pleasure in a dazzling and ostentatious pageantry; to mistake show for substance, vain pomp for power; to hedge round the throne itself with a barren and burdensome ceremonial, the counterfeit of real majesty.

Even this, however, was an advance in refinement compared with the rude manners of the earlier Aztecs. The change may, doubtless, be referred in some degree to the personal influence of Montezuma. In his younger days he had tempered the fierce habits of the soldier with the milder profession of religion. In later life he had withdrawn himself still more from the brutalising occupations of war, and his manners acquired a refinement tinctured, it may be added, with an effeminacy unknown to his martial predecessors.

The condition of the empire, too, under his reign, was favourable to this change. The dismemberment of the Tezcucan kingdom, on the death of the great Nezahualpilli, had left the Aztec monarchy without a rival; and it soon spread its colossal arms over the furthest limits of Anahuac. The aspiring mind of Montezuma rose with the acquisition of wealth and power; and he displayed the consciousness of new importance by the assumption of unprecedented state. He affected a reserve unknown to his predecessors; withdrew his person from the vulgar eye, and fenced himself round with an elaborate and courtly etiquette. When he went abroad it was in state, on some public occasion, usually to the great temple to take part in the religious services; and, as he passed along, he exacted from his people, as we have seen, the homage of an adulation worthy of an Oriental despot. His haughty demeanour touched the pride of his more potent vassals, particularly those who at a distance felt themselves nearly independent of his authority. His exactions, demanded by the profuse expenditure of his palace, scattered broadcast the seeds of discontent; and, while the empire seemed towering in its most palmy and prosperous state, the canker had eaten deepest into its heart.

CHAPTER II

Market of Mexico—Great Temple—Interior Sanctuaries—
Spanish Quarters

1519

FOUR DAYS HAD ELAPSED since the Spaniards made their entry into Mexico. Whatever schemes their commander may have revolved in his mind, he felt that he could determine on no plan of operations till he had seen more of the capital, and ascertained by his own inspection the nature of its resources. He accordingly, as was observed at the close of the last book, sent to Montezuma, asking permission to visit the great *teocalli,* and some other places in the city.

The friendly monarch consented without difficulty. He even prepared to go in person to the great temple, to receive his guests there—it may be, to shield the shrine of his tutelar deity from any attempted profanation. He was acquainted, as we have already seen, with the proceedings of the Spaniards on similar occasions in the course of their march. Cortés put himself at the head of his little corps of cavalry, and nearly all the Spanish foot, as usual, and followed the caciques sent by Montezuma to guide him. They proposed first to conduct him to the great market of Tlatelolco in the western part of the city.

On the way the Spaniards were struck, in the same manner as they had been on entering the capital, with the appearance of the inhabitants, and their great superiority in the style and quality of their dress over the people of the lower countries. The *tilmatli,* or cloak, thrown over the shoulders, and tied round the neck, made of cotton of different degrees of fineness, according to the condition of the wearer, and the ample sash around the loins, were often wrought in rich and elegant figures, and edged with a deep fringe or tassel. As the weather was now growing cool, mantles of fur or of the gorgeous featherwork were sometimes substituted. The latter combined the advantage of great warmth with beauty. The Mexicans had also the art of spinning a fine thread of the hair of the rabbit and other animals, which they wove into a delicate web that took a permanent dye.

The women, as in other parts of the country, seemed to go about as freely as the men. They wore several skirts or petticoats of different lengths, with highly ornamented borders, and sometimes over them loose flowing robes, which reached to the ankles. These also were made of cotton, for the wealthier classes, of a fine texture, prettily embroidered. No veils were worn here, as in some other parts of Anahuac, where they were made of the aloe thread, or of the light web of hair above noticed. The Aztec women had their faces exposed; and their dark raven tresses floated luxuriantly over their shoulders, revealing features which, although of a dusky or rather cinnamon hue, were not unfrequently pleasing, while touched with the serious, even sad expression, characteristic of the national physiognomy.

On drawing near to the *tianguez,* or great market, the Spaniards were astonished at the throng of people pressing towards it, and, on entering the place, their surprise was still further heightened by the sight of the multitudes assembled there, and the dimensions of the inclosure, thrice as large as the celebrated square of Salamanca. Here were met together traders from all parts, with the products and manufactures peculiar to their countries; the goldsmiths of Azcapozalco; the potters and jewellers of Cholula, the painters of Tezcuco, the stone-cutters of Tenajocan, the hunters of Xilotepec, the fishermen of Cuitlahuac, the fruiterers of the warm countries, the mat and chair-makers of Quauhtitlan, and the florists of Xochimilco—all busily engaged in recommending their respective wares, and in chaffering with purchasers.

The market-place was surrounded by deep porticoes, and the several articles had each its own quarter allotted to it. Here might be seen cotton piled up in bales, or manufactured into dresses and articles of domestic use, as tapestry, curtains, coverlets, and the like. The richly stained and nice fabrics reminded Cortés of the *alcayceria,* or silk market of Granada. There was the quarter assigned to the goldsmiths, where the purchaser might find various articles of ornament or use formed of the precious metals, or curious toys, such as we have already had occasion to notice, made in imitation of birds and fishes, with scales and feathers alternately of gold and silver, and with movable heads and bodies. These fantastic little trinkets were often garnished with precious stones, and showed a patient, puerile ingenuity in the manufacture, like that of the Chinese.

In an adjoining quarter were collected specimens of pottery coarse and fine, vases of wood elaborately carved, varnished or gilt, of curious and sometimes graceful forms. There were also hatchets made of copper alloyed with tin, the substitute, and, as it proved, not a bad one, for iron. The soldier found here all the implements of his trade. The casque fashioned into the head of some wild animal, with its grinning defences of teeth, and bristling crest dyed with the rich tint of the cochineal; the *escaupil,* or quilted doublet of cotton, the rich surcoat of feather-mail, and weapons of all sorts, copper-headed lances and arrows, and the broad *maquahuitl,* the Mexican sword, with its sharp blades of *itztli.* Here were razors and mirrors of this same hard and polished mineral which served so many of the purposes of steel with the Aztecs. In the square were also to be found booths occupied by barbers, who used these same razors in their vocation. For the Mexicans, contrary to the popular and erroneous notions respecting the aborigines of the New World, had beards, though scanty ones. Other shops or booths were tenanted by apothecaries, well provided with drugs, roots, and different medicinal preparations. In other places, again, blank books or maps for the hieroglyphical picture-writing were to be seen, folded together like fans, and made of cotton, skins, or more commonly the fibres of the agave, the Aztec papyrus.

Under some of the porticoes they saw hides raw and dressed, and various articles for domestic or personal use made of the leather. Animals, both wild and tame, were offered for sale, and near them, perhaps, a gang of slaves, with collars round their necks, intimating they were likewise on sale—a spectacle unhappily not confined to the barbarian markets of Mexico, though the evils of their condition were aggravated there by the consciousness that a life of degradation might be consummated at any moment by the dreadful doom of sacrifice.

The heavier materials for building, as stone, lime, timber, were considered too bulky to be allowed a place in the square, and were deposited in the adjacent streets on the borders of the canals. It would be tedious to enumerate all the various articles, whether for luxury or daily use, which were collected from all quarters in this vast bazaar. I must not omit to mention, however, the display of provisions, one of the most attractive features of the *tianguez;* meats of all kinds, domestic poultry, game from the neighbouring mountains, fish from the lakes and streams, fruits in all the delicious abundance of these temperate regions, green vegetables, and the unfailing maize. There was many a viand, too, ready dressed, which sent up its savoury steams provoking the appetite of the idle passenger; pastry, bread of the Indian corn, cakes, and confectionery. Along with these were to be seen cooling or stimulating beverages, the spicy foaming *chocolatl,* with its delicate aroma of vanilla, and the inebriating *pulque,* the fermented juice of the aloe. All these commodities, and every stall and portico, were set out, or rather smothered, with flowers, showing, on a much greater scale, indeed, a taste similar to that displayed in the markets of modern Mexico. Flowers seem to be the spontaneous growth of this luxuriant soil; which, instead of noxious weeds, as in other regions, is ever ready, without the aid of man, to cover up its nakedness with this rich and variegated livery of nature.

I will spare the reader the repetition of all the particulars enumerated by the bewildered Spaniards, which are of some interest as evincing the various mechanical skill and the polished wants, resembling those of a refined community, rather than of a nation of savages. It was the *material* civilisation, which belongs neither to the one nor the other. The Aztec had plainly reached that middle station, as far above the rude races of the New World as it was below the cultivated communities of the Old.

As to the numbers assembled in the market, the estimates differ, as usual. The Spaniards often visited the place, and no one states the amount at less than forty thousand! Some carry it much higher. Without relying too much on the arithmetic of the Conquerors, it is certain that on this occasion, which occurred every fifth day, the city swarmed with a motley crowd of strangers, not only from the vicinity, but from many leagues around; the causeways were thronged, and the lake was darkened by canoes filled with traders flocking to the great *tianguez.* It resembled indeed the periodical fairs in Europe, not as they exist now, but as they existed in the Middle Ages, when, from the difficulties of intercommunication, they served as the great central marts for commercial intercourse, exercising a most important and salutary influence on the community.

The exchanges were conducted partly by barter, but more usually in the currency of the country. This consisted of bits of tin stamped with a character like a T, bags of cacao, the value of which was regulated by their size, and lastly quills filled with gold dust. Gold was part of the regular currency, it seems, in both hemispheres. In their dealings it is singular that they should have had no knowledge of scales and weights. The quantity was determined by measure and number.

The most perfect order reigned throughout this vast assembly. Officers patrolled the square, whose business it was to keep the peace, to collect the duties imposed on the different articles of merchandise, to see that no false measures or fraud of any kind were used, and to bring offenders at once to justice. A court of twelve judges sat in one part of the *tianguez,* clothed with those ample and summary powers, which, in despotic countries, are often delegated even to petty tribunals. The extreme severity with which they exercised these powers, in more than one instance, proves that they were not a dead letter.

The *tianguez* of Mexico was naturally an object of great interest, as well as wonder, to the Spaniards. For in it they saw converged into one focus, as it were, all the rays of civilisation scattered throughout the land. Here they beheld the various evidences of mechanical skill, of domestic industry, the multiplied resources, of whatever kind, within the compass of the natives. It could not fail to impress them with high ideas of the magnitude of these resources, as well as of the commercial activity and social subordination by which the whole community was knit together; and their admiration is fully evinced by the minuteness and energy of their descriptions.

From this bustling scene the Spaniards took their way to the great *teocalli,* in the neighbourhood of their own quarters. It covered, with the subordinate edifices, as the reader has already seen, the large tract of ground now occupied by the cathedral, part of the market-place, and some of the adjoining streets. It was the spot which had been consecrated to the same object, probably, ever since the foundation of the city. The present building, however, was of no great antiquity, having been constructed by Ahuitzotl, who celebrated its dedication in 1486, by that hecatomb of victims, of which such incredible reports are to be found in the chronicles.

It stood in the midst of a vast area, encompassed by a wall of stone and lime, about eight feet high, ornamented on the outer side by figures of serpents, raised in relief, which gave it the name of the *coatepantli,* or "wall of serpents." This emblem was a common one in the sacred sculpture of Anahuac, as well as of Egypt. The wall, which was quadrangular, was pierced by huge battlemented gateways, opening on the four principal streets of the capital. Over each of the gates was a kind of arsenal, filled with arms and warlike gear; and, if we may credit the report of the Conquerors, there were barracks adjoining, garrisoned by ten thousand soldiers, who served as a sort of military police for the capital, supplying the emperor with a strong arm in case of tumult or sedition.

The *teocalli* itself was a solid pyramidal structure of earth and pebbles, coated on the outside with hewn stones, probably of the light, porous kind employed in the buildings of the city. It was probably square, with its sides facing the cardinal points. It was divided into five bodies or stories, each one receding so as to be of smaller dimensions than that immediately below it; the usual form of the Aztec *teocallis,* as already described, and bearing obvious resemblance to some of the primitive pyramidal structures in the Old World. The ascent was by a flight of steps on the outside, which reached to the narrow terrace or platform at the base of the second story, passing quite round the building, when a second stairway conducted to a similar landing at the base of the third. The breadth of this walk was just so much space as was left by the retreating story next above it. From this construction the visitor was obliged to pass round the whole edifice four times, in order to reach the top. This had a most imposing effect in the religious ceremonials, when the pompous procession of priests with their wild minstrelsy came sweeping round the huge sides of the pyramid, as they rose higher and higher in the presence of gazing multitudes, towards the summit.

The dimensions of the temple cannot be given with any certainty. The Conquerors judged by the eye, rarely troubling themselves with anything like an accurate measurement. It was, probably, not much less than three hundred feet square at the base; and, as the Spaniards counted a hundred and fourteen steps, was probably less than one hundred feet in height.

When Cortés arrived before the *teocalli,* he found two priests and several caciques commissioned by Montezuma to save him the fatigue of the ascent by bearing him on their shoulders, in the same manner as had been done to the emperor. But the general declined the compliment, preferring to march up at the head of his men. On reaching the summit they found it a vast area, paved with broad flat stones. The first object that met their view was a large block of jasper, the peculiar shape of which showed it was the stone on which the bodies of the unhappy victims were stretched for sacrifice. Its convex surface, by raising the breast, enabled the priest to perform more easily his diabolical task of removing the heart. At the other end of the area were two towers or sanctuaries, consisting of three stories, the lower one of stone and stucco, the two upper of wood elaborately carved. In the lower division stood the images of their gods; the apartments above were filled with utensils for their religious services, and with the ashes of some of their Aztec princes, who had fancied this airy sepulchre. Before each sanctuary stood an altar with that undying fire upon it, the extinction of which boded as much evil to the empire as that of the Vestal flame would have done in ancient Rome. Here, also, was the huge cylindrical drum made of serpents' skins, and struck only on extraordinary occasions, when it sent forth a melancholy sound that might be heard for miles—a sound of woe in after times to the Spaniards.

Montezuma, attended by the high priest, came forward to receive Cortés as he mounted the area. "You are weary, Malintzin," said he to him, "with climbing up our great temple." But Cortés, with a politic vaunt, assured him "the Spaniards were never weary!" Then, taking him by the hand, the emperor pointed out the localities of the neighbourhood. The temple on which they stood, rising high above all other edifices in the capital, afforded the most elevated as well as central point of view. Below them the city lay spread out like a map, with its streets and canals intersecting each other at right angles, its terraced roofs blooming like so many parterres of flowers. Every place seemed alive with business and bustle; canoes were glancing up and down the canals, the streets were crowded with people in their gay, picturesque costume, while from the market-place they had so lately left, a confused hum of many sounds and voices rose upon the air. They could distinctly trace the symmetrical plan of the city, with its principal avenues issuing, as it were, from the four gates of the *coatepantli;* and connecting themselves with the causeways, which formed the grand entrances to the capital. This regular and beautiful arrangement was imitated in many of the inferior towns, where the great roads converged towards the chief *teocalli,* or cathedral, as to a common focus. They could discern the insular position of the metropolis, bathed on all sides by the salt floods of the Tezcuco, and in the distance the clear fresh waters of the Chalco; far beyond stretched a wide prospect of fields and waving woods, with the burnished walls of many a lofty temple rising high above the trees, and crowning the distant hilltops. The view reached in an unbroken line to the very base of the circular range of mountains, whose frosty peaks glittered as if touched with fire in the morning ray; while long, dark wreaths of vapour, rolling up from the hoary head of Popocatepetl, told that the destroying element was, indeed, at work in the bosom of the beautiful valley.

Cortés was filled with admiration at this grand and glorious spectacle, and gave utterance to his feelings in animated language to the emperor, the lord of these flourishing domains. His thoughts, however, soon took another direction; and, turning to Father Olmedo, who stood by his side, he suggested that the area would afford a most conspicuous position for the Christian Cross, if Montezuma would but allow it to be planted there. But the discreet ecclesiastic, with the good sense which on these occasions seems to have been so lamentably deficient in his commander, reminded him that such a request, at present, would be exceedingly ill-timed, as the Indian monarch had shown no dispositions as yet favourable to Christianity.

Cortés then requested Montezuma to allow him to enter the sanctuaries, and behold the shrines of his gods. To this the latter, after a short conference with the priests, assented, and conducted the Spaniards into the building. They found themselves in a spacious apartment incrusted on the sides with stucco, on which various figures were sculptured, representing the Mexican calendar, perhaps, or the priestly ritual. At one end of the saloon was a recess with a roof of timber richly carved and gilt. Before the altar in this sanctuary stood the colossal image of Huitzilo-potchli, the tutelary deity and war-god of the Aztecs. His countenance was distorted into hideous lineaments of symbolical import. In his right hand he wielded a bow, and in his left a bunch of golden arrows, which a mystic legend had connected with the victories of his people. The huge folds of a serpent, consisting of pearls and precious stones, were coiled round his waist, and the same rich materials were profusely sprinkled over his person. On his left foot were the delicate feathers of the humming-bird, which, singularly enough, gave its name to the dread deity. The most conspicuous ornament was a chain of gold and silver hearts alternate, suspended round his neck, emblematical of the sacrifice in which he most delighted. A more unequivocal evidence of this was afforded by three human hearts smoking and almost palpitating, as if recently torn from the victims, and now lying on the altar before him!

The adjoining sanctuary was dedicated to a milder deity. This was Tezcatlipoca, next in honour to that invisible Being, the Supreme God, who was represented by no image, and confined by no temple. It was Tezcatlipoca who created the world, and watched over it with a providential care. He was represented as a young man, and his image, of polished black stone, was richly garnished with gold plates and ornaments; among which a shield, burnished like a mirror, was the most characteristic emblem, as in it he saw reflected all the doings of the world. But the homage to this god was not always of a more refined or merciful character than that paid to his carnivorous brother; for five bleeding hearts were also seen in a golden platter on his altar.

The walls of both these chapels were stained with human gore. "The stench was more intolerable," exclaims Diaz, "than that of the slaughter-houses in Castile!" And the frantic forms of the priests, with their dark robes clotted with blood, as they flitted to and fro, seemed to the Spaniards to be those of the very ministers of Satan!

From this foul abode they gladly escaped into the open air; when Cortés, turning to Montezuma, said with a smile, "I do not comprehend how a great and wise prince like you can put faith in such evil spirits as these idols, the representatives of the devil! If you will but permit us to erect here the true Cross, and place the images of the blessed Virgin and her Son in your sanctuaries, you will soon see how your false gods will shrink before them!"

Montezuma was greatly shocked at this sacrilegious address. "These are the gods," he answered, "who have led the Aztecs on to victory since they were a nation, and who send the seed-time and harvest in their seasons. Had I thought you would have offered them this outrage, I would not have admitted you into their presence!"

Cortés, after some expressions of concern at having wounded the feelings of the emperor, took his leave. Montezuma remained, saying that he must expiate, if possible, the crime of exposing the shrines of the divinities to such profanation by the strangers.

On descending to the court, the Spaniards took a leisurely survey of the other edifices in the inclosure. The area was protected by a smooth stone pavement, so polished, indeed, that it was with difficulty the horses could keep their legs. There were several other *teocallis,* built generally on the model of the great one, though of much inferior size, dedicated to the different Aztec deities. On their summits were the altars crowned with perpetual flames, which, with those on the numerous temples in other quarters of the capital, shed a brilliant illumination over its streets, through the long nights.

Among the *teocallis* in the inclosure was one consecrated to Quetzal-coatl, circular in its form, and having an entrance in imitation of a dragon's mouth, bristling with sharp fangs and dripping with blood. As the Spaniards cast a furtive glance into the throat of this horrible monster, they saw collected there implements of sacrifice and other abominations of fearful import. Their bold hearts shuddered at the spectacle, and they designated the place not inaptly as the "Hell."

One other structure may be noticed as characteristic of the brutish nature of their religion. This was a pyramidal mound or tumulus, having a complicated framework of timber on its broad summit. On this was strung an immense number of human skulls, which belonged to the victims, mostly prisoners of war, who had perished on the accursed stone of sacrifice. One of the soldiers had the patience to count the number of these ghastly trophies, and reported it to be one hundred and thirty-six thousand! Belief might well be staggered, did not the Old World present a worthy counterpart in the pyramidal Golgothas which commemorated the triumphs of Tamerlane.

There were long ranges of buildings in the inclosure, appropriated as the residence of the priests and others engaged in the offices of religion. The whole number of them was said to amount to several thousand. Here were, also, the principal seminaries for the instruction of youth of both sexes, drawn chiefly from the higher and wealthier classes. The girls were taught by elderly women, who officiated as priestesses in the temples, a custom familiar also to Egypt. The Spaniards admit that the greatest care for morals, and the most blameless deportment, were maintained in these institutions. The time of the pupils was chiefly occupied, as in most monastic establishments, with the minute and burdensome ceremonial of their religion. The boys were likewise taught such elements of science as were known to their teachers, and the girls initiated in the mysteries of embroidery and weaving, which they employed in decorating the temples. At a suitable age they generally went forth into the world to assume the occupations fitted to their condition, though some remained permanently devoted to the services of religion.

The spot was also covered by edifices of a still different character. There were granaries filled with the rich produce of the church-lands, and with the first-fruits and other offerings of the faithful. One large mansion was reserved for strangers of eminence, who were on a pilgrimage to the great *teocalli*. The inclosure was ornamented with gardens, shaded by ancient trees, and watered by fountains and reservoirs from the copious streams of Chapultepec. The little community was thus provided with almost everything requisite for its own maintenance and the services of the temple.

It was a microcosm of itself—a city within a city; and, according to the assertion of Cortés, embraced a tract of ground large enough for five hundred houses. It presented in this brief compass the extremes of barbarism, blended with a certain civilisation, altogether characteristic of the Aztecs. The rude Conquerors saw only the evidence of the former. In the fantastic and symbolical features of the deities, they beheld the literal lineaments of Satan; in the rites and frivolous ceremonial, his own especial code of damnation; and in the modest deportment and careful nurture of the inmates of the seminaries, the snares by which he was to beguile his deluded victims. Before a century had elapsed, the descendants of these same Spaniards discerned in the mysteries of the Aztec religion the features, obscured and defaced, indeed, of the Jewish and Christian revelations! Such were the opposite conclusions of the unlettered soldier and of the scholar. A philosopher, untouched by superstition, might well doubt which of the two was the most extraordinary.

The sight of the Indian abominations seems to have kindled in the Spaniards a livelier feeling for their own religion; since, on the following day, they asked leave of Montezuma to convert one of the halls in their residence into a chapel, that they might celebrate the services of the Church there. The monarch, in whose bosom the feelings of resentment seem to have soon subsided, easily granted their request, and sent some of his own artisans to aid them in the work.

While it was in progress, some of the Spaniards observed what appeared to be a door recently plastered over. It was a common rumour that Montezuma still kept the treasures of his father, King Axayacatl, in this ancient palace. The Spaniards, acquainted with this fact, felt no scruple in gratifying their curiosity by removing the plaster. As was anticipated, it concealed a door. On forcing this they found the rumour was no exaggeration. They beheld a large hall filled with rich and beautiful stuffs, articles of curious workmanship of various kinds, gold and silver in bars and in the ore, and many jewels of value. It was the private hoard of Montezuma, the contributions, it may be, of tributary cities, and once the property of his father. "I was a young man," says Diaz, who was one of those that obtained a sight of it, "and it seemed to me as if all the riches of the world were in that room!" The Spaniards, notwithstanding their elation at the discovery of this precious deposit, seem to have felt some commendable scruples as to appropriating it to their own use—at least for the present. And Cortés, after closing up the wall as it was before, gave strict injunctions that nothing should be said of the matter, unwilling that the knowledge of its existence by his guests should reach the ears of Montezuma.

Three days sufficed to complete the chapel; and the Christians had the satisfaction to see themselves in possession of a temple where they might worship God in their own way, under the protection of the Cross, and the blessed Virgin. Mass was regularly performed by the fathers, Olmedo and Diaz, in the presence of the assembled army, who were most earnest and exemplary in their devotions, partly, says the chronicler above quoted, from the propriety of the thing, and partly for its edifying influence on the benighted heathen.

CHAPTER III

*Anxiety of Cortés—Seizure of Montezuma—His Treatment
by the Spaniards—Execution of His Officers—Montezuma in Irons—Reflections*

1519

THE SPANIARDS had been now a week in Mexico. During this time they had experienced the most friendly treatment from the emperor. But the mind of Cortés was far from easy. He felt that it was quite uncertain how long this amiable temper would last. A hundred circumstances might occur to change it. He might very naturally feel the maintenance of so large a body too burdensome on his treasury. The people of the capital might become dissatisfied at the presence of so numerous an armed force within their walls. Many causes of disgust might arise betwixt the soldiers and the citizens. Indeed, it was scarcely possible that a rude, licentious soldiery, like the Spaniards, could be long kept in subjection without active employment. The danger was even greater with the Tlascalans, a fierce race now brought into daily contact with the nation who held them in loathing and detestation. Rumours were already rife among the allies, whether well founded or not, of murmurs among the Mexicans, accompanied by menaces of raising the bridges.

Even should the Spaniards be allowed to occupy their present quarters unmolested, it was not advancing the great object of the expedition. Cortés was not a whit nearer gaining the capital, so essential to his meditated subjugation of the country; and any day he might receive tidings that the Crown, or, what he most feared, the governor of Cuba, had sent a force of superior strength to wrest from him a conquest but half achieved. Disturbed by these anxious reflections, he resolved to extricate himself from his embarrassment by one bold stroke. But he first submitted the affair to a council of the officers in whom he most confided, desirous to divide with them the responsibility of the act, and no doubt to interest them more heartily in its execution, by making it in some measure the result of their combined judgments.

When the general had briefly stated the embarrassments of their position, the council was divided in opinion. All admitted the necessity of some instant action. One party were for retiring secretly from the city, and getting beyond the causeways before their march could be intercepted. Another advised that it should be done openly, with the knowledge of the emperor, of whose good will they had had so many proofs. But both these measures seemed alike impolitic. A retreat under these circumstances, and so abruptly made, would have the air of a flight. It would be construed into distrust of themselves; and anything like timidity on their part would be sure not only to bring on them the Mexicans, but the contempt of their allies, who would, doubtless, join in the general cry.

As to Montezuma, what reliance could they place on the protection of a prince so recently their enemy, and who, in his altered bearing, must have taken counsel of his fears rather than his inclinations?

Even should they succeed in reaching the coast, their situation would be little better. It would be proclaiming to the world that, after all their lofty vaunts, they were unequal to the enterprise. Their only hopes of their sovereign's favour, and of pardon for their irregular proceedings, were founded on success. Hitherto, they had only made the discovery of Mexico; to retreat would be to leave conquest and the fruits of it to another. In short, to stay and to retreat seemed equally disastrous.

In this perplexity Cortés proposed an expedient, which none but the most daring spirit, in the most desperate extremity, would have conceived. This was to march to the royal palace, and bring Montezuma to the Spanish quarters, by fair means if they could persuade him, by force if necessary—at all events to get possession of his person. With such a pledge, the Spaniards would be secure from the assault of the Mexicans, afraid by acts of violence to compromise the safety of their prince. If he came by his own consent, they would be deprived of all apology for doing so. As long as the emperor remained among the Spaniards, it would be easy, by allowing him a show of sovereignty, to rule in his name, until they had taken measures for securing their safety, and the success of their enterprise. The idea of employing a sovereign as a tool for the government of his own kingdom, if a new one in the age of Cortés, is certainly not so in ours.

A plausible pretext for the seizure of the hospitable monarch—for the

most barefaced action seeks to veil itself under some show of decency—
was afforded by a circumstance of which Cortés had received intelligence
at Cholula. He had left, as we have seen, a faithful officer, Juan de
Escalante, with a hundred and fifty men in garrison at Vera Cruz, on
his departure for the capital. He had not been long absent when his lieutenant received a message from an Aztec chief named Quauhpopoca,
governor of a district to the north of the Spanish settlement, declaring
his desire to come in person and tender his allegiance to the Spanish
authorities at Vera Cruz. He requested that four of the white men might
be sent to protect him against certain unfriendly tribes through which
his road lay. This was not an uncommon request, and excited no suspicion in Escalante. The four soldiers were sent; and on their arrival two
of them were murdered by the false Aztec. The other two made their
way back to the garrison.

The commander marched at once, with fifty of his men, and several
thousand Indian allies, to take vengeance on the cacique. A pitched battle
followed. The allies fled from the redoubted Mexicans. The few Spaniards stood firm, and with the aid of their firearms and the blessed Virgin,
who was distinctly seen hovering over their ranks in the van, they made
good the field against the enemy. It cost them dear, however, since seven
or eight Christians were slain, and among them the gallant Escalante
himself, who died of his injuries soon after his return to the fort. The
Indian prisoners captured in the battle spoke of the whole proceeding as
having taken place at the instigation of Montezuma.

One of the Spaniards fell into the hands of the natives, but soon after
perished of his wounds. His head was cut off and sent to the Aztec
emperor. It was uncommonly large and covered with hair; and, as Montezuma gazed on the ferocious features, rendered more horrible by death,
he seemed to read in them the dark lineaments of the destined destroyers
of his house. He turned from it with a shudder, and commanded that it
should be taken from the city, and not offered at the shrine of any of his
gods.

Although Cortés had received intelligence of this disaster at Cholula,
he had concealed it within his own breast, or communicated it to very
few only of his most trusty officers, from apprehension of the ill effect it
might have on the spirits of the common soldiers.

The cavaliers whom Cortés now summoned to the council were men
of the same mettle with their leader. Their bold chivalrous spirit seemed
to court danger for its own sake. If one or two, less adventurous, were

startled by the proposal he made, they were soon overruled by the others, who, no doubt, considered that a desperate disease required as desperate a remedy.

That night, Cortés was heard pacing his apartment to and fro, like a man oppressed by thought, or agitated by strong emotion. He may have been ripening in his mind the daring scheme for the morrow. In the morning the soldiers heard Mass as usual, and Father Olmedo invoked the blessing of Heaven on their hazardous enterprise. Whatever might be the cause in which he was embarked, the heart of the Spaniard was cheered with the conviction that the Saints were on his side.

Having asked an audience from Montezuma, which was readily granted, the general made the necessary arrangements for his enterprise. The principal part of his force was drawn up in the courtyard, and he stationed a considerable detachment in the avenues leading to the palace, to check any attempt at rescue by the populace. He ordered twenty-five or thirty of the soldiers to drop in at the palace, as if by accident, in groups of three or four at a time, while the conference was going on with Montezuma. He selected five cavaliers, in whose courage and coolness he placed most trust, to bear him company: Pedro de Alvarado, Gonzalo de Sandoval, Francisco de Lujo, Velasquez de Leon, and Alonso de Avila—brilliant names in the annals of the Conquest. All were clad, as well as the common soldiers, in complete armour, a circumstance of too familiar occurrence to excite suspicion.

The little party were graciously received by the emperor, who soon, with the aid of the interpreters, became interested in a sportive conversation with the Spaniards, while he indulged his natural munificence by giving them presents of gold and jewels. He paid the Spanish general the particular compliment of offering him one of his daughters as his wife; an honour which the latter respectfully declined, on the ground that he was already accommodated with one in Cuba, and that his religion forbade a plurality.

When Cortés perceived that a sufficient number of his soldiers were assembled, he changed his playful manner, and with a serious tone briefly acquainted Montezuma with the treacherous proceedings in the *tierra caliente,* and the accusation of him as their author. The emperor listened to the charge with surprise; and disavowed the act, which he said could only have been imputed to him by his enemies. Cortés expressed his belief in his declaration, but added, that, to prove it true, it would be necessary to send for Quauhpopoca and his accomplices, that they might be examined and dealt with according to their deserts. To this Montezuma made no objection. Taking from his wrist, to which it was attached, a precious stone, the royal signet, on which was cut the figure of the war-god, he gave it to one of his nobles, with orders to show it to the Aztec governor, and require his instant presence in the capital, together with all those who had been accessory to the murder of the Spaniards. If he resisted, the officer was empowered to call in the aid of the neighbouring towns to enforce the mandate.

When the messenger had gone, Cortés assured the monarch that this prompt compliance with his request convinced him of his innocence. But it was important that his own sovereign should be equally convinced of it. Nothing would promote this so much as for Montezuma to transfer his residence to the palace occupied by the Spaniards, till on the arrival of Quauhpopoca the affair could be fully investigated. Such an act of condescension would, of itself, show a personal regard for the Spaniards, incompatible with the base conduct alleged against him, and would fully absolve him from all suspicion!

Montezuma listened to this proposal, and the flimsy reasoning with which it was covered, with looks of profound amazement. He became pale as death; but in a moment his face flushed with resentment, as with the pride of offended dignity, he exclaimed, "When was it ever heard that a great prince, like myself, voluntarily left his own palace to become a prisoner in the hands of strangers!"

Cortés assured him he would not go as a prisoner. He would experience nothing but respectful treatment from the Spaniards; would be surrounded by his own household, and hold intercourse with his people as usual. In short, it would be but a change of residence, from one of his palaces to another, a circumstance of frequent occurrence with him. It was in vain. "If I should consent to such a degradation," he answered, "my subjects never would!" When further pressed, he offered to give up one of his sons and one of his daughters to remain as hostages with the Spaniards, so that he might be spared this disgrace.

Two hours passed in this fruitless discussion, till a high-mettled cavalier, Velasquez de Leon, impatient of the long delay, and seeing that the attempt, if not the deed, must ruin them, cried out, "Why do we waste words on this barbarian? We have gone too far to recede now. Let us seize him, and, if he resists, plunge our swords into his body!" The fierce tone and menacing gestures with which this was uttered alarmed the monarch, who inquired of Marina what the angry Spaniard said. The interpreter explained it in as gentle a manner as she could, beseeching him, "to accompany the white men to their quarters, where he would be treated with all respect and kindness, while to refuse them would but expose himself to violence, perhaps to death." Marina, doubtless, spoke to her sovereign as she thought, and no one had better opportunity of knowing the truth than herself.

This last appeal shook the resolution of Montezuma. It was in vain that the unhappy prince looked around for sympathy or support. As his eyes wandered over the stern visages and iron forms of the Spaniards, he felt that his hour was indeed come; and, with a voice scarcely audible from emotion, he consented to accompany the strangers—to quit the palace, whither he was never more to return. Had he possessed the spirit of the first Montezuma, he would have called his guards around him, and left his life-blood on the threshold, sooner than have been dragged a dishonoured captive across it. But his courage sank under circumstances. He felt he was the instrument of an irresistible Fate!

No sooner had the Spaniards got his consent, than orders were given for the royal litter. The nobles, who bore and attended it, could scarcely believe their senses, when they learned their master's purpose. But pride now came to Montezuma's aid, and, since he must go, he preferred that it should appear to be with his own free-will. As the royal retinue, escorted by the Spaniards, marched through the street with downcast eyes and dejected mien, the people assembled in crowds, and a rumour ran among them that the emperor was carried off by force to the quarters of the white men. A tumult would have soon arisen but for the intervention of Montezuma himself, who called out to the people to disperse, as he was visiting his friends of his own accord; thus sealing his ignominy by a declaration which deprived his subjects of the only excuse for resistance. On reaching the quarters, he sent out his nobles with similar assurances to the mob, and renewed orders to return to their homes.

He was received with ostentatious respect by the Spaniards, and selected the suite of apartments which best pleased him. They were soon furnished with fine cotton tapestries, featherwork, and all the elegances of Indian upholstery. He was attended by such of his household as he chose, his wives and his pages, and was served with his usual pomp and luxury at his meals. He gave audience, as in his own palace, to his subjects, who were admitted to his presence, few, indeed, at a time, under the pretext of greater order and decorum. From the Spaniards themselves he met with a formal deference. No one, not even the general himself, approached him without doffing his casque, and rendering the obeisance due to his rank. Nor did they ever sit in his presence, without being invited by him to do so.

With all this studied ceremony and show of homage there was one circumstance which too clearly proclaimed to his people that their sovereign was a prisoner. In the front of the palace a patrol of sixty men was established, and the same number in the rear. Twenty of each corps mounted guard at once, maintaining a careful watch day and night. Another body, under command of Velasquez de Leon, was stationed in the royal antechamber. Cortés punished any departure from duty, or relaxation of vigilance, in these sentinels, with the utmost severity. He felt, as, indeed, every Spaniard must have felt, that the escape of the emperor now would be their ruin. Yet the task of this unintermitting watch sorely added to their fatigues. "Better this dog of a king should die," cried a soldier one day, "than that we should wear out our lives in this manner." The words were uttered in the hearing of Montezuma, who gathered something of their import, and the offender was severely chastised by order of the general. Such instances of disrespect, however, were very rare. Indeed, the amiable deportment of the monarch, who seemed to take pleasure in the society of his jailers, and who never allowed a favour or attention from the meanest soldier to go unrequited, inspired the Spaniards with as much attachment as they were capable of feeling— for a barbarian.

Things were in this posture when the arrival of Quauhpopoca from the coast was announced. He was accompanied by his son and fifteen Aztec chiefs. He had travelled all the way, borne, as became his high rank, in a litter. On entering Montezuma's presence, he threw over his dress the coarse robe of *nequen,* and made the usual humiliating acts of obeisance. The poor parade of courtly ceremony was the more striking when placed in contrast with the actual condition of the parties.

The Aztec governor was coldly received by his master, who referred the affair (had he the power to do otherwise?) to the examination of Cortés. It was, doubtless, conducted in a sufficiently summary manner. To the general's query, whether the cacique was the subject of Montezuma, he replied, "And what other sovereign could I serve?" implying that his sway was universal. He did not deny his share in the transaction, nor did he seek to shelter himself under the royal authority, till sentence of death was passed on him and his followers, when they all laid the blame of their proceedings on Montezuma. They were condemned to be burnt alive in the area before the palace. The funeral piles were made of heaps of arrows, javelins, and other weapons, drawn by the emperor's permission from the arsenals round the great *teocalli*, where they had been stored to supply means of defence in times of civic tumult or insurrection. By this politic precaution Cortés proposed to remove a ready means of annoyance in case of hostilities with the citizens.

To crown the whole of these extraordinary proceedings, Cortés, while preparations for the execution were going on, entered the emperor's apartment, attended by a soldier bearing fetters in his hands. With a severe aspect he charged the monarch with being the original contriver of the violence offered to the Spaniards, as was now proved by the declaration of his own instruments. Such a crime, which merited death in a subject, could not be atoned for, even by a sovereign, without some punishment. So saying, he ordered the soldier to fasten the fetters on Montezuma's ankles. He coolly waited till it was done; then, turning his back on the monarch, quitted the room.

Montezuma was speechless under the infliction of this last insult. He was like one struck down by a heavy blow that deprives him of all his faculties. He offered no resistance. But, though he spoke not a word, low, ill-suppressed moans, from time to time, intimated the anguish of his spirit. His attendants, bathed in tears, offered him their consolations. They tenderly held his feet in their arms, and endeavoured, by inserting their shawls and mantles, to relieve them from the pressure of the iron. But they could not reach the iron which had penetrated into his soul. He felt that he was no more a king.

Meanwhile, the execution of the dreadful doom was going forward in the courtyard. The whole Spanish force was under arms, to check any interruption that might be offered by the Mexicans. But none was attempted. The populace gazed in silent wonder, regarding it as the sentence of the emperor. The manner of the execution, too, excited less surprise, from their familiarity with similar spectacles, aggravated, indeed, by additional horrors in their own diabolical sacrifices. The Aztec lord and his companions, bound hand and foot to the blazing piles, submitted without a cry or a complaint to their terrible fate. Passive fortitude is the virtue of the Indian warrior; and it was the glory of the Aztec, as of the other races on the North American continent, to show how the spirit of the brave man may triumph over torture and the agonies of death.

When this dismal tragedy was ended, Cortés re-entered Montezuma's apartment. Kneeling down he unclasped his shackles with his own hand, expressing at the same time his regret that so disagreeable a duty as that of subjecting him to such a punishment had been imposed on him. This last indignity had entirely crushed the spirit of Montezuma; and the monarch, whose frown, but a week since, would have made the nations of Anahuac tremble to their remotest borders, was now craven enough to thank his deliverer for his freedom, as for a great and unmerited boon!

Not long after, the Spanish general, conceiving that his royal captive was sufficiently humbled, expressed his willingness that he should return, if he inclined, to his own palace. Montezuma declined it; alleging, it is said, that his nobles had more than once importuned him to resent his injuries by taking arms against the Spaniards; and that, were he in the midst of them, it would be difficult to avoid it, or to save his capital from bloodshed and anarchy. The reason did honour to his heart, if it was the one which influenced him. It is probable that he did not care to trust his safety to those haughty and ferocious chieftains who had witnessed the degradation of their master, and must despise his pusillanimity as a thing unprecedented in an Aztec monarch. It is also said that, when Marina conveyed to him the permission of Cortés, the other interpreter, Aguilar, gave him to understand the Spanish officers never would consent that he should avail himself of it.

Whatever were his reasons, it is certain that he declined the offer; and the general, in a well-feigned, or real ecstasy, embraced him, declaring, "that he loved him as a brother, and that every Spaniard would be zealously devoted to his interests, since he had shown himself so mindful of theirs!" Honeyed words, "which," says the shrewd old chronicler who was present, "Montezuma was wise enough to know the worth of."

The events recorded in this chapter are certainly some of the most extraordinary on the page of history. That a small body of men, like the Spaniards, should have entered the palace of a mighty prince, have seized his person in the midst of his vassals, have borne him off a captive to their quarters—that they should have put to an ignominious death before his face his high officers, for executing probably his own commands, and have crowned the whole by putting the monarch in irons like a common malefactor—that this should have been done, not to a drivelling dotard in the decay of his fortunes, but to a proud monarch in the plenitude of his power, in the very heart of his capital, surrounded by thousands and tens of thousands who trembled at his nod, and would have poured out their blood like water in his defence—that all this should have been done by a mere handful of adventurers is a thing too extravagant, altogether too improbable, for the pages of romance! It is, nevertheless, literally true. Yet we shall not be prepared to acquiesce in the judgments of contemporaries, who regarded these acts with admiration. We may well distrust any grounds on which it is attempted to justify the kidnapping of a friendly sovereign—by those very persons, too, who were reaping the full benefit of his favours.

To view the matter differently, we must take the position of the Conquerors, and assume with them the original right of conquest. Regarded from this point of view many difficulties vanish. If conquest were a duty, whatever was necessary to effect it was right also. Right and expedient become convertible terms. And it can hardly be denied that the capture of the monarch was expedient if the Spaniards would maintain their hold on the empire.

The execution of the Aztec governor suggests other considerations. If he were really guilty of the perfidious act imputed to him by Cortés, and if Montezuma disavowed it, the governor deserved death, and the general was justified by the law of nations in inflicting it. It is by no means so clear, however, why he should have involved so many in this sentence; most, perhaps all, of whom must have acted under his authority. The cruel manner of the death will less startle those who are familiar with the established penal codes in most civilised nations in the sixteenth century.

But, if the governor deserved death, what pretence was there for the outrage on the person of Montezuma? If the former was guilty, the latter surely was not. But if the cacique only acted in obedience to orders, the responsibility was transferred to the sovereign who gave the orders. They could not both stand in the came category.

It is vain, however, to reason on the matter, on any abstract principles of right and wrong, or to suppose that the Conquerors troubled themselves with the refinements of casuistry. Their standard of right and wrong, in reference to the natives, was a very simple one. Despising them as an outlawed race, without God in the world, they, in common with their age, held it to be their "mission" (to borrow the cant phrase of our own day) to conquer and to convert. The measures they adopted certainly facilitated the first great work of conquest. By the execution of the caciques, they struck terror not only into the capital, but throughout the country. It proclaimed that not a hair of a Spaniard was to be touched with impunity! By rendering Montezuma contemptible in his own eyes and those of his subjects, Cortés deprived him of the support of his people, and forced him to lean on the arm of the stranger. It was a politic proceeding—to which few men could have been equal, who had a touch of humanity in their natures.

A good criterion of the moral sense of the actors in these events is afforded by the reflections of Bernal Diaz, made some fifty years, it will be remembered, after the events themselves, when the fire of youth had become extinct, and the eye, glancing back through the vista of half a century, might be supposed to be unclouded by the passions and prejudices which throw their mist over the present. "Now that I am an old man," says the veteran, "I often entertain myself with calling to mind the heroical deeds of early days, till they are as fresh as the events of yesterday. I think of the seizure of the Indian monarch, his confinement in irons, and the execution of his officers, till all these things seem actually passing before me. And, as I ponder on our exploits, I feel that it was not of ourselves that we performed them, but that it was the providence of God which guided us. Much food is there here for meditation!" There is so, indeed, and for a meditation not unpleasing, as we reflect on the advance, in speculative morality, at least, which the nineteenth century has made over the sixteenth. But should not the consciousness of this teach us charity? Should it not make us the more distrustful of applying the standard of the present to measure the actions of the past?

CHAPTER IV

*Montezuma's Deportment—His Life in the Spanish Quarters
—Meditated Insurrection—Lord of Tezcuco Seized—
Further Measures of Cortés*

1520

THE SETTLEMENT of La Villa Rica de Vera Cruz was of the last importance to the Spaniards. It was the port by which they were to communicate with Spain; the strong post on which they were to retreat in case of disaster, and which was to bridle their enemies and give security to their allies; the *point d'appui* for all their operations in the country. It was of great moment, therefore, that the care of it should be intrusted to proper hands.

A cavalier, named Alonso de Grado, had been sent by Cortés to take the place made vacant by the death of Escalante. He was a person of greater repute in civil than military matters, and would be more likely, it was thought, to maintain peaceful relations with the natives, than a person of more belligerent spirit. Cortés made—what was rare with him—a bad choice. He soon received such accounts of troubles in the settlement from the exactions and negligence of the new governor that he resolved to supersede him.

He now gave the command to Gonzalo de Sandoval, a young cavalier, who had displayed through the whole campaign singular intrepidity united with sagacity and discretion, while the good humour with which he bore every privation, and his affable manners, made him a favourite with all, privates as well as officers. Sandoval accordingly left the camp for the coast. Cortés did not mistake his man a second time.

Notwithstanding the actual control exercised by the Spaniards through their royal captive, Cortés felt some uneasiness when he reflected that it was in the power of the Indians, at any time, to cut off his communications with the surrounding country, and hold him a prisoner in the capital. He proposed, therefore, to build two vessels of sufficient size to transport his forces across the lake, and thus to render himself independent of the causeways. Montezuma was pleased with the idea of seeing those wonderful "water-houses," of which he had heard so much, and readily gave permission to have the timber in the royal forests felled for the purpose. The work was placed under the direction of Martin Lopez, an experienced shipbuilder. Orders were also given to Sandoval to send up from the coast a supply of cordage, sails, iron, and other necessary materials, which had been judiciously saved on the destruction of the fleet.

The Aztec emperor, meanwhile, was passing his days in the Spanish quarters in no very different manner from what he had been accustomed to in his own palace. His keepers were too well aware of the value of their prize not to do everything which could make his captivity comfortable, and disguise it from himself. But the chain will gall, though wreathed with roses. After Montezuma's breakfast, which was a light meal of fruits or vegetables, Cortés or some of his officers usually waited on him, to learn if he had any commands for them. He then devoted some time to business. He gave audience to those of his subjects who had petitions to prefer, or suits to settle. The statement of the party was drawn up on the hieroglyphic scrolls, which were submitted to a number of counsellors or judges, who assisted him with their advice on these occasions. Envoys from foreign states or his own remote provinces and cities were also admitted, and the Spaniards were careful that the same precise and punctilious. etiquette should be maintained towards the royal puppet as when in the plenitude of his authority.

After business was despatched, Montezuma often amused himself with seeing the Castilian troops go through their military exercises. He, too, had been a soldier, and in his prouder days had led armies in the field. It was very natural he should take an interest in the novel display of European tactics and discipline. At other times he would challenge Cortés or his officers to play at some of the national games. A favourite one was called *totoloque,* played with golden balls aimed at a target or mark of the same metal. Montezuma usually staked something of value—precious stones or ingots of gold. He lost with good humour; indeed it was of little consequence whether he won or lost, since he generally gave away his winnings to his attendants. He had, in truth, a most munificent spirit. His enemies accused him of avarice. But, if he were avaricious, it could have been only that he might have the more to give away.

Each of the Spaniards had several Mexicans, male and female, who attended to his cooking and various other personal offices. Cortés, considering that the maintenance of this host of menials was a heavy tax on the royal exchequer, ordered them to be dismissed, excepting one to be retained for each soldier. Montezuma, on learning this, pleasantly remonstrated with the general on his careful economy, as unbecoming a royal establishment, and, countermanding the order, caused additional accommodations to be provided for the attendants, and their pay to be doubled.

On another occasion a soldier purloined some trinkets of gold from the treasure kept in the chamber, which, since Montezuma's arrival in the Spanish quarters, had been reopened. Cortés would have punished the man for the theft, but the emperor, interfering, said to him, "Your countrymen are welcome to the gold and other articles, if you will but spare those belonging to the gods." Some of the soldiers, making the most of his permission, carried off several hundred loads of fine cotton to their quarters. When this was represented to Montezuma, he only replied, "What I have once given I never take back again."

While thus indifferent to his treasures, he was keenly sensitive to personal slight or insult. When a common soldier once spoke to him angrily, the tears came into the monarch's eyes, as it made him feel the true character of his impotent condition. Cortés, on becoming acquainted with it, was so much incensed that he ordered the soldier to be hanged; but, on Montezuma's intercession, commuted this severe sentence for a flogging. The general was not willing that any one but himself should treat his royal captive with indignity. Montezuma was desired to procure a further mitigation of the punishment. But he refused, saying, "that, if a similar insult had been offered by any one of his subjects to Malintzin, he would have resented it in like manner."

Such instances of disrespect were very rare. Montezuma's amiable and inoffensive manners, together with his liberality, the most popular of virtues with the vulgar, made him generally beloved by the Spaniards. The arrogance, for which he had been so distinguished in his prosperous days, deserted him in his fallen fortunes. His character in captivity seems to have undergone something of that change which takes place in the wild animals of the forest, when caged within the walls of the menagerie.

The Indian monarch knew the name of every man in the army, and was careful to discriminate his proper rank. For some he showed a strong partiality. He obtained from the general a favourite page, named Orteguilla, who, being in constant attendance on his person, soon learned enough of the Mexican language to be of use to his countrymen. Montezuma took great pleasure, also, in the society of Velasquez de León, the captain of his guard, and Pedro de Alvarado, *Tonatiuh,* or "the Sun," as he was called by the Aztecs, from his yellow hair and sunny countenance. The sunshine, as events afterwards showed, could sometimes be the prelude to a terrible tempest.

Notwithstanding the care taken to cheat him of the tedium of captivity, the royal prisoner cast a wistful glance now and then beyond the walls of his residence to the ancient haunts of business or pleasure. He intimated a desire to offer up his devotions at the great temple, where he was once so constant in his worship. The suggestion startled Cortés. It was too reasonable, however, for him to object to it, without wholly discarding the appearances which he was desirous to maintain. But he secured Montezuma's return by sending an escort with him of a hundred and fifty soldiers under the same resolute cavaliers who had aided in his seizure. He told him also that, in case of any attempt to escape, his life would instantly pay the forfeit. Thus guarded, the Indian prince visited the *teocalli,* where he was received with the usual state, and, after performing his devotions, he returned again to his quarters.

It may well be believed that the Spaniards did not neglect the opportunity afforded by his residence with them of instilling into him some notions of the Christian doctrine. Fathers Diaz and Olmedo exhausted all their battery of logic and persuasion to shake his faith in his idols, but in vain. He, indeed, paid a most edifying attention, which gave promise of better things. But the conferences always closed with the declaration that "the God of the Christians was good, but the gods of his own country were the true gods for him." It is said, however, they extorted a promise from him that he would take part in no more human sacrifices. Yet such sacrifices were of daily occurrence in the great temples of the capital; and the people were too blindly attached to their bloody abominations for the Spaniards to deem it safe, for the present at least, openly to interfere.

Montezuma showed, also, an inclination to engage in the pleasures of the chase, of which he once was immoderately fond. He had large forests reserved for the purpose on the other side of the lake. As the Spanish brigantines were now completed, Cortés proposed to transport him and his suite across the water in them. They were of a good size, strongly built. The largest was mounted with four falconets, or small guns. It was protected by a gaily coloured awning stretched over the deck, and the royal ensign of Castile floated proudly from the mast. On board of this vessel, Montezuma, delighted with the opportunity of witnessing the nautical skill of the white men, embarked with a train of Aztec nobles and a numerous guard of Spaniards. A fresh breeze played on the waters, and the vessel soon left behind it the swarms of light pirogues which darkened their surface. She seemed like a thing of life in the eyes of the astonished natives, who saw her, as if disdaining human agency, sweeping by with snowy pinions as if on the wings of the wind, while the thunders from her sides, now for the first time breaking on the silence of this "inland sea," showed that the beautiful phantom was clothed in terror.

The royal chase was well stocked with game; some of which the emperor shot with arrows, and others were driven by the numerous attendants into nets. In these woodland exercises, while he ranged over his wild domain, Montezuma seemed to enjoy again the sweets of liberty. It was but the shadow of liberty, however; as in his quarters at home he enjoyed but the shadow of royalty. At home or abroad the eye of the Spaniard was always upon him.

But while he resigned himself without a struggle to his inglorious fate, there were others who looked on it with very different emotions. Among them was his nephew Cacama, lord of Tezcuco, a young man not more than twenty-five years of age, but who enjoyed great consideration from his high personal qualities, especially his intrepidity of character. He was the same prince who had been sent by Montezuma to welcome the Spaniards on their entrance into the valley; and, when the question of their reception was first debated in the council, he had advised to admit them honourably as ambassadors of a foreign prince, and, if they should prove different from what they pretended, it would be time enough then to take up arms against them. That time, he thought, had now come.

In a former part of this work, the reader has been made acquainted with the ancient history of the Acolhuan or Tezcucan monarchy, once the proud rival of the Aztec in power, and greatly its superior in civilisation. Under its last sovereign, Nezahualpilli, its territory is said to have been grievously clipped by the insidious practices of Montezuma, who fomented dissensions and insubordination among his subjects. On the death of the Tezcucan prince, the succession was contested, and a bloody war ensued between his eldest son, Cacama, and an ambitious younger brother, Ixtlilxochitl. This was followed by a partition of the kingdom, in which the latter chieftain held the mountain districts north of the capital, leaving the residue to Cacama. Though shorn of a large part of his hereditary domain, the city was itself so important that the lord of Tezcuco still held a high rank among the petty princes of the valley. His capital, at the time of the Conquest, contained, according to Cortés, a hundred and fifty thousand inhabitants. It was embellished with noble buildings, rivalling those of Mexico itself, and the ruins still to be met with on its ancient site attest that it was once the abode of princes.

The young Tezcucan chief beheld, with indignation and no slight contempt, the abject condition of his uncle. He endeavoured to rouse him to manly exertion, but in vain. He then set about forming a league with several of the neighbouring caciques to rescue his kinsman, and to break the detested yoke of the strangers. He called on the lord of Iztapalapan, Montezuma's brother, the lord of Tlacopan, and some others of most authority, all of whom entered heartily into his views. He then urged the Aztec nobles to join them, but they expressed an unwillingness to take any step not first sanctioned by the emperor. They entertained, undoubtedly, a profound reverence for their master; but it seems probable that jealousy of the personal views of Cacama had its influence on their determination. Whatever were their motives, it is certain that by this refusal they relinquished the best opportunity ever presented for retrieving their sovereign's independence, and their own.

These intrigues could not be conducted so secretly as not to reach the ears of Cortés, who, with his characteristic promptness, would have marched at once on Tezcuco, and trodden out the spark of "rebellion," before it had time to burst into a flame. But from this he was dissuaded by Montezuma, who represented that Cacama was a man of resolution, backed by a powerful force, and not to be put down without a desperate struggle. He consented, therefore, to negotiate, and sent a message of amicable expostulation to the cacique. He received a haughty answer in return. Cortés rejoined in a more menacing tone, asserting the supremacy of his own sovereign, the emperor of Castile. To this Cacama replied, "He acknowledged no such authority; he knew nothing of the Spanish sovereign nor his people, nor did he wish to know anything of them." Montezuma was not more successful in his application to Cacama to come to Mexico, and allow him to mediate his differences with the Spaniards, with whom he assured the prince he was residing as a friend. But the young lord of Tezcuco was not to be so duped. He understood the position of his uncle, and replied, "that, when he did visit his capital, it would be to rescue it, as well as the emperor himself, and their common gods, from bondage. He should come, not with his hand in his bosom, but on his sword—to drive out the detested strangers who had brought such dishonour on their country."

Cortés, incensed at this tone of defiance, would again have put himself in motion to punish it, but Montezuma interposed with his more politic arts. He had several of the Tezcucan nobles, he said, in his pay; and it would be easy, through their means, to secure Cacama's person, and thus break up the confederacy at once, without bloodshed. The maintaining of a corps of stipendiaries in the courts of neighbouring princes was a refinement which showed that the western barbarian understood the science of political intrigue, as well as some of his royal brethren on the other side of the water.

By the contrivance of these faithless nobles, Cacama was induced to hold a conference, relative to the proposed invasion, in a villa which overhung the Tezcucan lake, not far from his capital. Like most of the principal edifices, it was raised so as to admit the entrance of boats beneath it. In the midst of the conference Cacama was seized by the conspirators, hurried on board a bark in readiness for the purpose, and transported to Mexico. When brought into Montezuma's presence the high-spirited chief abated nothing of his proud and lofty bearing. He taxed his uncle with his perfidy, and a pusillanimity so unworthy of his former character and of the royal house from which he was descended. By the emperor he was referred to Cortés, who, holding royalty but cheap in an Indian prince, put him in fetters.

There was at this time in Mexico a brother of Cacama, a stripling much younger than himself. At the instigation of Cortés, Montezuma, pretending that his nephew had forfeited the sovereignty by his late *rebellion,* declared him to be deposed, and appointed Cuicuitzca in his place. The Aztec sovereigns had always been allowed a paramount authority in questions relating to the succession. But this was a most unwarrantable exercise of it. The Tezcucans acquiesced, however, with a ready ductility, which showed their allegiance hung but lightly on them, or, what is more probable, that they were greatly in awe of the Spaniards; and the new prince was welcomed with acclamations to his capital.

Cortés still wanted to get into his hands the other chiefs who had entered into the confederacy with Cacama. This was no difficult matter. Montezuma's authority was absolute everywhere but in his own palace. By his command, the caciques were seized, each in his own city, and brought in chains to Mexico, where Cortés placed them in strict confinement with their leader.

He had now triumphed over all his enemies. He had set his foot on the necks of princes; and the great chief of the Aztec empire was but a convenient tool in his hands for accomplishing his purposes. His first use of this power was to ascertain the actual resources of the monarchy. He sent several parties of Spaniards, guided by the natives, to explore the regions where gold was obtained. It was gleaned mostly from the beds of rivers, several hundred miles from the capital.

His next object was to learn if there existed any good natural harbour for shipping on the Atlantic coast, as the road of Vera Cruz left no protection against the tempests that at certain seasons swept over these seas. Montezuma showed him a chart on which the shores of the Mexican Gulf were laid down with tolerable accuracy. Cortés, after carefully inspecting it, sent a commission, consisting of ten Spaniards, several of them pilots, and some Aztecs, who descended to Vera Cruz, and made a careful survey of the coast for nearly sixty leagues south of that settlement, as far as the great river Coatzacualco, which seemed to offer the best, indeed the only, accommodations for a safe and suitable harbour. A spot was selected as the site of a fortified post, and the general sent a detachment of a hundred and fifty men, under Velasquez de Leon, to plant a colony there.

He also obtained a grant of an extensive tract of land in the fruitful province of Oaxaca, where he proposed to lay out a plantation for the crown. He stocked it with the different kinds of domesticated animals peculiar to the country, and with such indigenous grains and plants as would afford the best articles for export. He soon had the estate under such cultivation that he assured his master, the emperor, Charles the Fifth, it was worth twenty thousand ounces of gold.

CHAPTER V

Montezuma Swears Allegiance to Spain—Royal Treasures—
Their Division—Christian Worship in the Teocalli—
Discontent of the Aztecs

1520

CORTÉS now felt his authority sufficiently assured to demand from Montezuma a formal recognition of the supremacy of the Spanish emperor. The Indian monarch had intimated his willingness to acquiesce in this, on their very first interview. He did not object, therefore, to calling together his principal caciques for the purpose. When they were assembled, he made them an address, briefly stating the object of the meeting. They were all acquainted, he said, with the ancient tradition that the great Being, who had once ruled over the land, had declared, on his departure, that he should return at some future time and resume his sway. That time had now arrived. The white men had come from the quarter where the sun rises, beyond the ocean, to which the good deity had withdrawn. They were sent by their master to reclaim the obedience of his ancient subjects. For himself he was ready to acknowledge his authority. "You have been faithful vassals of mine," continued Montezuma, "during the many years that I have sat on the throne of my fathers. I now expect that you will show me this last act of obedience by acknowledging the great king beyond the waters to be your lord, also, and that you will pay him tribute in the same manner as you have hitherto done to me." As he concluded his voice was nearly stifled by his emotion, and the tears fell fast down his cheeks.

His nobles, many of whom, coming from a distance, had not kept pace with the changes which had been going on in the capital, were filled with astonishment as they listened to his words, and beheld the voluntary abasement of their master, whom they had hitherto reverenced as the omnipotent lord of Anahuac. They were the more affected, therefore, by the sight of his distress. His will, they told him, had always been their law. It should be so now; and, if he thought the sovereign of the strangers was the ancient lord of their country, they were willing to acknowledge him as such still. The oaths of allegiance were then administered with all due solemnity, attested by the Spaniards present, and a full record of the proceedings was drawn up by the royal notary, to be sent to Spain. There was something deeply touching in the ceremony by which an independent and absolute monarch, in obedience less to the dictates of fear than of conscience, thus relinquished his hereditary rights in favour of an unknown and mysterious power. It even moved those hard men who were thus unscrupulously availing themselves of the confiding ignorance of the natives; and, though "it was in the regular way of their own business," says an old chronicler, "there was not a Spaniard who could look on the spectacle with a dry eye!"

The rumour of these strange proceedings was soon circulated through the capital and the country. Men read in them the finger of Providence. The ancient tradition of Quetzalcoatl was familiar to all; and where it had slept scarcely noticed in the memory, it was now revived with many exaggerated circumstances. It was said to be part of the tradition that the royal line of the Aztecs was to end with Montezuma; and his name, the literal signification of which is "sad" or "angry lord," was construed into an omen of his evil destiny.

Having thus secured this great feudatory to the crown of Castile, Cortés suggested that it would be well for the Aztec chiefs to send his sovereign such a gratuity as would conciliate his good will by convincing him of the loyalty of his new vassals. Montezuma consented that his collectors should visit the principal cities and provinces, attended by a number of Spaniards, to receive the customary tributes, in the name of the Castilian sovereign. In a few weeks most of them returned, bringing back large quantities of gold and silver plate, rich stuffs, and the various commodities in which the taxes were usually paid.

To this store Montezuma added, on his own account, the treasure of Axayacatl, previously noticed, some part of which had been already given to the Spaniards. It was the fruit of long and careful hoarding—of extortion, it may be—by a prince who little dreamed of its final destination. When brought into the quarters, the gold alone was sufficient to make three great heaps. It consisted partly of native grains; part had been melted into bars; but the greatest portion was in utensils, and various kinds of ornaments and curious toys, together with imitations of birds, insects, or flowers, executed with uncommon truth and delicacy. There were also quantities of collars, bracelets, wands, fans, and other trinkets, in which the gold and featherwork were richly powdered with pearls and precious stones. Many of the articles were even more admirable for the workmanship than for the value of the materials; such, indeed—if we may take the report of Cortés to one who would himself have soon an opportunity to judge of its veracity, and whom it would not be safe to trifle with—as no monarch in Europe could boast in his dominions!

Magnificent as it was, Montezuma expressed his regret that the treasure was no larger. But he had diminished it, he said, by his former gifts to the white men. "Take it," he added, "Malintzin, and let it be recorded in your annals that Montezuma sent this present to your master."

The Spaniards gazed with greedy eyes on the display of riches, now their own, which far exceeded all hitherto seen in the New World, and fell nothing short of the *El Dorado* which their glowing imaginations had depicted. It may be that they felt somewhat rebuked by the contrast which their own avarice presented to the princely munificence of the barbarian chief. At least they seemed to testify their sense of his superiority by the respectful homage which they rendered him, as they poured forth the fulness of their gratitude. They were not so scrupulous, however, as to manifest any delicacy in appropriating to themselves the donative, a small part of which was to find its way into the royal coffers. They clamoured loudly for an immediate division of the spoil, which the general would have postponed till the tributes from the remoter provinces had been gathered in. The goldsmiths of Azcapozalco were sent for to take in pieces of the larger and coarser ornaments, leaving untouched those of more delicate workmanship. Three days were consumed in this labour, when the heaps of gold were cast into ingots and stamped with the royal arms.

Some difficulty occurred in the division of the treasure, from the want of weights, which, strange as it appears, considering their advancement in the arts, were, as already observed, unknown to the Aztecs. The deficiency was soon supplied by the Spaniards, however, with scales and weights of their own manufacture, probably not the most exact. With the aid of these they ascertained the value of the royal fifth to be thirty-two thousand and four hundred *pesos de oro*. Diaz swells it to nearly four times that amount. But their desire of securing the emperor's favour makes it improbable that the Spaniards should have defrauded the exchequer of any part of its due; while, as Cortés was responsible for the sum admitted in his letter, he would be still less likely to overstate it. His estimate may be received as the true one.

The whole amounted, therefore, to one hundred and sixty-two thousand *pesos de oro,* independently of the fine ornaments and jewellery, the value of which Cortés computes at five hundred thousand ducats more. There were, besides, five hundred marks of silver, chiefly in plate, drinking cups, and other articles of luxury. The inconsiderable quantity of the silver, as compared with the gold, forms a singular contrast to the relative proportions of the two metals since the occupation of the country by the Europeans. The whole amount of the treasure, reduced to our own currency, and making allowance for the change in the value of gold since the beginning of the sixteenth century, was about six million three hundred thousand dollars, or one million four hundred and seventeen thousand pounds sterling; a sum large enough to show the incorrectness of the popular notion that little or no wealth was found in Mexico. It was, indeed, small in comparison with that obtained by the conquerors in Peru. But few European monarchs of that day could boast a larger treasure in their coffers.

The division of the spoil was a work of some difficulty. A perfectly equal division of it among the Conquerors would have given them more than three thousand pounds sterling apiece; a magnificent booty! But one-fifth was to be deducted for the crown. An equal portion was reserved for the general, pursuant to the tenor of his commission. A large sum was then allowed to indemnify him and the governor of Cuba for the charges of the expedition and the loss of the fleet. The garrison of Vera Cruz was also to be provided for. Ample compensation was made to the principal cavaliers. The cavalry, arquebusiers, and crossbow-men, each received double pay. So that when the turn of the common soldiers came, there remained not more than a hundred *pesos de oro* for each; a sum so insignificant, in comparison with their expectations, that several refused to accept it.

Loud murmurs now rose among the men. "Was it for this," they said, "that we left our homes and families, perilled our lives, submitted to fatigue and famine, and all for so contemptible a pittance! Better to have stayed in Cuba, and contented ourselves with the gains of a safe and easy traffic. When we gave up our share of the gold at Vera Cruz it was on the assurance that we should be amply requited in Mexico. We have, indeed, found the riches we expected; but no sooner seen, than they are snatched from us by the very men who pledged us their faith!" The malcontents even went so far as to accuse their leaders of appropriating to themselves several of the richest ornaments, before the partition had been made; an accusation that receives some countenance from a dispute which arose between Mexia, the treasurer for the crown, and Velasquez de Leon, a relation of the governor, and a favourite of Cortés. The treasurer accused this cavalier of purloining certain pieces of plate before they were submitted to the royal stamp. From words the parties came to blows. They were good swordsmen; several wounds were given on both sides, and the affair might have ended fatally, but for the interference of Cortés, who placed both under arrest.

He then used all his authority and insinuating eloquence to calm the passions of his men. It was a delicate crisis. He was sorry, he said, to see them so unmindful of the duty of loyal soldiers, and cavaliers of the Cross, as to brawl like common banditti over their booty. The division, he assured them, had been made on perfectly fair and equitable principles. As to his own share, it was no more than was warranted by his commission. Yet, if they thought it too much, he was willing to forego his just claims, and divide with the poorest soldier. Gold, however welcome, was not the chief object of his ambition. If it were theirs, they should still reflect that the present treasure was little in comparison with what awaited them hereafter; for had they not the whole country and its mines at their disposal? It was only necessary that they should not give an opening to the enemy, by their discord, to circumvent and to crush them. With these honeyed words, of which he had good store for all fitting occasions, says an old soldier, for whose benefit, in part, they were intended, he succeeded in calming the storm for the present; while in private he took more effectual means, by presents judiciously administered, to mitigate the discontents of the importunate and refractory. And, although there were a few of more tenacious temper, who treasured this in their memories against a future day, the troops soon returned to their usual subordination. This was one of those critical conjunctures which taxed all the address and personal authority of Cortés. He never shrank from them, but on such occasions was true to himself. At Vera Cruz he had persuaded his followers to give up what was but the earnest of future gains. Here he persuaded them to relinquish these gains themselves. It was snatching the prey from the very jaws of the lion. Why did he not turn and rend him?

To many of the soldiers, indeed, it mattered little whether their share of the booty were more or less. Gaming is a deep-rooted passion in the

Spaniard, and the sudden acquisition of riches furnished both the means and the motive for its indulgence. Cards were easily made out of old parchment drumheads, and in a few days most of the prize money, obtained with so much toil and suffering, had changed hands, and many of the improvident soldiers closed the campaign as poor as they had commenced it. Others, it is true, more prudent, followed the example of their officers, who, with the aid of the royal jewellers, converted their gold into chains, services of plate, and other portable articles of ornament or use.

Cortés seemed now to have accomplished the great objects of the expedition. The Indian monarch had declared himself the feudatory of the Spanish. His authority, his revenues, were at the disposal of the general. The Conquest of Mexico seemed to be achieved, and that without a blow. But it was far from being achieved. One important step yet remained to be taken, towards which the Spaniards had hitherto made little progress—the conversion of the natives. With all the exertions of Father Olmedo, backed by the polemic talents of the general, neither Montezuma nor his subjects showed any disposition to abjure the faith of their fathers. The bloody exercises of their religion, on the contrary, were celebrated with all the usual circumstance and pomp of sacrifice before the eyes of the Spaniards.

Unable further to endure these abominations, Cortés, attended by several of his cavaliers, waited on Montezuma. He told the emperor that the Christians could no longer consent to have the services of their religion shut up within the narrow walls of the garrison. They wished to spread its light far abroad, and to open to the people a full participation in the blessings of Christianity. For this purpose they requested that the great *teocalli* should be delivered up, as a fit place where their worship might be conducted in the presence of the whole city.

Montezuma listened to the proposal with visible consternation. Amidst all his troubles he had leaned for support on his own faith, and, indeed, it was in obedience to it that he had shown such deference to the Spaniards as the mysterious messengers predicted by the oracles. "Why," said he, "Malintzin, why will you urge matters to an extremity that must surely bring down the vengeance of our gods, and stir up an insurrection among my people, who will never endure this profanation of their temples?"

Cortés, seeing how greatly he was moved, made a sign to his officers to withdraw. When left alone with the interpreters, he told the emperor that he would use his influence to moderate the zeal of his followers, and persuade them to be contented with one of the sanctuaries of the *teocalli*. If that were not granted, they should be obliged to take it by force, and to roll down the images of his false deities in the face of the city. "We fear not for our lives," he added, "for, though our numbers are few, the arm of the true God is over us." Montezuma, much agitated, told him that he would confer with the priests.

The result of the conference was favourable to the Spaniards, who were allowed to occupy one of the sanctuaries as a place of worship. The tidings spread great joy throughout the camp. They might now go forth in open day and publish their religion to the assembled capital. No time was lost in availing themselves of the permission. The sanctuary was cleansed of its disgusting impurities. An altar was raised, surmounted by a crucifix and the image of the Virgin. Instead of the gold and jewels which blazed on the neighbouring pagan shrine, its walls were decorated with fresh garlands of flowers; and an old soldier was stationed to watch over the chapel, and guard it from intrusion.

When these arrangements were completed, the whole army moved in solemn procession up the winding ascent of the pyramid. Entering the sanctuary, and clustering round its portals, they listened reverently to the service of the Mass, as it was performed by the fathers Olmedo and Diaz. And as the beautiful *Te Deum* rose towards Heaven, Cortés and his soldiers kneeling on the ground, with tears streaming from their eyes, poured forth their gratitude to the Almighty for this glorious triumph of the Cross.

It was a striking spectacle—that of these rude warriors lifting up their orisons on the summit of this mountain temple, in the very capital of heathendom, on the spot especially dedicated to its unhallowed mysteries. Side by side the Spaniard and the Aztec knelt down in prayer; and the Christian hymn mingled its sweet tones of love and mercy with the wild chant raised by the Indian priest in honour of the war-god of Anahuac! It was an unnatural union, and could not long abide.

A nation will endure any outrage sooner than that on its religion. This is an outrage both on its principles and its prejudices; on the ideas instilled into it from childhood, which have strengthened with its growth, until they become a part of its nature—which have to do with its highest interests here, and with the dread hereafter. Any violence to the religious sentiment touches all alike, the old and the young, the rich and the poor, the noble and the plebeian. Above all, it touches the priests, whose personal consideration rests on that of their religion; and who, in a semi-civilised state of society, usually hold an unbounded authority. Thus it was with the Brahmins of India, the Magi of Persia, the Roman Catholic clergy in the Dark Ages, the priests of ancient Egypt and Mexico.

The people had borne with patience all the injuries and affronts hitherto put on them by the Spaniards. They had seen their sovereign dragged as a captive from his own palace; his ministers butchered before his eyes; his treasures seized and appropriated; himself in a manner deposed from his royal supremacy. All this they had seen without a struggle to prevent it. But the profanation of their temples touched a deeper feeling, of which the priesthood were not slow to take advantage.

The first intimation of this change of feeling was gathered from Montezuma himself. Instead of his usual cheerfulness, he appeared grave and abstracted, and instead of seeking, as he was wont, the society of the Spaniards, seemed rather to shun it. It was noticed, too, that conferences were more frequent between him and the nobles, and especially the priests. His little page, Orteguilla, who had now picked up a tolerable acquaintance with the Aztec, contrary to Montezuma's usual practice, was not allowed to attend him at these meetings. These circumstances could not fail to awaken most uncomfortable apprehensions in the Spaniards.

Not many days elapsed, however, before Cortés received an invitation, or rather a summons, from the emperor, to attend him in his apartment. The general went with some feelings of anxiety and distrust, taking with him Olid, captain of the guard, and two or three other trusty cavaliers. Montezuma received them with cold civility, and, turning to the general, told him that all his predictions had come to pass. The gods of his country had been offended by the violation of their temples. They had threatened the priests that they would forsake the city, if the sacrilegious strangers were not driven from it, or rather sacrificed on the altars, in expiation of their crimes. The monarch assured the Christians it was from regard to their safety that he communicated this; and, "if you have any regard for it yourselves," he concluded, "you will leave the country without delay. I have only to raise my finger, and every Aztec in the land will rise in arms against you." There was no reason to doubt his sincerity; for Montezuma, whatever evils had been brought on him by the white men, held them in reverence as a race more highly gifted than his own, while for several, as we have seen, he had conceived an attachment, flowing, no doubt, from their personal attentions and deference to himself.

Cortés was too much master of his feelings to show how far he was startled by this intelligence. He replied with admirable coolness that he should regret much to leave the capital so precipitately, when he had no vessels to take him from the country. If it were not for this, there could be no obstacle to his leaving it at once. He should also regret another step to which he should be driven, if he quitted it under these circumstances—that of taking the emperor along with him.

Montezuma was evidently troubled by this last suggestion. He inquired how long it would take to build the vessels, and finally consented to send a sufficient number of workmen to the coast, to act under the orders of the Spaniards; meanwhile, he would use his authority to restrain the impatience of the people, under the assurance that the white men would leave the land, when the means for it were provided. He kept his word. A large body of Aztec artisans left the capital with the most experienced Castilian shipbuilders, and, descending to Vera Cruz, began at once to fell the timber and build a sufficient number of ships to transport the Spaniards back to their own country. The work went forward with apparent alacrity. But those who had the direction of it, it is said, received private instructions from the general to interpose as many delays as possible, in hopes of receiving in the meantime such reinforcements from Europe as would enable him to maintain his ground.

The whole aspect of things was now changed in the Castilian quarters. Instead of the security and repose in which the troops had of late indulged, they felt a gloomy apprehension of danger, not the less oppressive to the spirits, that it was scarcely visible to the eye—like the faint speck just descried above the horizon by the voyager in the tropics, to the common gaze seeming only a summer cloud, but which to the experienced mariner bodes the coming of the hurricane. Every precaution that prudence could devise was taken to meet it. The soldier, as he threw himself on his mats for repose, kept on his armour. He ate, drank, slept, with his weapons by his side. His horse stood ready caparisoned, day and night, with the bridle hanging at the saddle-bow. The guns were carefully planted, so as to command the great avenues. The sentinels were doubled, and every man, of whatever rank, took his turn in mounting guard. The garrison was in a state of siege. Such was the uncomfortable position of the army when, in the beginning of May, 1520, six months after their arrival in the capital, tidings came from the coast which gave greater alarm to Cortés than even the menaced insurrection of the Aztecs.

CHAPTER VI

*Fate of Cortés' Emissaries—Proceedings in the Castilian Court
—Preparations of Velasquez—Narvaez Lands in Mexico
—Politic Conduct of Cortés—He Leaves the Capital*

1520

BEFORE explaining the nature of the tidings alluded to in the preceding chapter, it will be necessary to cast a glance over some of the transactions of an earlier period. The vessel, which, as the reader may remember, bore the envoys Puertocarrero and Montejo with the despatches from Vera Cruz, after touching, contrary to orders, at the northern coast of Cuba, and spreading the news of the late discoveries, held on its way uninterrupted towards Spain, and early in October, 1519, reached the little port of San Lucar. Great was the sensation caused by her arrival and the tidings which she brought; a sensation scarcely inferior to that created by the original discovery of Columbus. For now, for the first time, all the magnificent anticipations formed of the New World seemed destined to be realised.

Unfortunately, there was a person in Seville, at this time, named Benito Martin, chaplain of Velasquez, the governor of Cuba. No sooner did this man learn the arrival of the envoys, and the particulars of their story, than he lodged a complaint with the *Casa de Contratacion*—the Royal India House—charging those on board the vessel with mutiny and rebellion against the authorities of Cuba, as well as with treason to the crown. In consequence of his representations, the ship was taken possession of by the public officers, and those on board were prohibited from moving their own effects or anything else from her. The envoys were not even allowed the funds necessary for the expenses of the voyage, nor a considerable sum remitted by Cortés to his father, Don Martin. In this embarrassment they had no alternative but to present themselves, as speedily as possible, before the emperor, deliver the letters with which they had been charged by the colony, and seek redress for their own grievances. They first sought out Martin Cortés, residing at Medellin, and with him made the best of their way to court.

Charles the Fifth was then on his first visit to Spain after his accession. It was not a long one; long enough, however, to disgust his subjects, and, in a great degree, to alienate their affections. He had lately received intelligence of his election to the imperial crown of Germany. From that hour his eyes were turned to that quarter. His stay in the Peninsula was prolonged only that he might raise supplies for appearing with splendour on the great theatre of Europe. Every act showed too plainly that the diadem of his ancestors was held lightly in comparison with the imperial bauble in which neither his countrymen nor his own posterity could have the slightest interest. The interest was wholly personal.

Contrary to established usage, he had summoned the Castilian *cortes* to meet at Compostella, a remote town in the north, which presented no other advantage than that of being near his place of embarkation. On his way thither he stopped some time at Tordesillas, the residence of his unhappy mother, Joanna "The Mad." It was here that the envoys from Vera Cruz presented themselves before him, in March, 1520. At nearly the same time, the treasures brought over by them reached the court, where they excited unbounded admiration. Hitherto, the returns from the New World had been chiefly in vegetable products, which, if the surest, are also the slowest, sources of wealth. Of gold they had as yet seen but little, and that in its natural state, or wrought into the rudest trinkets. The courtiers gazed with astonishment on the large masses of the precious metal, and the delicate manufacture of the various articles, especially of the richly tinted featherwork. And, as they listened to the accounts, written and oral, of the great Aztec empire, they felt assured that the Castilian ships had, at length, reached the golden Indies, which hitherto had seemed to recede before them.

In this favourable mood there is little doubt the monarch would have granted the petition of the envoys, and confirmed the irregular proceedings of the Conquerors, but for the opposition of a person who held the highest office in the Indian department. This was Juan Rodriguez de Fonseca, formerly dean of Seville, now bishop of Burgos. He was a man of noble family, and had been intrusted with the direction of the colonial concerns, on the discovery of the New World. On the establishment of the Royal Council of the Indies by Ferdinand the Catholic he had been made its president, and had occupied that post ever since. His long continuance in a position of great importance and difficulty is evidence of capacity for business. It was no uncommon thing in that age to find ecclesiastics in high civil, and even military, employments. Fonseca appears to have been an active, efficient person, better suited to a secular than to a religious vocation. He had, indeed, little that was religious in his temper; quick to take offence, and slow to forgive. His resentments seem to have been nourished and perpetuated like a part of his own nature. Unfortunately his peculiar position enabled him to display them towards some of the most illustrious men of his time. From pique at some real or fancied slight from Columbus, he had constantly thwarted the plans of the great navigator. He had shown the same unfriendly feeling towards the admiral's son, Diego, the heir of his honours; and he now, and from this time forward, showed a similar spirit towards the Conqueror of Mexico. The immediate cause of this was his own personal relations with Velasquez, to whom a near relative was betrothed.

Through this prelate's representations, Charles, instead of a favourable answer to the envoys, postponed his decision till he should arrive at Coruña, the place of embarkation. But here he was much pressed by the troubles which his impolitic conduct had raised, as well as by preparations for his voyage. The transaction of the colonial business, which, long postponed, had greatly accumulated on his hands, was reserved for the last week in Spain. But the affairs of the "young admiral" consumed so large a portion of this that he had no time to give to those of Cortés; except, indeed, to instruct the board at Seville to remit to the envoys so much of their funds as was required to defray the charges of the voyage. On May 16, 1520, the impatient monarch bade adieu to his distracted kingdom, without one attempt to settle the dispute between his belligerent vassals in the New World, and without an effort to promote the magnificent enterprise which was to secure to him the possession of an empire. What a contrast to the policy of his illustrious predecessors, Ferdinand and Isabella!

The governor of Cuba, meanwhile, without waiting for support from home, took measures for redress into his own hands. We have seen, in a preceding chapter, how deeply he was moved by the reports of the proceedings of Cortés, and of the treasures which his vessel was bearing to Spain. Rage, mortification, disappointed avarice, distracted his mind. He could not forgive himself for trusting the affair to such hands. On the very week in which Cortés had parted from him to take charge of the fleet, a *capitulation* had been signed by Charles the Fifth, conferring on

Velasquez the title of *adelantado,* with great augmentation of his original powers. The governor resolved, without loss of time, to send such a force to the Aztec coast as should enable him to assert his new authority to its full extent, and to take vengeance on his rebellious officer. He began his preparations as early as October. At first he proposed to assume the command in person. But his unwieldy size, which disqualified him for the fatigues incident to such an expedition, or, according to his own account, tenderness for his Indian subjects, then wasted by an epidemic, induced him to devolve the command on another.

The person whom he selected was a Castilian hidalgo, named Pánfilo de Narvaez. He had assisted Velasquez in the reduction of Cuba, where his conduct cannot be wholly vindicated from the charge of inhumanity, which too often attaches to the early Spanish adventurers. From that time he continued to hold important posts under the government, and was a decided favourite with Velasquez. He was a man of some military capacity, though negligent and lax in his discipline. He possessed undoubted courage, but it was mingled with an arrogance, or rather overweening confidence in his own powers, which made him deaf to the suggestions of others more sagacious than himself. He was altogether deficient in that prudence and calculating foresight demanded in a leader who was to cope with an antagonist like Cortés.

The governor and his lieutenant were unwearied in their efforts to assemble an army. They visited every considerable town in the island, fitting out vessels, laying in stores and ammunition, and encouraging volunteers to enlist by liberal promises. But the most effectual bounty was the assurance of the rich treasures that awaited them in the golden regions of Mexico. So confident were they in this expectation, that all classes and ages vied with one another in eagerness to embark in the expedition, until it seemed as if the whole white population would desert the island, and leave it to its primitive occupants.

The report of these proceedings soon spread through the islands, and drew the attention of the Royal Audience of St. Domingo. This body was intrusted, at that time, not only with the highest judicial authority in the colonies, but with a civil jurisdiction, which, as "the Admiral" complained, encroached on his own rights. The tribunal saw with alarm the proposed expedition of Velasquez, which, whatever might be its issue in regard to the parties, could not fail to compromise the interests of the crown. They chose accordingly one of their number, the licentiate Ayllon, a man of prudence and resolution, and despatched him to Cuba, with instructions to interpose his authority, and stay, if possible, the proceedings of Velasquez.

On his arrival he found the governor in the western part of the island busily occupied in getting the fleet ready for sea. The licentiate explained to him the purport of his mission, and the views entertained of the proposed enterprise by the Royal Audience. The conquest of a powerful country like Mexico required the whole force of the Spaniards, and, if one half were employed against the other, nothing but ruin could come of it. It was the governor's duty, as a good subject, to forego all private animosities, and to sustain those now engaged in the great work by sending them the necessary supplies. He might, indeed, proclaim his own powers, and demand obedience to them. But, if this were refused, he should leave the determination of his dispute to the authorised tribunals, and employ his resources in prosecuting discovery in another direction, instead of hazarding all by hostilities with his rival.

This admonition, however sensible and salutary, was not at all to the taste of the governor. He professed, indeed, to have no intention of coming to hostilities with Cortés. He designed only to assert his lawful jurisdiction over territories discovered under his own auspices. At the same time he denied the right of Ayllon or of the Royal Audience to interfere in the matter. Narvaez was still more refractory; and, as the fleet was now ready, proclaimed his intention to sail in a few hours. In this state of things the licentiate, baffled in his first purpose of staying the expedition, determined to accompany it in person, that he might prevent, if possible, by his presence, an open rupture between the parties.

The squadron consisted of eighteen vessels, large and small. It carried nine hundred men, eighty of whom were cavalry, eighty more arquebusiers, one hundred and fifty crossbow-men, with a number of heavy guns, and a large supply of ammunition and military stores. There were, besides, a thousand Indians, natives of the island, who went probably in a menial capacity. So gallant an armada—with one exception—never before rode in the Indian seas. None to compare with it had ever been fitted out in the Western World.

Leaving Cuba early in March, 1520, Narvaez held nearly the same course as Cortés, and running down what was then called the "Island of Yucatan," after a heavy tempest, in which some of his smaller vessels foundered, anchored, April 23, off San Juan de Ulua. It was the place where Cortés also had first landed; the sandy waste covered by the present city of Vera Cruz.

Here the commander met with a Spaniard, one of those sent by the general from Mexico, to ascertain the resources of the country, especially its mineral products. This man came on board the fleet, and from him the Spaniards gathered the particulars of all that had occurred since the departure of the envoys from Vera Cruz—the march into the interior, the bloody battles with the Tlascalans, the occupation of Mexico, the rich treasures found in it, and the seizure of the monarch, by means of which, concluded the soldier, "Cortés rules over the land like its own sovereign, so that a Spaniard may travel unarmed from one end of the country to the other, without insult or injury." His audience listened to this marvellous report with speechless amazement, and the loyal indignation of Narvaez waxed stronger and stronger, as he learned the value of the prize which had been snatched from his employer.

He now openly proclaimed his intention to march against Cortés, and punish him for his rebellion. He made this vaunt so loudly that the natives who had flocked in numbers to the camp, which was soon formed on shore, clearly comprehended that the new-comers were not friends, but enemies, of the preceding. Narvaez determined, also—though in opposition to the counsel of the Spaniard, who quoted the example of Cortés—to establish a settlement on this unpromising spot: and he made the necessary arrangements to organise a municipality. He was informed by the soldier of the existence of the neighbouring colony at Villa Rica, commanded by Sandoval, and consisting of a few invalids, who, he was assured, would surrender on the first summons. Instead of marching against the place, however, he determined to send a peaceful embassy to display his powers, and demand the submission of the garrison.

These successive steps gave serious displeasure to Ayllon, who saw they must lead to inevitable collision with Cortés. But it was in vain he remonstrated, and threatened to lay the proceedings of Narvaez before the government. The latter, chafed by his continued opposition and sour rebuke, determined to rid himself of a companion who acted as a spy on his movements. He caused him to be seized and sent back to Cuba. The licentiate had the address to persuade the captain of the vessel to change her destination for St. Domingo; and, when he arrived there, a formal report of his proceedings, exhibiting in strong colours the disloyal conduct of the governor and his lieutenant, was prepared and despatched by the Royal Audience to Spain.

Sandoval, meanwhile, had not been inattentive to the movements of Narvaez. From the time of his first appearance on the coast, that vigilant officer, distrusting the object of the armament, had kept his eye on him. No sooner was he apprised of the landing of the Spaniards, than the commander of Villa Rica sent off his few disabled soldiers to a place of safety in the neighbourhood. He then put his works in the best posture of defence that he could, and prepared to maintain the place to the last extremity. His men promised to stand by him, and, the more effectually to fortify the resolution of any who might falter, he ordered a gallows to be set up in a conspicuous part of the town! The constancy of his men was not put to the trial.

The only invaders of the place were a priest, a notary, and four other Spaniards, selected for the mission, already noticed, by Narvaez. The ecclesiastic's name was Guevara. On coming before Sandoval, he made him a formal address, in which he pompously enumerated the services and claims of Velasquez, taxed Cortés and his adherents with rebellion, and demanded of Sandoval to tender his submission as a loyal subject to the newly constituted authority of Narvaez.

The commander of La Villa Rica was so much incensed at this unceremonious mention of his companions in arms, that he assured the reverend envoy that nothing but respect for his cloth saved him from the chastisement he merited. Guevara now waxed wroth in his turn, and called on the notary to read the proclamation. But Sandoval interposed, promising that functionary that, if he attempted to do so, without first producing a warrant of his authority from the crown, he should be soundly flogged. Guevara lost all command of himself at this, and, stamping on the ground, repeated his orders in a more peremptory tone than before. Sandoval was not a man of many words; he simply remarked that the instrument should be read to the general himself in Mexico. At the same time he ordered his men to procure a number of sturdy *tamanes,* or Indian porters, on whose backs the unfortunate priest and his companions were bound like so many bales of goods. They were then placed under a guard of twenty Spaniards, and the whole caravan took its march for the capital. Day and night they travelled, stopping only to obtain fresh relays of carriers; and as they passed through populous towns, forests and cultivated fields, vanishing as soon as seen, the Spaniards, bewildered by the strangeness of the scene, as well as of their novel mode of conveyance, hardly knew whether they were awake or in a dream. In this way, at the end of the fourth day, they reached the Tezcucan lake in view of the Aztec capital.

Its inhabitants had already been made acquainted with the fresh arrival

of white men on the coast. Indeed, directly on their landing, intelligence
had been communicated to Montezuma, who is said (it does not seem
probable) to have concealed it some days from Cortés. At length, inviting
him to an interview, he told him there was no longer any obstacle to his
leaving the country, as a fleet was ready for him. To the inquiries of the
astonished general, Montezuma replied by pointing to a hieroglyphical
map sent him from the coast, on which the ships, the Spaniards themselves, and their whole equipment, were minutely delineated. Cortés, suppressing all emotions but those of pleasure, exclaimed, "Blessed be the
Redeemer for his mercies!" On returning to his quarters, the tidings were
received by the troops with loud shouts, the firing of cannon, and other
demonstrations of joy. They hailed the new-comers as a reinforcement
from Spain. Not so their commander. From the first he suspected them
to be sent by his enemy, the governor of Cuba. He communicated his
suspicions to his officers, through whom they gradually found their way
among the men. The tide of joy was instantly checked. Alarming apprehensions succeeded, as they dwelt on the probability of this suggestion, and
on the strength of the invaders. Yet their constancy did not desert them;
and they pledged themselves to remain true to their cause, and, come
what might, to stand by their leader. It was one of those occasions that
proved the entire influence which Cortés held over these wild adventurers.
All doubts were soon dispelled by the arrival of the prisoners from Villa
Rica.

One of the convoy, leaving the party in the suburbs, entered the city,
and delivered a letter to the general from Sandoval, acquainting him with
all the particulars. Cortés instantly sent to the prisoners, ordered them
to be released, and furnished them with horses to make their entrance into
the capital—a more creditable conveyance than the backs of *tamanes*. On
their arrival he received them with marked courtesy, apologised for the
rude conduct of his officers, and seemed desirous by the most assiduous
attentions to soothe the irritation of their minds. He showed his good will
still further by lavishing presents on Guevara and his associates, until he
gradually wrought such a change in their dispositions that, from enemies,
he converted them into friends, and drew forth many important particulars respecting not merely the designs of their leader, but the feelings of
his army. The soldiers, in general, they said, far from desiring a rupture
with those of Cortés, would willingly co-operate with them, were it not
for their commander. They had no feelings of resentment to gratify.
Their object was gold. The personal influence of Narvaez was not great,

and his arrogance and penurious temper had already gone far to alienate from him the affections of his followers. These hints were not lost on the general.

He addressed a letter to his rival in the most conciliatory terms. He besought him not to proclaim their animosity to the world, and, by kindling a spirit of insubordination in the natives, unsettle all that had been so far secured. A violent collision must be prejudicial even to the victor, and might be fatal to both. It was only in union that they could look for success. He was ready to greet Narvaez as a brother in arms, to share with him the fruits of conquest, and, if he could produce a royal commission, to submit to his authority. Cortés well knew he had no such commission to show.

Soon after the departure of Guevara and his comrades, the general determined to send a special envoy of his own. The person selected for this delicate office was Father Olmedo, who, through the campaign, had shown a practical good sense, and a talent for affairs not always to be found in persons of his spiritual calling. He was intrusted with another epistle to Narvaez, of similar import with the preceding. Cortés wrote, also, to the licentiate Ayllon, with whose departure he was not acquainted, and to Andrés de Duero, former secretary of Velasquez, and his own friend, who had come over in the present fleet. Olmedo was instructed to converse with these persons in private, as well as with the principal officers and soldiers, and, as far as possible, to infuse into them a spirit of accommodation. To give greater weight to his arguments, he was furnished with a liberal supply of gold.

During this time, Narvaez had abandoned his original design of planting a colony on the sea-coast, and had crossed the country to Cempoalla, where he had taken up his quarters. He was here when Guevara returned, and presented the letter of Cortés.

Narvaez glanced over it with a look of contempt, which was changed into one of stern displeasure, as his envoy enlarged on the resources and formidable character of his rival, counselling him, by all means, to accept his proffers of amity. A different effect was produced on the troops, who listened with greedy ears to the accounts given of Cortés, his frank and liberal manners, which they involuntarily contrasted with those of their own commander, the wealth in his camp, where the humblest private could stake his ingot and chain of gold at play, where all revelled in plenty, and the life of the soldier seemed to be one long holiday. Guevara had been admitted only to the sunny side of the picture.

The impression made by these accounts was confirmed by the presence of Olmedo. The ecclesiastic delivered his missives, in like manner, to Narvaez, who ran through their contents with feelings of anger which found vent in the most opprobrious invectives against his rival; while one of his captains, named Salvatierra, openly avowed his intention to cut off the rebel's ears, and broil them for his breakfast! Such impotent sallies did not alarm the stout-hearted friar, who soon entered into communication with many of the officers and soldiers, whom he found better inclined to an accommodation. His insinuating eloquence, backed by his liberal largesses, gradually opened a way into their hearts, and a party was formed under the very eyes of their chief, better affected to his rival's interests than to his own. The intrigue could not be conducted so secretly as wholly to elude the suspicions of Narvaez, who would have arrested Olmedo and placed him under confinement, but for the interposition of Duero. He put a stop to his further machinations by sending him back again to his master. But the poison was left to do its work.

Narvaez made the same vaunt as at his landing, of his design to march against Cortés and apprehend him as a traitor. The Cempoallans learned with astonishment that their new guests were enemies of their own countrymen. Narvaez also proclaimed his intention to release Montezuma from captivity, and restore him to his throne. It is said he received a rich present from the Aztec emperor, who entered into a correspondence with him. That Montezuma should have treated him with his usual munificence, supposing him to be the friend of Cortés, is very probable. But that he should have entered into a secret communication, hostile to the general's interests, is too repugnant to the whole tenor of his conduct, to be lightly admitted.

These proceedings did not escape the watchful eyes of Sandoval. He gathered the particulars partly from deserters, who fled to Villa Rica, and partly from his own agents, who in the disguise of natives mingled in the enemy's camp. He sent a full account of them to Cortés, acquainted him with the growing defection of the Indians, and urged him to take speedy measures for the defence of Villa Rica, if he would not see it fall into the enemy's hands. The general felt that it was time to act.

Yet the selection of the course to be pursued was embarrassing in the extreme. If he remained in Mexico and awaited there the attack of his rival, it would give the latter time to gather round him the whole forces of the empire, including those of the capital itself, all willing, no doubt, to serve under the banners of a chief who proposed the liberation of their master. The odds were too great to be hazarded.

If he marched against Narvaez, he must either abandon the city and the emperor, the fruit of all his toils and triumphs, or, by leaving a garrison to hold them in awe, must cripple his strength, already far too weak to cope with that of his adversary. Yet on this latter course he decided. He trusted less, perhaps, to an open encounter of arms, than to the influence of his personal address and previous intrigues, to bring about an amicable arrangement. But he prepared himself for either result.

In the preceding chapter it was mentioned that Velasquez de Leon was sent with a hundred and fifty men to plant a colony on one of the great rivers emptying into the Mexican Gulf. Cortés, on learning of the arrival of Narvaez, had despatched a messenger to his officer to acquaint him with the fact and to arrest his further progress. But Velasquez had already received notice of it from Narvaez himself, who, in a letter written soon after his landing, had adjured him in the name of his kinsman, the governor of Cuba, to quit the banners of Cortés, and come over to him. That officer, however, had long since buried the feelings of resentment which he had once nourished against his general, to whom he was now devotedly attached, and who had honoured him throughout the campaign with particular regard. Cortés had early seen the importance of securing this cavalier to his interests. Without waiting for orders, Velasquez abandoned his expedition, and commenced a countermarch on the capital, when he received the general's commands to wait him in Cholula.

Cortés had also sent to the distant province of Chinantla, situated far to the south-east of Cholula, for a reinforcement of two thousand natives. They were a bold race, hostile to the Mexicans, and had offered their services to him since his residence in the metropolis. They used a long spear in battle, longer, indeed, than that borne by the Spanish or German infantry. Cortés ordered three hundred of their double-headed lances to be made for him, and to be tipped with copper instead of *itztli*. With this formidable weapon he proposed to foil the cavalry of his enemy.

The command of the garrison, in his absence, he intrusted to Pedro de Alvarado—the *Tonatiuh* of the Mexicans—a man possessed of many commanding qualities, of an intrepid, though somewhat arrogant spirit, and his warm personal friend. He inculcated on him moderation and forbearance. He was to keep a close watch on Montezuma, for on the possession of the royal person rested all their authority in the land. He was to show him the deference alike due to his high station, and demanded by policy. He was to pay uniform respect to the usages and the prejudices of the people; remembering that though his small force would be large enough to overawe them in times of quiet, yet, should they be once roused, it would be swept away like chaff before the whirlwind.

From Montezuma he exacted a promise to maintain the same friendly relations with his lieutenant which he had preserved towards himself. This, said Cortés, would be most grateful to his own master, the Spanish sovereign. Should the Aztec prince do otherwise, and lend himself to any hostile movement, he must be convinced that he would fall the first victim of it.

The emperor assured him of his continued good will. He was much perplexed, however, by the recent events. Were the Spaniards at his court, or those just landed, the true representatives of their sovereign? Cortés, who had hitherto maintained a reserve on the subject, now told him that the latter were indeed his countrymen, but traitors to his master. As such it was his painful duty to march against them, and, when he had chastised their rebellion, he should return, before his departure from the land, in triumph to the capital. Montezuma offered to support him with five thousand Aztec warriors; but the general declined it, not choosing to encumber himself with a body of doubtful, perhaps disaffected auxiliaries.

He left in garrison, under Alvarado, one hundred and forty men, two-thirds of his whole force. With these remained all the artillery, the greater part of the little body of horse, and most of the arquebusiers. He took with him only seventy soldiers, but they were men of the most mettle in the army and his staunch adherents. They were lightly armed, and encumbered with as little baggage as possible. Everything depended on celerity of movement.

Montezuma, in his royal litter, borne on the shoulders of his nobles, and escorted by the whole Spanish infantry, accompanied the general to the causeway. There, embracing him in the most cordial manner, they parted, with all the external marks of mutual regard. It was about the middle of May, 1520, more than six months since the entrance of the Spaniards into Mexico. During this time they had lorded it over the land with absolute sway. They were now leaving the city in hostile array, not against an Indian foe, but their own countrymen. It was the beginning of a long career of calamity—chequered, indeed, by occasional triumphs—which was yet to be run before the Conquest could be completed.

CHAPTER VII

Cortés Descends from the Tableland—Negotiates with Narvaez—Prepares to Assault Him—Quarters of Narvaez—Attacked by Night—Narvaez Defeated

1520

TRAVERSING THE SOUTHERN CAUSEWAY, by which they had entered the capital, the little party were soon on their march across the beautiful valley. They climbed the mountain-screen which nature has so ineffectually drawn around it; passed between the huge volcanoes that, like faithless watch-dogs on their posts, have long since been buried in slumber; threaded the intricate defiles where they had before experienced such bleak and tempestuous weather; and, emerging on the other side, descended the eastern slope which opens on the wide expanse of the fruitful plateau of Cholula.

They heeded little of what they saw on their rapid march, nor whether it was cold or hot. The anxiety of their minds made them indifferent to outward annoyances; and they had fortunately none to encounter from the natives, for the name of Spaniard was in itself a charm—a better guard than helm or buckler to the bearer.

In Cholula, Cortés had the inexpressible satisfaction of meeting Velasquez de Leon, with the hundred and twenty soldiers intrusted to his command for the formation of a colony. That faithful officer had been some time at Cholula, waiting for the general's approach. Had he failed, the enterprise of Cortés must have failed also. The idea of resistance, with his own handful of followers, would have been chimerical. As it was, his little band was now trebled, and acquired a confidence in proportion.

Cordially embracing their companions in arms, now knit together more closely than ever by the sense of a great and common danger, the combined troops traversed with quick step the streets of the sacred city, where many a dark pile of ruins told of their disastrous visit on the preceding autumn. They kept the high road to Tlascala; and, at not many leagues' distance from that capital, fell in with Father Olmedo and his companions on their return from the camp of Narvaez, to which, it will be remembered, they had been sent as envoys. The ecclesiastic bore a letter from that commander, in which he summoned Cortés and his followers to submit to his authority, as captain-general of the country, menacing them with condign punishment, in case of refusal or delay. Olmedo gave many curious particulars of the state of the enemy's camp. Narvaez he described as puffed up by authority, and negligent of precautions against a foe whom he held in contempt. He was surrounded by a number of pompous conceited officers, who ministered to his vanity, and whose braggart tones, the good father; who had an eye for the ridiculous, imitated, to the no small diversion of Cortés and the soldiers. Many of the troops, he said, showed no great partiality for their commander, and were strongly disinclined to a rupture with their countrymen; a state of feeling much promoted by the accounts they had received of Cortés, by his own arguments and promises, and by the liberal distribution of the gold with which he had been provided. In addition to these matters, Cortés gathered much important intelligence respecting the position of the enemy's force, and his general plan of operations.

At Tlascala the Spaniards were received with a frank and friendly hospitality. It is not said whether any of the Tlascalan allies accompanied them from Mexico. If they did, they went no further than their native city. Cortés requested a reinforcement of six hundred fresh troops to attend him on his present expedition. It was readily granted; but, before the army had proceeded many miles on its route, the Indian auxiliaries fell off, one after another, and returned to their city. They had no personal feeling of animosity to gratify in the present instance, as in a war against Mexico. It may be, too, that although intrepid in a contest with the bravest of the Indian races, they had had too fatal experience of the prowess of the white men to care to measure swords with them again. At any rate, they deserted in such numbers that Cortés dismissed the remainder at once, saying, good-humouredly, "He had rather part with them then, than in the hour of trial."

The troops soon entered on that wild district in the neighbourhood of Perote, strewed with the wreck of volcanic matter, which forms so singular a contrast to the general character of beauty with which the scenery is stamped. It was not long before their eyes were gladdened by the approach of Sandoval and about sixty soldiers from the garrison of

Vera Cruz, including several deserters from the enemy. It was a most important reinforcement, not more on account of the numbers of the men than of the character of the commander, in every respect one of the ablest captains in the service. He had been compelled to fetch a circuit, in order to avoid falling in with the enemy, and had forced his way through thick forests and wild mountain passes, till he had fortunately, without accident, reached the appointed place of rendezvous, and stationed himself once more under the banner of his chieftain.

At the same place, also, Cortés was met by Tobillos, a Spaniard whom he had sent to procure the lances from Chinantla. They were perfectly well made, after the pattern which had been given; double-headed spears, tipped with copper, and of great length. Tobillos drilled the men in the exercise of this weapon, the formidable uses of which, especially against horse, had been fully demonstrated, towards the close of the last century, by the Swiss battalions, in their encounters with the Burgundian cavalry, the best in Europe.

Cortés now took a review of his army—if so paltry a force may be called an army—and found their numbers were two hundred and sixty-six, only five of whom were mounted. A few muskets and crossbows were sprinkled among them. In defensive armour they were sadly deficient. They were for the most part cased in the quilted doublet of the country, thickly stuffed with cotton, the *escaupil,* recommended by its superior lightness, but which, though competent to turn the arrow of the Indian, was ineffectual against a musket-ball. Most of this cotton mail was exceedingly out of repair, giving evidence, in its unsightly gaps, of much rude service, and hard blows. Few, in this emergency, but would have given almost any price—the best of the gold chains which they wore in tawdry display over their poor habiliments—for a steel morion or cuirass, to take the place of their own hacked and battered armour.

Under this coarse covering, however, they bore hearts stout and courageous as ever beat in human bosoms. For they were the heroes, still invincible, of many a hard-fought field, where the odds had been incalculably against them. They had large experience of the country and of the natives; knew well the character of their own commander, under whose eye they had been trained, till every movement was in obedience to him. The whole body seemed to constitute but a single individual, in respect of unity of design and of action. Thus its real effective force was incredibly augmented; and, what was no less important, the humblest soldier felt it to be so.

The troops now resumed their march across the tableland, until reaching the eastern slope their labours were lightened, as they descended towards the broad plains of the *tierra caliente,* spread out like a boundless ocean of verdure below them. At some fifteen leagues' distance from Cempoalla, where Narvaez, as has been noticed, had established his quarters, they were met by another embassy from that commander. It consisted of the priest, Guevara, Andrés de Duero, and two or three others. Duero, the fast friend of Cortés, had been the person most instrumental, originally, in obtaining him his commission from Velasquez. They now greeted each other with a warm embrace, and it was not till after much preliminary conversation on private matters that the secretary disclosed the object of his visit.

He bore a letter from Narvaez, couched in terms somewhat different from the preceding. That officer required, indeed, the acknowledgment of his paramount authority in the land, but offered his vessels to transport all who desired it, from the country, together with their treasures and effects, without molestation or inquiry. The more liberal tenor of these terms was, doubtless, to be ascribed to the influence of Duero. The secretary strongly urged Cortés to comply with them, as the most favourable that could be obtained, and as the only alternative affording him a chance of safety in his desperate condition. "For, however valiant your men may be, how can they expect," he asked, "to face a force so much superior in numbers and equipment as that of their antagonists?" But Cortés had set his fortunes on the cast, and he was not the man to shrink from it. "If Narvaez bears a royal commission," he returned, "I will readily submit to him. But he has produced none. He is a deputy of my rival, Velasquez. For myself I am a servant of the king, I have conquered the country for him; and for him I and my brave followers will defend it, be assured, to the last drop of our blood. If we fall, it will be glory enough to have perished in the discharge of our duty."

His friend might have been somewhat puzzled to comprehend how the authority of Cortés rested on a different ground from that of Narvaez; and if they both held of the same superior, the governor of Cuba, why that dignitary should not be empowered to supersede his own officer in case of dissatisfaction, and appoint a substitute. But Cortés here reaped the full benefit of that legal fiction, if it may be so termed, by which his commission, resigned to the self-constituted municipality of Vera Cruz, was again derived through that body from the crown. The device, indeed, was too palpable to impose on any but those who chose to be blinded.

Most of the army were of this number. To them it seemed to give additional confidence, in the same manner as a strip of painted canvas, when substituted, as it has sometimes been, for a real parapet of stone, has been found not merely to impose on the enemy, but to give a sort of artificial courage to the defenders concealed behind it.

Duero had arranged with his friend in Cuba, when he took command of the expedition, that he himself was to have a liberal share of the profits. It is said that Cortés confirmed this arrangement at the present juncture, and made it clearly for the other's interest that he should prevail in the struggle with Narvaez. This was an important point, considering the position of the secretary. From this authentic source the general derived much information respecting the designs of Narvaez, which had escaped the knowledge of Olmedo. On the departure of the envoys, Cortés intrusted them with a letter for his rival, a counterpart of that which he had received from him. This show of negotiation intimated a desire on his part to postpone if not avoid hostilities, which might the better put Narvaez off his guard. In the letter he summoned that commander and his followers to present themselves before him without delay, and to acknowledge his authority as the representative of his sovereign. He should otherwise be compelled to proceed against them as rebels to the crown! With this missive, the vaunting tone of which was intended quite as much for his own troops as the enemy, Cortés dismissed the envoys. They returned to disseminate among their comrades their admiration of the general and of his unbounded liberality, of which he took care they should experience full measure, and they dilated on the riches of his adherents, who, over their wretched attire, displayed with ostentatious profusion jewels, ornaments of gold, collars, and massive chains winding several times round their necks and bodies, the rich spoil of the treasury of Montezuma.

The army now took its way across the level plains of the *tierra caliente,* on which nature has exhausted all the wonders of creation; it was covered more thickly then than at the present day with noble forests, where the towering cotton-wood tree, the growth of ages, stood side by side with the light bamboo, or banana, the product of a season, each in its way attesting the marvellous fecundity of the soil, while innumerable creeping flowers, muffling up the giant branches of the trees, waved in bright festoons above their heads, loading the air with odours. But the senses of the Spaniards were not open to the delicious influences of nature. Their minds were occupied by one idea.

Coming upon an open reach of meadow, of some extent, they were, at length, stopped by a river or rather stream, called *rio de canoas,* "the river of canoes," of no great volume ordinarily, but swollen at this time by excessive rains. It had rained hard that day, although at intervals the sun had broken forth with intolerable fervour, affording a good specimen of those alternations of heat and moisture, which give such activity to vegetation in the tropics, where the process of forcing seems to be always going on.

The river was about a league distant from the camp of Narvaez. Before seeking out a practical ford, by which to cross it, Cortés allowed his men to recruit their exhausted strength by stretching themselves on the ground. The shades of evening had gathered round; and the rising moon, wading through dark masses of cloud, shone with a doubtful and interrupted light. It was evident that the storm had not yet spent its fury. Cortés did not regret this. He had made up his mind to an assault that very night, and in the darkness and uproar of the tempest his movements would be most effectually concealed.

Before disclosing his design, he addressed his men in one of those stirring, soldierly harangues, to which he had recourse in emergencies of great moment, as if to sound the depths of their hearts, and, where any faltered, to re-animate them with his own heroic spirit. He briefly recapitulated the great events of the campaign, the dangers they had surmounted, the victories they had achieved over the most appalling odds, the glorious spoil they had won. But of this they were now to be defrauded; not by men holding a legal warrant from the crown, but by adventurers, with no better title than that of superior force. They had established a claim on the gratitude of their country and their sovereign. This claim was now to be dishonoured; their very services were converted into crimes, and their names branded with infamy as those of traitors. But the time had at last come for vengeance. God would not desert the soldier of the Cross. Those, whom he had carried victorious through greater dangers, would not be left to fail now. And, if they should fail, better to die like brave men on the field of battle, than, with fame and fortune cast away, to perish ignominiously like slaves on the gibbet. This last point he urged home upon his hearers; well knowing there was not one among them so dull as not to be touched by it.

They responded with hearty acclamations, and Velasquez de Leon, and de Lugo, in the name of the rest, assured their commander, if they failed, it should be his fault, not theirs. They would follow wherever he led. The general was fully satisfied with the temper of his soldiers, as he felt that his difficulty lay not in awakening their enthusiasm, but in giving it a right direction. One thing is remarkable. He made no allusion to the defection which he knew existed in the enemy's camp. He would have his soldiers, in this last pinch, rely on nothing but themselves.

He announced his purpose to attack the enemy that very night, when he should be buried in slumber, and the friendly darkness might throw a veil over their own movements, and conceal the poverty of their numbers. To this the troops, jaded though they were by incessant marching, and half famished, joyfully assented. In their situation, suspense was the worst of evils. He next distributed the commands among his captains. To Gonzalo de Sandoval he assigned the important office of taking Narvaez. He was commanded, as *alguacil mayor,* to seize the person of that officer as a rebel to his sovereign, and, if he made resistance, to kill him on the spot. He was provided with sixty picked men to aid him in this difficult task, supported by several of the ablest captains, among whom were two of the Alvarados, de Avila and Ordaz. The largest division of the force was placed under Christoval de Olid, or, according to some authorities, of Pizarro, one of that family so renowned in the subsequent conquest of Peru. He was to get possession of the artillery, and to cover the assault of Sandoval by keeping those of the enemy at bay who would interfere with it. Cortés reserved only a body of twenty men for himself, to act on any point that occasion might require. The watchword was *Espíritu Santo,* it being the evening of Whitsunday. Having made these arrangements, he prepared to cross the river.

During the interval thus occupied by Cortés, Narvaez had remained at Cempoalla, passing his days in idle and frivolous amusement. From this he was at length roused, after the return of Duero, by the remonstrances of the old cacique of the city. "Why are you so heedless?" exclaims the latter; "do you think Malintzin is so? Depend on it, he knows your situation exactly, and, when you least dream of it, he will be upon you."

Alarmed at these suggestions and those of his friends, Narvaez at length put himself at the head of his troops, and, on the very day on which Cortés arrived at the River of Canoes, sallied out to meet him. But, when he had reached this barrier, Narvaez saw no sign of an enemy. The rain, which fell in torrents, soon drenched the soldiers to the skin. Made somewhat effeminate by their long and luxurious residence at Cempoalla, they murmured at their uncomfortable situation. "Of what use was it to remain there fighting with the elements? There was no sign of an enemy, and little reason to apprehend his approach in such tempestuous weather. It would be wiser to return to Cempoalla, and in the morning they should be all fresh for action, should Cortés make his appearance."

Narvaez took counsel of these advisers, or rather of his own inclinations. Before retracing his steps, he provided against surprise, by stationing a couple of sentinels at no great distance from the river, to give notice of the approach of Cortés. He also detached a body of forty horse in another direction, by which he thought it not improbable the enemy might advance on Cempoalla. Having taken these precautions, he fell back again before night on his own quarters.

He there occupied the principal *teocalli*. It consisted of a stone building on the usual pyramidal basis; and the ascent was by a flight of steep steps on one of the faces of the pyramid. In the edifice or sanctuary above he stationed himself with a strong party of arquebusiers and crossbowmen. Two other *teocallis* in the same area were garrisoned by large detachments of infantry. His artillery, consisting of seventeen or eighteen small guns, he posted in the area below, and protected it by the remainder of his cavalry. When he had thus distributed his forces, he returned to his own quarters, and soon after to repose, with as much indifference as if his rival had been on the other side of the Atlantic, instead of a neighbouring stream.

That stream was now converted by the deluge of waters into a furious torrent. It was with difficulty that a practicable ford could be found. The slippery stones, rolling beneath the feet, gave way at every step. The difficulty of the passage was much increased by the darkness and driving tempest. Still, with their long pikes, the Spaniards contrived to make good their footing, at least all but two, who were swept down by the fury of the current. When they had reached the opposite side, they had new impediments to encounter in traversing a road never good, now made doubly difficult by the deep mire and the tangled brushwood with which it was overrun.

Here they met with a cross, which had been raised by them on their former march into the interior. They hailed it as a good omen; and Cortés, kneeling before the blessed sign, confessed his sins, and declared his great object to be the triumph of the holy Catholic faith. The army followed his example, and, having made a general confession, received absolution from Father Olmedo, who invoked the blessing of Heaven on the warriors who had consecrated their swords to the glory of the Cross. Then rising up and embracing one another, as companions in the good cause, they found themselves wonderfully invigorated and refreshed. The incident is curious, and well illustrates the character of the time—in which war, religion, and rapine were so intimately blended together. Adjoining the road was a little coppice; and Cortés, and the few who had horses, dismounting, fastened the animals to the trees, where they might find some shelter from the storm. They deposited there, too, their baggage and such superfluous articles as would encumber their movement. The general then gave them a few last words of advice. "Everything," said he, "depends on obedience. Let no man, from desire of distinguishing himself, break his ranks. On silence, despatch, and, above all, obedience to your officers, the success of our enterprise depends."

Silently and stealthily they held on their way without beat of drum or sound of trumpet, when they suddenly came on the two sentinels who had been stationed by Narvaez to give notice of their approach. This had been so noiseless, that the videttes were both of them surprised on their posts, and one only, with difficulty, effected his escape. The other was brought before Cortés. Every effort was made to draw from him some account of the present position of Narvaez. But the man remained obstinately silent; and, though threatened with the gibbet, and having a noose actually drawn round his neck, his Spartan heroism was not to be vanquished. Fortunately no change had taken place in the arrangements of Narvaez since the intelligence previously derived from Duero.

The other sentinel, who had escaped, carried the news of the enemy's approach to the camp. But his report was not credited by the lazy soldiers, whose slumbers he had disturbed. "He had been deceived by his fears," they said, "and mistaken the noise of the storm, and the waving of the bushes, for the enemy. Cortés and his men were far enough on the other side of the river, which they would be slow to cross in such a night." Narvaez himself shared in the same blind infatuation, and the discredited sentinel slunk abashed to his own quarters, vainly menacing them with the consequences of their incredulity.

Cortés, not doubting that the sentinel's report must alarm the enemy's camp, quickened his pace. As he drew near, he discerned a light in one of the lofty towers of the city. "It is the quarters of Narvaez," he exclaimed to Sandoval, "and that light must be your beacon." On entering the suburbs, the Spaniards were surprised to find no one stirring, and no symptom of alarm. Not a sound was to be heard, except the measured tread of their own footsteps, half-drowned in the howling of the tempest. Still they could not move so stealthily as altogether to elude notice, as they defiled through the streets of this populous city. The tidings were quickly conveyed to the enemy's quarters, where, in an instant, all was bustle and confusion. The trumpets sounded to arms. The dragoons sprang to their steeds, the artillerymen to their guns. Narvaez hastily buckled on his armour, called his men around him, and summoned those in the neighbouring *teocallis* to join him in the area. He gave his orders with coolness; for, however wanting in prudence, he was not deficient in presence of mind or courage.

All this was the work of a few minutes. But in those minutes the Spaniards had reached the avenue leading to the camp. Cortés ordered his men to keep close to the walls of the buildings, that the cannon-shot might have free range. No sooner had they presented themselves before the enclosure than the artillery of Narvaez opened a general fire. Fortunately the pieces were pointed so high that most of the balls passed over their heads, and three men only were struck down. They did not give the enemy time to reload. Cortés shouting the watchword of the night, *"Espíritu Santo! Espíritu Santo!* Upon them!" in a moment Olid and his division rushed on the artillerymen, whom they pierced or knocked down with their pikes, and got possession of their guns. Another division engaged the cavalry, and made a diversion in favour of Sandoval, who with his gallant little band sprang up the great stairway of the temple. They were received with a shower of missiles—arrows and musket-balls, which, in the hurried aim, and the darkness of the night, did little mischief. The next minute the assailants were on the platform, engaged hand to hand with their foes. Narvaez fought bravely in the midst, encouraging his followers. His standard-bearer fell by his side, run through the body. He himself received several wounds; for his short sword was no match for the long pikes of the assailants. At length, he received a blow from a spear, which struck out his left eye. "Santa María!" exclaimed the unhappy man, "I am slain!" The cry was instantly taken up by the followers of Cortés, who shouted, "Victory!"

Disabled, and half-mad with agony from his wound, Narvaez was withdrawn by his men into the sanctuary. The assailants endeavoured to force an entrance, but it was stoutly defended. At length a soldier, getting possession of a torch, or firebrand, flung it on the thatched roof, and in a few moments the combustible materials of which it was composed were in a blaze. Those within were driven out by the suffocating heat and smoke. A soldier named Farfan grappled with the wounded commander, and easily brought him to the ground; when he was speedily dragged down the steps, and secured with fetters. His followers, seeing the fate of their chief, made no further resistance.

During this time Cortés and the troops of Olid had been engaged with the cavalry, and had discomfited them, after some ineffectual attempts on the part of the latter to break through the dense array of pikes, by which several of their number were unhorsed and some of them slain. The general then prepared to assault the other *teocallis,* first summoning the garrisons to surrender. As they refused, he brought up the heavy guns to bear on them, thus turning the artillery against its own masters. He accompanied this menacing movement with offers of the most liberal import; an amnesty of the past, and a full participation in all the advantages of the Conquest. One of the garrisons was under the command of Salvatierra, the same officer who talked of cutting off the ears of Cortés. From the moment he had learned the fate of his own general, the hero was seized with a violent fit of illness which disabled him from further action. The garrison waited only for one discharge of the ordnance, when they accepted the terms of capitulation. Cortés, it is said, received, on this occasion, a support from an unexpected auxiliary. The air was filled with the *cocuyos*—a species of large beetle which emits an intense phosphoric light from its body, strong enough to enable one to read by it. These wandering fires, seen in the darkness of the night, were converted by the excited imaginations of the besieged into an army with matchlocks. Such is the report of an eye-witness. But the facility with which the enemy surrendered may quite as probably be referred to the cowardice of the commander, and the disaffection of the soldiers, not unwilling to come under the banners of Cortés.

The body of cavalry posted, it will be remembered, by Narvaez on one of the roads to Cempoalla, to intercept his rival, having learned what had been passing, were not long in tendering their submission. Each of the soldiers in the conquered army was required, in token of his obedience, to deposit his arms in the hands of the *alguacils,* and to take the oaths to Cortés as Chief Justice and captain-general of the colony.

The number of the slain is variously reported. It seems probable that not more than twelve perished on the side of the vanquished, and of the victors half that number. The small amount may be explained by the short duration of the action, and the random aim of the missiles in the darkness. The number of the wounded was much more considerable.

The field was now completely won. A few brief hours had sufficed to change the condition of Cortés from that of a wandering outlaw at the head of a handful of needy adventurers, a rebel with a price upon his head, to that of an independent chief, with a force at his disposal strong enough not only to secure his present conquests, but to open a career for still loftier ambition. While the air rang with the acclamations of the soldiery, the victorious general, assuming a deportment corresponding with his change of fortune, took his seat in a chair of state, and, with a rich embroidered mantle thrown over his shoulders, received, one by one, the officers and soldiers, as they came to tender their congratulations. The privates were graciously permitted to kiss his hand. The officers he noticed with words of compliment or courtesy; and, when Duero, Bermudez the treasurer, and some others of the vanquished party, his old friends, presented themselves, he cordially embraced them.

Narvaez, Salvatierra, and two or three of the hostile leaders were led before him in chains. It was a moment of deep humiliation for the former commander, in which the anguish of the body, however keen, must have been forgotten in that of the spirit. "You have great reason, Señor Cortés," said the discomfited warrior, "to thank fortune for having given you the day so easily, and put me in your power." "I have much to be thankful for," replied the general; "but for my victory over you, I esteem it as one of the least of my achievements since my coming into the country!" He then ordered the wounds of the prisoners to be cared for, and sent them under a strong guard to Vera Cruz.

Notwithstanding the proud humility of his reply, Cortés could scarcely have failed to regard his victory over Narvaez as one of the most brilliant achievements in his career. With a few scores of followers, badly clothed, worse fed, wasted by forced marches, under every personal disadvantage, deficient in weapons and military stores, he had attacked in their own quarters, routed, and captured the entire force of the enemy, thrice his superior in numbers, well provided with cavalry and artillery, admirably equipped, and complete in all the munitions of war! The amount of troops engaged on either side was, indeed, inconsiderable. But the proportions are not affected by this: and the relative strength of the parties made a result so decisive one of the most remarkable events in the annals of war.

It is true there were some contingencies on which the fortunes of the day depended, that could not be said to be entirely within his control. Something was the work of chance. If Velasquez de Leon, for example, had proved false, the expedition must have failed. If the weather, on the night of the attack, had been fair, the enemy would have had certain notice of his approach, and been prepared for it. But these are the chances that enter more or less into every enterprise. He is the skilful general who knows how to turn them to account; to win the smiles of Fortune, and make even the elements fight on his side.

If Velasquez de Leon was, as it proved, the very officer whom the general should have trusted with the command, it was his sagacity which originally discerned this, and selected him for it. It was his address that converted this dangerous foe into a friend; and one so fast that, in the hour of need, he chose rather to attach himself to his desperate fortunes than to those of the governor of Cuba, powerful as the latter was, and his near kinsman. It was the same address which gained Cortés such an ascendancy over his soldiers, and knit them to him so closely, that, in the darkest moment, not a man offered to desert him. If the success of the assault may be ascribed mainly to the dark and stormy weather which covered it, it was owing to him that he was in a condition to avail himself of this. The shortest possible time intervened between the conception of his plan and its execution. In a very few days he descended by extraordinary marches from the capital to the sea-coast. He came like a torrent from the mountains, pouring on the enemy's camp and sweeping everything away, before a barrier could be raised to arrest it. This celerity of movement—the result of a clear head and determined will, has entered into the strategy of the greatest captains, and forms a prominent feature in their most brilliant military exploits. It was undoubtedly, in the present instance, a great cause of success.

But it would be taking a limited view of the subject to consider the battle which decided the fate of Narvaez as wholly fought at Cempoalla. It was begun in Mexico. With that singular power which he exercised over all who came near him, Cortés converted the very emissaries of Narvaez into his own friends and agents. The reports of Guevara and his companions, the intrigues of Father Olmedo, and the general's gold, were all busily at work to shake the loyalty of the soldiers, and the battle was half won before a blow had been struck. It was fought quite as much with gold as with steel. Cortés understood this so well, that he made it his great object to seize the person of Narvaez. In such an event, he had full confidence that indifference to their own cause and partiality to himself would speedily bring the rest of the army under his banner. He was not deceived. Narvaez said truly enough, therefore, some years after this event, that "he had been beaten by his own troops, not by those of his rival; that his followers had been bribed to betray him." This affords the only explanation of their brief and ineffectual resistance.

CHAPTER VIII

Discontent of the Troops—Insurrection in the Capital—Return of Cortés—General Signs of Hostility—Massacre by Alvarado—Rising of the Aztecs

1520

THE TEMPEST that had raged so wildly during the night passed away with the morning, which rose bright and unclouded on the field of battle. As the light advanced, it revealed more strikingly the disparity of the two forces so lately opposed to each other. Those of Narvaez could not conceal their chagrin; and murmurs of displeasure became audible, as they contrasted their own superior numbers and perfect appointments with the way-worn visages and rude attire of their handful of enemies! It was with some satisfaction, therefore, that the general beheld his dusky allies from Chinantla, two thousand in number, arrive upon the field. They were a fine athletic set of men; and, as they advanced in a sort of promiscuous order, so to speak, with their gay banners of feather-work, and their long lances tipped with *itztli* and copper, glistening in the morning sun, they had something of an air of military discipline. They came too late for the action, indeed, but Cortés was not sorry to exhibit to his new followers the extent of his resources in the country. As he had now no occasion for his Indian allies, after a courteous reception and a liberal recompense, he dismissed them to their homes.

He then used his utmost endeavours to allay the discontent of the troops. He addressed them in his most soft and insinuating tones, and was by no means frugal of his promises. He suited the action to the word. There were few of them but had lost their accoutrements, or their baggage, or horses taken and appropriated by the victors. This last article was in great request among the latter, and many a soldier, weary with the long marches hitherto made on foot, had provided himself, as he imagined, with a much more comfortable as well as creditable conveyance for the rest of the campaign. The general now commanded everything to be restored. "They were embarked in the same cause," he said, "and should share with one another equally." He went still further; and distributed among the soldiers of Narvaez a quantity of gold and other precious commodities gathered from the neighbouring tribes, or found in his rival's quarters.

These proceedings, however politic in reference to his new followers, gave great disgust to his old. "Our commander," they cried, "has forsaken his friends for his foes. We stood by him in his hour of distress, and are rewarded with blows and wounds, while the spoil goes to our enemies!" The indignant soldiery commissioned the priest Olmedo and Alonso de Avila to lay their complaints before Cortés. The ambassadors stated them without reserve, comparing their commander's conduct to the ungrateful proceeding of Alexander, who, when he gained a victory, usually gave away more to his enemies than to the troops who enabled him to beat them. Cortés was greatly perplexed. Victorious or defeated, his path seemed equally beset with difficulties!

He endeavoured to soothe their irritation by pleading the necessity of the case. "Our new comrades," he said, "are formidable from their numbers; so much so, that we are even now much more in their power than they are in ours. Our only security is to make them not merely confederates, but friends. On any cause of disgust, we shall have the whole battle to fight over again; and, if they are united, under a much greater disadvantage than before. I have considered your interests," he added, "as much as my own. All that I have is yours. But why should there be any ground for discontent, when the whole country, with its riches, is before us? And our augmented strength must henceforth secure the undisturbed control of it!"

But Cortés did not rely wholly on argument for the restoration of tranquillity. He knew this to be incompatible with inaction; and he made arrangements to divide his forces at once, and to employ them on distant services. He selected a detachment of two hundred men, under Diego de Ordaz, whom he ordered to form the settlement before meditated on the Coatzacualco. A like number was sent with Velasquez de Leon, to secure the province of Panuco, some three degrees to the north, on the Mexican Gulf. Twenty in each detachment were drafted from his own veterans.

Two hundred men he despatched to Vera Cruz, with orders to have the rigging, iron, and everything portable on board of the fleet of Narvaez brought on shore, and the vessels completely dismantled. He appointed a person named Cavallero superintendent of the marine, with instructions that if any ships hereafter should enter the port, they should be dismantled in like manner, and their officers imprisoned on shore.

But while he was thus occupied with new schemes of discovery and conquest, he received such astounding intelligence from Mexico, as compelled him to concentrate all his faculties and his forces on that one point. The city was in a state of insurrection. No sooner had the struggle with his rival been decided, than Cortés despatched a courier with the tidings to the capital. In less than a fortnight, the same messenger returned with letters from Alvarado, conveying the alarming information that the Mexicans were in arms, and had vigorously assaulted the Spaniards in their own quarters. The enemy, he added, had burned the brigantines, by which Cortés had secured the means of retreat in case of the destruction of the bridges. They had attempted to force the defences, and had succeeded in partially undermining them, and they had overwhelmed the garrison with a tempest of missiles, which had killed several, and wounded a great number. The letter concluded with beseeching his commander to hasten to their relief, if he would save them, or keep his hold on the capital.

These tidings were a heavy blow to the general—the heavier, it seemed, coming, as they did, in the hour of triumph, when he had thought to have all his enemies at his feet. There was no room for hesitation. To lose their footing in the capital, the noblest city in the Western World, would be to lose the country itself, which looked up to it as its head. He opened the matter fully to his soldiers, calling on all who would save their countrymen to follow him. All declared their readiness to go; showing an alacrity, says Diaz, which some would have been slow to manifest, had they foreseen the future.

Cortés now made preparations for instant departure. He countermanded the orders previously given to Velasquez and Ordaz, and directed them to join him with their forces at Tlascala. He recalled the troops from Vera Cruz, leaving only a hundred men in garrison there, under command of one Rodrigo Rangre: for he could not spare the services of Sandoval at this crisis. He left his sick and wounded at Cempoalla, under charge of a small detachment, directing that they should follow as soon as they were in marching order. Having completed these arrangements, he set out from Cempoalla, well supplied with provisions by its hospitable cacique, who attended him some leagues on his way. The Totonac chief seems to have had an amiable facility of accommodating himself to the powers that were in the ascendant.

Nothing worthy of notice occurred during the first part of the march. The troops everywhere met with a friendly reception from the peasantry, who readily supplied their wants. Some time before reaching Tlascala, the route lay through a country thinly settled, and the army experienced considerable suffering from want of food, and still more from that of water. Their distress increased to an alarming degree, as, in the hurry of their forced march, they travelled with the meridian sun beating fiercely on their heads. Several faltered by the way, and, throwing themselves down by the roadside, seemed incapable of further effort, and almost indifferent to life.

In this extremity Cortés sent forward a small detachment of horse to procure provisions in Tlascala, and speedily followed in person. On arriving, he found abundant supplies already prepared by the hospitable natives. They were sent back to the troops; the stragglers were collected one by one; refreshments were administered; and the army, restored in strength and spirits, entered the republican capital.

Here they gathered little additional news respecting the events in Mexico, which a popular rumour attributed to the secret encouragement and machinations of Montezuma. Cortés was commodiously lodged in the quarters of Maxixca, one of the four chiefs of the republic. They readily furnished him with two thousand troops. There was no want of heartiness, when the war was with their ancient enemy, the Aztec.

The Spanish commander, on reviewing his forces, after the junction with his two captains, found that they amounted to about a thousand foot, and one hundred horse, besides the Tlascalan levies. In the infantry were nearly a hundred arquebusiers, with as many crossbow-men; and the part of the army brought over by Narvaez was admirably equipped. It was inferior, however, to his own veterans in what is better than any outward appointments—military training, and familiarity with the peculiar service in which they were engaged.

Leaving these friendly quarters, the Spaniards took a more northerly route, as more direct than that by which they had before penetrated into the valley. It was the road to Tezcuco. It still compelled them to climb the same bold range of the Cordilleras, which attains its greatest elevation in the two mighty *volcans* at whose base they had before travelled. The sides of the sierra were clothed with dark forests of pine, cypress, and cedar, through which glimpses now and then opened into fathomless dells and valleys, whose depths, far down in the sultry climate of the tropics, were lost in a glowing wilderness of vegetation. From the crest of the mountain-range the eye travelled over the broad expanse of country, which they had lately crossed, far away to the green plains of Cholula. Towards the west they looked down on the Mexican Valley, from a point of view wholly different from that which they had before occupied, but still offering the same beautiful spectacle, with its lakes trembling in the light, its gay cities and villas floating on their bosom, its burnished *teocallis* touched with fire, its cultivated slopes and dark hills of porphyry stretching away in dim perspective to the verge of the horizon. At their feet lay the city of Tezcuco, which, modestly retiring behind her deep groves of cypress, formed a contrast to her more ambitious rival on the other side of the lake, who seemed to glory in the unveiled splendours of her charms, as Mistress of the Valley.

As they descended into the populous plains, their reception by the natives was very different from that which they had experienced on the preceding visit. There were no groups of curious peasantry to be seen gazing at them as they passed, and offering their simple hospitality. The supplies they asked were not refused, but granted with an ungracious air, that showed the blessing of the giver did not accompany them. This air of reserve became still more marked as the army entered the suburbs of the ancient capital of the Acolhuans. No one came forth to greet them, and the population seemed to have dwindled away—so many of them were withdrawn to the neighbouring scene of hostilities at Mexico. Their cold reception was a sensible mortification to the veterans of Cortés, who, judging from the past, had boasted to their new comrades of the sensation their presence would excite among the natives. The cacique of the place, who, as it may be remembered, had been created through the influence of Cortés, was himself absent. The general drew an ill omen from all these circumstances, which even raised an uncomfortable apprehension in his mind respecting the fate of the garrison in Mexico.

But his doubts were soon dispelled by the arrival of a messenger in a canoe from that city, whence he had escaped through the remissness of the enemy, or, perhaps, with their connivance. He brought despatches from Alvarado, informing his commander that the Mexicans had for the last fortnight desisted from active hostilities, and converted their operations into a blockade. The garrison had suffered greatly, but Alvarado expressed his conviction that the siege would be raised, and tranquillity restored, on the approach of his countrymen. Montezuma sent a message, also, to the same effect. At the same time, he exculpated himself from any part in the late hostilities, which he said had not only been conducted without his privity, but contrary to his inclination and efforts.

The Spanish general, having halted long enough to refresh his wearied troops, took up his march along the southern margin of the lake, which led him over the same causeway by which he had before entered the capital. It was the day consecrated to St. John the Baptist, June 24, 1520. But how different was the scene from that presented on his former entrance! No crowds now lined the roads, no boats swarmed on the lake, filled with admiring spectators. A single pirogue might now and then be seen in the distance, like a spy stealthily watching their movements, and darting away the moment it had attracted notice. A death-like stillness brooded over the scene—a stillness that spoke louder to the heart than the acclamations of multitudes.

Cortés rode on moodily at the head of his battalions, finding abundant food for meditation, doubtless, in this change of circumstances. As if to dispel these gloomy reflections, he ordered his trumpets to sound, and their clear, shrill notes, borne across the waters, told the inhabitants of the beleaguered fortress that their friends were at hand. They were answered by a joyous peal of artillery, which seemed to give a momentary exhilaration to the troops, as they quickened their pace, traversed the great drawbridges, and once more found themselves within the walls of the imperial city.

The appearance of things here was not such as to allay their apprehensions. In some places they beheld the smaller bridges removed, intimating too plainly, now that their brigantines were destroyed, how easy it would be to cut off their retreat. The town seemed even more deserted than Tezcuco. Its once busy and crowded population had mysteriously vanished. And, as the Spaniards defiled through the empty streets, the tramp of their horses' feet upon the pavement was answered by dull and melancholy echoes that fell heavily on their hearts. With saddened feelings they reached the great gates of the palace of Axayacatl. The gates were thrown open, and Cortés and his veterans, rushing in, were cordially embraced by their companions in arms, while both parties soon forgot the present in the interesting recapitulation of the past.

The first inquiries of the general were respecting the origin of the tumult. The accounts were various. Some imputed it to the desire of the Mexicans to release their sovereign from confinement; others to the design of cutting off the garrison while crippled by the absence of Cortés and their countrymen. All agreed, however, in tracing the immediate cause to the violence of Alvarado. It was common for the Aztecs to celebrate an annual festival in May, in honour of their patron war-god. It was called the "incensing of Huitzilopotchli," and was commemorated by sacrifice, religious songs, and dances, in which most of the nobles engaged, for it was one of the great festivals which displayed the pomp of the Aztec ritual. As it was held in the court of the *teocalli,* in the immediate neighbourhood of the Spanish quarters, and as a part of the temple itself was reserved for a Christian chapel, the caciques asked permission of Alvarado to perform their rites there. They requested also, it is said, to be allowed the presence of Montezuma. This latter petition Alvarado declined, in obedience to the injunctions of Cortés; but acquiesced in the former, on condition that the Aztecs should celebrate no human sacrifices, and should come without weapons.

They assembled accordingly on the day appointed, to the number of six hundred, at the smallest computation. They were dressed in their most magnificent gala costumes, with their graceful mantles of feather-work, sprinkled with precious stones, and their necks, arms, and legs ornamented with collars and bracelets of gold. They had that love of gaudy splendour which belongs to semi-civilised nations, and on these occasions displayed all the pomp and profusion of their barbaric ward-robes.

Alvarado and his soldiers attended as spectators, some of them taking their station at the gates, as if by chance, and others mingling in the crowd. They were all armed, a circumstance which, as it was usual, excited no attention. The Aztecs were soon engrossed by the exciting movement of the dance, accompanied by their religious chant, and wild, discordant minstrelsy. While thus occupied, Alvarado and his men, at a concerted signal, rushed with drawn swords on their victims. Unprotected by armour or weapons of any kind, they were hewn down without resistance by their assailants, who, in their bloody work, says a contemporary, showed no touch of pity or compunction. Some fled to the gates, but were caught on the long pikes of the soldiers. Others, who attempted to scale the *Coatepantli,* or Wall of Serpents, as it was called, which surrounded the area, shared the like fate, or were cut to pieces, or shot by the ruthless soldiery. The pavement, says a writer of the age, ran with streams of blood, like water in a heavy shower. Not an Aztec of all that gay company was left alive! It was repeating the dreadful scene of Cholula, with the disgraceful addition that the Spaniards, not content with slaughtering their victims, rifled them of the precious ornaments on their persons! On this sad day fell the flower of the Aztec nobility. Not a family of note but had mourning and desolation brought within its walls; and many a doleful ballad, rehearsing the tragic incidents of the story, and adapted to the plaintive national airs, continued to be chanted by the natives long after the subjugation of the country.

Various explanations have been given of this atrocious deed; but few historians have been content to admit that of Alvarado himself. According to this, intelligence had been obtained through his spies—some of them Mexicans—of an intended rising of the Indians. The celebration of this festival was fixed on as the period for its execution, when the caciques would be met together, and would easily rouse the people to support them. Alvarado, advised of all this, had forbidden them to wear arms at their meeting. While affecting to comply, they had secreted their weapons in the neighbouring arsenals, whence they could readily withdraw them. But his own blow, by anticipating theirs, defeated the design, and, as he confidently hoped, would deter the Aztecs from a similar attempt in future.

Such is the account of the matter given by Alvarado. But, if true, why did he not verify his assertion by exposing the arms thus secreted? Why did he not vindicate his conduct in the eyes of the Mexicans generally, by publicly avowing the treason of the nobles, as was done by Cortés at Cholula? The whole looks much like an apology devised after the commission of the deed, to cover up its atrocity.

Some contemporaries assign a very different motive for the massacre, which, according to them, originated in the cupidity of the Conquerors, as shown by their plundering the bodies of their victims. Bernal Diaz, who, though not present, had conversed familiarly with those who were, vindicates them from the charge of this unworthy motive. According to him, Alvarado struck the blow in order to intimidate the Aztecs from any insurrectionary movement. But whether he had reason to apprehend such, or even affected to do so before the massacre, the old chronicler does not inform us.

On reflection, it seems scarcely possible that so foul a deed, and one involving so much hazard to the Spaniards themselves, should have been perpetrated from the mere desire of getting possession of the baubles worn on the persons of the natives. It is more likely this was an afterthought, suggested to the rapacious soldiery by the display of the spoil before them. It is not improbable that Alvarado may have gathered rumours of a conspiracy among the nobles—rumours, perhaps, derived through the Tlascalans, their inveterate foes, and for that reason very little deserving of credit. He proposed to defeat it by imitating the example of his commander at Cholula. But he omitted to imitate his leader in taking precautions against the subsequent rising of the populace. And he grievously miscalculated, when he confounded the bold and warlike Aztec with the effeminate Cholulan.

No sooner was the butchery accomplished, than the tidings spread like wildfire through the capital. Men could scarcely credit their senses. All they had hitherto suffered, the desecration of their temples, the imprisonment of their sovereign, the insults heaped on his person, all were forgotten in this one act. Every feeling of long smothered hostility and rancour now burst forth in the cry for vengeance. Every former sentiment of superstitious dread was merged in that of inextinguishable hatred. It required no effort of the priests—though this was not wanting —to fan these passions into a blaze. The city rose in arms to a man; and on the following dawn, almost before the Spaniards could secure themselves in their defences, they were assaulted with desperate fury. Some of the assailants attempted to scale the walls; others succeeded in partially undermining and in setting fire to the works. Whether they would have succeeded in carrying the place by storm is doubtful. But, at the prayers of the garrison, Montezuma himself interfered, and mounting the battlements addressed the populace, whose fury he endeavoured to mitigate by urging considerations for his own safety. They respected their monarch so far as to desist from further attempts to storm the fortress, but changed their operations into a regular blockade. They threw up works around the palace to prevent the egress of the Spaniards. They suspended the *tianguez,* or market, to preclude the possibility of their enemy's obtaining supplies; and they then quietly sat down, with feelings of sullen desperation, waiting for the hour when famine should throw their victims into their hands.

The condition of the besieged, meanwhile, was sufficiently distressing. Their magazines of provisions, it is true, were not exhausted; but they suffered greatly from want of water, which, within the inclosure, was exceedingly brackish, for the soil was saturated with the salt of the surrounding element. In this extremity, they discovered, it is said, a spring of fresh water in the area. Such springs were known in some other parts of the city; but, discovered first under these circumstances, it was accounted as nothing less than a miracle. Still they suffered much from their past encounters. Seven Spaniards, and many Tlascalans, had fallen, and there was scarcely one of either nation who had not received several wounds. In this situation, far from their own countrymen, without expectation of succour from abroad, they seemed to have no alternative before them, but a lingering death by famine, or one more dreadful on the altar of sacrifice. From this gloomy state they were relieved by the coming of their comrades.

Cortés calmly listened to the explanation made by Alvarado. But, before it was ended, the conviction must have forced itself on his mind that he had made a wrong selection for this important post. Yet the mistake was natural. Alvarado was a cavalier of high family, gallant and chivalrous, and his warm personal friend. He had talents for action, was possessed of firmness and intrepidity, while his frank and dazzling manners made the *Tonatiuh* an especial favourite with the Mexicans. But, underneath this showy exterior, the future conqueror of Guatemala concealed a heart rash, rapacious, and cruel. He was altogether destitute of that moderation, which, in the delicate position he occupied, was a quality of more worth than all the rest.

When Alvarado had concluded his answers to the several interrogatories of Cortés, the brow of the latter darkened, as he said to his lieutenant, "You have done badly. You have been false to your trust. Your conduct has been that of a madman!" And, turning abruptly on his heel, he left him in undisguised displeasure.

Yet this was not a time to break with one so popular, and in many respects so important to him, as this captain, much less to inflict on him the punishment he merited. The Spaniards were like mariners labouring in a heavy tempest, whose bark nothing but the dexterity of the pilot, and the hearty co-operation of the crew, can save from foundering. Dissensions at such a moment must be fatal. Cortés, it is true, felt strong in his present resources. He now found himself at the head of a force which could scarcely amount to less than twelve hundred and fifty Spaniards, and eight thousand native warriors, principally Tlascalans. But, though relying on this to overawe resistance, the very augmentations of numbers increased the difficulty of subsistence. Discontented with himself, disgusted with his officer, and embarrassed by the disastrous consequences in which Alvarado's intemperance had involved him, he became irritable, and indulged in a petulance by no means common; for, though a man of lively passions by nature, he held them habitually under control.

On the day that Cortés arrived, Montezuma had left his own quarters to welcome him. But the Spanish commander, distrusting, as it would seem, however unreasonably, his good faith, received him so coldly that the Indian monarch withdrew, displeased and dejected, to his apartment. As the Mexican populace made no show of submission, and brought no supplies to the army, the general's ill-humour with the emperor continued. When, therefore, Montezuma sent some of the nobles to ask an interview with Cortés, the latter, turning to his own officers, haughtily exclaimed, "What have I to do with this dog of a king, who suffers us to starve before his eyes!"

His captains, among whom were Olid, de Avila, and Velasquez de Leon, endeavoured to mitigate his anger, reminding him, in respectful terms, that, had it not been for the emperor, the garrison might even now have been overwhelmed by the enemy. This remonstrance only chafed him the more. "Did not the dog," he asked, repeating the opprobrious epithet, "betray us in his communications with Narvaez? And does he not now suffer his markets to be closed, and leave us to die of famine?" Then, turning fiercely to the Mexicans, he said, "Go, tell your master and his people to open the markets, or we will do it for them, at their cost!" The chiefs, who had gathered the import of his previous taunt on their sovereign, from his tone and gesture, or perhaps from some comprehensions of his language, left his presence swelling with resentment; and, in communicating his message, took care it should lose none of its effect.

Shortly after, Cortés, at the suggestion, it is said, of Montezuma, released his brother Cuitlahua, lord of Iztapalapan, who, it will be remembered, had been seized on suspicion of co-operating with the chief of Tezcuco in his meditated revolt. It was thought he might be of service in allaying the present tumult, and bringing the populace to a better state of feeling. But he returned no more to the fortress. He was a bold, ambitious prince, and the injuries he had received from the Spaniards rankled deep in his bosom. He was presumptive heir to the crown, which, by the Aztec laws of succession, descended much more frequently in a collateral than in a direct line. The people welcomed him as the representative of their reign, and chose him to supply the place of Montezuma during his captivity. Cuitlahua willingly accepted the post of honour and of danger. He was an experienced warrior, and exerted himself to reorganise the disorderly levies, and to arrange a more efficient plan of operations. The effect was soon visible.

Cortés, meanwhile, had so little doubt of his ability to overawe the insurgents, that he wrote to that effect to the garrison of Villa Rica, by the same despatches in which he informed them of his safe arrival in the capital. But scarcely had his messenger been gone half an hour, when he returned breathless with terror, and covered with wounds.

"The city," he said, "was all in arms! The drawbridges were raised, and the enemy would soon be upon them!" He spoke truth. It was not long before a hoarse, sullen sound became audible like that of the roaring of distant waters. It grew louder and louder; till, from the parapet surrounding the inclosure, the great avenues which led to it might be seen dark with the masses of warriors, who came rolling on in a confused tide towards the fortress. At the same time the terraces and *azoteas* or flat roofs, in the neighbourhood, were thronged with combatants brandishing their missiles, who seemed to have risen up as if by magic! It was a spectacle to appal the stoutest. But the dark storm to which it was the prelude, and which gathered deeper and deeper round the Spaniards during the remainder of their residence in the capital, must form the subject of a separate book.

EXPULSION FROM MEXICO

CHAPTER I

*Desperate Assault on the Quarters—Fury of the Mexicans—
Sally of the Spaniards—Montezuma Addresses the People—Dangerously Wounded*

1520

THE PALACE OF AXAYACATL, in which the Spaniards were quartered,
was, as the reader may remember, a vast, irregular pile of stone buildings, having but one floor, except in the centre, where another story was
added, consisting of a suite of apartments which rose like turrets on the
main building of the edifice. A vast area stretched around, encompassed
by a stone wall of no great height. This was supported by towers or
bulwarks at certain intervals, which gave it some degree of strength, not,
indeed, as compared with European fortifications, but sufficient to resist
the rude battering enginery of the Indians. The parapet had been pierced
here and there with embrasures for the artillery, which consisted of
thirteen guns; and smaller apertures were made in other parts for the
convenience of the arquebusiers. The Spanish forces found accommodations within the great building; but the numerous body of Tlascalan
auxiliaries could have had no other shelter than what was afforded by
barracks or sheds hastily constructed for the purpose in the spacious
courtyard. Most of them, probably, bivouacked under the open sky, in a
climate milder than that to which they were accustomed among the rude
hills of their native land. Thus crowded into a small compact compass,
the whole army could be assembled at a moment's notice; and, as the
Spanish commander was careful to enforce the strictest discipline and
vigilance, it was scarcely possible that he could be taken by surprise. No
sooner, therefore, did the trumpet call to arms, as the approach of the
enemy was announced, than every soldier was at his post, the cavalry
mounted, the artillerymen at their guns, and the archers and arquebusiers
stationed so as to give the assailants a warm reception.

On they came, with the companies, or irregular masses, into which the

287

multitude was divided, rushing forward each in its own dense column, with many a gay banner displayed, and many a bright gleam of light reflected from helmet, arrow, and spear-head, as they were tossed about in their disorderly array. As they drew near the inclosure, the Aztecs set up a hideous yell, or rather that shrill whistle used in fight by the nations of Anahuac, which rose far above the sound of shell and atabal, and their other rude instruments of warlike melody. They followed this by a tempest of missiles—stones, darts, and arrows—which fell thick as rain on the besieged, while volleys of the same kind descended from the crowded terraces of the neighbourhood.

The Spaniards waited until the foremost column had arrived within the best distance for giving effect to their fire, when a general discharge of artillery and arquebuses swept the ranks of the assailants, and mowed them down by hundreds. The Mexicans were familiar with the report of these formidable engines, as they had been harmlessly discharged on some holiday festival; but never till now had they witnessed their murderous power. They stood aghast for a moment, as with bewildered looks they staggered under the fury of the fire; but, soon rallying, the bold barbarians uttered a piercing cry, and rushed forward over the prostrate bodies of their comrades. A second and a third volley checked their career, and threw them into disorder, but still they pressed on, letting off clouds of arrows; while their comrades on the roofs of the houses took more deliberate aim at the combatants in the courtyard. The Mexicans were particularly expert in the use of the sling; and the stones which they hurled from their elevated positions on the heads of their enemies did even greater execution than the arrows. They glanced, indeed, from the mail-covered bodies of the cavaliers, and from those who were sheltered under the cotton panoply, or *escaupil*. But some of the soldiers, especially the veterans of Cortés, and many of their Indian allies, had but slight defences, and suffered greatly under this stony tempest.

The Aztecs, meanwhile, had advanced close under the walls of the intrenchment; their ranks broken and disordered, and their limbs mangled by the unintermitting fire of the Christians. But they still pressed on, under the very muzzle of the guns. They endeavoured to scale the parapet, which from its moderate height was in itself a work of no great difficulty. But the moment they showed their heads above the rampart, they were shot down by the unerring marksmen within, or stretched on the ground by a blow of a Tlascalan *naquahuitl*. Nothing daunted, others soon appeared to take the place of the fallen, and strove, by raising themselves on the writhing bodies of their dying comrades, or by fixing their spears in the crevices of the wall, to surmount the barrier. But the attempt proved equally vain.

Defeated here, they tried to effect a breach in the parapet by battering it with heavy pieces of timber. The works were not constructed on those scientific principles by which one part is made to overlook and protect another. The besiegers, therefore, might operate at their pleasure, with but little molestation from the garrison within, whose guns could not be brought into a position to bear on them, and who could mount no part of their own works for their defence, without exposing their persons to the missiles of the whole besieging army. The parapet, however, proved too strong for the efforts of the assailants. In their despair, they endeavoured to set the Christian quarters on fire, shooting burning arrows into them, and climbing up so as to dart their firebrands through the embrasures. The principal edifice was of stone. But the temporary defences of the Indian allies, and other parts of the exterior works, were of wood. Several of these took fire, and the flame spread rapidly among the light combustible materials. This was a disaster for which the besieged were wholly unprepared. They had little water, scarcely enough for their own consumption. They endeavoured to extinguish the flames by heaping on earth; but in vain. Fortunately the great building was of materials which defied the destroying element. But the fire raged in some of the outworks, connected with the parapet, with a fury which could only be checked by throwing down a part of the wall itself, thus laying open a formidable breach. This, by the general's order, was speedily protected by a battery of heavy guns, and a file of arquebusiers, who kept up an incessant volley through the opening on the assailants.

The fight now raged with fury on both sides. The walls around the palace belched forth an unintermitting sheet of flame and smoke. The groans of the wounded and dying were lost in the fiercer battle-cries of the combatants, the roar of the artillery, the sharper rattle of the musketry, and the hissing sound of Indian missiles. It was the conflict of the European with the American; of civilised man with the barbarian; of the science of the one with the rude weapons and warfare of the other. And as the ancient walls of Tenochtitlan shook under the thunders of the artillery—it announced that the white man, the destroyer, had set his foot within her precincts.

Night at length came, and drew her friendly mantle over the contest.

The Aztec seldom fought by night. It brought little repose, however, to the Spaniards, in hourly expectation of an assault; and they found abundant occupation in restoring the breaches in their defences, and in repairing their battered armour. The beleaguering host lay on their arms through the night, giving token of their presence, now and then, by sending a stone or shaft over the battlements, or by a solitary cry of defiance from some warrior more determined than the rest, till all other sounds were lost in the vague, indistinct murmurs which float upon the air in the neighbourhood of a vast assembly.

The ferocity shown by the Mexicans seems to have been a thing for which Cortés was wholly unprepared. His past experience, his uninterrupted career of victory with a much feebler force at his command, had led him to underrate the military efficiency, if not the valour, of the Indians. The apparent facility with which the Mexicans had acquiesced in the outrages on their sovereign and themselves had led him to hold their courage, in particular, too lightly. He could not believe the present assault to be anything more than a temporary ebullition of the populace, which would soon waste itself by its own fury. And he proposed, on the following day, to sally out and inflict such chastisement on his foes as should bring them to their senses, and show who was master in the capital.

With early dawn, the Spaniards were up and under arms; but not before their enemies had given evidence of their hostility by the random missiles, which, from time to time, were sent into the inclosure. As the grey light of morning advanced, it showed the besieging army far from being diminished in numbers, filing up the great square and neighbouring avenues, in more dense array than on the preceding evening. Instead of a confused, disorderly rabble, it had the appearance of something like a regular force, with its battalions distributed under their respective banners, the devices of which showed a contribution from the principal cities and districts in the valley. High above the rest was conspicuous the ancient standard of Mexico, with its well-known cognisance, an eagle pouncing on an ocelot, emblazoned on a rich mantle of featherwork. Here and there priests might be seen mingling in the ranks of the besiegers, and, with frantic gestures, animating them to avenge their insulted deities.

The greater part of the enemy had little clothing save the *maxtlatl,* or sash, round the loins. They were variously armed, with long spears tipped with copper, or flint, or sometimes merely pointed and hardened in the fire. Some were provided with slings, and others with darts having two or three points, with long strings attached to them, by which, when discharged, they could be torn away again from the body of the wounded. This was a formidable weapon, much dreaded by the Spaniards. Those of a higher order wielded the terrible *maquahuitl,* with its sharp and brittle blades of obsidian. Amidst the motley bands of warriors were seen many whose showy dress and air of authority intimated persons of high military consequence. Their breasts were protected by plates of metal, over which was thrown the gay surcoat of featherwork. They wore casques resembling, in their form, the head of some wild and ferocious animal, crested with bristly hair, or overshadowed by tall and graceful plumes of many a brilliant colour. Some few were decorated with the red fillet bound round the hair, having tufts of cotton attached to it, which denoted by their number that of the victories they had won, and their own pre-eminent rank among the warriors of the nation. The motley assembly plainly showed that priest, warrior, and citizen had all united to swell the tumult.

Before the sun had shot his beams into the Castilian quarters, the enemy were in motion, evidently preparing to renew the assault of the preceding day. The Spanish commander determined to anticipate them by a vigorous sortie, for which he had already made the necessary disposi- tions. A general discharge of ordnance and musketry sent death far and wide into the enemy's ranks, and, before they had time to recover from their confusion, the gates were thrown open, and Cortés, sallying out at the head of his cavalry, supported by a large body of infantry and several thousand Tlascalans, rode at full gallop against them. Taken thus by surprise, it was scarcely possible to offer much resistance. Those who did were trampled down under the horses' feet, cut to pieces with the broadswords, or pierced with the lances of the riders. The infantry followed up the blow, and the rout for the moment was general.

But the Aztecs fled only to take refuge behind a barricade, or strong work of timber and earth, which had been thrown across the great street through which they were pursued. Rallying on the other side, they made a gallant stand, and poured in turn a volley of their light weapons on the Spaniards, who, saluted with a storm of missiles at the same time, from the terraces of the houses, were checked in their career, and thrown into some disorder.

Cortés, thus impeded, ordered up a few pieces of heavy ordnance, which soon swept away the barricades, and cleared a passage for the army. But it had lost the momentum acquired in its rapid advance. The enemy had time to rally and to meet the Spaniards on more equal terms. They were attacked in flank, too, as they advanced, by fresh battalions, who swarmed in from the adjoining streets and lanes. The canals were alive with boats filled with warriors, who, with their formidable darts, searched every crevice or weak place in the armour of proof, and made havoc on the unprotected bodies of the Tlascalans. By repeated and vigorous charges, the Spaniards succeeded in driving the Indians before them; though many, with a desperation which showed they loved vengeance better than life, sought to embarrass the movements of their horses by clinging to their legs, or more successfully strove to pull the riders from their saddles. And woe to the unfortunate cavalier who was thus dismounted—to be despatched by the brutal *maquahuitl,* or to be dragged on board a canoe to the bloody altar of sacrifice!

But the greatest annoyance which the Spaniards endured was from the missiles from the *azoteas,* consisting often of large stones, hurled with a force that would tumble the stoutest rider from his saddle. Galled in the extreme by these discharges, against which even their shields afforded no adequate protection, Cortés ordered fire to be set to the buildings. This was no very difficult matter, since, although chiefly of stone, they were filled with mats, canework, and other combustible materials, which were soon in a blaze. But the buildings stood separated from one, another by canals and drawbridges, so that the flames did not easily communicate to the neighbouring edifices. Hence the labour of the Spaniards was incalculably increased, and their progress in the work of destruction—fortunately for the city—was comparatively slow. They did not relax their efforts, however, till several hundred houses had been consumed, and the miseries of a conflagration, in which the wretched inmates perished equally with the defenders, were added to the other horrors of the scene.

The day was now far spent. The Spaniards had been everywhere victorious. But the enemy, though driven back on every point, still kept the field. When broken by the furious charges of the cavalry, he soon rallied behind the temporary defences, which, at different intervals, had been thrown across the streets, and, facing about, renewed the fight with undiminished courage, till the sweeping away of the barriers by the cannon of the assailants left a free passage for the movements of their horse. Thus the action was a succession of rallying and retreating, in which both parties suffered much, although the loss inflicted on the Indians was probably tenfold greater than that of the Spaniards. But the Aztecs could better afford the loss of a hundred lives than their antagonists that of one. And, while the Spaniards showed an array broken, and obviously thinned in numbers, the Mexican army, swelled by the tributary levies which flowed in upon it from the neighbouring streets, exhibited, with all its losses, no sign of diminution. At length, sated with carnage, and exhausted by toil and hunger, the Spanish commander drew off his men, and sounded a retreat.

On his way back to his quarters, he beheld his friend, the secretary Duero, in a street adjoining, unhorsed, and hotly engaged with a body of Mexicans, against whom he was desperately defending himself with his poniard. Cortés, roused at the sight, shouted his war-cry, and, dashing into the midst of the enemy, scattered them like chaff by the fury of his onset; then recovering his friend's horse, he enabled him to remount, and the two cavaliers, striking their spurs into their steeds, burst through their opponents and joined the main body of the army. Such displays of generous gallantry were not uncommon in these engagements, which called forth more feats of personal adventure than battles with antagonists better skilled in the science of war. The chivalrous bearing of the general was emulated in full measure by Sandoval, de Leon, Olid, Alvarado, Ordaz, and his other brave companions, who won such glory under the eyes of their leader, as prepared the way for the independent commands which afterwards placed provinces and kingdoms at their disposal.

The undaunted Aztecs hung on the rear of their retreating foes, annoying them at every step by fresh flights of stones and arrows; and when the Spaniards had re-entered their fortress, the Indian host encamped around it, showing the same dogged resolution as on the preceding evening. Though true to their ancient habits of inaction during the night, they broke the stillness of the hour by insulting cries and menaces, which reached the ears of the besieged. "The gods have delivered you, at last, into our hands," they said; "Huitzilopotchli has long cried for his victims. The stone of sacrifice is ready. The knives are sharpened. The wild beasts in the palace are roaring for their offal. And the cages," they added, taunting the Tlascalans with their leanness, "are waiting for the false sons of Anahuac, who are to be fattened for the festival." These dismal menaces, which sounded fearfully in the ears of the besieged, who understood too well their import, were mingled with piteous lamentations for their sovereign, whom they called on the Spaniards to deliver up to them.

Cortés suffered much from a severe wound which he had received in the hand in the late action. But the anguish of his mind must have been still greater, as he brooded over the dark prospect before him. He had mistaken the character of the Mexicans. Their long and patient endurance had been a violence to their natural temper, which, as their whole history proves, was arrogant and ferocious beyond that of most of the races of Anahuac. The restraint which, in deference to their monarch, more than to their own fears, they had so long put on their natures, being once removed, their passions burst forth with accumulated violence. The Spaniards had encountered in the Tlascalan an open enemy, who had no grievance to complain of, no wrong to redress. He fought under the vague apprehension only of some coming evil to his country. But the Aztec, hitherto the proud lord of the land, was goaded by insult and injury, till he had reached that pitch of self-devotion which made life cheap in comparison with revenge. Armed thus with the energy of despair, the savage is almost a match for the civilised man; and a whole nation, moved to its depths by a common feeling which swallows up all selfish considerations of personal interest and safety, becomes, whatever be its resources, like the earthquake and the tornado, the most formidable among the agencies of nature.

Considerations of this kind may have passed through the mind of Cortés, as he reflected on his own impotence to restrain the fury of the Mexicans, and resolved in despite of his late supercilious treatment of Montezuma, to employ his authority to allay the tumult—an authority so successfully exerted in behalf of Alvarado, at an earlier stage of the insurrection. He was the more confirmed in his purpose, on the following morning, when the assailants, redoubling their efforts, succeeded in scaling the works in one quarter, and effecting an entrance into the inclosure. It is true, they were met with so resolute a spirit, that not a man of those who entered was left alive. But in the impetuosity of the assault, it seemed, for a few moments, as if the place was to be carried by storm.

Cortés now sent to the Aztec emperor to request his interposition with his subjects in behalf of the Spaniards. But Montezuma was not in the humour to comply. He had remained moodily in his quarters ever since the general's return. Disgusted with the treatment he had received, he had still further cause for mortification in finding himself the ally of those who were the open enemies of his nation. From his apartment he had beheld the tragical scenes in his capital, and seen another, the presumptive heir to his throne, taking the place which he should have occupied at the head of his warriors, and fighting the battles of his country. Distressed by his position, indignant at those who had placed him in it, he coldly answered, "What have I to do with Malintzin? I do not wish to hear from him. I desire only to die. To what a state has my willingness to serve him reduced me!" When urged still further to comply by Olid and Father Olmedo, he added, "It is of no use. They will neither believe me, nor the false words and promises of Malintzin. You will never leave these walls alive." On being assured, however, that the Spaniards would willingly depart, if a way were opened to them by their enemies, he at length—moved, probably, more by the desire to spare the blood of his subjects than of the Christians—consented to expostulate with his people.

In order to give the greater effect to his presence, he put on his imperial robes. The *tilmatli,* his mantle of white and blue, flowed over his shoulders, held together by its rich clasp of the green *chalchivitl.* The same precious gem, with emeralds of uncommon size, set in gold, profusely ornamented other parts of his dress. His feet were shod with the golden sandals, and his brows covered by the *copilli,* or Mexican diadem, resembling in form the pontifical tiara. Thus attired, and surrounded by a guard of Spaniards and several Aztec nobles, and preceded by the golden wand, the symbol of sovereignty, the Indian monarch ascended the central turret of the palace. His presence was instantly recognised by the people, and, as the royal retinue advanced along the battlements, a change, as if by magic, came over the scene. The clang of instruments, the fierce cries of the assailants, were hushed, and a death-like stillness pervaded the whole assembly, so fiercely agitated but a few moments before by the wild tumult of war! Many prostrated themselves on the ground; others bent the knee; and all turned with eager expectation towards the monarch, whom they had been taught to reverence with slavish awe, and from whose countenance they had been wont to turn away as from the intolerable splendours of divinity! Montezuma saw his advantage; and, while he stood thus confronted with his awe-struck people, he seemed to recover all his former authority and confidence as he felt himself to be still a king. With a calm voice, easily heard over the silent assembly, he is said by the Castilian writers to have thus addressed them:

"Why do I see my people here in arms against the palace of my fathers? Is it that you think your sovereign a prisoner, and wish to release him? If so, you have acted rightly. But you are mistaken. I am no prisoner. The strangers are my guests. I remain with them only from choice, and can leave them when I list. Have you come to drive them from the city? That is unnecessary. They will depart of their own accord, if you will open a way for them. Return to your homes, then. Lay down your arms. Show your obedience to me who have a right to it. The white men shall go back to their own land; and all shall be well again within the walls of Tenochtitlan."

As Montezuma announced himself the friend of the detested strangers, a murmur ran through the multitude; a murmur of contempt for the pusillanimous prince who could show himself so insensible to the insults and injuries for which the nation was in arms! The swollen tide of their passions swept away all the barriers of ancient reverence, and, taking a new direction, descended on the head of the unfortunate monarch, so far degenerated from his warlike ancestors. "Base Aztec," they exclaimed, "woman, coward, the white men have made you a woman—fit only to weave and spin!" These bitter taunts were soon followed by still more hostile demonstrations. A chief, it is said, of high rank, bent a bow or brandished a javelin with an air of defiance against the emperor, when, in an instant, a cloud of stones and arrows descended on the spot where the royal train was gathered. The Spaniards appointed to protect his person had been thrown off their guard by the respectful deportment of the people during their lord's address. They now hastily interposed their bucklers. But it was too late. Montezuma was wounded by three of the missiles, one of which, a stone, fell with such violence on his head, near the temple, as brought him senseless to the ground. The Mexicans, shocked at their own sacrilegious act, experienced a sudden revulsion of feeling, and, setting up a dismal cry, dispersed panic-struck in different directions. Not one of the multitudinous array remained in the great square before the palace!

The unhappy prince, meanwhile, was borne by his attendants to his apartments below. On recovering from the insensibility caused by the blow, the wretchedness of his condition broke upon him. He had tasted the last bitterness of degradation. He had been reviled, rejected, by his people. The meanest of the rabble had raised their hands against him. He had nothing more to live for. It was in vain that Cortés and his officers endeavoured to soothe the anguish of his spirit and fill him with better thoughts. He spoke not a word in answer. His wound, though dangerous, might still, with skilful treatment, not prove mortal. But

Montezuma refused all the remedies prescribed for it. He tore off the bandages as often as they were applied, maintaining all the while the most determined silence. He sat with eyes dejected, brooding over his fallen fortunes, over the image of ancient majesty and present humiliation. He had survived his honour. But a spark of his ancient spirit seemed to kindle in his bosom, as it was clear he did not mean to survive his disgrace. From this painful scene the Spanish general and his followers were soon called away by the new dangers which menaced the garrison.

CHAPTER II

Storming of the Great Temple—Spirit of the Aztecs—Distresses of the Garrison—Sharp Combats in the City—Death of Montezuma

1520

OPPOSITE TO THE SPANISH QUARTERS, at only a few rods' distance, stood the great *teocalli* of Huitzilopotchli. This pyramidal mound, with the sanctuaries that crowned it, rising altogether to the height of nearly a hundred and fifty feet, afforded an elevated position that completely commanded the palace of Axayacatl, occupied by the Christians. A body of five or six hundred Mexicans, many of them nobles and warriors of the highest rank, had got possession of the *teocalli,* whence they discharged such a tempest of arrows on the garrison, that no one could leave his defences for a moment without imminent danger; while the Mexicans, under shelter of the sanctuaries, were entirely covered from the fire of the besieged. It was obviously necessary to dislodge the enemy, if the Spaniards would remain longer in their quarters.

Cortés assigned this service to his chamberlain Escobar, giving him a hundred men for the purpose, with orders to storm the *teocalli,* and set fire to the sanctuaries. But that officer was thrice repulsed in the attempt, and, after the most desperate efforts, was obliged to return with considerable loss and without accomplishing his object.

Cortés, who saw the immediate necessity of carrying the place, determined to lead the storming party himself. He was then suffering much from the wound in his left hand, which had disabled it for the present. He made the arm serviceable, however, by fastening his buckler to it, and, thus crippled, sallied out at the head of three hundred chosen cavaliers, and several thousand of his auxiliaries.

In the courtyard of the temple he found a numerous body of Indians prepared to dispute his passage. He briskly charged them, but the flat, smooth stones of the pavement were so slippery that the horses lost their footing and many of them fell. Hastily dismounting, they sent back the animals to their quarters, and, renewing the assault, the Spaniards succeeded without much difficulty in dispersing the Indian warriors, and opening a free passage for themselves to the *teocalli*. This building, as the reader may remember, was a large pyramidal structure, about three hundred feet square at the base. A flight of stone steps on the outside, at one of the angles of the mound, led to a platform, or terraced walk, which passed round the building until it reached a similar flight of stairs directly over the preceding, that conducted to another landing as before. As there were five bodies or divisions of the *teocalli,* it became necessary to pass round its whole extent four times, or nearly a mile, in order to reach the summit, which, it may be recollected, was an open area, crowned only by the two sanctuaries dedicated to the Aztec deities.

Cortés, having cleared a way for the assault, sprang up the lower stairway, followed by Alvarado, Sandoval, Ordaz, and the other gallant cavaliers of his little band, leaving a file of arquebusiers and a strong corps of Indian allies to hold the enemy in check at the foot of the monument. On the first landing, as well as on the several galleries above, and on the summit, the Aztec warriors were drawn up to dispute his passage. From their elevated position they showered down volleys of lighter missiles, together with heavy stones, beams, and burning rafters, which, thundering along the stairway, overturned the ascending Spaniards, and carried desolation through their ranks. The more fortunate, eluding or springing over these obstacles, succeeded in gaining the first terrace, where, throwing themselves on their enemies, they compelled them, after a short resistance, to fall back. The assailants pressed on, effectually supported by a brisk fire of the musketeers from below, which so much galled the Mexicans in their exposed situation, that they were glad to take shelter on the broad summit of the *teocalli*.

Cortés and his comrades were close upon their rear, and the two parties soon found themselves face to face on this aerial battlefield, engaged in mortal combat in presence of the whole city, as well as of the troops in the courtyard, who paused, as if by mutual consent, from their own hostilities, gazing in silent expectation on the issue of those above. The area, though somewhat smaller than the base of the *teocalli,* was large enough to afford a fair field of fight for a thousand combatants. It was paved with broad, flat stones. No impediment occurred over its surface, except the huge sacrificial block, and the temples of stone which rose to the height of forty feet, at the further extremity of the arena. One of these had been consecrated to the Cross; the other was still occupied by the Mexican war-god. The Christian and the Aztec contended for their religions under the very shadow of their respective shrines; while the Indian priests, running to and fro, with their hair wildly streaming over their sable mantles, seemed hovering in mid air, like so many demons of darkness urging on the work of slaughter!

The parties closed with the desperate fury of men who had no hope but in victory. Quarter was neither asked nor given; and to fly was impossible. The edge of the area was unprotected by parapet or battlement. The least slip would be fatal; and the combatants, as they struggled in mortal agony, were sometimes seen to roll over the sheer sides of the precipice together. Cortés himself is said to have had a narrow escape from this dreadful fate. Two warriors, of strong, muscular frames, seized on him, and were dragging him violently towards the brink of the pyramid. Aware of their intention, he struggled with all his force, and, before they could accomplish their purpose, succeeded in tearing himself from their grasp, and hurling one of them over the walls with his own arm! The story is not improbable in itself, for Cortés was a man of uncommon agility and strength. It has been often repeated, but not by contemporary history.

The battle lasted with unintermitting fury for three hours. The number of the enemy was double that of the Christians; and it seemed as if it were a contest which must be determined by numbers and brute force, rather than by superior science. But it was not so. The invulnerable armour of the Spaniard, his sword of matchless temper, and his skill in the use of it, gave him advantages which far outweighed the odds of physical strength and numbers. After doing all that the courage of despair could enable men to do, resistance grew fainter and fainter on the side of the Aztecs. One after another they had fallen. Two or three priests only survived to be led away in triumph by the victors. Every other combatant was stretched a corpse on the bloody arena, or had been hurled from the giddy heights. Yet the loss of the Spaniards was not inconsiderable. It amounted to forty-five of their best men, and nearly all the remainder were more or less injured in the desperate conflict.

The victorious cavaliers now rushed towards the sanctuaries. The lower story was of stone; the two upper were of wood. Penetrating into their recesses, they had the mortification to find the image of the Virgin and the Cross removed. But in the other edifice they still beheld the grim figure of Huitzilopotchli, with his censer of smoking hearts, and the walls of his oratory reeking with gore—not improbably of their own countrymen! With shouts of triumph the Christians tore the uncouth monster from his niche, and tumbled him, in the presence of the horror-struck Aztecs, down the steps of the *teocalli*. They then set fire to the accursed building. The flame speedily ran up the slender towers, sending forth an ominous light over city, lake, and valley, to the remotest hut among the mountains. It was the funeral pyre of paganism, and pro-claimed the fall of that sanguinary religion which had so long hung like a dark cloud over the fair regions of Anahuac!

Having accomplished this good work, the Spaniards descended the winding slopes of the *teocalli* with more free and buoyant step, as if conscious that the blessing of Heaven now rested on their arms. They passed through the dusky files of Indian warriors in the courtyard, too much dismayed by the appalling scenes they had witnessed to offer resistance; and reached their own quarters in safety. That very night they followed up the blow by a sortie on the sleeping town, and burned three hundred houses, the horrors of conflagration being made still more impressive by occurring at the hour when the Aztecs, from their own system of warfare, were least prepared for them.

Hoping to find the temper of the natives somewhat subdued by these reverses, Cortés now determined, with his usual policy, to make them a vantage-ground for proposing terms of accommodation. He accordingly invited the enemy to a parley, and, as the principal chiefs, attended by their followers, assembled in the great square, he mounted the turret before occupied by Montezuma, and made signs that he would address them. Marina, as usual, took her place by his side, as his interpreter. The multitude gazed with earnest curiosity on the Indian girl, whose influence with the Spaniards was well known, and whose connection with the general, in particular, had led the Aztecs to designate him by her Mexican name of Malinche. Cortés, speaking through the soft, musical tones of his mistress, told his audience they must now be convinced that they had nothing further to hope from opposition to the Spaniards. They had seen their gods trampled in the dust, their altars broken, their dwell-ings burned, their warriors falling on all sides. "All this," continued he, "you have brought on yourselves by your rebellion. Yet for the affection the sovereign, whom you have so unworthily treated, still bears you, I would willingly stay my hand, if you will lay down your arms, and return once more to your obedience. But, if you do not," he concluded,

"I will make your city a heap of ruins, and leave not a soul alive to mourn over it!"

But the Spanish commander did not yet comprehend the character of the Aztecs, if he thought to intimidate them by menaces. Calm in their exterior and slow to move, they were the more difficult to pacify when roused; and now that they had been stirred to their inmost depths, it was no human voice that could still the tempest. It may be, however, that Cortés did not so much misconceive the character of the people. He may have felt that an authoritative tone was the only one he could assume with any chance of effect, in his present position, in which milder and more conciliatory language would, by intimating a consciousness of inferiority, have too certainly defeated its own object.

It was true, they answered, he had destroyed their temples, broken in pieces their gods, massacred their countrymen. Many more, doubtless, were yet to fall under their terrible swords. But they were content so long as for every thousand Mexicans they could shed the blood of a single white man! "Look out," they continued, "on our terraces and streets, see them still thronged with warriors as far as your eyes can reach. Our numbers are scarcely diminished by our losses. Yours, on the contrary, are lessening every hour. You are perishing from hunger and sickness. Your provisions and water are failing. You must soon fall into our hands. *The bridges are broken down, and you cannot escape!* There will be too few of you left to glut the vengeance of our gods!" As they concluded, they sent a volley of arrows over the battlements, which compelled the Spaniards to descend and take refuge in their defences.

The fierce and indomitable spirit of the Aztecs filled the besieged with dismay. All, then, that they had done and suffered, their battles by day, their vigils by night, the perils they had braved, even the victories they had won, were of no avail. It was too evident that they had no longer the spring of ancient superstition to work upon in the breasts of the natives, who, like some wild beast that has burst the bonds of his keeper, seemed now to swell and exult in the full consciousness of their strength. The annunciation respecting the bridges fell like a knell on the ears of the Christians. All that they had heard was too true—and they gazed on one another with looks of anxiety and dismay.

The same consequences followed, which sometimes take place among the crew of a shipwrecked vessel. Subordination was lost in the dreadful sense of danger. A spirit of mutiny broke out, especially among the recent levies drawn from the army of Narvaez. They had come into the country from no motive of ambition, but attracted simply by the glowing reports of its opulence, and they had fondly hoped to return in a few months with their pockets well lined with the gold of the Aztec monarch. But how different had been their lot! From the first hour of their landing, they had experienced only trouble and disaster, privations of every description, sufferings unexampled, and they now beheld in perspective a fate yet more appalling. Bitterly did they lament the hour when they left the sunny fields of Cuba for these cannibal regions! And heartily did they curse their own folly in listening to the call of Velasquez, and still more in embarking under the banner of Cortés!

They now demanded with noisy vehemence to be led instantly from the city, and refused to serve longer in defence of a place where they were cooped up like sheep in the shambles, waiting only to be dragged to slaughter. In all this they were rebuked by the more orderly soldier-like conduct of the veterans of Cortés. These latter had shared with their general the day of his prosperity, and they were not disposed to desert him in the tempest. It was, indeed, obvious, on a little reflection, that the only chance of safety, in the existing crisis, rested on subordination and union; and that even this chance must be greatly diminished under any other leader than their present one.

Thus pressed by enemies without and by factions within, that leader was found, as usual, true to himself. Circumstances so appalling as would have paralysed a common mind only stimulated his to higher action, and drew forth all its resources. He combined what is most rare, singular coolness and constancy of purpose, with a spirit of enterprise that might well be called romantic. His presence of mind did not now desert him. He calmly surveyed his condition, and weighed the difficulties which surrounded him, before coming to a decision. Independently of the hazard of a retreat in the face of a watchful and desperate foe, it was a deep mortification to surrender up the city, where he had so long lorded it as a master; to abandon the rich treasures which he had secured to himself and his followers; to forego the very means by which he had hoped to propitiate the favour of his sovereign, and secure an amnesty for his irregular proceedings. This, he well knew, must, after all, be dependent on success. To fly now was to acknowledge himself further removed from the conquest than ever. What a close was this to a career so auspiciously begun! What a contrast to his magnificent vaunts! What a triumph would it afford to his enemies! The governor of Cuba would be amply revenged.

But, if such humiliating reflections crowded on his mind, the alternative of remaining, in his present crippled condition, seemed yet more desperate. With his men daily diminishing in strength and numbers, their provisions reduced so low that a small daily ration of bread was all the sustenance afforded to the soldier under his extraordinary fatigues, with the breaches every day widening in his feeble fortifications, with his ammunition, in fine, nearly expended, it would be impossible to maintain the place much longer—and none but men of iron constitutions and tempers, like the Spaniards, could have held out so long—against the enemy. The chief embarrassment was as to the time and manner in which it would be expedient to evacuate the city. The best route seemed to be that of Tlacopan (Tacuba). For the causeway, the most dangerous part of the road, was but two miles long in that direction, and would therefore place the fugitives much sooner than either of the other great avenues on terra firma. Before his final departure, however, he proposed to make another sally in that direction, in order to reconnoitre the ground, and, at the same time, divert the enemy's attention from his real purpose by a show of active operations.

For some days his workmen had been employed in constructing a military machine of his own invention. It was called a *manta,* and was contrived somewhat on the principle of the mantelets used in the wars of the Middle Ages. It was, however, more complicated, consisting of a tower made of light beams and planks, having two chambers, one over the other. These were to be filled with musketeers, and the sides were provided with loopholes, through which a fire could be kept up on the enemy. The great advantage proposed by this contrivance was to afford a defence to the troops against the missiles hurled from the terraces. These machines, three of which were made, rested on rollers, and were provided with strong ropes, by which they were to be dragged along the streets by the Tlascalan auxiliaries.

The Mexicans gazed with astonishment on this warlike machinery, and, as the rolling fortresses advanced, belching forth fire and smoke from their entrails, the enemy, incapable of making an impression on those within, fell back in dismay. By bringing the *mantas* under the walls of the houses, the Spaniards were enabled to fire with effect on the mischievous tenants of the *azoteas,* and when this did not silence them, by letting a ladder, or light drawbridge, fall on the roof from the top of the *manta,* they opened a passage to the terrace, and closed with the combatants hand to hand. They could not, however, thus approach the higher buildings, from which the Indian warriors threw down such heavy masses of stone and timber as dislodged the planks that covered the machines, or, thundering against their sides, shook the frail edifices to their foundations, threatening all within with indiscriminate ruin. Indeed, the success of the experiment was doubtful, when the intervention of a canal put a stop to their further progress.

The Spaniards now found the assertion of their enemies too well confirmed. The bridge which traversed the opening had been demolished; and, although the canals which intersected the city were in general of no great width or depth, the removal of the bridges not only impeded the movements of the general's clumsy machines, but effectually disconcerted those of his cavalry. Resolving to abandon the *mantas,* he gave orders to fill up the chasm with stone, timber, and other rubbish drawn from the ruined buildings, and to make a new passage-way for the army. While this labour was going on, the Aztec slingers and archers on the other side of the opening kept up a galling discharge on the Christians, the more defenceless from the nature of their occupation. When the work was completed, and a safe passage secured, the Spanish cavaliers rode briskly against the enemy, who, unable to resist the shock of the steel-clad column, fell back with precipitation to where another canal afforded a similar strong position for defence.

There were no less than seven of these canals, intersecting the great street of Tlacopan, and at every one the same scene was renewed, the Mexicans making a gallant stand, and inflicting some loss, at each, on their persevering antagonists. These operations consumed two days, when, after incredible toil, the Spanish general had the satisfaction to find the line of communication completely re-established through the whole length of the avenue, and the principal bridges placed under strong detachments of infantry. At this juncture, when he had driven the foe before him to the furthest extremity of the street, where it touches on the causeway, he was informed that the Mexicans, disheartened by their reverses, desired to open a parley with him respecting the terms of an accommodation, and that their chiefs awaited his return for that purpose at the fortress. Overjoyed at the intelligence, he instantly rode back, attended by Alvarado, Sandoval, and about sixty of the cavaliers, to his quarters.

The Mexicans proposed that he should release the two priests captured in the temple, who might be the bearers of his terms, and serve as agents for conducting the negotiation. They were accordingly sent with the requisite instructions to their countrymen. But they did not return. The whole was an artifice of the enemy, anxious to procure the liberation of their religious leaders, one of whom was their *teoteuctli,* or high priest, whose presence was indispensable in the probable event of a new coronation.

Cortés, meanwhile, relying on the prospects of a speedy arrangement, was hastily taking some refreshment with his officers, after the fatigues of the day, when he received the alarming tidings that the enemy were in arms again, with more fury than ever; that they had overpowered the detachments posted under Alvarado at three of the bridges, and were busily occupied in demolishing them. Stung with shame at the facility with which he had been duped by his wily foe, or rather by his own sanguine hopes, Cortés threw himself into the saddle, and, followed by his brave companions, galloped back at full speed to the scene of action. The Mexicans recoiled before the impetuous charge of the Spaniards. The bridges were again restored; and Cortés and his chivalry rode down the whole extent of the great street, driving the enemy, like frightened deer, at the points of their lances. But before he could return on his steps, he had the mortification to find that the indefatigable foe, gathering from the adjoining lanes and streets, had again closed on his infantry, who, worn down by fatigue, were unable to maintain their position at one of the principal bridges. New swarms of warriors now poured in on all sides, overwhelming the little band of Christian cavaliers with a storm of stones, darts, and arrows, which rattled like hail on their armour and on that of their well-barbed horses. Most of the missiles, indeed, glanced harmless from the good panoplies of steel, or thick quilted cotton; but, now and then, one better aimed penetrated the joints of the harness, and stretched the rider on the ground.

The confusion became greater around the broken bridge. Some of the horsemen were thrown into the canal, and their steeds floundered wildly about without a rider. Cortés himself, at this crisis, did more than any other to cover the retreat of his followers. While the bridge was repairing, he plunged boldly into the midst of the barbarians, striking down an enemy at every vault of his charger, cheering on his own men, and spreading terror through the ranks of his opponents by the well-known sound of his battle-cry. Never did he display greater hardihood, or more freely expose his person, emulating, says an old chronicler, the feats of the Roman Cocles. In this way he stayed the tide of assailants, till the last man had crossed the bridge, when, some of the planks having given way, he was compelled to leap a chasm of full six feet in width, amidst a cloud of missiles, before he could place himself in safety. A report ran through the army that the general was slain. It soon spread through the city, to the great joy of the Mexicans, and reached the fortress, where the besieged were thrown into no less consternation. But, happily for them, it was false. He, indeed, received two severe contusions on the knee, but in other respects remained uninjured. At no time, however, had he been in such extreme danger; and his escape, and that of his companions, were esteemed little less than a miracle. More than one grave historian refers the preservation of the Spaniards to the watchful care of their patron Apostle, St. James, who, in these desperate conflicts, was beheld career-ing on his milk-white steed at the head of the Christian squadrons, with his sword flashing lightning, while a lady robed in white—supposed to be the Virgin—was distinctly seen by his side, throwing dust in the eyes of the infidel! The fact is attested both by Spaniards and Mexicans—by the latter after their conversion to Christianity. Surely never was there a time when the interposition of their tutelar saint was more strongly demanded.

The coming of night dispersed the Indian battalions, which, vanishing like birds of ill-omen from the field, left the well-contested pass in possession of the Spaniards. They returned, however, with none of the joyous feelings of conquerors, to their citadel, but with slow step and dispirited, with weapons hacked, armour battered, and fainting under the loss of blood, fasting, and fatigue. In this condition they had yet to learn the tidings of a fresh misfortune in the death of Montezuma.

The Indian monarch had rapidly declined, since he had received his injury, sinking, however, quite as much under the anguish of a wounded spirit, as under disease. He continued in the same moody state of insensi-bility as that already described; holding little communication with those around him, deaf to consolation, obstinately rejecting all medical reme-dies, as well as nourishment. Perceiving his end approach, some of the cavaliers present in the fortress, whom the kindness of his manners had personally attached to him, were anxious to save the soul of the dying prince from the sad doom of those who perish in the darkness of unbelief. They accordingly waited on him, with Father Olmedo at their head, and in the most earnest manner implored him to open his eyes to the error of his creed, and consent to be baptized. But Montezuma—whatever may have been suggested to the contrary—seems never to have faltered in his hereditary faith, or to have contemplated becoming an apostate; for surely he merits that name in its most odious application, who, whether Christian or pagan, renounces his religion without conviction of its falsehood. Indeed, it was a too implicit reliance on its oracles, which had led him to give such easy confidence to the Spaniards. His intercourse with them had, doubtless, not sharpened his desire to embrace their communion; and the calamities of his country he might consider as sent by his gods to punish him for his hospitality to those who had desecrated and destroyed their shrines.

When Father Olmedo, therefore, kneeling at his side, with the uplifted crucifix, affectionately besought him to embrace the sign of man's redemption, he coldly repulsed the priest, exclaiming, "I have but a few moments to live; and will not at this hour desert the faith of my fathers." One thing, however, seemed to press heavily on Montezuma's mind. This was the fate of his children, especially of three daughters, whom he had by his two wives; for there were certain rites of marriage, which distinguished the lawful wife from the concubine. Calling Cortés to his bedside, he earnestly commended these children to his care, as "the most precious jewels that he could leave him." He besought the general to interest his master, the emperor, in their behalf, and to see that they should not be left destitute, but be allowed some portion of their rightful inheritance. "Your lord will do this," he concluded, "if it were only for the friendly offices I have rendered the Spaniards, and, for the love I have shown them—though it has brought me to this condition! But for this I bear them no ill-will." Such, according to Cortés himself, were the words of the dying monarch. Not long after, on June 30, 1520, he expired in the arms of some of his own nobles, who still remained faithful in their attendance on his person. "Thus," exclaims a native historian, one of his enemies, a Tlascalan, "thus died the unfortunate Montezuma, who had swayed the sceptre with such consummate policy and wisdom; and who was held in greater reverence and awe than any other prince of his lineage, or any, indeed, that ever sat on a throne in this Western World. With him may be said to have terminated the royal line of the Aztecs, and the glory to have passed away from the empire, which under him had reached the zenith of its prosperity." "The tidings of his death," says the old Castilian chronicler Diaz, "were received with real grief by every cavalier and soldier in the army who had had access to his person; for we all loved him as a father—and no wonder, seeing how good he was." This simple, but emphatic, testimony to his desert, at such a time, is in itself the best refutation of the suspicions occasionally entertained of his fidelity to the Christians.

It is not easy to depict the portrait of Montezuma in its true colours, since it has been exhibited to us under two aspects, of the most opposite and contradictory character. In the accounts gathered of him by the Spaniards, on coming into the country, he was uniformly represented as bold and warlike, unscrupulous as to the means of gratifying his ambition, hollow and perfidious, the terror of his foes, with a haughty bearing which made him feared even by his own people. They found him, on the contrary, not merely affable and gracious, but disposed to waive all the advantages of his own position, and to place them on a footing with himself; making their wishes his law; gentle even to effeminacy in his deportment, and constant in his friendship, while his whole nation was in arms against them. Yet these traits, so contradictory, were truly enough drawn. They are to be explained by the extraordinary circumstances of his position.

When Montezuma ascended the throne, he was scarcely twenty-three years of age. Young, and ambitious of extending his empire, he was continually engaged in war, and is said to have been present himself in nine pitched battles. He was greatly renowned for his martial prowess, for he belonged to the *Quachictin,* the highest military order of his nation, and one into which but few even of its sovereigns had been admitted. In later life, he preferred intrigue to violence, as more consonant to his character and priestly education. In this he was as great an adept as any prince of his time, and, by arts not very honourable to himself, succeeded in filching away much of the territory of his royal kinsman of Tezcuco. Severe in the administration of justice, he made important reforms in the arrangement of the tribunals. He introduced other innovations in the royal household, creating new offices, introducing a lavish magnificence and forms of courtly etiquette unknown to his ruder predecessors. He was, in short, most attentive to all that concerned the exterior and pomp of royalty. Stately and decorous, he was careful of his own dignity, and might be said to be as great an "actor of majesty" among the barbarian potentates of the New World, as Louis the Fourteenth was among the polished princes of Europe.

He was deeply tinctured, moreover, with that spirit of bigotry, which threw such a shade over the latter days of the French monarch. He received the Spaniards as the beings predicted by his oracles. The anxious dread, with which he had evaded their proffered visit, was founded on the same feelings which led him so blindly to resign himself to them on their approach. He felt himself rebuked by their superior genius. He at once conceded all that they demanded—his treasures, his power, even his person. For their sake he forsook his wonted occupations, his pleasures, his most familiar habits. He might be said to forego his nature; and, as his subjects asserted, to change his sex and become a woman. If we cannot refuse our contempt for the pusillanimity of the Aztec monarch, it should be mitigated by the consideration that his pusillanimity sprang from his superstition, and that superstition in the savage is the substitute for religious principle in the civilised man.

It is not easy to contemplate the fate of Montezuma without feelings of the strongest compassion; to see him thus borne along the tide of events beyond his power to avert or control; to see him, like some stately tree, the pride of his own Indian forests, towering aloft in the pomp and majesty of its branches, by its very eminence a mark for the thunderbolt, the first victim of the tempest which was to sweep over its native hills! When the wise king of Tezcuco addressed his royal relative at his coronation, he exclaimed, "Happy the empire, which is now in the meridian of its prosperity, for the sceptre is given to one whom the Almighty has in his keeping; and the nations shall hold him in reverence!" Alas! the subject of this auspicious invocation lived to see his empire melt away like the winter's wreath; to see a strange race drop, as it were, from the clouds on his land; to find himself a prisoner in the palace of his fathers, the companion of those who were the enemies of his gods and his people; to be insulted, reviled, trodden in the dust, by the meanest of his subjects, by those who, a few months previous, had trembled at his glance; drawing his last breath in the halls of the stranger, a lonely outcast in the heart of his own capital! He was the sad victim of destiny—a destiny as dark and irresistible in its march, as that which broods over the mythic legends of antiquity!

Montezuma, at the time of his death, was about forty-one years old, of which he reigned eighteen. His person and manners have been already described. He left a numerous progeny by his various wives, most of whom, having lost their consideration after the Conquest, fell into obscurity as they mingled with the mass of the Indian population. Two of them, however, a son and a daughter, who embraced Christianity, became the founders of noble houses in Spain. The government, willing to show its gratitude for the large extent of empire derived from their ancestor, conferred on them ample estates, and important hereditary honours; and the Counts of Montezuma and Tula, intermarrying with the best blood of Castile, intimated by their names and titles their illustrious descent from the royal dynasty of Mexico.

Montezuma's death was a misfortune to the Spaniards. While he lived, they had a precious pledge in their hands, which, in extremity, they might possibly have turned to account. Now the last link was snapped which connected them with the natives of the country. But independently of interested feelings, Cortés and his officers were much affected by his death from personal considerations; and, when they gazed on the cold remains of the ill-starred monarch, they may have felt a natural compunction as they contrasted his late flourishing condition with that to which his friendship for them had now reduced him.

The Spanish commander showed all respect for his memory. His body, arrayed in its royal robes, was laid decently on a bier, and borne on the shoulders of his nobles to his subjects in the city. What honours, if any, indeed, were paid to his remains, is uncertain. A sound of wailing, distinctly heard in the western quarters of the capital, was interpreted by the Spaniards into the moans of a funeral procession, as it bore the body to be laid among those of his ancestors, under the princely shades of Chapultepec. Others state that it was removed to a burial-place in the city named Copalco, and there burnt with the usual solemnities and signs of lamentation by his chiefs, but not without some unworthy insults from the Mexican populace. Whatever be the fact, the people, occupied with the stirring scenes in which they were engaged, were probably not long mindful of the monarch, who had taken no share in their late patriotic movements. Nor is it strange that the very memory of his sepulchre should be effaced in the terrible catastrophe which afterwards overwhelmed the capital, and swept away every landmark from its surface.

CHAPTER III

*Council of War—Spaniards Evacuate the City—Noche Triste,
or "The Melancholy Night"—Terrible Slaughter—Halt
for the Night—Amount of Losses*

1520

THERE was no longer any question as to the expediency of evacuating
the capital. The only doubt was as to the time of doing so, and the route.
The Spanish commander called a council of officers to deliberate on these
matters. It was his purpose to retreat on Tlascala, and in that capital to
decide according to circumstances on his future operations. After some
discussion, they agreed on the causeway of Tlacopan as the avenue by
which to leave the city. It would, indeed, take them back by a circuitous
route, considerably longer than either of those by which they had
approached the capital. But, for that reason, it would be less likely to
be guarded, as least suspected; and the causeway itself being shorter than
either of the other entrances, would sooner place the army in comparative security on the main land.

There was some difference of opinion in respect to the hour of
departure. The daytime, it was argued by some, would be preferable,
since it would enable them to see the nature and extent of their danger,
and to provide against it. Darkness would be much more likely to embarrass their own movements than those of the enemy, who were familiar
with the ground. A thousand impediments would occur in the night,
which might prevent their acting in concert, or obeying, or even ascertaining, the orders of the commander. But on the other hand it was
urged that the night presented many obvious advantages in dealing with
a foe who rarely carried his hostilities beyond the day. The late active
operations of the Spaniards had thrown the Mexicans off their guard,
and it was improbable they would anticipate so speedy a departure of
their enemies. With celerity and caution they might succeed, therefore,
in making their escape from the town, possibly over the causeway, before

their retreat should be discovered; and, could they once get beyond that pass of peril, they felt little apprehension for the rest.

These views were fortified, it is said, by the counsels of a soldier named Botello, who professed the mysterious science of judicial astrology. He had gained credit with the army by some predictions which had been verified by the events; those lucky hits which make chance pass for calculation with the credulous multitude. This man recommended to his countrymen by all means to evacuate the place in the night, as the hour most propitious to them, although he should perish in it. The event proved the astrologer better acquainted with his own horoscope than with that of others.

It is possible Botello's predictions had some weight in determining the opinion of Cortés. Superstition was the feature of the age, and the Spanish general, as we have seen, had a full measure of its bigotry. Seasons of gloom, moreover, dispose the mind to a ready acquiescence in the marvellous. It is, however, quite as probable that he made use of the astrologer's opinion, finding it coincided with his own, to influence that of his men, and inspire them with higher confidence. At all events, it was decided to abandon the city that very night.

The general's first care was to provide for the safe transportation of the treasure. Many of the common soldiers had converted their share of the prize, as we have seen, into gold chains, collars, or other ornaments, which they easily carried about their persons. But the royal fifth, together with that of Cortés himself, and much of the rich booty of the principal cavaliers had been converted into bars and wedges of solid gold, and deposited in one of the strong apartments of the palace. Cortés delivered the share belonging to the crown to the royal officers, assigning them one of the strongest horses, and a guard of Castilian soldiers to transport it. Still, much of the treasure belonging both to the crown and to individuals was necessarily abandoned, from the want of adequate means of conveyance. The metal lay scattered in shining heaps along the floor, exciting the cupidity of the soldiers. "Take what you will of it," said Cortés to his men. "Better you should have it than these Mexican hounds. But be careful not to overload yourselves. He travels safest in the dark night who travels lightest." His own more wary followers took heed to his counsel, helping themselves to a few articles of least bulk, though, it might be, of greatest value. But the troops of Narvaez, pining for riches, of which they had heard so much, and hitherto seen so little, showed no such discretion. To them it seemed as if the very mines of

Mexico were turned up before them, and, rushing on the treacherous spoil, they greedily loaded themselves with as much of it, not merely as they could accommodate about their persons, but as they could stow away in wallets, boxes, or any other mode of conveyance at their disposal.

Cortés next arranged the order of march. The van, composed of two hundred Spanish foot, he placed under the command of the valiant Gonzalo de Sandoval, supported by Diego de Ordaz, Francisco de Lujo, and about twenty other cavaliers. The rear-guard, constituting the strength of the infantry, was intrusted to Pedro de Alvarado and Velasquez de Leon. The general himself took charge of the "battle," or centre, in which went the baggage, some of the heavy guns, most of which, however, remained in the rear, the treasure, and the prisoners. These consisted of a son and two daughters of Montezuma, Cacama, the deposed lord of Tezcuco, and several other nobles, whom Cortés retained as important pledges in his future negotiations with the enemy. The Tlascalans were distributed pretty equally among the three divisions; and Cortés had under his immediate command a hundred picked soldiers, his own veterans most attached to his service, who, with Christoval de Olid, Francisco de Morla, Alonso de Avila, and two or three other cavaliers, formed a select corps, to act wherever occasion might require.

The general had already superintended the construction of a portable bridge to be laid over the open canals in the causeway. This was given in charge to an officer named Magarino, with forty soldiers under his orders, all pledged to defend the passage to the last extremity. The bridge was to be taken up when the entire army had crossed one of the breaches, and transported to the next. There were three of these openings in the causeway, and most fortunate would it have been for the expedition, if the foresight of the commander had provided the same number of bridges. But the labour would have been great, and time was short.

At midnight the troops were under arms, in readiness for the march. Mass was performed by Father Olmedo, who invoked the protection of the Almighty through the awful perils of the night. The gates were thrown open, and, on July 1, 1520, the Spaniards for the last time sallied forth from the walls of the ancient fortress, the scene of so much suffering and such indomitable courage.

The night was cloudy, and a drizzling rain, which fell without intermission, added to the obscurity. The great square before the palace was deserted, as, indeed, it had been since the fall of Montezuma. Steadily, and as noiselessly as possible, the Spaniards held their way along the great street of Tlacopan, which so lately had resounded to the tumult of battle. All was now hushed in silence; and they were only reminded of the past by the occasional presence of some solitary corpse, or a dark heap of the slain, which too plainly told where the strife had been hottest. As they passed along the lanes and alleys which opened into the great street, or looked down the canals, whose polished surface gleamed with a sort of ebon lustre through the obscurity of night, they easily fancied that they discerned the shadowy forms of their foe lurking in ambush, and ready to spring on them. But it was only fancy; and the city slept undisturbed even by the prolonged echoes of the tramp of the horses, and the hoarse rumbling of the artillery and baggage trains. At length a lighter space beyond the dusky line of buildings showed the van of the army that it was emerging on the open causeway. They might well have congratulated themselves on having thus escaped the dangers of an assault in the city itself, and that a brief time would place them in comparative safety on the opposite shore. But the Mexicans were not all asleep.

As the Spaniards drew near the spot where the street opened on the causeway, and were preparing to lay the portable bridge across the uncovered breach which now met their eyes, several Indian sentinels, who had been stationed at this, as at the other approaches to the city, took the alarm, and fled, rousing their countrymen by their cries. The priests, keeping their night watch on the summit of the *teocallis*, instantly caught the tidings and sounded their shells, while the huge drum in the desolate temple of the war-god sent forth those solemn tones, which, heard only in seasons of calamity, vibrated through every corner of the capital. The Spaniards saw that no time was to be lost. The bridge was brought forward and fitted with all possible expedition. Sandoval was the first to try its strength, and, riding across, was followed by his little body of chivalry, his infantry, and Tlascalan allies, who formed the first division of the army. Then came Cortés and his squadrons, with the baggage, ammunition waggons, and a part of the artillery. But before they had time to defile across the narrow passage, a gathering sound was heard, like that of a mighty forest agitated by the winds. It grew louder and louder, while on the dark waters of the lake was heard a splashing noise, as of many oars. Then came a few stones and arrows striking at random among the hurrying troops. They fell every moment faster and more furious, till they thickened into a terrible tempest, while the very heavens were rent with the yells and war-cries of myriads of combatants, who seemed all at once to be swarming over land and lake!

The Spaniards pushed steadily on through this arrowy sleet, though the barbarians, dashing their canoes against the sides of the causeway, clambered up and broke in upon their ranks. But the Christians, anxious only to make their escape, declined all combat except for self-preservation. The cavaliers, spurring forward their steeds, shook off their assailants, and rode over their prostrate bodies, while the men on foot with their good swords or the butts of their pieces drove them headlong again down the sides of the dike.

But the advance of several thousand men, marching, probably, on a front of not more than fifteen or twenty abreast, necessarily required much time, and the leading files had already reached the second breach in the causeway before those in the rear had entirely traversed the first. Here they halted; as they had no means of effecting a passage, smarting all the while under unintermitting volleys from the enemy, who were clustered thick on the waters around this second opening. Sorely distressed, the vanguard sent repeated messages to the rear to demand the portable bridge. At length the last of the army had crossed, and Magarino and his sturdy followers endeavoured to raise the ponderous framework. But it stuck fast in the sides of the dike. In vain they strained every nerve. The weight of so many men and horses, and above all of the heavy artillery, had wedged the timbers so firmly in the stones and earth, that it was beyond their power to dislodge them. Still they laboured amidst a torrent of missiles, until, many of them slain, and all wounded, they were obliged to abandon the attempt.

The tidings soon spread from man to man, and no sooner was their dreadful import comprehended, than a cry of despair arose, which for a moment drowned all the noise of conflict. All means of retreat were cut off. Scarcely hope was left. The only hope was in such desperate exertions as each could make for himself. Order and subordination were at an end. Intense danger produced intense selfishness. Each thought only of his own life. Pressing forward, he trampled down the weak and the wounded, heedless whether it were friend or foe. The leading files, urged on by the rear, were crowded on the brink of the gulf. Sandoval, Ordaz, and the other cavaliers dashed into the water. Some succeeded in swimming their horses across; others failed, and some, who reached the opposite bank, being overturned in the ascent, rolled headlong with their steeds into the lake. The infantry followed pellmell, heaped promiscuously on one another, frequently pierced by the shafts, or struck down by the war-clubs of the Aztecs; while many an unfortunate victim was dragged half-stunned on board their canoes, to be reserved for a protracted, but more dreadful death.

The carnage raged fearfully along the length of the causeway. Its shadowy bulk presented a mark of sufficient distinctness for the enemy's missiles, which often prostrated their own countrymen in the blind fury of the tempest. Those nearest the dike, running their canoes alongside, with a force that shattered them to pieces, leaped on the land and grappled with the Christians, until both come rolling down the side of the causeway together. But the Aztec fell among his friends, while his antagonist was borne away in triumph to the sacrifice. The struggle was long and deadly. The Mexicans were recognised by their white cotton tunics, which showed faint through the darkness. Above the combatants rose a wild and discordant clamour, in which horrid shouts of vengeance were mingled with groans of agony, with invocations of the saints and the blessed Virgin, and with the screams of women; for there were several women, both native and Spaniards, who had accompanied the Christian camp. Among these, one named María de Estrada is particularly noticed for the courage she displayed, battling with broadsword and target like the staunchest of the warriors.

The opening in the causeway, meanwhile, was filled up with the wreck of matter which had been forced into it, ammunition-waggons, heavy guns, bales of rich stuffs scattered over the waters, chests of solid ingots, and bodies of men and horses, till over this dismal ruin a passage was gradually formed, by which those in the rear were enabled to clamber to the other side. Cortés, it is said, found a place that was fordable, where halting with the water up to his saddle-girths, he endeavoured to check the confusion, and lead his followers by a safer path to the opposite bank. But his voice was lost in the wild uproar, and finally, hurrying on with the tide, he pressed forwards with a few trusty cavaliers, who remained near his person, to the van; but not before he had seen his favourite page, Juan de Salazar, struck down, a corpse, by his side. Here he found Sandoval and his companions, halting before the third and last breach, endeavouring to cheer on their followers to surmount it. But their resolution faltered. It was wide and deep; though the passage was not so closely beset by the enemy as the preceding ones. The cavaliers again set the example by plunging into the water. Horse and foot followed as they could, some swimming, others with dying grasp clinging to the manes and tails of the struggling animals. Those fared best, as the general had predicted, who travelled lightest; and many were the unfortunate wretches, who, weighed down by the fatal gold which they loved so well, were buried with it in the salt floods of the lake. Cortés, with his gallant comrades, Olid, Morla, Sandoval, and some few others, still kept in the advance, leading his broken remnant off the fatal causeway. The din of battle lessened in the distance; when the rumour reached them that the rear-guard would be wholly overwhelmed without speedy relief. It seemed almost an act of desperation; but the generous hearts of the Spanish cavaliers did not stop to calculate danger when the cry for succour reached them. Turning their horses' bridles, they galloped back to the theatre of action, worked their way through the press, swam the canal, and placed themselves in the thick of the *mêlée* on the opposite bank.

The first grey of the morning was now coming over the waters. It showed the hideous confusion of the scene which had been shrouded in the obscurity of night. The dark masses of combatants, stretching along the dike, were seen struggling for mastery, until the very causeway on which they stood appeared to tremble, and reel to and fro, as if shaken by an earthquake; while the bosom of the lake, as far as the eye could reach, was darkened by canoes crowded with warriors, whose spears and bludgeons, armed with blades of "volcanic glass," gleamed in the morning light.

The cavaliers found Alvarado unhorsed, and defending himself with a poor handful of followers against an overwhelming tide of the enemy. His good steed, which had borne him through many a hard fight, had fallen under him. He was himself wounded in several places, and was striving in vain to rally his scattered column, which was driven to the verge of the canal by the fury of the enemy, then in possession of the whole rear of the causeway, where they were reinforced every hour by fresh combatants from the city. The artillery in the earlier part of the engagement had not been idle, and its iron shower, sweeping along the dike, had mowed down the assailants by hundreds. But nothing could resist their impetuosity. The front ranks, pushed on by those behind, were at length forced up to the pieces, and, pouring over them like a torrent, overthrew men and guns in one general ruin. The resolute charge of the Spanish cavaliers, who had now arrived, created a temporary check, and gave time for their countrymen to make a feeble rally. But they were speedily borne down by the returning flood. Cortés and his companions were compelled to plunge again into the lake—though all did not escape. Alvarado stood on the brink for a moment, hesitating what to do. Unhorsed as he was, to throw himself into the water in the face of the hostile canoes that now swarmed around the opening, afforded but a desperate chance of safety. He had but a second for thought. He was a man of powerful frame, and despair gave him unnatural energy. Setting his long lance firmly on the wreck which strewed the bottom of the lake, he sprang forward with all his might, and cleared the wide gap at a leap! Aztecs and Tlascalans gazed in stupid amazement, exclaiming, as they beheld the incredible feat, "This is truly the *Tonatiuh*—the child of the Sun!"—The breadth of the opening is not given. But it was so great that the valorous Captain Diaz, who well remembered the place, says the leap was impossible to any man. Other contemporaries, however, do not discredit the story. It was, beyond doubt, matter of popular belief at the time; it is to this day familiarly known to every inhabitant of the capital; and the name of the *Salto de Alvarado,* "Alvarado's leap," given to the spot, still commemorates an exploit which rivalled those of the demigods of Grecian fable.

Cortés and his companions now rode forward to the front, where the troops in a loose, disorderly manner, were marching off the fatal causeway. A few only of the enemy hung on their rear, or annoyed them by occasional flights of arrows from the lake. The attention of the Aztecs was diverted by the rich spoil that strewed the battleground; fortunately for the Spaniards, who, had their enemy pursued with the same ferocity with which he had fought, would, in their crippled condition, have been cut off, probably to a man. But little molested, therefore, they were allowed to defile through the adjacent village, or suburbs, it might be called, of Popotla.

The Spanish commander there dismounted from his jaded steed, and, sitting down on the steps of an Indian temple, gazed mournfully on the broken files as they passed before him. What a spectacle did they present! The cavalry, most of them dismounted, were mingled with the infantry, who dragged their feeble limbs along with difficulty; their shattered mail and tattered garments dripping with the salt ooze, showing through their rents many a bruise and ghastly wound; their bright arms soiled, their proud crests and banners gone, the baggage, artillery—all, in short, that constitutes the pride and panoply of glorious war, for ever lost. Cortés, as he looked wistfully on their thinned and disordered ranks, sought in vain for many a familiar face, and missed more than one dear companion who had stood side by side with him through all the perils of the Conquest. Though accustomed to control his emotions, or, at least, to conceal them, the sight was too much for him. He covered his face with his hands, and the tears which trickled down revealed too plainly the anguish of his soul.

He found some consolation, however, in the sight of several of the cavaliers on whom he most relied. Alvarado, Sandoval, Olid, Ordaz, Avila were yet safe. He had the inexpressible satisfaction, also, of learning the safety of the Indian interpreter, Marina, so dear to him, and so important to the army. She had been committed, with a daughter of a Tlascalan chief, to several of that nation. She was fortunately placed in the van, and her faithful escort had carried her securely through all the dangers of the night. Aguilar, the other interpreter, had also escaped; and it was with no less satisfaction that Cortés learned the safety of the shipbuilder, Martin Lopez. The general's solicitude for the fate of this man, so indispensable, as he proved, to the success of his subsequent operations, showed that amidst all his affliction his indomitable spirit was looking forward to the hour of vengeance.

Meanwhile, the advancing column had reached the neighbouring city of Tlacopan (Tacuba), once the capital of an independent principality. There it halted in the great street, as if bewildered and altogether uncertain what course to take; like a herd of panic-struck deer, who, flying from the hunters, with the cry of hound and horn still ringing in their ears, look wildly around for some glen or copse in which to plunge for concealment. Cortés, who had hastily mounted and rode on to the front again, saw the danger of remaining in a populous place, where the inhabitants might sorely annoy the troops from the *azoteas,* with little risk to themselves. Pushing forward, therefore, he soon led them into the country. There he endeavoured to reform his disorganised battalions, and bring them to something like order.

Hard by, at no great distance on the left, rose an eminence, looking towards a chain of mountains which fences in the valley on the west. It was called the Hill of Otoncalpolco, and sometimes the Hill of Montezuma. It was crowned with an Indian *teocalli,* with its large outworks of stone covering an ample space, and by its strong position, which commanded the neighbouring plain, promised a good place of refuge for the exhausted troops. But the men, disheartened and stupefied by their late reverses, seemed for the moment incapable of further exertion; and the

place was held by a body of armed Indians. Cortés saw the necessity of
dislodging them, if he would save the remains of his army from entire
destruction. The event showed he still held a control over their wills
stronger than circumstances themselves. Cheering them on, and supported by his gallant cavaliers, he succeeded in infusing into the most
sluggish something of his own intrepid temper, and led them up the
ascent in face of the enemy. But the latter made slight resistance, and
after a few feeble volleys of missiles which did little injury left the ground
to the assailants.

It was covered by a building of considerable size, and furnished ample
accommodations for the diminished numbers of the Spaniards. They found
there some provisions; and more, it is said, were brought to them in the
course of the day from some friendly Otomie villages in the neighbourhood. There was, also, a quantity of fuel in the courts, destined to the
uses of the temple. With this they made fires to dry their drenched garments, and busily employed themselves in dressing one another's wounds,
stiff and extremely painful from exposure and long exertion. Thus
refreshed, the weary soldiers threw themselves down on the floor and
courts of the temple, and soon found the temporary oblivion which
nature seldom denies even in the greatest extremity of suffering.

There was one eye in that assembly, however, which we may well
believe did not so speedily close. For what agitating thoughts must have
crowded on the mind of their commander, as he beheld his poor remnant
of followers thus huddled together in this miserable bivouac! And this
was all that survived of the brilliant array with which but a few weeks
since he had entered the capital of Mexico! Where now were his dreams
of conquest and empire? And what was he but a luckless adventurer, at
whom the finger of scorn would be uplifted as at a madman? Whichever
way he turned, the horizon was almost equally gloomy, with scarcely
one light spot to cheer him. He had still a weary journey before him,
through perilous and unknown paths, with guides of whose fidelity he
could not be assured. And how could he rely on his reception at Tlascala, the place of his destination; the land of his ancient enemies; where,
formerly as a foe, and now as a friend, he had brought desolation to
every family within its borders?

Yet these agitating and gloomy reflections, which might have crushed
a common mind, had no power over that of Cortés; or rather, they only
served to renew his energies, and quicken his perceptions, as the war of
the elements purifies and gives elasticity to the atmosphere. He looked

with an unblenching eye on his past reverses; but, confident in his own resources, he saw a light through the gloom which others could not. Even in the shattered relics which lay around him, resembling in their haggard aspect and wild attire a horde of famished outlaws, he discerned the materials out of which to reconstruct his ruined fortunes. In the very hour of discomfiture and general despondency, there is no doubt that his heroic spirit was meditating the plan of operations which he afterwards pursued with such dauntless constancy.

The loss sustained by the Spaniards on this fatal night, like every other event in the history of the Conquest, is reported with the greatest discrepancy. If we believe Cortés' own letter, it did not exceed one hundred and fifty Spaniards and two thousand Indians. But the general's bulletins, while they do full justice to the difficulties to be overcome, and the importance of the results, are less scrupulous in stating the extent either of his means or of his losses. Thoan Cano, one of the cavaliers present, estimates the slain at eleven hundred and seventy Spaniards, and eight thousand allies. But this is a greater number than we have allowed for the whole army. Perhaps we may come nearest the truth by taking the computation of Gomara, the chaplain of Cortés, who had free access, doubtless, not only to the general's papers, but to other authentic sources of information. According to him, the number of Christians killed and missing was four hundred and fifty, and that of natives four thousand. This, with the loss sustained in the conflicts of the previous week, may have reduced the former to something more than a third, and the latter to a fourth, or, perhaps, fifth, of the original force with which they entered the capital. The brunt of the action fell on the rear-guard, few of whom escaped. It was formed chiefly of the soldiers of Narvaez, who fell the victims in some measure of their cupidity. Forty-six of the cavalry were cut off, which with previous losses reduced the number in this branch of the service to twenty-three, and some of these in very poor condition. The greater part of the treasure, the baggage, the general's papers, including his accounts, and a minute diary of transactions since leaving Cuba—which, to posterity, at least, would have been of more worth than the gold—had been swallowed up by the waters. The ammunition, the beautiful little train of artillery, with which Cortés had entered the city, were all gone. Not a musket even remained, the men having thrown them away, eager to disencumber themselves of all that might retard their escape on that disastrous night. Nothing, in short, of their military apparatus was left, but their swords, their crippled cavalry, and a few damaged crossbows, to assert the superiority of the European over the barbarian.

The prisoners, including, as already noticed, the children of Montezuma and the cacique of Tezcuco, all perished by the hands of their ignorant countrymen, it is said, in the indiscriminate fury of the assault. There were, also, some persons of consideration among the Spaniards, whose names were inscribed on the same bloody roll of slaughter. Such was Francisco de Morla, who fell by the side of Cortés, on returning with him to the rescue. But the greatest loss was that of Juan Velasquez de Leon, who, with Alvarado, had command of the rear. It was the post of danger on that night, and he fell, bravely defending it, at an early part of the retreat. He was an excellent officer, possessed of many knightly qualities, though somewhat haughty in his bearing, being one of the best connected cavaliers in the army. The near relation of the governor of Cuba, he looked coldly at first on the pretensions of Cortés; but, whether from a conviction that the latter had been wronged, or from personal preference, he afterwards attached himself zealously to his leader's interests. The general requited this with a generous confidence, assigning him, as we have seen, a separate and independent command, where misconduct, or even a mistake, would have been fatal to the expedition. Velasquez proved himself worthy of the trust; and there was no cavalier in the army, with the exception, perhaps, of Sandoval and Alvarado, whose loss would have been so deeply deplored by the commander. Such were the disastrous results of this terrible passage of the causeway; more disastrous than those occasioned by any other reverse which has stained the Spanish arms in the New World; and which have branded the night on which it happened, in the national annals, with the name of the *noche triste,* "the sad or melancholy night."

CHAPTER IV

Retreat of the Spaniards—Distresses of the Army—Pyramids of Teotihuacan—Great Battle of Otumba

1520

THE MEXICANS, during the day which followed the retreat of the Spaniards, remained, for the most part, quiet in their own capital, where they found occupation in cleansing the streets and causeways from the dead, which lay festering in heaps that might have bred a pestilence. They may have been employed, also, in paying the last honours to such of their warriors as had fallen, solemnising the funeral rites by the sacrifice of their wretched prisoners, who, as they contemplated their own destiny, may well have envied the fate of their companions who left their bones on the battle-field. It was most fortunate for the Spaniards, in their extremity, that they had this breathing-time allowed them by the enemy. But Cortés knew that he could not calculate on its continuance, and, feeling how important it was to get the start of his vigilant foe, he ordered his troops to be in readiness to resume their march by midnight. Fires were left burning, the better to deceive the enemy; and at the appointed hour, the little army, without sound of drum or trumpet, but with renewed spirits, sallied forth from the gates of the *teocalli,* within whose hospitable walls they had found such seasonable succour. The place is now indicated by a Christian church, dedicated to the Virgin, under the title of *Nuestra Señora de los Remedios,* whose miraculous image—the very same, *it is said,* brought over by the followers of Cortés —still extends her beneficent sway over the neighbouring capital; and the traveller, who pauses within the precincts of the consecrated fane, may feel that he is standing on the spot made memorable by the refuge it afforded to the Conquerors in the hour of their deepest despondency.

It was arranged that the sick and wounded should occupy the centre, transported on litters, or on the backs of the *tamanes,* while those who were strong enough to keep their seats should mount behind the cavalry.

The able-bodied soldiers were ordered to the front and rear, while others protected the flanks, thus affording all the security possible to the invalids.

The retreating army held on its way unmolested under cover of the darkness. But, as morning dawned, they beheld parties of the natives moving over the heights, or hanging at a distance, like a cloud of locusts on their rear. They did not belong to the capital; but were gathered from the neighbouring country, where the tidings of their route had already penetrated. The charm, which had hitherto covered the white men, was gone. The dread *Teules* were no longer invincible.

The Spaniards, under the conduct of their Tlascalan guides, took a circuitous route to the north, passing through Quauhtitlan, and round Lake Tzompanco (Zumpango), thus lengthening their march, but keeping at a distance from the capital. From the eminences, as they passed along, the Indians rolled down heavy stones, mingled with volleys of darts and arrows on the heads of the soldiers. Some were even bold enough to descend into the plain and assault the extremities of the column. But they were soon beaten off by the horse, and compelled to take refuge among the hills, where the ground was too rough for the rider to follow. Indeed, the Spaniards did not care to do so, their object being rather to fly than to fight.

In this way they slowly advanced, halting at intervals to drive off their assailants when they became too importunate, and greatly distressed by their missiles and their desultory attacks. At night, the troops usually found shelter in some town or hamlet, whence the inhabitants, in anticipation of their approach, had been careful to carry off all the provisions. The Spaniards were soon reduced to the greatest straits for subsistence. Their principal food was the wild cherry, which grew in the woods or by the roadside. Fortunate were they if they found a few ears of corn unplucked. More frequently nothing was left but the stalks; and with them, and the like unwholesome fare, they were fain to supply the cravings of appetite. When a horse happened to be killed, it furnished an extraordinary banquet; and Cortés himself records the fact of his having made one of a party who thus sumptuously regaled themselves, devouring the animal even to his hide.

The wretched soldiers, faint with famine and fatigue, were sometimes seen to drop down lifeless on the road. Others loitered behind unable to keep up with the march, and fell into the hands of the enemy, who followed in a track of the army like a flock of famished vultures, eager to pounce on the dying and the dead. Others, again, who strayed too far, in their eagerness to procure sustenance, shared the same fate. The number of these, at length, and the consciousness of the cruel lot for which they were reserved, compelled Cortés to introduce stricter discipline, and to enforce it by sterner punishments than he had hitherto done—though too often ineffectually, such was the indifference to danger, under the overwhelming pressure of present calamity.

In their prolonged distresses, the soldiers ceased to set a value on those very things for which they had once been content to hazard life itself. More than one, who had brought his golden treasure safe through the perils of the *noche triste,* now abandoned it as an intolerable burden; and the rude Indian peasant gleaned up, with wondering delight, the bright fragments of the spoils of the capital.

Through these weary days Cortés displayed his usual serenity and fortitude. He was ever in the post of danger, freely exposing himself in encounters with the enemy; in one of which he received a severe wound in the head, that afterwards gave him much trouble. He fared no better than the humblest soldier, and strove, by his own cheerful countenance and counsels, to fortify the courage of those who faltered, assuring them that their sufferings would soon be ended by their arrival in the hospitable "land of bread." His faithful officers co-operated with him in these efforts; and the common file, indeed, especially his own veterans, must be allowed, for the most part, to have shown a full measure of the constancy and power of endurance so characteristic of their nation—justifying the honest boast of an old chronicler, "that there was no people so capable of supporting hunger as the Spaniards, and none of them who were ever more severely tried than the soldiers of Cortés." A similar fortitude was shown by the Tlascalans, trained in a rough school that made them familiar with hardships and privations. Although they sometimes threw themselves on the ground, in the extremity of famine, imploring their gods not to abandon them, they did their duty as warriors; and, far from manifesting coldness towards the Spaniards as the cause of their distresses, seemed only the more firmly knit to them by the sense of a common suffering.

On the seventh morning, the army had reached the mountain rampart which overlooks the plains of Otompan, or Otumba, as commonly called, from the Indian city—now a village—situated in them. The distance from the capital is hardly nine leagues. But the Spaniards had travelled more than thrice that distance, in their circuitous march round the lakes. This had been performed so slowly that it consumed a week; two nights

of which had been passed in the same quarters, from the absolute necessity of rest. It was not, therefore, till July 7 that they reached the
heights commanding the plains which stretched far away towards the
territory of Tlascala, in full view of the venerable pyramids of Teotihuacan, two of the most remarkable monuments of the antique American
civilisation now existing north of the Isthmus. During all the preceding
day, they had seen parties of the enemy hovering like dark clouds above
the highlands, brandishing their weapons, and calling out in vindictive
tones, "Hasten on! You will soon find yourselves where you cannot
escape!" words of mysterious import, which they were made fully to
comprehend on the following morning.

The monuments of San Juan Teotihuacan are, with the exception of
the temple of Cholula, the most ancient remains, probably, on the Mexican soil. They were found by the Aztecs, according to their traditions,
on their entrance into the country, when Teotihuacan, *the habitation of
the gods,* now a paltry village, was a flourishing city, the rival of Tula,
the great Toltec capital. The two principal pyramids were dedicated to
Tonatiuh, the Sun, and *Meztli,* the Moon. The former, which is considerably the larger, is found by recent measurements to be six hundred
and eighty-two feet long at the base, and one hundred and eighty feet
high, dimensions not inferior to those of some of the kindred monuments
of Egypt. They were divided into four stories, of which three are now
discernible, while the vestiges of the intermediate gradations are nearly
effaced. In fact, time has dealt so roughly with them, and the materials
have been so much displaced by the treacherous vegetation of the Tropics,
muffling up with its flowery mantle the ruin which it causes, that it is not
easy to discern, at once, the pyramidal form of the structures. The huge
masses bear such resemblance to the North American mounds, that some
have fancied them to be only natural eminences shaped by the hand of
man into a regular form, and ornamented with the temples and terraces,
the wreck of which still covers their slopes. But others, seeing no example
of a similar elevation in the wide plain in which they stand, infer, with
more probability, that they are wholly of an artificial construction.

The interior is composed of clay mixed with pebbles, incrusted on the
surface with the light porous stone *tetzontli,* so abundant in the neighbouring quarries. Over this was a thick coating of stucco, resembling, in
its reddish colour, that found in the ruins of Palenque. According to
tradition, the pyramids are hollow, but hitherto the attempt to discover
the cavity in that dedicated to the Sun has been unsuccessful. In the

smaller mound, an aperture has been found on the southern side, at two-thirds of the elevation. It is formed by a narrow gallery, which, after penetrating to the distance of several yards, terminates in two pits or wells. The largest of these is about fifteen feet deep; and the sides are faced with unbaked bricks; but to what purpose it was devoted, nothing is left to show. It may have been to hold the ashes of some powerful chief, like the solitary apartment discovered in the great Egyptian pyramid. That these monuments were dedicated to religious uses there is no doubt; and it would be only conformable to the practice of antiquity in the eastern continent that they should have served for tombs as well as temples.

Distinct traces of the latter destination are said to be visible on the summit of the smaller pyramid, consisting of the remains of stone walls, showing a building of considerable size and strength. There are no remains on the top of the pyramid of the Sun. But the traveller, who will take the trouble to ascend its bald summit, will be amply compensated by the glorious view it will open to him—towards the south-east, the hills of Tlascala, surrounded by their green plantations and cultivated corn-fields, in the midst of which stands the little village, once the proud capital of the republic. Somewhat further to the south, the eye passes across the beautiful plains lying around the city of Puebla de los Angeles, founded by the old Spaniards, and still rivalling, in the splendour of its churches, the most brilliant capitals of Europe; and far in the west he may behold the Valley of Mexico, spread out like a map, with its diminished lakes, its princely capital rising in still greater glory from its ruins, and its rugged hills gathering darkly around it, as in the days of Montezuma.

The summit of this larger mound is said to have been crowned by a temple, in which was a colossal statue of its presiding deity, the Sun, made of one entire block of stone, and facing the east. Its breast was protected by a plate of burnished gold and silver, on which the first rays of the rising luminary rested. An antiquary, in the early part of the last century, speaks of having seen some fragments of the statue. It was still standing, according to report, on the invasion of the Spaniards, and was demolished by the indefatigable Bishop Zumarraga, whose hand fell more heavily than that of Time itself on the Aztec monuments.

Around the principal pyramids are a great number of smaller ones, rarely exceeding thirty feet in height, which, according to tradition, were dedicated to the stars, and served as sepulchres for the great men of the nation. They are arranged symmetrically in avenues terminating at the sides of the great pyramids, which face the cardinal points. The plain on which they stand was called *Micoatl,* or "Path of the Dead." The labourer, as he turns up the ground, still finds there numerous arrowheads, and blades of obsidian, attesting the warlike character of its primitive population.

What thoughts must crowd on the mind of the traveller, as he wanders amidst these memorials of the past; as he treads over the ashes of the generations who reared these colossal fabrics, which take us from the present into the very depths of time! But who were their builders? Was it the shadowy Olmecs, whose history, like that of the ancient Titans, is lost in the mists of fable? or as commonly reported, the peaceful and industrious Toltecs, of whom all that we can glean rests on traditions hardly more secure? What has become of the races who built them? Did they remain on the soil, and mingle and become incorporated with the fierce Aztecs who succeeded them? Or did they pass on to the south, and find a wider field for the expansion of their civilisation, as shown by the higher character of the architectural remains in the distant regions of Central America and Yucatan? It is all a mystery—over which Time has thrown an impenetrable veil that no mortal hand may raise. A nation has passed away—powerful, populous, and well advanced in refinement, as attested by their monuments—but it has perished without a name. It has died and made no sign!

Such speculations, however, do not seem to have disturbed the minds of the Conquerors, who have not left a single line respecting these time-honoured structures, though they passed in full view of them—perhaps, under their very shadows. In the sufferings of the present, they had little leisure to bestow on the past. Indeed, the new and perilous position, in which at this very spot they found themselves, must naturally have excluded every other thought from their bosoms, but that of self-preservation.

As the army was climbing the mountain steeps which shut in the Valley of Otompan, the videttes came in with the intelligence that a powerful body was encamped on the other side, apparently awaiting their approach. The intelligence was soon confirmed by their own eyes, as they turned the crest of the sierra, and saw spread out, below, a mighty host, filling up the whole depth of the valley, and giving to it the appearance, from the white cotton mail of the warriors, of being covered with snow. It consisted of levies from the surrounding country, and especially the populous territory of Tezcuco, drawn together at the instance of Cuitla-huac, Montezuma's successor, and now concentrated on this point to dispute the passage of the Spaniards. Every chief of note had taken the field with his whole array gathered under his standard, proudly display-ing all the pomp and rude splendour of his military equipment. As far as the eye could reach, were to be seen shields and waving banners, fantastic helmets, forests of shining spears, the bright feather-mail of the chief, and the coarse cotton panoply of his follower, all mingled together in wild confusion, and tossing to and fro like the billows of a troubled ocean. It was a sight to fill the stoutest heart among the Christians with dismay, heightened by the previous expectation of soon reaching the friendly land which was to terminate their wearisome pilgrimage. Even Cortés, as he contrasted the tremendous array before him with his own diminished squadrons, wasted by disease and enfeebled by hunger and fatigue, could not escape the conviction that his last hour had arrived.

But his was not the heart to despond; and he gathered strength from the very extremity of his situation. He had no room for hesitation; for there was no alternative left to him. To escape was impossible. He could not retreat on the capital, from which he had been expelled. He must advance—cut through the enemy, or perish. He hastily made his dis-positions for the fight. He gave his force as broad a front as possible, protecting it on each flank by his little body of horse, now reduced to twenty. Fortunately, he had not allowed the invalids, for the last two days, to mount behind the riders, from a desire to spare the horses, so that these were now in tolerable condition; and, indeed, the whole army had been refreshed by halting, as we have seen, two nights and a day in the same place, a delay, however, which had allowed the enemy time to assemble in such force to dispute its progress.

Cortés instructed his cavaliers not to part with their lances, and to direct them at the face. The infantry were to thrust, not strike, with their swords; passing them, at once, through the bodies of their enemies. They were, above all, to aim at the leaders, as the general well knew how much depends on the life of the commander in the wars of bar-barians, whose want of subordination makes them impatient of any con-trol but that to which they are accustomed.

He then addressed to his troops a few words of encouragement, as customary with him on the eve of an engagement. He reminded them of the victories they had won with odds nearly as discouraging as the pres-ent; thus establishing the superiority of science and discipline over numbers. Numbers, indeed, were of no account, where the arm of the Almighty was on their side. And he bade them have full confidence that He, who had carried them safely through so many perils, would not now abandon them and His own good cause, to perish by the hand of the infidel. His address was brief, for he read in their looks that settled resolve which rendered words unnecessary. The circumstances of their position spoke more forcibly to the heart of every soldier than any eloquence could have done, filling it with that feeling of desperation, which makes the weak arm strong, and turns the coward into a hero. After they had earnestly commended themselves, therefore, to the protection of God, the Virgin, and St. James, Cortés led his battalions straight against the enemy.

It was a solemn moment—that in which the devoted little band, with steadfast countenances, and their usual intrepid step, descended on the plain to be swallowed up, as it were, in the vast ocean of their enemies. The latter rushed on with impetuosity to meet them, making the mountains ring to their discordant yells and battle-cries, and sending forth volleys of stones and arrows which for a moment shut out the light of day. But, when the leading files of the two armies closed, the superiority of the Christians was felt, as their antagonists, falling back before the charges of cavalry, were thrown into confusion by their own numbers who pressed on them from behind. The Spanish infantry followed up the blow, and a wide lane was opened in the ranks of the enemy, who, receding on all sides, seemed willing to allow a free passage for their opponents. But it was to return on them with accumulated force, as, rallying, they poured upon the Christians, enveloping the little army on all sides, which with its bristling array of long swords and javelins, stood firm—in the words of a contemporary—like an islet against which the breakers, roaring and surging, spend their fury in vain. The struggle was desperate of man against man. The Tlascalan seemed to renew his strength, as he fought almost in view of his own native hills; as did the Spaniard, with the horrible doom of the captive before his eyes. Well did the cavaliers do their duty on that day; charging, in little bodies or four or five abreast, deep into the enemy's ranks, riding over the broken files, and by this temporary advantage giving strength and courage to the infantry. Not a lance was there which did not reek with the blood of an infidel. Among the rest, the young captain Sandoval is particularly commemorated for his daring prowess. Managing his fiery steed with easy horsemanship, he darted, when least expected, into the thickest of the *mêlée,* overturning the staunchest warriors, and rejoicing in danger, as if it were his natural element.

But these gallant displays of heroism served only to ingulf the Spaniards deeper and deeper in the mass of the enemy, with scarcely any more chance of cutting their way through his dense and interminable battalions, than of hewing a passage with their swords through the mountains. Many of the Tlascalans and some of the Spaniards had fallen, and not one but had been wounded. Cortés himself had received a second cut on the head, and his horse was so much injured that he was compelled to dismount, and take one from the baggage train, a strong-boned animal, who carried him well through the turmoil of the day. The contest had now lasted several hours. The sun rode high in the heavens, and shed an intolerable fervour over the plain. The Christians, weakened by previous sufferings, and faint with loss of blood, began to relax in their desperate exertions. Their enemies, constantly supported by fresh relays from the rear, were still in good heart, and, quick to perceive their advantage, pressed with redoubled force on the Spaniards. The horse fell back, crowded on the foot; and the latter, in vain seeking a passage amidst the dusky throngs of the enemy, who now closed up the rear, were thrown into some disorder. The tide of battle was setting rapidly against the Christians. The fate of the day would soon be decided; and all that now remained for them seemed to be to sell their lives as dearly as possible.

At this critical moment, Cortés, whose restless eye had been roving round the field in quest of any object that might offer him the means of arresting the coming ruin, rising in his stirrups, descried at a distance, in the midst of the throng, the chief who, from his dress and military cortège, he knew must be the commander of the barbarian forces. He was covered with a rich surcoat of featherwork; and a panache of beautiful plumes, gorgeously set in gold and precious stones, floated above his head. Rising above this, and attached to his back, between the shoulders, was a short staff bearing a golden net for a banner—the singular, but customary, symbol of authority for an Aztec commander. The cacique, whose name was Cihuaca, was borne on a litter, and a body of young warriors, whose gay and ornamented dresses showed them to be the flower of the Indian nobles, stood round as a guard of his person and the sacred emblem.

The eagle eye of Cortés no sooner fell on this personage, than it lighted up with triumph. Turning quickly round to the cavaliers at his side, among whom were Sandoval, Olid, Alvarado, and Avila, he pointed out the chief, exclaiming, "There is our mark! Follow and support me!" Then crying his war-cry, and striking his iron heel into his weary steed, he plunged headlong into the thickest of the press. His enemies fell back, taken by surprise and daunted by the ferocity of the attack. Those who did not were pierced through with his lance, or borne down by the weight of his charger. The cavaliers followed close in the rear. On they swept, with the fury of a thunderbolt, cleaving the solid ranks asunder, strewing their path with the dying and the dead, and bounding over every obstacle in their way. In a few minutes they were in the presence of the Indian commander, and Cortés, overturning his supporters, sprang forward with the strength of a lion, and, striking him through with his lance, hurled him to the ground. A young cavalier, Juan de Salamanca, who had kept close by his general's side, quickly dismounted and despatched the fallen chief. Then tearing away his banner, he presented it to Cortés, as a trophy to which he had the best claim. It was all the work of a moment. The guard, overpowered by the suddenness of the onset, made little resistance, but, flying, communicated their own panic to their comrades. The tidings of the loss soon spread over the field. The Indians, filled with consternation, now thought only of escape. In their blind terror, their numbers augmented their confusion. They trampled on one another, fancying it was the enemy in their rear.

The Spaniards and Tlascalans were not slow to avail themselves of the marvellous change in their affairs. Their fatigue, their wounds, hunger, thirst, all were forgotten in the eagerness for vengeance; and they followed up the flying foe, dealing death at every stroke, and taking ample retribution for all they had suffered in the bloody marshes of Mexico. Long did they pursue, till, the enemy having abandoned the field, they returned sated with slaughter to glean the booty which he had left. It was great, for the ground was covered with the bodies of chiefs, at whom the Spaniards, in obedience to the general's instructions, had particularly aimed; and their dresses displayed all the barbaric pomp of ornament, in which the Indian warrior delighted. When his men had thus indemnified themselves, in some degree, for their late reverses, Cortés called them again under their banners; and, after offering up a grateful acknowledgment to the Lord of Hosts for their miraculous preservation, they renewed their march across the now deserted valley. The sun was declining in the heavens, but before the shades of evening had gathered around, they reached an Indian temple on an eminence, which afforded a strong and commodious position for the night.

Such was the famous battle of Otompan—or Otumba, as commonly called from the Spanish corruption of the name. It was fought on July 8, 1520. The whole amount of the Indian force is reckoned by Castilian writers at two hundred thousand! that of the slain at twenty thousand! Those who admit the first part of the estimate will find no difficulty in receiving the last. It is about as difficult to form an accurate calculation of the numbers of a disorderly savage multitude, as of the pebbles on the beach, or the scattered leaves in autumn. Yet it was, undoubtedly, one of the most remarkable victories ever achieved in the New World. And this, not merely on account of the disparity of the forces, but of their unequal condition. For the Indians were in all their strength, while the Christians were wasted by disease, famine, and long-protracted sufferings; without cannon or firearms, and deficient in the military apparatus which had so often struck terror into their barbarian foe—deficient even in the terrors of a victorious name. But they had discipline on their side, desperate resolve, and implicit confidence in their commander. That they should have triumphed against such odds furnishes an inference of the same kind as that established by the victories of the European over the semi-civilised hordes of Asia.

Yet even here all must not be referred to superior discipline and tactics. For the battle would certainly have been lost, had it not been for the fortunate death of the Indian general. And, although the selection of the victim may be called the result of calculation, yet it was by the most precarious chance that he was thrown in the way of the Spaniards. It is, indeed, one among many examples of the influence of fortune in determining the fate of military operations. The star of Cortés was in the ascendant. Had it been otherwise, not a Spaniard would have survived that day to tell the bloody tale of the battle of Otumba.

CHAPTER V

ON THE FOLLOWING MORNING the army broke up its encampment at an early hour. The enemy do not seem to have made an attempt to rally. Clouds of skirmishers, however, were seen during the morning, keeping at a respectful distance, though occasionally venturing near enough to salute the Spaniards with a volley of missiles.

On a rising ground they discovered a fountain, a blessing not too often met with in these arid regions, and gratefully commemorated by the Christians, for the refreshment afforded by its cool and abundant waters. A little further on, they descried the rude works which served as the bulwark and boundary of the Tlascalan territory. At the sight, the allies sent up a joyous shout of congratulation, in which the Spaniards heartily joined, as they felt they were soon to be on friendly and hospitable ground.

But these feelings were speedily followed by others of a different nature; and, as they drew nearer the territory, their minds were disturbed with the most painful apprehensions as to their reception by the people among whom they were bringing desolation and mourning, and who might so easily, if ill-disposed, take advantage of their present crippled condition. "Thoughts like these," says Cortés, "weighed as heavily on my spirit as any which I ever experienced in going to battle with the Aztecs." Still he put, as usual, a good face on the matter, and encouraged his men to confide in their allies, whose past conduct had afforded every ground for trusting to their fidelity in future. He cautioned them, however, as their own strength was so much impaired, to be most careful to give no umbrage, or ground for jealousy, to their high-spirited allies. "Be but on your guard," continued the intrepid general, "and we have still

337

stout hearts and strong hands to carry us through the midst of them!"
With these anxious surmises, bidding adieu to the Aztec domain, the
Christian army crossed the frontier, and once more trod the soil of the
Republic.

The first place at which they halted was the town of Huejotlipan, a
place of about twelve or fifteen thousand inhabitants. They were kindly
greeted by the people, who came out to receive them, inviting the troops
to their habitations, and administering all the relief of their simple hospitality. Yet this was not so disinterested, according to some of the
Spaniards, as to prevent their expecting in requital a share of the plunder
taken in the late action. Here the weary forces remained two or three
days, when the news of their arrival having reached the capital, not more
than four or five leagues distant, the old chief, Maxixca, their efficient
friend on their former visit, and Xicotencatl, the young warrior who, it
will be remembered, had commanded the troops of his nation in their
bloody encounters with the Spaniards, came with a numerous concourse
of the citizens to welcome the fugitives to Tlascala. Maxixca, cordially
embracing the Spanish commander, testified the deepest sympathy for his
misfortunes. That the white men could so long have withstood the con-
federated power of the Aztecs was proof enough of their marvellous
prowess. "We have made common cause together," said the lord of Tlascala, "and we have common injuries to avenge; and, come weal or come
woe, be assured we will prove true and loyal friends, and stand by you to
the death."

This cordial assurance and sympathy, from one who exercised a control over the public counsels beyond any other ruler, effectually dispelled
the doubts that lingered in the mind of Cortés. He readily accepted his
invitation to continue his march at once to the capital, where he would
find so much better accommodations for his army, than in a small town
on the frontier. The sick and wounded, placed in hammocks, were borne
on the shoulders of the friendly natives; and, as the troops drew near the
city, the inhabitants came flocking out in crowds to meet them, rending
the air with joyous acclamations and wild bursts of their rude Indian
minstrelsy. Amidst the general jubilee, however, were heard sounds of
wailing and sad lament, as some unhappy relative or friend, looking
earnestly into the diminished files of their countrymen, sought in vain for
some dear and familiar countenance, and, as they turned disappointed
away, gave utterance to their sorrow in tones that touched the heart of
every soldier in the army. With these mingled accompaniments of joy

and woe—the motley web of human life—the way-worn columns of Cortés at length re-entered the republican capital.

The general and his suite were lodged in the rude, but spacious, palace of Maxixca. The rest of the army took up their quarters in the district over which the Tlascalan lord presided. Here they continued several weeks, until, by the attentions of the hospitable citizens, and such medical treatment as their humble science could supply, the wounds of the soldiers were healed, and they recovered from the debility to which they had been reduced by their long and unparalleled sufferings. Cortés was one of those who suffered severely. He lost the use of two of the fingers of his left hand. He had received, besides, two injuries on the head; one of which was so much exasperated by his subsequent fatigues and excitement of mind, that it assumed an alarming appearance. A part of the bone was obliged to be removed. A fever ensued, and for several days the hero, who had braved danger and death in their most terrible forms, lay stretched on his bed, as helpless as an infant. His excellent constitution, however, got the better of disease, and he was, at length, once more enabled to resume his customary activity. The Spaniards, with politic generosity, requited the hospitality of their hosts by sharing with them the spoils of their recent victory; and Cortés especially rejoiced the heart of Maxixca, by presenting him with the military trophy which he had won from the Indian commander.

But while the Spaniards were thus recruiting their health and spirits under the friendly treatment of their allies, and recovering the confidence and tranquillity of mind which had sunk under their hard reverses, they received tidings, from time to time, which showed that their late disaster had not been confined to the Mexican capital. On his descent from Mexico to encounter Narvaez, Cortés had brought with him a quantity of gold, which he left for safe keeping at Tlascala. To this was added a considerable sum, collected by the unfortunate Velasquez de Leon, in his expedition to the coast, as well as contributions from other sources. From the unquiet state of the capital, the general thought it best, on his return there, still to leave the treasure under the care of a number of invalid soldiers, who, when in marching condition, were to rejoin him in Mexico. A party from Vera Cruz, consisting of five horsemen and forty foot, had since arrived at Tlascala, and, taking charge of the invalids and treasure, undertook to escort them to the capital. He now learned that they had been intercepted on the route, and all cut off, with the entire loss of the treasure. Twelve other soldiers, marching in the same direction, had been massacred in the neighbouring province of Tepeaca; and accounts continually arrived of some unfortunate Castilian, who, presuming on the respect hitherto shown to his countrymen, and ignorant of the disasters in the capital, had fallen a victim to the fury of the enemy.

These dismal tidings filled the mind of Cortés with gloomy apprehensions for the fate of the settlement at Villa Rica—the last stay of their hopes. He despatched a trusty messenger, at once, to that place; and had the inexpressible satisfaction to receive a letter in return from the commander of the garrison, acquainting him with the safety of the colony, and its friendly relations with the neighbouring Totonacs. It was the best guarantee of the fidelity of the latter, that they had offended the Mexicans too deeply to be forgiven.

While the affairs of Cortés wore so gloomy an aspect without, he had to experience an annoyance scarcely less serious from the discontents of his followers. Many of them had fancied that their late appalling reverses would put an end to the expedition; or, at least, postpone all thoughts of resuming it for the present. But they knew little of Cortés who reasoned thus. Even while tossing on his bed of sickness, he was ripening in his mind fresh schemes for retrieving his honour, and for recovering the empire which had been lost more by another's rashness than his own. This was apparent, as he became convalescent, from the new regulations he made respecting the army, as well as from the orders sent to Vera Cruz for fresh reinforcements.

The knowledge of all this occasioned much disquietude to the disaffected soldiers. They were, for the most part, the ancient followers of Narvaez, on whom, as we have seen, the brunt of war had fallen the heaviest. Many of them possessed property in the islands, and had embarked on this expedition chiefly from the desire of increasing it. But they had gathered neither gold nor glory in Mexico. Their present service filled them only with disgust; and the few, comparatively, who had been so fortunate as to survive, languished to return to their rich mines and pleasant farms in Cuba, bitterly cursing the day when they had left them.

Finding their complaints little heeded by the general, they prepared a written remonstrance, in which they made their demand more formally. They represented the rashness of persisting in the enterprise in his present impoverished state, without arms or ammunition, almost without men; and this, too, against a powerful enemy, who had been more than a match for him, with all the strength of his late resources. It was madness to think of it. The attempt would bring them all to the sacrifice-block. Their only course was to continue their march to Vera Cruz. Every hour of delay might be fatal. The garrison in that place might be overwhelmed from want of strength to defend itself; and thus their last hope would be annihilated. But, once there, they might wait in comparative security for such reinforcements as would join them from abroad; while, in case of failure, they could the more easily make their escape. They concluded with insisting on being permitted to return, at once, to the port of Villa Rica. This petition, or rather remonstrance, was signed by all the disaffected soldiers, and, after being formally attested by the royal notary, was presented to Cortés.

It was a trying circumstance for him. What touched him most nearly was to find the name of his friend, the secretary Duero, to whose good offices he had chiefly owed his command, at the head of the paper. He was not, however, to be shaken from his purpose for a moment; and while all outward resources seemed to be fading away, and his own friends faltered or failed him, he was still true to himself. He knew that to retreat to Vera Cruz would be to abandon the enterprise. Once there, his army would soon find a pretext and a way for breaking up, and returning to the islands. All his ambitious schemes would be blasted. The great prize, already once in his grasp, would then be lost for ever. He would be a ruined man.

In his celebrated letter to Charles the Fifth, he says that, in reflecting on his position, he felt the truth of the adage, "that fortune favours the brave. The Spaniards were the followers of the Cross; and, trusting in the infinite goodness and mercy of God, he could not believe that He would suffer them and His own good cause thus to perish among the heathen. He was resolved, therefore, not to descend to the coast, but at all hazards to retrace his steps and beard the enemy again in his capital."

It was in the same resolute tone that he answered his discontented followers. He urged every argument which could touch their pride or honour as cavaliers. He appealed to that ancient Castilian valour which had never been known to falter before an enemy; besought them not to discredit the great deeds which had made their name ring throughout Europe; not to leave the emprise half achieved, for others more daring and adventurous to finish. How could they with any honour, he asked, desert their allies whom they had involved in the war, and leave them unprotected to the vengeance of the Aztecs? To retreat but a single step towards Villa Rica would be to proclaim their own weakness. It would dishearten their friends, and give confidence to their foes. He implored them to resume the confidence in him which they had ever shown, and to reflect that, if they had recently met with reverses, he had up to that point accomplished all, and more than all, that he had promised. It would be easy now to retrieve their losses, if they would have patience, and abide in this friendly land until the reinforcements, which would be ready to come in at his call, should enable them to act on the offensive. If, however, there were any so insensible to the motives which touch a brave man's heart, as to prefer ease at home to the glory of this great achievement, he would not stand in their way. Let them go in God's name. Let them leave their general in his extremity. He should feel stronger in the service of a few brave spirits, than if surrounded by a host of the false or the faint-hearted.

The disaffected party, as already noticed, was chiefly drawn from the troops of Narvaez. When the general's own veterans heard this appeal, their blood warmed with indignation at the thoughts of abandoning him or the cause at such a crisis. They pledged themselves to stand by him to the last; and the malcontents silenced, if not convinced, by this generous expression of sentiment from their comrades, consented to postpone their departure for the present, under the assurance that no obstacle should be thrown in their way, when a more favourable season should present itself.

Scarcely was this difficulty adjusted, when Cortés was menaced with one more serious, in the jealousy springing up between his soldiers and their Indian allies. Notwithstanding the demonstrations of regard by Maxixca and his immediate followers, there were others of the nation who looked with an evil eye on their guests, for the calamities in which they had involved them; and they tauntingly asked if, in addition to this, they were now to be burdened by the presence and maintenance of the strangers? The sallies of discontent were not so secret as altogether to escape the ears of the Spaniards, in whom they occasioned no little disquietude. They proceeded, for the most part, it is true, from persons of little consideration, since the four great chiefs of the Republic appear to have been steadily secured to the interests of Cortés. But they derived some importance from the countenance of the warlike Xicotencatl, in whose bosom still lingered the embers of that implacable hostility which he had displayed so courageously on the field of battle; and sparkles of this fiery temper occasionally gleamed forth in the intimate intercourse into which he was now reluctantly brought with his ancient opponents.

Cortés, who saw with alarm the growing feelings of estrangement, which must sap the very foundations on which he was to rest the lever for future operations, employed every argument which suggested itself to restore the confidence of his own men. He reminded them of the good services they had uniformly received from the great body of the nation. They had a sufficient pledge of the future constancy of the Tlascalans in their long cherished hatred of the Aztecs, which the recent disasters they had suffered from the same quarter could serve only to sharpen. And he urged with much force that, if any evil designs had been meditated by them against the Spaniards, the Tlascalans would doubtless have taken advantage of their late disabled condition, and not waited till they had recovered their strength and means of resistance.

While Cortés was thus endeavouring, with somewhat doubtful success, to stifle his own apprehensions, as well as those in the bosoms of his followers, an event occurred which happily brought the affair to an issue, and permanently settled the relations in which the two parties were to stand to each other. This will make it necessary to notice some events which had occurred in Mexico since the expulsion of the Spaniards.

On Montezuma's death, his brother Cuitlahuac, lord of Iztapalapan, conformably to the usage regulating the descent of the Aztec crown, was chosen to succeed him. He was an active prince, of large experience in military affairs, and, by the strength of his character, was well fitted to sustain the tottering fortunes of the monarchy. He appears, moreover, to have been a man of liberal and what may be called enlightened taste, to judge from the beautiful gardens which he had filled with rare exotics, and which so much attracted the admiration of the Spaniards in his city of Iztapalapan. Unlike his predecessor, he held the white men in detestation; and had probably the satisfaction of celebrating his own coronation by the sacrifice of many of them. From the moment of his release from the Spanish quarters, where he had been detained by Cortés, he entered into the patriotic movements of his people. It was he who conducted the assaults both in the streets of the city, and on the "Melancholy Night"; and it was at his instigation that the powerful force had been assembled to dispute the passage of the Spaniards in the Vale of Otumba.

Since the evacuation of the capital, he had been busily occupied in repairing the mischief it had received—restoring the buildings and the bridges, and putting it in the best posture of defence. He had endeavoured to improve the discipline and arms of his troops. He introduced the long spear among them, and, by attaching the sword-blades taken from the Christians to long poles, contrived a weapon that should be formidable against cavalry. He summoned his vassals, far and near, to hold themselves in readiness to march to the relief of the capital, if necessary, and, the better to secure their good will, relieved them from some of the burdens usually laid on them. But he was now to experience the instability of a government which rested not on love, but on fear. The vassals in the neighbourhood of the valley remained true to their allegiance; but others held themselves aloof, uncertain what course to adopt; while others, again, in the more distant provinces, refused obedience altogether, considering this a favourable moment for throwing off the yoke which had so long galled them.

In this emergency, the government sent a deputation to its ancient enemies, the Tlascalans. It consisted of six Aztec nobles, bearing a present of cotton cloth, salt, and other articles rarely seen, of late years, in the Republic. The lords of the state, astonished at this unprecedented act of condescension in their ancient foe, called the council or senate of the great chiefs together, to give the envoys audience.

Before this body, the Aztecs stated the purpose of their mission. They invited the Tlascalans to bury all past grievances in oblivion, and to enter into a treaty with them. All the nations of Anahuac should make common cause in defence of their country against the white men. The Tlascalans would bring down on their own heads the wrath of the gods, if they longer harboured the strangers who had violated and destroyed their temples. If they counted on the support and friendship of their guests, let them take warning from the fate of Mexico, which had received them kindly within its walls, and which, in return, they had filled with blood and ashes. They conjured them, by their reverence for their common religion, not to suffer the white men, disabled as they now were, to escape from their hands, but to sacrifice them at once to the gods, whose temples they had profaned. In that event, they proffered them their alliance, and the renewal of that friendly traffic which would restore to the Republic the possession of the comforts and luxuries of which it had been so long deprived.

The proposals of the ambassadors produced different effects on their audience. Xicotencatl was for embracing them at once. Far better was it, he said, to unite with their kindred, with those who held their own language, their faith and usages, than to throw themselves into the arms of the fierce strangers, who, however they might talk of religion, worshipped no god but gold. This opinion was followed by that of the younger warriors, who readily caught the fire of his enthusiasm. But the elder chiefs, especially his blind old father, one of the four rulers of the state, who seem to have been all heartily in the interests of the Spaniards, and one of them, Maxixca, their staunch friend, strongly expressed their aversion to the proposed alliance with the Aztecs. They were always the same, said the latter—fair in speech, and false in heart. They now proffered friendship to the Tlascalans. But it was fear which drove them to it, and, when that fear was removed, they would return to their old hostility. Who was it, but these insidious foes, that had so long deprived the country of the very necessaries of life, of which they were now so lavish in their offers? Was it not owing to the white men that the nation at length possessed them? Yet they were called on to sacrifice the white men to the gods!—the warriors who, after fighting the battles of the Tlascalans, now threw themselves on their hospitality. But the gods abhorred perfidy. And were not their guests the very beings whose coming had been so long predicted by the oracles? "Let us avail ourselves of it," he concluded, "and unite and make common cause with them, until we have humbled our haughty enemy."

This discourse provoked a sharp rejoinder from Xicotencatl, till the passion of the elder chieftain got the better of his patience, and, substituting force for argument, he thrust his younger antagonist with some violence from the council chamber. A proceeding so contrary to the usual decorum of Indian debate astonished the assembly. But, far from bringing censure on its author, it effectually silenced opposition. Even the hot-headed followers of Xicotencatl shrank from supporting a leader who had incurred such a mark of contemptuous displeasure from the ruler whom they most venerated. His own father openly condemned him; and the patriotic young warrior, gifted with a truer foresight into futurity than his countrymen, was left without support in the council, as he had formerly been on the field of battle. The proffered alliance of the Mexicans was unanimously rejected; and the envoys, fearing that even the sacred character with which they were invested might not protect them from violence, made their escape secretly from the capital.

The result of the conference was of the last importance to the Spaniards, who, in their present crippled condition, especially if taken .

unawares, would have been, probably, at the mercy of the Tlascalans. At all events, the union of these latter with the Aztecs would have settled the fate of the expedition; since, in the poverty of his own resources, it was only by adroitly playing off one part of the Indian population against the other that Cortés could ultimately hope for success.

CHAPTER VI

War with the Surrounding Tribes—Successes of the Spaniards —Death of Maxixca—Arrival of Reinforcements—Return in Triumph to Tlascala

1520

THE SPANISH COMMANDER, reassured by the result of the deliberations in the Tlascalan senate, now resolved on active operations, as the best means of dissipating the spirit of faction and discontent inevitably fostered by a life of idleness. He proposed to exercise his troops, at first, against some of the neighbouring tribes who had laid violent hands on such of the Spaniards as, confiding in their friendly spirit, had passed through their territories. Among these were the Tepeacans, a people often engaged in hostility with the Tlascalans, and who, as mentioned in a preceding chapter, had lately massacred twelve Spaniards in their march to the capital. An expedition against them would receive the ready support of his allies, and would assert the dignity of the Spanish name, much dimmed in the estimation of the natives by the late disasters.

The Tepeacans were a powerful tribe of the same primitive stock as the Aztecs, to whom they acknowledged allegiance. They had transferred this to the Spaniards, on their first march into the country, intimidated by the bloody defeats of their Tlascalan neighbours. But, since the troubles in the capital, they had again submitted to the Aztec sceptre. Their capital, now a petty village, was a flourishing city at the time of the Conquest, situated in the fruitful plains that stretch far away towards the base of Orizaba. The province contained, moreover, several towns of considerable size, filled with a bold and warlike population.

As these Indians had once acknowledged the authority of Castile, Cortés and his officers regarded their present conduct in the light of rebellion, and, in a council of war, it was decided that those engaged in the late massacre had fairly incurred the doom of slavery. Before proceeding against them, however, the general sent a summons requiring their submission, and offering full pardon for the past, but, in case of refusal, menacing them with the severest retribution. To this the Indians, now in arms, returned a contemptuous answer, challenging the Spaniards to meet them in fight, as they were in want of victims for their sacrifices.

Cortés, without further delay, put himself at the head of his small corps of Spaniards, and a large reinforcement of Tlascalan warriors. They were led by the younger Xicotencatl, who now appeared willing to bury his recent animosity, and desirous to take a lesson in war under the chief who had so often foiled him in the field.

The Tepeacans received their enemy on their borders. A bloody battle followed, in which the Spanish horse were somewhat embarrassed by the tall maize that covered part of the plain. They were successful in the end, and the Tepeacans, after holding their ground like good warriors, were at length routed with great slaughter. A second engagement, which took place a few days after, was followed by like decisive results; and the victorious Spaniards with their allies, marching straightway on the city of Tepeaca, entered it in triumph. No further resistance was attempted by the enemy, and the whole province, to avoid further calamities, eagerly tendered its submission. Cortés, however, inflicted the meditated chastisement on the places implicated in the massacre. The inhabitants were branded with a hot iron as slaves, and, after the royal fifth had been reserved, were distributed between his own men and the allies. The Spaniards were familiar with the system of *repartimientos* established in the islands; but this was the first example of slavery in New Spain. It was justified, in the opinion of the general and his military casuists, by the aggravated offences of the party. The sentence, however, was not countenanced by the crown, which, as the colonial legislation abundantly shows, was ever at issue with the craving and mercenary spirit of the colonist.

Satisfied with this display of his vengeance, Cortés now established his headquarters at Tepeaca, which, situated in a cultivated country, afforded easy means for maintaining an army, while its position on the Mexican frontier made it a good *point d'appui* for future operations.

The Aztec government, since it had learned the issue of its negotiations at Tlascala, had been diligent in fortifying its frontier in that quarter. The garrisons usually maintained there were strengthened, and large bodies of men were marched in the same direction, with orders to occupy the strong positions on the borders. The conduct of these troops was in their usual style of arrogance and extortion, and greatly disgusted the inhabitants of the country.

Among the places thus garrisoned by the Aztecs was Quauhque-chollan, a city containing thirty thousand inhabitants, according to the historians, and lying to the south-west twelve leagues or more from the Spanish quarters. It stood at the extremity of a deep valley, resting against a bold range of hills, or rather mountains, and flanked by two rivers with exceedingly high and precipitous banks. The only avenue by which the town could be easily approached was protected by a stone wall more than twenty feet high, and of great thickness. Into this place, thus strongly defended by art as well as by nature, the Aztec emperor had thrown a garrison of several thousand warriors, while a much more formidable force occupied the heights commanding the city.

The cacique of this strong post, impatient of the Mexican yoke, sent to Cortés, inviting him to march to his relief, and promising a co-operation of the citizens in an assault on the Aztec quarters. The general eagerly embraced the proposal, and detached Christoval de Olid, with two hundred Spaniards and a strong body of Tlascalans, to support the friendly cacique. On the way, Olid was joined by many volunteers from the Indian city and from the neighbouring capital of Cholula, all equally pressing their services. The number and eagerness of these auxiliaries excited suspicions in the bosom of the cavalier. They were strengthened by the surmises of the soldiers of Narvaez, whose imaginations were still haunted, it seems, by the horrors of the *noche triste,* and who saw in the friendly alacrity of their new allies evidence of an insidious understanding with the Aztecs. Olid, catching this distrust, made a countermarch on Cholula, where he seized the suspected chiefs, who had been most forward in offering their services, and sent them under a strong guard to Cortés.

The general, after a careful examination, was satisfied of the integrity of the suspected parties. He, expressing his deep regret at the treatment they had received, made them such amends as he could by liberal presents; and, as he now saw the impropriety of committing an affair of such importance to other hands, put himself at the head of his remaining force, and effected a junction with his officer in Cholula.

He had arranged with the cacique of the city against which he was marching that, on the appearance of the Spaniards, the inhabitants should rise on the garrison. Everything succeeded as he had planned. No sooner had the Christian battalions defiled on the plain before the town than the inhabitants attacked the garrison with the utmost fury. The latter, abandoning the outer defences of the place, retreated to their own quarters in the principal *teocalli,* where they maintained a hard struggle with their adversaries. In the heat of it, Cortés, at the head of his little body of horse, rode into the place, and directed the assault in person. The Aztecs made a fierce defence. But fresh troops constantly arriving to support the assailants, the works were stormed, and every one of the garrison was put to the sword.

The Mexican forces, meanwhile, stationed on the neighbouring eminences, had marched down to the support of their countrymen in the town, and formed in order of battle in the suburbs, where they were encountered by the Tlascalan levies. "They mustered," says Cortés, speaking of the enemy, "at least thirty thousand men, and it was a brave sight for the eye to look on—such a beautiful array of warriors glistening with gold and jewels and variegated featherwork!" The action was well contested between the two Indian armies. The suburbs were set on fire, and, in the midst of the flames, Cortés and his squadrons, rushing on the enemy, at length broke their array, and compelled them to fall back in disorder into the narrow gorge of the mountain, from which they had lately descended. The pass was rough and precipitous. Spaniards and Tlascalans followed close in the rear, and the light troops, scaling the high wall of the valley, poured down on the enemy's flanks. The heat was intense, and both parties were so much exhausted by their efforts that it was with difficulty, says the chronicler, that the one could pursue, or the other fly. They were not too weary, however, to slay. The Mexicans were routed with terrible slaughter. They found no pity from their Indian foes, who had a long account of injuries to settle with them. Some few sought refuge by flying higher up into the fastnesses of the sierra. They were followed by their indefatigable enemy, until, on the bald summit of the ridge, they reached the Mexican encampment. It covered a wide tract of ground. Various utensils, ornamented dresses, and articles of luxury were scattered round, and the number of slaves in attendance showed the barbaric pomp with which the nobles of Mexico went to their campaigns. It was a rich booty for the victors, who spread over the deserted camp, and loaded themselves with the spoil, until the gathering darkness warned them to descend.

Cortés followed up the blow by assaulting the strong town of Itzocan, held also by a Mexican garrison, and situated in the depths of a green valley watered by artificial canals, and smiling in all the rich abundance of this fruitful region of the plateau. The place, though stoutly defended, was stormed and carried; the Aztecs were driven across a river which ran below the town, and, although the light bridges that traversed it were broken down in the flight, whether by design or accident, the Spaniards, fording and swimming the stream as they could, found their way to the opposite bank, following up the chase with the eagerness of bloodhounds. Here, too, the booty was great; and the Indian auxiliaries flocked by thousands to the banners of the chief who so surely led them on to victory and plunder.

Soon afterwards, Cortés returned to his headquarters at Tepeaca. Thence he detached his officers on expeditions which were usually successful. Sandoval, in particular, marched against a large body of the enemy lying between the camp and Vera Cruz; defeated them in two decisive battles, and thus restored the communications with the port.

The result of these operations was the reduction of that populous and cultivated territory which lies between the great *volcan,* on the west, and the mighty skirts of Orizaba, on the east. Many places, also, in the neighbouring province of Mixtecapan acknowledged the authority of the Spaniards, and others from the remote region of Oaxaca sent to claim their protection. The conduct of Cortés towards his allies had gained him great credit for disinterestedness and equity. The Indian cities in the adjacent territory appealed to him, as their umpire, in their differences with one another, and cases of disputed succession in their governments were referred to his arbitration. By his discreet and moderate policy, he insensibly acquired an ascendency over their counsels, which had been denied to the ferocious Aztec. His authority extended wider and wider every day; and a new empire grew up in the very heart of the land, forming a counterpoise to the colossal power which had so long overshadowed it.

Cortés now felt himself strong enough to put in execution the plans for recovering the capital, over which he had been brooding ever since the hour of his expulsion. He had greatly undervalued the resources of the Aztec monarchy. He was now aware, from bitter experience, that, to vanquish it, his own forces, and all he could hope to muster, would be incompetent, without a very extensive support from the Indians themselves. A large army would, moreover, require large supplies for its maintenance, and these could not be regularly obtained, during a protracted siege, without the friendly co-operation of the natives. On such support he might now safely calculate from Tlascala, and the other

Indian territories, whose warriors were so eager to serve under his banners. His past acquaintance with them had instructed him in their national character and system of war; while the natives who had fought under his command, if they had caught little of the Spanish tactics, had learned to act in concert with the white men, and to obey him implicitly as their commander. This was a considerable improvement in such wild and disorderly levies, and greatly augmented the strength derived from numbers.

Experience showed that in a future conflict with the capital it would not do to trust to the causeways, but that to succeed, he must command the lake. He proposed, therefore, to build a number of vessels, like those constructed under his orders in Montezuma's time, and afterwards destroyed by the inhabitants. For this he had still the services of the same experienced shipbuilder, Martin Lopez, who, as we have seen, had fortunately escaped the slaughter of the "Melancholy Night." Cortés now sent this man to Tlascala, with orders to build thirteen brigantines, which might be taken to pieces and carried on the shoulders of the Indians to be launched on the waters of Lake Tezcuco. The sails, rigging, and ironwork were to be brought from Vera Cruz, where they had been stored since their removal from the dismantled ships. It was a bold conception, that of constructing a fleet to be transported across forest and mountain before it was launched on its destined waters! But it suited the daring genius of Cortés, who, with the co-operation of his staunch Tlascalan confederates, did not doubt his ability to carry it into execution.

It was with no little regret that the general learned at this time of the death of his good friend Maxixca, the old lord of Tlascala, who had stood by him so steadily in the hour of adversity. He had fallen a victim to that terrible epidemic, the small-pox, which was now sweeping over the land like fire over the prairies, smiting down prince and peasant, and adding another to the long train of woes that followed the march of the white men. It was imported into the country, it is said, by a Negro slave, in the fleet of Narvaez. It first broke out in Cempoalla. The poor natives, ignorant of the best mode of treating the loathsome disorder, sought relief in their usual practice of bathing in cold water, which greatly aggravated their trouble. From Cempoalla it spread rapidly over the neighbouring country, and, penetrating through Tlascala, reached the Aztec capital, where Montezuma's successor, Cuitlahuac, fell one of its first victims. Thence it swept down towards the borders of the Pacific, leaving its path strewn with the dead bodies of the natives, who, in the strong language of a contemporary, perished in heaps like cattle stricken with the murrain. It does not seem to have been fatal to the Spaniards, many of whom, probably, had already had the disorder, and who were, at all events, acquainted with the proper method of treating it.

The death of Maxixca was deeply regretted by the troops, who lost in him a true and most efficient ally. With his last breath, he commended them to his son and successor, as the great beings whose coming into the country had been so long predicted by the oracles. He expressed a desire to die in the profession of the Christian faith. Cortés no sooner learned his condition than he despatched Father Olmedo to Tlascala. The friar found that Maxixca had already caused a crucifix to be placed before his sick couch, as the object of his adoration. After explaining, as intelligibly as he could, the truths of revelation, he baptised the dying chieftain; and the Spaniards had the satisfaction to believe that the soul of their benefactor was exempted from the doom of eternal perdition that hung over the unfortunate Indian who perished in his unbelief.

Their late brilliant successes seem to have reconciled most of the disaffected soldiers to the prosecution of the war. There were still a few among them, the secretary Duero, Bermudez the treasurer, and others high in office, or wealthy hidalgos, who looked with disgust on another campaign, and now loudly reiterated their demand of a free passage to Cuba. To this Cortés, satisfied with the support on which he could safely count, made no further objection. Having once given his consent, he did all in his power to facilitate their departure, and provide for their comfort. He ordered the best ship at Vera Cruz to be placed at their disposal, to be well supplied with provisions and everything necessary for the voyage, and sent Alvarado to the coast to superintend the embarkation. He took the most courteous leave of them, with assurances of his own unalterable regard. But, as the event proved, those who could part from him at this crisis had little sympathy with his fortunes; and we find Duero not long afterwards in Spain, supporting the claims of Velasquez before the emperor, in opposition to those of his former friend and commander.

The loss of these few men was amply compensated by the arrival of others, whom Fortune—to use no higher term—most unexpectedly threw in his way. The first of these came in a small vessel sent from Cuba by the governor, Velasquez, with stores for the colony at Vera

Cruz. He was not aware of the late transactions in the country, and of the discomfiture of his officer. In the vessel came despatches, it is said, from Fonseca, bishop of Burgos, instructing Narvaez to send Cortés, if he had not already done so, for trial to Spain. The alcalde of Vera Cruz, agreeably to the general's instructions, allowed the captain of the bark to land, who had no doubt that the country was in the hands of Narvaez. He was undeceived by being seized, together with his men, so soon as they had set foot on shore. The vessel was then secured; and the commander and his crew, finding out their error, were persuaded without much difficulty to join their countrymen in Tlascala.

A second vessel, sent soon after by Velasquez, shared the same fate, and those on board consented also to take their chance in the expedition under Cortés.

About the same time, Garay, the governor of Jamaica, fitted out three ships with an armed force to plant a colony on the Panuco, a river which pours into the Gulf a few degrees north of Villa Rica. Garay persisted in establishing this settlement, in contempt of the claims of Cortés, who had already entered into a friendly communication with the inhabitants of that region. But the crews experienced such a rough reception from the natives on landing, and lost so many men, that they were glad to take to their vessels again. One of these foundered in a storm. The others put into the port of Vera Cruz to restore the men, much weakened by hunger and disease. Here they were kindly received, their wants supplied, their wounds healed; when they were induced, by the liberal promises of Cortés, to abandon the disastrous service of their employer, and enlist under his own prosperous banner. The reinforcements obtained from these sources amounted to full a hundred and fifty men, well provided with arms and ammunition, together with twenty horses. By this strange concurrence of circumstances, Cortés saw himself in possession of the supplies he most needed; that, too, from the hands of his enemies, whose costly preparations were thus turned to the benefit of the very man whom they were designed to ruin.

His good fortune did not stop here. A ship from the Canaries touched at Cuba, freighted with arms and military stores for the adventurers in the New World. Their commander heard there of the recent discoveries in Mexico, and, thinking it would afford a favourable market for him, directed his course to Vera Cruz. He was not mistaken. The alcalde, by the general's orders, purchased both ship and cargo; and the crews, catching the spirit of adventure, followed their countrymen into the interior. There seemed to be a magic in the name of Cortés, which drew all who came within hearing of it under his standard.

Having now completed the arrangements for settling his new conquests, there seemed to be no further reason for postponing his departure to Tlascala. He was first solicited by the citizens of Tepeaca to leave a garrison with them, to protect them from the vengeance of the Aztecs. Cortés acceded to the request, and, considering the central position of the town favourable for maintaining his conquests, resolved to plant a colony there. For this object he selected sixty of his soldiers, most of whom were disabled by wounds or infirmity. He appointed the alcaldes, regidores, and other functionaries of a civic magistracy. The place he called *Segura de la Frontera* or Security of the Frontier. It received valuable privileges as a city, a few years later, from the emperor Charles the Fifth; and rose to some consideration in the age of the Conquest. But its consequence soon after declined. Even its Castilian name, with the same caprice which has decided the fate of more than one name in our own country, was gradually supplanted by its ancient one, and the little village of Tepeaca is all that now commemorates the once flourishing Indian capital, and the second Spanish colony in Mexico.

While at Segura, Cortés wrote that celebrated letter to the emperor— the second in the series—so often cited in the preceding pages. It takes up the narrative with the departure from Vera Cruz, and exhibits in a brief and comprehensive form the occurrences up to the time at which we are now arrived. In the concluding page, the general, after noticing the embarrassments under which he labours, says, in his usual manly spirit, that he holds danger and fatigue light in comparison with the attainment of his object; and that he is confident a short time will restore the Spaniards to their former position, and repair all their losses.

He notices the resemblance of Mexico, in many of its features and productions, to the mother country, and requests that it may henceforth be called, "New Spain of the Ocean Sea." He finally requests that a commission may be sent out at once, to investigate his conduct, and to verify the accuracy of his statements.

This letter, which was printed at Seville the year after its reception, has been since reprinted and translated more than once. It excited a great sensation at the court, and among the friends of science generally. The previous discoveries of the New World had disappointed the expectations which had been formed after the solution of the grand problem of its existence. They had brought to light only rude tribes, which, however gentle and inoffensive in their manners, were still in the primitive stages of barbarism. Here was an authentic account of a vast nation, potent and populous, exhibiting an elaborate social polity, well advanced in the arts of civilisation, occupying a soil that teemed with mineral treasures and with a boundless variety of vegetable products, stores of wealth, both natural and artificial, that seemed, for the first time, to realise the golden dreams in which the great discoverer of the New World had so fondly, and in his own day so fallaciously, indulged. Well might the scholar of that age exult in the revelation of these wonders, which so many had long, but in vain, desired to see.

With this letter went another to the emperor, signed, as it would seem, by nearly every officer and soldier in the camp. It expatiated on the obstacles thrown in the way of the expedition by Velasquez and Narvaez, and the great prejudice this had caused to the royal interests. It then set forth the services of Cortés, and besought the emperor to confirm him in his authority, and not to allow any interference with one who, from his personal character, his intimate knowledge of the land and its people, and the attachment of his soldiers, was the man best qualified in all the world to achieve the conquest of the country.

It added not a little to the perplexities of Cortés that he was still in entire ignorance of the light in which his conduct was regarded in Spain. He had not even heard whether his despatches, sent the year preceding from Vera Cruz, had been received. Mexico was as far removed from all intercourse with the civilised world, as if it had been placed at the antipodes. Few vessels had entered, and none had been allowed to leave its ports. The governor of Cuba, an island distant but a few days' sail, was yet ignorant, as we have seen, of the fate of his armament. On the arrival of every new vessel or fleet on these shores, Cortés might well doubt whether it brought aid to his undertaking, or a royal commission to supersede him. His sanguine spirit relied on the former; though the latter was much the more probable, considering the intimacy of his enemy, the governor, with Bishop Fonseca, a man jealous of his authority, and one who, from his station at the head of the Indian department, held a predominant control over the affairs of the New World. It was the policy of Cortés, therefore, to lose no time; to push forward his preparations, lest another should be permitted to snatch the laurel now almost within his grasp. Could he but reduce the Aztec capital, he felt that he should be safe; and that, in whatever light his irregular proceedings might now be viewed, his services in that event would far more than counterbalance them in the eyes both of the crown and of the country.

The general wrote, also, to the Royal Audience at St. Domingo, in order to interest them in his cause. He sent four vessels to the same island, to obtain a further supply of arms and ammunition; and, the better to stimulate the cupidity of adventurers, and allure them to the expedition, he added specimens of the beautiful fabrics of the country, and of its precious metals. The funds for procuring these important supplies were probably derived from the plunder gathered in the late battles, and the gold which, as already remarked, had been saved from the general wreck by the Castilian convoy.

It was the middle of December, when Cortés, having completed all his arrangements, set out on his return to Tlascala, ten or twelve leagues distant. He marched in the van of the army, and took the way of Cholula. How different was his condition from that in which he had left the republican capital not five months before! His march was a triumphal procession, displaying the various banners and military ensigns taken from the enemy, long files of captives, and all the rich spoils of conquest gleaned from many a hard-fought field. As the army passed through the towns and villages, the inhabitants poured out to greet them, and, as they drew near to Tlascala, the whole population, men, women, and children, came forth celebrating their return with songs, dancing, and music. Arches decorated with flowers were thrown across the streets through which they passed, and a Tlascalan orator addressed the general, on his entrance into the city, in a lofty panegyric on his late achievements, proclaiming him the "avenger of the nation." Amidst this pomp and triumphal show, Cortés and his principal officers were seen clad in deep mourning in honour of their friend Maxixca. And this tribute of respect to the memory of their venerated ruler touched the Tlascalans more sensibly than all the proud display of military trophies.

The general's first act was to confirm the son of his deceased friend in the succession, which had been contested by an illegitimate brother. The youth was but twelve years of age; and Cortés prevailed on him without difficulty to follow his father's example, and receive baptism. He afterwards knighted him with his own hand; the first instance, probably, of the order of chivalry being conferred on an American Indian. The elder Xicotencatl was also persuaded to embrace Christianity; and the example of their rulers had its obvious effect in preparing the minds of the people for the reception of the truth. Cortés, whether from the suggestions of

Olmedo, or from the engrossing nature of his own affairs, did not press the work of conversion further at this time, but wisely left the good seed, already sown, to ripen in secret, till time should bring forth the harvest.

The Spanish commander, during his short stay in Tlascala, urged forward the preparations for the campaign. He endeavoured to drill the Tlascalans, and give them some idea of European discipline and tactics. He caused new arms to be made, and the old ones to be put in order. Powder was manufactured with the aid of sulphur obtained by some adventurous cavaliers from the smoking throat of Popocatepetl. The construction of the brigantines went forward prosperously under the direction of Lopez, with the aid of the Tlascalans. Timber was cut in the forests, and pitch, an article unknown to the Indians, was obtained from the pines on the neighbouring Sierra de Malinche. The rigging and other appurtenances were transported by the Indian *tamanes* from Villa Rica; and by Christmas, the work was so far advanced, that it was no longer necessary for Cortés to delay the march to Mexico.

CHAPTER VII

Guatemozin, Emperor of the Aztecs—Preparations for the March—Military Code—Spaniards Cross the Sierra—Enter Tezcuco—Prince Ixtlilxochitl

1520

WHILE the events related in the preceding chapter were passing, an important change had taken place in the Aztec monarchy. Montezuma's brother and successor, Cuitlahuac, had suddenly died of the small-pox after a brief reign of four months—brief, but glorious, for it had witnessed the overthrow of the Spaniards and their expulsion from Mexico. On the death of their warlike chief, the electors were convened, as usual, to supply the vacant throne. It was an office of great responsibility in the dark hour of their fortunes. The *teoteuctli,* or high-priest, invoked the blessing of the supreme God on their deliberations. His prayer is still extant. It was the last one ever made on a similar occasion in Anahuac, and a few extracts from it may interest the reader, as a specimen of Aztec eloquence.

"O Lord! thou knowest that the days of our sovereign are at an end, for thou hast placed him beneath thy feet. He abides in the place of his retreat; he has trodden the path which we are all to tread; he has gone to the house whither we are all to follow—the house of eternal darkness, where no light cometh. He is gathered to his rest, and no one henceforth shall disquiet him. . . . All these were the princes, his predecessors, who sat on the imperial throne, directing the affairs of thy kingdom; for thou art the universal lord and emperor, by whose will and movement the whole world is directed; thou needest not the counsel of another. They laid down the intolerable burden of government, and left it to him, their successor. Yet he sojourned but a few days in his kingdom—but a few days had we enjoyed his presence, when thou summonedst him away to follow those who had ruled over the land before him. And great cause has he for thankfulness, that thou hast relieved him from so grievous a load, and placed him in tranquillity and rest. . . . Who now shall order matters for the good of the people and the realm? Who shall appoint the judges to administer justice to thy people? Who now shall bid the drum and the flute to sound, and gather together the veteran soldiers and the men mighty in battle? Our Lord and our Defence! wilt thou, in thy wisdom, elect one who shall be worthy to sit on the throne of thy kingdom; one who shall bear the grievous burden of government; who shall comfort and cherish thy poor people, even as the mother cherisheth her offspring? . . . O Lord, most merciful! pour forth thy light and thy splendour over this thine empire! . . . Order it so that thou shalt be served in all, and through all."

The choice fell on Quauhtemotzin, or Guatemozin, as euphoniously corrupted by the Spaniards. He was nephew to the two last monarchs, and married his cousin, the beautiful princess Tecuichpo, Montezuma's daughter. "He was not more than twenty-five years old, and elegant in his person for an Indian," says one who had seen him often; "valiant, and so terrible, that his followers trembled in his presence." He did not shrink from the perilous post that was offered to him; and, as he saw the tempest gathering darkly around, he prepared to meet it like a man. Though young, he had ample experience in military matters, and had distinguished himself above all others in the bloody conflicts of the capital. He bore a sort of religious hatred to the Spaniards, like that which Hannibal is said to have sworn, and which he certainly cherished, against his Roman foes.

By means of his spies, Guatemozin made himself acquainted with the movements of the Spaniards, and their design to besiege the capital. He prepared for it by sending away the useless part of the population, while he called in his potent vassals from the neighbourhood. He continued the plans of his predecessor for strengthening the defences of the city, reviewed his troops, and stimulated them by prizes to excel in their exercises. He made harangues to his soldiers to rouse them to a spirit of desperate resistance. He encouraged his vassals throughout the empire to attack the white men wherever they were to be met with, setting a price on their heads, as well as on the persons of all who should be brought alive to him in Mexico. And it was no uncommon thing for the Spaniards to find hanging up in the temples of the conquered places the arms and accoutrements of their unfortunate countrymen who had been seized and sent to the capital for sacrifice. Such was the young monarch who was now called to the tottering throne of the Aztecs; worthy, by his bold and magnanimous nature, to sway the sceptre of his country, in the most flourishing period of her renown; and now, in her distress, devoting himself in the true spirit of a patriotic prince to uphold her falling fortunes, or bravely perish with them.

We must now return to the Spaniards in Tlascala, where we left them preparing to resume their march on Mexico. Their commander had the satisfaction to see his troops tolerably complete in their appointments; varying, indeed, according to the condition of the different reinforcements which had arrived from time to time; but on the whole, superior to those of the army with which he had first invaded the country. His whole force fell little short of six hundred men; forty of whom were cavalry, together with eighty arquebusiers and crossbow-men. The rest were armed with sword and target, and with the copper-headed pike of Chinantla. He had nine cannon of a moderate calibre, and was indifferently supplied with powder.

As his forces were drawn up in order of march, Cortés rode through the ranks, exhorting his soldiers, as usual with him on these occasions, to be true to themselves, and the enterprise in which they were embarked. He told them, they were to march against *rebels,* who had once acknowledged allegiance to the Spanish sovereign; against barbarians, the enemies of their religion. They were to fight the battles of the Cross and of the crown; to fight their own battles, to wipe away the stain from their arms, to avenge their injuries, and the loss of the dear companions who had been butchered on the field or on the accursed altar of their sacrifice. Never was there a war which offered higher incentives to the Christian cavalier; a war which opened to him riches and renown in this life, and an imperishable glory in that to come.

Thus did the politic chief touch all the secret springs of devotion, honour, and ambition in the bosoms of his martial audience, waking the mettle of the most sluggish before leading him on the perilous emprise. They answered with acclamations that they were ready to die in defence of the faith; and would either conquer, or leave their bones with those of their countrymen, in the waters of the Tezcuco.

The army of the allies next passed in review before the general. It is variously estimated by writers from a hundred and ten to a hundred and fifty thousand soldiers! The palpable exaggeration, no less than the discrepancy, shows that little reliance can be placed on any estimate. It is certain, however, that it was a multitudinous array, consisting not only of the flower of the Tlascalan warriors, but of those of Cholula,

Tepeaca, and the neighbouring territories, which had submitted to the Castilian crown.

They were armed after the Indian fashion, with bows and arrows, the glassy *maquahuitl,* and the long pike, which formidable weapon, Cortés, as we have seen, had introduced among his own troops. They were divided into battalions, each having its own banner, displaying the appropriate arms or emblem of its company. The four great chiefs of the nation marched in the van; three of them venerable for their years, and showing in the insignia which decorated their persons the evidence of many a glorious feat in arms. The panache of many coloured plumes floated from their casques, set in emeralds or other precious stones. Their *escaupil,* or stuffed doublet of cotton, was covered with the graceful surcoat of featherwork, and their feet were protected by sandals embossed with gold. Four young pages followed, bearing their weapons, and four others supported as many standards, on which were emblazoned the armorial bearings of the four great divisions of the republic. The Tlascalans, though frugal in the extreme, and rude in their way of life, were as ambitious of display in their military attire as any of the races on the plateau. As they defiled before Cortés, they saluted him by waving their banners and by a flourish of their wild music, which the general acknowledged by courteously raising his cap as they passed. The Tlascalan warriors, and especially the younger Xicotencatl, their commander, affected to imitate their European masters, not merely in their tactics, but in minuter matters of military etiquette.

Cortés, with the aid of Marina, made a brief address to his Indian allies. He reminded them that he was going to fight their battles against their ancient enemies. He called on them to support him in a manner worthy of their renowned republic. To those who remained at home, he committed the charge of aiding in the completion of the brigantines, on which the success of the expedition so much depended; and he requested that none would follow his banner, who were not prepared to remain till the final reduction of the capital. This address was answered by shouts, or rather yells, of defiance, showing the exultation felt by his Indian confederates at the prospect of at last avenging their manifold wrongs, and humbling their haughty enemy.

Before setting out on the expedition, Cortés published a code of ordinances, as he terms them, or regulations for the army, too remarkable to be passed over in silence. The preamble sets forth that in all institutions, whether divine or human—if the latter have any worth—

order is the great law. The ancient chronicles inform us that the greatest captains in past times owed their successes quite as much to the wisdom of their ordinances, as to their own valour and virtue. The situation of the Spaniards eminently demanded such a code; a mere handful of men as they were, in the midst of countless enemies, most cunning in the management of their weapons and in the art of war. The instrument then reminds the army that the conversion of the heathen is the work most acceptable in the eye of the Almighty, and one that will be sure to receive his support. It calls on every soldier to regard this as the prime object of the expedition, *without which the war would be manifestly unjust, and every acquisition made by it a robbery.*

The general solemnly protests that the principal motive which operates in his own bosom is the desire to wean the natives from their gloomy idolatry, and to impart to them the knowledge of a purer faith; and next, to recover for his master, the emperor, the dominions which of right belong to him.

The ordinances then prohibit all blasphemy against God or the saints; a vice much more frequent among Catholic than Protestant nations, arising, perhaps, less from difference of religion, than of physical temperament, for the warm sun of the South, under which Catholicism prevails, stimulates the sensibilities to the more violent expression of passion.

Another law is directed against gaming, to which the Spaniards in all ages have been peculiarly addicted. Cortés, making allowance for the strong national propensity, authorises it under certain limitations; but prohibits the use of dice altogether. Then follow other laws against brawls and private combats, against personal taunts and the irritating sarcasms of rival companies; rules for the more perfect discipline of the troops, whether in camp or the field. Among others is one prohibiting any captain, under pain of death, from charging the enemy without orders; a practice noticed as most pernicious and of too frequent occurrence—showing the impetuous spirit and want of true military subordination in the bold cavaliers who followed the standard of Cortés.

The last ordinance prohibits any man, officer or private, from securing to his own use any of the booty taken from the enemy, whether it be gold, silver, precious stones, featherwork, stuffs, slaves, or other commodity, however or wherever obtained, in the city or in the field; and requires him to bring it forthwith to the presence of the general, or the officer appointed to receive it. The violation of this law was punished with death and confiscation of property. So severe an edict may be thought to prove that, however much the *Conquistador* may have been influenced by spiritual considerations, he was by no means insensible to those of a temporal character.

These provisions were not suffered to remain a dead letter. The Spanish commander, soon after their proclamation, made an example of two of his own slaves, whom he hanged for plundering the natives. A similar sentence was passed on a soldier for the like offence, though he allowed him to be cut down before the sentence was entirely executed. Cortés knew well the character of his followers; rough and turbulent spirits, who required to be ruled with an iron hand. Yet he was not eager to assert his authority on light occasions. The intimacy into which they were thrown by their peculiar situation, perils, and sufferings, in which all equally shared, and a common interest in the adventure, induced a familiarity between men and officers, most unfavourable to military discipline. The general's own manners, frank and liberal, seemed to invite this freedom, which on ordinary occasions he made no attempt to repress; perhaps finding it too difficult, or at least impolitic, since it afforded a safety-valve for the spirits of a licentious soldiery, that, if violently coerced, might have burst forth into open mutiny. But the limits of his forbearance were clearly defined; and any attempt to overstep them, or to violate the established regulations of the camp, brought a sure and speedy punishment on the offender. By thus tempering severity with indulgence, masking an iron will under the open bearing of a soldier—Cortés established a control over his band of bold and reckless adventurers, such as a pedantic martinet, scrupulous in enforcing the minutiæ of military etiquette, could never have obtained.

The ordinances, dated on December 22, were proclaimed to the assembled army on the 26th. Two days afterwards, the troops were on their march, and Cortés, at the head of his battalions, with colours flying and music playing, issued forth from the gates of the republican capital, which had so generously received him in his distress, and which now, for the second time, supplied him with the means for consummating his great enterprise. The population of the city, men, women, and children, hung on the rear of the army, taking a last leave of their countrymen, and imploring the gods to crown their arms with victory.

Notwithstanding the great force mustered by the Indian confederates, the Spanish general allowed but a small part of them now to attend him. He proposed to establish his headquarters at some place on the Tezcucan lake, whence he could annoy the Aztec capital, by reducing the surrounding country, cutting off the supplies, and thus placing the city in a state of blockade.

The direct assault on Mexico, itself, he intended to postpone, until the arrival of the brigantines should enable him to make it with the greatest advantage. Meanwhile, he had no desire to encumber himself with a superfluous multitude, whom it would be difficult to feed; and he preferred to leave them at Tlascala, whence they might convey the vessels, when completed, to the camp, and aid him in his future operations.

Three routes presented themselves to Cortés, by which he might penetrate into the valley. He chose the most difficult, traversing the bold sierra which divides the eastern plateau from the western, and so rough and precipitous, as to be scarcely practicable for the march of an army. He wisely judged that he should be less likely to experience annoyance from the enemy in this direction, as they might naturally confide in the difficulties of the ground for their protection.

The first day the troops advanced five or six leagues, Cortés riding in the van at the head of his little body of cavalry. They halted at the village of Tetzmellocan, at the base of the mountain chain which traverses the country, touching at its southern limit the mighty Iztaccihuatl, or "White Woman"—white with the snows of ages. At this village they met with a friendly reception, and on the following morning began the ascent of the sierra.

The path was steep and exceedingly rough. Thick matted bushes covered its surface, and the winter torrents had broken it into deep, stony channels, hardly practicable for the passage of artillery, while the straggling branches of the trees, flung horizontally across the road, made it equally difficult for cavalry. The cold, as they rose higher, became intense. It was keenly felt by the Spaniards, accustomed of late to a warm, or at least temperate climate; though the extreme toil with which they forced their way upward furnished the best means of resisting the weather. The only vegetation to be seen in these higher regions was the pine, dark forests of which clothed the sides of the mountains, till even these dwindled into a thin and stunted growth. It was night before the way-worn soldiers reached the bald crest of the sierra, where they lost no time in kindling their fires; and, huddling round their bivouacs, they warmed their frozen limbs, and prepared their evening repast.

With the earliest dawn, the troops were again in motion. Mass was said, and they began their descent, more difficult and painful than their ascent on the day preceding; for, in addition to the natural obstacles of the road, they found it strewn with huge pieces of timber and trees, obviously felled for the purpose by the natives. Cortés ordered up a body of light troops to clear away the impediments, and the army again resumed its march, but with the apprehension that the enemy had prepared an ambuscade, to surprise them when they should be entangled in the pass. They moved cautiously forward, straining their vision to pierce the thick gloom of the forests, where the wily foe might be lurking. But they saw no living thing, except only the wild inhabitants of the woods, and flocks of the *zopilote,* the voracious vulture of the country, which, in anticipation of a bloody banquet, hung like a troop of evil spirits on the march of the army.

As they descended, the Spaniards felt a sensible and most welcome change in the temperature. The character of the vegetation changed with it, and the funereal pine, their only companion of late, gave way to the sturdy oak, to the sycamore, and lower down, to the graceful pepper-tree mingling its red berry with the dark foliage of the forest; while, in still lower depths, the gaudy-coloured creepers might be seen flinging their gay blossoms over the branches, and telling of a softer and more luxurious climate.

At length, the army emerged on an open level, where the eye, unobstructed by intervening wood or hill-top, could range far and wide over the Valley of Mexico. There it lay bathed in the golden sunshine, stretched out as it were in slumber, in the arms of the giant hills, which clustered like a phalanx of guardian genii around it. The magnificent vision, new to many of the spectators, filled them with rapture. Even the veterans of Cortés could not withhold their admiration, though this was soon followed by a bitter feeling, as they recalled the sufferings which had befallen them within these beautiful, but treacherous precincts. "It made us feel," says the lion-hearted Conqueror in his letters, "that we had no choice but victory or death; and our minds once resolved, we moved forward with as light a step as if we had been going on an errand of certain pleasure."

As the Spaniards advanced, they beheld the neighbouring hill-tops blazing with beacon-fires, showing that the country was already alarmed and mustering to oppose them. The general called on his men to be mindful of their high reputation; to move in order, closing up their ranks, and to obey implicitly the commands of their officers. At every turn among

the hills, they expected to meet the forces of the enemy drawn up to
dispute their passage. And, as they were allowed to pass the defiles
unmolested, and drew near to the open plains, they were prepared to see
them occupied by a formidable host, who would compel them to fight
over again the battle of Otumba. But, although clouds of dusky warriors
were seen, from time to time, hovering on the highlands, as if watching
their progress, they experienced no interruption, till they reached a
barranca, or deep ravine, through which flowed a little river, crossed
by a bridge partly demolished. On the opposite side a considerable body
of Indians was stationed, as if to dispute the passage; but, whether
distrusting their own numbers, or intimidated by the steady advance of
the Spaniards they offered them no annoyance, and were quickly dispersed
by a few resolute charges of cavalry. The army then proceeded, without
molestation, to a small town, called Coatepec, where they halted for the
night. Before retiring to his own quarters, Cortés made the rounds of the
camp, with a few trusty followers, to see that all was safe. He seemed to
have an eye that never slumbered, and a frame incapable of fatigue. It
was the indomitable spirit within, which sustained him.

Yet he may well have been kept awake through the watches of the
night, by anxiety and doubt. He was now but three leagues from
Tezcuco, the far-famed capital of the Acolhuans. He proposed to establish his headquarters, if possible, at this place. Its numerous dwellings
would afford ample accommodations for his army. An easy communication with Tlascala, by a different route from that which he had traversed, would furnish him with the means of readily obtaining supplies
from that friendly country, and for the safe transportation of the
brigantines, when finished, to be launched on the waters of the Tezcuco.
But he had good reason to distrust the reception he should meet with in
the capital; for an important revolution had taken place there, since the
expulsion of the Spaniards from Mexico, of which it will be necessary
to give some account.

The reader will remember that the cacique of that place, named
Cacama, was deposed by Cortés, during his first residence in the Aztec
metropolis, in consequence of a projected revolt against the Spaniards,
and that the crown had been placed on the head of a younger brother,
Cuicuitzca. The deposed prince was among the prisoners carried away
by Cortés, and perished with the others, in the terrible passage of the
causeway, on the *noche triste.* His brother, afraid, probably, after the

flight of the Spaniards, of continuing with his own vassals, whose sympathies were altogether with the Aztecs, accompanied his friends in their retreat, and was so fortunate as to reach Tlascala in safety.

Meanwhile, a second son of Nezahualpilli, named Coanaco, claimed the crown, on his elder brother's death, as his own rightful inheritance. As he heartily joined his countrymen and the Aztecs in their detestation of the white men, his claims were sanctioned by the Mexican emperor. Soon after his accession, the new lord of Tezcuco had an opportunity of showing his loyalty to his imperial patron in an effectual manner.

A body of forty-five Spaniards, ignorant of the disasters in Mexico, were transporting thither a large quantity of gold, at the very time their countrymen were on the retreat to Tlascala. As they passed through the Tezcucan territory, they were attacked by Coanaco's orders, most of them massacred on the spot, and the rest sent for sacrifice to Mexico. The arms and accoutrements of these unfortunate men were hung up as trophies in the temples, and their skins, stripped from their dead bodies, were suspended over the bloody shrines, as the most acceptable offering to the offended deities.

Some months after this event, the exiled prince, Cuicuitzca, wearied with his residence in Tlascala, and pining for his former royal state, made his way back secretly to Tezcuco, hoping, it would seem, to raise a party there in his favour. But if such were his expectations, they were sadly disappointed; for no sooner had he set foot in the capital, than he was betrayed to his brother, who, by the advice of Guatemozin, put him to death, as a traitor to his country. Such was the posture of affairs in Tezcuco, when Cortés, for the second time, approached its gates; and well might he doubt, not merely the nature of his reception there, but whether he would be permitted to enter it at all, without force of arms.

These apprehensions were dispelled the following morning, when, before the troops were well under arms, an embassy was announced from the lord of Tezcuco. It consisted of several nobles, some of whom were known to the companions of Cortés. They bore a golden flag in token of amity, and a present of no great value to Cortés. They brought also a message from the cacique, imploring the general to spare his territories, inviting him to take up his quarters in his capital, and promising on his arrival to become the vassal of the Spanish sovereign.

Cortés dissembled the satisfaction with which he listened to these overtures, and sternly demanded of the envoys an account of the Spaniards who had been massacred, insisting, at the same time, on the immediate restitution of the plunder. But the Indian nobles excused themselves, by throwing the whole blame upon the Aztec emperor, by whose orders the deed had been perpetrated, and who now had possession of the treasure. They urged Cortés not to enter the city that day, but to pass the night in the suburbs, that their master might have time to prepare suitable accommodations for him. The Spanish commander, however, gave no heed to this suggestion, but pushed forward his march, and, at noon, on December 31, 1520, entered, at the head of his legions, the venerable walls of Tezcuco, "the place of rest," as not inaptly denominated.

He was struck, as when he before visited this populous city, with the solitude and silence which reigned throughout its streets. He was conducted to the palace of Nezahualpilli, which was assigned as his quarters. It was an irregular pile of low buildings, covering a wide extent of ground, like the royal residence occupied by the troops in Mexico. It was spacious enough to furnish accommodations, not only for all the Spaniards, says Cortés, but for twice their number. He gave orders on his arrival that all regard should be paid to the persons and property of the citizens; and forbade any Spaniard to leave his quarters under pain of death.

His commands were not effectual to suppress some excesses of his Indian allies, if the report of the Tezcucan chronicler be correct, who states that the Tlascalans burned down one of the royal palaces, soon after their arrival. It was the depository of the national archives; and the conflagration, however it may have occurred, may well be deplored by the antiquary, who might have found in its hieroglyphic records some clue to the migrations of the mysterious races which first settled on the highlands of Anahuac.

Alarmed at the apparent desertion of the place, as well as by the fact that none of its principal inhabitants came to welcome him, Cortés ordered some soldiers to ascend the neighbouring *teocalli* and survey the city. They soon returned with the report that the inhabitants were leaving it in great numbers, with their families and effects, some in canoes upon the lake, others on foot towards the mountains. The general now comprehended the import of the cacique's suggestion, that the Spaniards should pass the night in the suburbs—in order to secure time for evacuating the city. He feared that the chief himself might have fled. He lost no time in detaching troops to secure the principal avenues, where they were to turn back the fugitives, and arrest the cacique, if he were among the number. But it was too late. Coanaco was already far on his way across the lake to Mexico.

Cortés now determined to turn this event to his own account, by placing another ruler on the throne, who should be more subservient to his interests. He called a meeting of the few principal persons still remaining in the city, and by their advice, and ostensible election, advanced a brother of the late sovereign to the dignity, which they declared vacant. The prince, who consented to be baptised, was a willing instrument in the hands of the Spaniards. He survived but a few months, and was succeeded by another member of the royal house, named Ixtlilxochitl, who, indeed, as general of his armies, may be said to have held the reins of government in his hands during his brother's lifetime. As this person was intimately associated with the Spaniards in their subsequent operations, to the success of which he essentially contributed, it is proper to give some account of his earlier history, which, in truth, is as much enveloped in the marvellous, as that of any fabulous hero of antiquity.

He was son, by a second queen, of the great Nezahualpilli. Some alarming prodigies at his birth, and the gloomy aspect of the planets, led the astrologers, who cast his horoscope, to advise the king, his father, to take away the infant's life, since, if he lived to grow up, he was destined to unite with the enemies of his country, and overturn its institutions and religion. But the old monarch replied, says the chronicler, that the time had arrived when the sons of Quetzalcoatl were to come from the East to take possession of the land; and, if the Almighty had selected his child to co-operate with them in the work, His will be done.

As the boy advanced in years, he exhibited a marvellous precocity not merely of talent, but of mischievous activity, which afforded an alarming prognostic for the future. When about twelve years old, he formed a little corps of followers of about his own age, or somewhat older, with whom he practised the military exercises of his nation, conducting mimic fights and occasionally assaulting the peaceful burghers, and throwing the whole city as well as palace into uproar and confusion. Some of his father's ancient counsellors, connecting this conduct with the predictions at his birth, saw in it such alarming symptoms that they repeated the advice of the astrologers, to take away the prince's life, if the monarch would not see his kingdom one day given up to anarchy. This unpleasant advice was reported to the juvenile offender, who was so much exasperated by it that he put himself at the head of a party of his young desperadoes, and, entering the houses of the offending counsellors, dragged them forth, and administered to them the *garrote*—the mode in which capital punishment was inflicted in Tezcuco.

He was seized and brought before his father. When questioned as to his extraordinary conduct, he coolly replied, "that he had done no more than he had a right to do. The guilty ministers had deserved their fate, by endeavouring to alienate his father's affections from him, for no other reason than his too great fondness for the profession of arms—the most honourable profession in the state, and the one most worthy of a prince. If they had suffered death, it was no more than they had intended for him." The wise Nezahualpilli, says the chronicler, found much force in these reasons; and, as he saw nothing low and sordid in the action, but rather the ebullition of a daring spirit, which in after life might lead to great things, he contented himself with bestowing a grave admonition on the juvenile culprit. Whether this admonition had any salutary effect on his subsequent demeanour, we are not informed. It is said, however, that as he grew older he took an active part in the wars of his country, and when no more than seventeen had won for himself the insignia of a valiant and victorious captain.

On his father's death, he disputed the succession with his elder brother, Cacama. The country was menaced with a civil war, when the affair was compromised by his brother's ceding to him that portion of his territories which lay among the mountains. On the arrival of the Spaniards, the young chieftain—for he was scarcely twenty years of age —made, as we have seen, many friendly demonstrations towards them, induced, no doubt, by his hatred of Montezuma, who had supported the pretensions of Cacama. It was not, however, till his advancement to the lordship of Tezcuco that he showed the full extent of his good will. From that hour, he became the fast friend of the Christians, supporting them with his personal authority, and the whole strength of his military array and resources, which, although much shorn of their ancient splendour since the days of his father, were still considerable, and made him a most valuable ally. His important services have been gratefully commemorated by the Castilian historians; and history should certainly not defraud him of his just meed of glory—the melancholy glory of having contributed more than any other chieftain of Anahuac to rivet the chains of the white man round the necks of his countrymen.

SIEGE AND SURRENDER OF MEXICO

CHAPTER I

Arrangements at Tezcuco—Sack of Iztapalapan—Advantages of the Spaniards—Wise Policy of Cortés—Transportation of the Brigantines

1521

THE CITY OF TEZCUCO was the best position, probably, which Cortés could have chosen for the headquarters of the army. It supplied all the accommodation for lodging a numerous body of troops, and all the facilities for subsistence, incident to a large and populous town. It furnished, moreover, a multitude of artisans and labourers for the uses of the army. Its territories, bordering on the Tlascalan, afforded a ready means of intercourse with the country of his allies, while its vicinity to Mexico enabled the general, without much difficulty, to ascertain the movements in that capital. Its central situation, in short, opened facilities for communication with all parts of the valley, and made it an excellent *point d'appui* for his future operations.

The first care of Cortés was to strengthen himself in the palace assigned to him, and to place his quarters in a state of defence, which might secure them against surprise, not only from the Mexicans, but from the Tezcucans themselves. Since the election of their new ruler, a large part of the population had returned to their homes, assured of protection in person and property. But the Spanish general, notwithstanding their show of submission, very much distrusted its sincerity; for he knew that many of them were united too intimately with the Aztecs, by marriage and other social relations, not to have their sympathies engaged in their behalf. The young monarch, however, seemed wholly in his interest; and, to secure him more effectually, Cortés placed several Spaniards near his person, whose ostensible province it was to instruct him in their language and religion, but who were in reality to watch over his conduct, and prevent his correspondence with those who might be unfriendly to the Spanish interests.

375

Tezcuco stood about half a league from the lake. It would be necessary to open a communication with it, so that the brigantines, when put together in the capital, might be launched upon its waters. It was proposed, therefore, to dig a canal, reaching from the gardens of Nezahualcoyotl, as they were called from the old monarch who planned them, to the edge of the basin. A little stream or rivulet, which flowed in that direction, was to be deepened sufficiently for the purpose; and eight thousand Indian labourers were forthwith employed on this great work, under the direction of the young Ixtlilxochitl.

Meanwhile Cortés received messages from several places in the neighbourhood, intimating their desire to become the vassals of his sovereign, and to be taken under his protection. The Spanish commander required, in return, that they should deliver up every Mexican who should set foot in their territories. Some noble Aztecs, who had been sent on a mission to these towns, were consequently delivered into his hands. He availed himself of it to employ them as bearers of a message to their master, the emperor. In it he deprecated the necessity of the present hostilities. Those who had most injured him, he said, were no longer among the living. He was willing to forget the past; and invited the Mexicans, by a timely submission, to save their capital from the horrors of a siege. Cortés had no expectation of producing any immediate result by this appeal. But he thought it might lie in the minds of the Mexicans, and that, if there was a party among them disposed to treat with him, it might afford them encouragement, as showing his own willingness to co-operate with their views. At this time, however, there was no division of opinion in the capital. The whole population seemed animated by a spirit of resistance, as one man.

In a former page I have mentioned that it was the plan of Cortés, on entering the valley, to commence operations by reducing the subordinate cities before striking at the capital itself, which, like some goodly tree, whose roots had been severed one after another, would be thus left without support against the fury of the tempest. The first point of attack which he selected was the ancient city of Iztapalapan; a place containing fifty thousand inhabitants, according to his own account, and situated about six leagues distant, on the narrow tongue of land which divides the waters of the great salt lake from those of the fresh. It was the private domain of the last sovereign of Mexico; where, as the reader may remember, he entertained the white men the night before their entrance into the capital, and astonished them by the display of his princely gardens. To this monarch they owed no good will, for he had conducted the operations on the *noche triste*. He was, indeed, no more; but the people of his city entered heartily into his hatred of the strangers, and were now the most loyal vassals of the Mexican crown.

In a week after his arrival at his new quarters, Cortés, leaving the command of the garrison to Sandoval, marched against this Indian city, at the head of two hundred Spanish foot, eighteen horse, and between three and four thousand Tlascalans. Their route lay along the eastern border of the lake, gemmed with many a bright town and hamlet, or, unlike its condition at the present day, darkened with overhanging groves of cypress and cedar, and occasionally opening a broad expanse to their view, with the Queen of the Valley rising gloriously from the waters, as if proudly conscious of her supremacy over the fair cities around her. Further on, the eye ranged along the dark line of causeway connecting Mexico with the main land, and suggesting many a bitter recollection to the Spaniards.

They quickened their step, and had advanced within two leagues of their point of destination, when they were encountered by a strong Aztec force, drawn up to dispute their progress. Cortés instantly gave them battle. The barbarians showed their usual courage; but, after some hard fighting, were compelled to give way before the steady valour of the Spanish infantry, backed by the desperate fury of the Tlascalans, whom the sight of an Aztec seemed to inflame almost to madness. The enemy retreated in disorder, closely followed by the Spaniards. When they had arrived within half a league of Iztapalapan, they observed a number of canoes filled with Indians, who appeared to be labouring on the mole which hemmed in the waters of the salt lake. Swept along in the tide of pursuit, they gave little heed to it, but, following up the chase, entered pell-mell with the fugitives into the city.

The houses stood some of them on dry ground, some on piles in the water. The former were deserted by the inhabitants, most of whom had escaped in canoes across the lake, leaving, in their haste, their effects behind them. The Tlascalans poured at once into the vacant dwellings and loaded themselves with booty; while the enemy, making the best of their way through this part of the town, sought shelter in the buildings erected over the water, or among the reeds which sprang from its shallow bottom. In the houses were many of the citizens also, who still lingered with their wives and children, unable to find the means of transporting themselves from the scene of danger.

Cortés, supported by his own men, and by such of the allies as could be brought to obey his orders, attacked the enemy in this last place of their retreat. Both parties fought up to their girdles in the water. A desperate struggle ensued, as the Aztec fought with the fury of a tiger driven to bay by the huntsmen. It was all in vain. The enemy was overpowered in every quarter. The citizen shared the fate of the soldier, and a pitiless massacre succeeded, without regard to sex or age. Cortés endeavoured to stop it. But it would have been as easy to call away the starving wolf from the carcass he was devouring, as the Tlascalan who had once tasted the blood of an enemy. More than six thousand, including women and children, according to the Conqueror's own statement, perished in the conflict.

Darkness meanwhile had set in; but it was dispelled in some measure by the light of the burning houses, which the troops had set on fire in different parts of the town. Their insulated position, it is true, prevented the flames from spreading from one building to another, but the solitary masses threw a strong and lurid glare over their own neighbourhood, which gave additional horror to the scene. As resistance was now at an end, the soldiers abandoned themselves to pillage, and soon stripped the dwellings of every portable article of any value.

While engaged in this work of devastation, a murmuring sound was heard as of the hoarse rippling of waters, and a cry soon arose among the Indians that the dikes were broken! Cortés now comprehended the business of the men whom he had seen in the canoes at work on the mole which fenced in the great basin of Lake Tezcuco. It had been pierced by the desperate Indians, who thus laid the country under an inundation, by suffering the waters of the salt lake to spread themselves over the lower level, through the opening. Greatly alarmed, the general called his men together, and made all haste to evacuate the city. Had they remained three hours longer, he says, not a soul could have escaped. They came staggering under the weight of booty, wading with difficulty through the water, which was fast gaining upon them. For some distance their path was illumin'ed by the glare of the burning buildings. But, as the light faded away in distance, they wandered with uncertain steps, sometimes up to their knees, at others up to their waists, in the water, through which they floundered on with the greatest difficulty. As they reached the opening in the dike, the stream became deeper, and flowed out with such a current that the men were unable to maintain their footing. The Spaniards, breasting the flood, forced their way through; but many of the Indians, unable to swim, were borne down by the waters. All the plunder was lost. The powder was spoiled; the arms and clothes of the soldiers were saturated with the brine, and the cold night wind, as it blew over them, benumbed their weary limbs till they could scarcely drag them along. At dawn they beheld the lake swarming with canoes, full of Indians, who had anticipated their disaster, and who now saluted them with showers of stones, arrows, and other deadly missiles. Bodies of light troops, hovering in the distance, disquieted the flanks of the army in like manner. The Spaniards had no desire to close with the enemy. They only wished to regain their comfortable quarters in Tezcuco, where they arrived on the same day, more disconsolate and fatigued than after many a long march and hard-fought battle.

The close of the expedition, so different from its brilliant commencement, greatly disappointed Cortés. His numerical loss had, indeed, not been great; but this affair convinced him how much he had to apprehend from the resolution of a people, who, with a spirit worthy of the ancient Hollanders, were prepared to bury their country under water rather than to submit. Still, the enemy had little cause for congratulation, since, independently of the number of slain, they had seen one of their most flourishing cities sacked, and in part, at least, laid in ruins—one of those, too, which in its public works displayed the nearest approach to civilisation. Such are the triumphs of war!

The expedition of Cortés, notwithstanding the disasters which chequered it, was favourable to the Spanish cause. The fate of Iztapalapan struck a terror throughout the valley. The consequences were soon apparent in the deputations sent by the different places eager to offer their submission. Its influence was visible, indeed, beyond the mountains. Among others, the people of Otumba, the town near which the Spaniards had gained their famous victory, sent to tender their allegiance, and to request the protection of the powerful strangers. They excused themselves, as usual, for the part they had taken in the late hostilities, by throwing the blame on the Aztecs.

But the place of most importance which thus claimed their protection was Chalco, situated on the eastern extremity of the lake of that name. It was an ancient city, peopled by a kindred tribe of the Aztecs, and once their formidable rival. The Mexican emperor, distrusting their loyalty, had placed a garrison within their walls to hold them in check. The rulers of the city now sent a message secretly to Cortés, proposing to put themselves under his protection, if he would enable them to expel the garrison.

The Spanish commander did not hesitate; but instantly detached a considerable force under Sandoval for this object. On the march his rear-guard, composed of Tlascalans, was roughly handled by some light troops of the Mexicans. But he took his revenge in a pitched battle, which took place with the main body of the enemy at no great distance from Chalco. They were drawn up on a level ground, covered with green crops of maize and maguey. The field is traversed by the road which at this day leads from the last-mentioned city of Tezcuco. Sandoval, charging the enemy at the head of his cavalry, threw them into disorder. But they quickly rallied, formed again, and renewed the battle with greater spirit than ever. In a second attempt he was more fortunate; and, breaking through their lines by a desperate onset, the brave cavalier succeeded, after a warm but ineffectual struggle on their part, in completely routing and driving them from the field. The conquering army continued its march to Chalco, which the Mexican garrison had already evacuated, and was received in triumph by the assembled citizens, who seemed eager to testify their gratitude for their deliverance from the Aztec yoke. After taking such measures as he could for the permanent security of the place, Sandoval returned to Tezcuco, accompanied by the two young lords of the city, sons of the late cacique.

They were courteously received by Cortés; and they informed him that their father had died full of years, a short time before. With his last breath he had expressed his regret that he should not have lived to see Malintzin. He believed that the white men were the beings predicted by the oracles, as one day to come from the East and take possession of the land; and he enjoined it on his children, should the strangers return to the valley, to render them their homage and allegiance. The young caciques expressed their readiness to do so; but, as this must bring on them the vengeance of the Aztecs, they implored the general to furnish a sufficient force for their protection.

Cortés received a similar application from various other towns, which were disposed, could they do so with safety, to throw off the Mexican yoke. But he was in no situation to comply with their request. He now felt, more sensibly than ever, the incompetency of his means to his undertaking. "I assure your Majesty," he writes in his letter to the emperor, "the greatest uneasiness which I feel after all my labours and fatigues is from my inability to succour and support our Indian friends, your Majesty's loyal vassals." Far from having a force competent to this, he had scarcely enough for his own protection. His vigilant enemy had an eye on all his movements, and, should he cripple his strength by sending away too many detachments, or by employing them at too great a distance, would be prompt to take advantage of it. His only expeditions, hitherto, had been in the neighbourhood, where the troops, after striking some sudden and decisive blow, might speedily regain their quarters. The utmost watchfulness was maintained there, and the Spaniards lived in as constant preparation for an assault, as if their camp was pitched under the walls of Mexico.

On two occasions the general had sallied forth and engaged the enemy in the environs of Tezcuco. At one time a thousand canoes, filled with Aztecs, crossed the lake to gather in a large crop of Indian corn, nearly ripe, on its borders. Cortés thought it important to secure this for himself. He accordingly marched out and gave battle to the enemy, drove them from the field, and swept away the rich harvest to the granaries of Tezcuco. Another time a strong body of Mexicans had established themselves in some neighbouring towns friendly to their interests. Cortés, again sallying, dislodged them from their quarters, beat them in several skirmishes, and reduced the places to obedience. But these enterprises demanded all his resources, and left him nothing to spare for his allies. In this exigency his fruitful genius suggested an expedient for supplying the deficiency of his means.

Some of the friendly cities without the valley, observing the numerous beacon-fires on the mountains, inferred that the Mexicans were mustering in great strength, and that the Spaniards must be hard pressed in their new quarters. They sent messengers to Tezcuco, expressing their apprehension, and offering reinforcements, which the general, when he set out on his march, had declined. He returned many thanks for the proffered aid; but, while he declined it for himself, as unnecessary, he indicated in what manner their services might be effectual for the defence of Chalco and the other places which had invoked his protection. But his Indian allies were in deadly feud with these places, whose inhabitants had too often fought under the Aztec banner not to have been engaged in repeated wars with the people beyond the mountains.

Cortés set himself earnestly to reconcile these differences. He told the hostile parties that they should be willing to forget their mutual wrongs, since they had entered into new relations. They were now vassals of the same sovereign, engaged in a common enterprise against a formidable foe who had so long trodden them in the dust. Singly they could do little, but united they might protect each other's weakness, and hold their enemy at bay till the Spaniards could come to their assistance. These arguments finally prevailed; and the politic general had the satisfaction to see the high-spirited and hostile tribes forego their long-cherished rivalry, and, resigning the pleasures of revenge, so dear to the barbarian, embrace one another as friends and champions in a common cause. To this wise policy the Spanish commander owed quite as much of his subsequent successes as to his arms.

Thus the foundations of the Mexican empire were hourly loosening, as the great vassals around the capital, on whom it most relied, fell off one after another from their allegiance. The Aztecs, properly so called, formed but a small part of the population of the valley. This was principally composed of cognate tribes, members of the same great family of the Nahuatlacs, who had come upon the plateau at nearly the same time. They were mutual rivals, and were reduced one after another by the more warlike Mexicans, who held them in subjection, often by open force, always by fear. Fear was the great principle of cohesion which bound together the discordant members of the monarchy; and this was now fast dissolving before the influence of a power more mighty than that of the Aztec. This, it is true, was not the first time that the conquered races had attempted to recover their independence; but all such attempts had failed for want of concert. It was reserved for the commanding genius of Cortés to extinguish their old hereditary feuds, and, combining their scattered energies, to animate them with a common principle of action.

Encouraged by this state of things, the Spanish general thought it a favourable moment to press his negotiations with the capital. He availed himself of the presence of some noble Mexicans, taken in the late action with Sandoval, to send another message to their master. It was in substance a repetition of the first, with a renewed assurance that, if the city would return to its allegiance to the Spanish crown, the authority of Guatemozin should be confirmed, and the persons and property of his subjects be respected. To this communication no reply was made. The young Indian emperor had a spirit as dauntless as that of Cortés himself. On his head descended the full effects of that vicious system of government bequeathed to him by his ancestors. But, as he saw his empire crumbling beneath him, he sought to uphold it by his own energy and resources. He anticipated the defection of some vassals by establishing garrisons within their walls. Others he conciliated by exempting them from tributes, or greatly lightening their burdens, or by advancing them to posts of honour and authority in the state. He showed, at the same time, his implacable animosity towards the Christians, by commanding that every one taken within his dominions should be straightway sent to the capital, where he was sacrificed with all the barbarous ceremonies prescribed by the Aztec ritual.

While these occurrences were passing, Cortés received the welcome intelligence that the brigantines were completed and waiting to be transported to Tezcuco. He detached a body for the service, consisting of two hundred Spanish foot and fifteen horse, which he placed under the command of Sandoval. This cavalier had been rising daily in the estimation both of the general and of the army. Though one of the youngest officers in the service, he possessed a cool head and a ripe judgment, which fitted him for the most delicate and difficult undertakings. There were others, indeed, as Alvarado and Olid, for example, whose intrepidity made them equally competent to achieve a brilliant coup-de-main. But the courage of Alvarado was too often carried to temerity, or perverted by passion; while Olid, dark and doubtful in his character, was not entirely to be trusted. Sandoval was a native of Medellin, the birthplace of Cortés himself. He was warmly attached to his commander, and had on all occasions proved himself worthy of his confidence. He was a man of few words, showing his worth rather by what he did, than what he said. His honest, soldier-like deportment made him a favourite with the troops, and had its influence even on his enemies. He unfortunately died in the flower of his age. But he discovered talents and military skill, which, had he lived to later life, would undoubtedly have placed his name on the roll with those of the greatest captains of his nation.

Sandoval's route was to lead him by Zoltepec, a small city where the massacre of the forty-five Spaniards, already noticed, had been perpetrated. The cavalier received orders to find out the guilty parties, if possible, and to punish them for their share in the transaction.

When the Spaniards arrived at the spot, they found that the inhabitants, who had previous notice of their approach, had all fled. In the deserted temples they discovered abundant traces of the fate of their countrymen; for, besides their arms and clothing, and the hides of their horses, the heads of several soldiers, prepared in such a way that they could be well preserved, were found suspended as trophies of the victory. In a neighbouring building, traced with charcoal on the walls, they found the following inscription in Castilian: "In this place the unfortunate Juan Juste, with many others of his company, was imprisoned." This hidalgo was one of the followers of Narvaez, and had come with him into the country in quest of gold, but had found, instead, an obscure and inglorious death. The eyes of the soldiers were suffused with tears, as they gazed on the gloomy record, and their bosoms swelled with indignation, as they thought of the horrible fate of the captives. Fortunately the inhabitants were not then before them. Some few, who subsequently fell into their hands, were branded as slaves. But the greater part of the population, who threw themselves, in the most abject manner, on the mercy of the Conquerors, imputing the blame of the affair to the Aztecs, the Spanish commander spared, from pity, or contempt.

He now resumed his march on Tlascala; but scarcely had he crossed the borders of the republic, when he descried the flaunting banners of the convoy which transported the brigantines, as it was threading its way through the defiles of the mountains. Great was his satisfaction at the spectacle, for he had feared a detention of some days at Tlascala, before the preparations for the march could be completed.

There were thirteen vessels in all, of different sizes. They had been constructed under the direction of the experienced shipbuilder, Martin Lopez, aided by three or four Spanish carpenters and the friendly natives, some of whom showed no mean degree of imitative skill. The brigantines, when completed, had been fairly tried on the waters of the Zahuapan. They were then taken to pieces, and, as Lopez was impatient of delay, the several parts, the timbers, anchors, ironwork, sails, and cordage were placed on the shoulders of the *tamanes,* and, under a numerous military escort, were thus far advanced on the way to Tezcuco. Sandoval dismissed a part of the Indian convoy as superfluous.

Twenty thousand warriors he retained, dividing them into two equal bodies for the protection of the *tamanes* in the centre. His own little body of Spaniards he distributed in like manner. The Tlascalans in the van marched under the command of a chief who gloried in the name of Chichemecatl. For some reason Sandoval afterwards changed the order of march, and placed this division in the rear—an arrangement which gave great umbrage to the doughty warrior that led it, who asserted his right to the front, the place which he and his ancestors had always occupied, as the post of danger. He was somewhat appeased by Sandoval's assurance that it was for that very reason he had been transferred to the rear, the quarter most likely to be assailed by the enemy. But even then he was greatly dissatisfied, on finding that the Spanish commander was to march by his side, grudging, it would seem, that any other should share the laurel with himself.

Slowly and painfully, encumbered with their heavy burden, the troops worked their way over steep eminences, and rough mountain-passes, presenting, one might suppose in their long line of march, many a vulnerable point to an enemy. But, although small parties of warriors were seen hovering at times on their flanks and rear, they kept at a respectful distance, not caring to encounter so formidable a foe. On the fourth day the warlike caravan arrived in safety before Tezcuco.

Their approach was beheld with joy by Cortés and the soldiers, who hailed it as a signal of a speedy termination of the war. The general, attended by his officers, all dressed in their richest attire, came out to welcome the convoy. It extended over a space of two leagues, and so slow was its progress that six hours elapsed before the closing files had entered the city. The Tlascalan chiefs displayed all their wonted bravery of apparel, and the whole array, composed of the flower of their warriors, made a brilliant appearance. They marched by the sound of atabal and cornet, and, as they traversed the streets of the capital amidst the acclamations of the soldiery, they made the city ring with the shouts of "Castile and Tlascala, long live our sovereign, the emperor."

"It was a marvellous thing," exclaims the Conqueror, in his letters, "that few have seen, or even heard of—this transportation of thirteen vessels of war on the shoulders of men, for nearly twenty leagues across the mountains!" It was, indeed, a stupendous achievement, and not easily matched in ancient or modern story; one which only a genius like that of Cortés could have devised, or a daring spirit like his have so successfully executed. Little did he foresee—when he ordered the destruction of the fleet which first brought him to the country, and with his usual forecast commanded the preservation of the ironwork and rigging—little did he foresee the important uses for which they were to be reserved. So important, that on their preservation may be said to have depended the successful issue of his great enterprise.

He greeted his Indian allies with the greatest cordiality, testifying his sense of their services by those honours and attentions which he knew would be most grateful to their ambitious spirits. "We come," exclaimed the hardy warriors, "to fight under your banner; to avenge our common quarrel, or to fall by your side"; and, with their usual impatience, they urged him to lead them at once against the enemy. "Wait," replied the general bluntly, "till you are rested, and you shall have your hands full."

CHAPTER II

Cortés Reconnoitres the Capital—Occupies Tacuba—Skirmishes with the Enemy—Expedition of Sandoval—Arrival of Reinforcements

1521

IN THE COURSE OF THREE OR FOUR DAYS, the Spanish general furnished the Tlascalans with the opportunity so much coveted, and allowed their boiling spirits to effervesce in active operations. He had, for some time, meditated an expedition to reconnoitre the capital and its environs, and to chastise, on the way, certain places which had sent him insulting messages of defiance, and which were particularly active in their hostilities. He disclosed his design to a few only of his principal officers, from his distrust of the Tezcucans, whom he suspected to be in correspondence with the enemy.

Early in the spring, he left Tezcuco, at the head of three hundred and fifty Spaniards and the whole strength of his allies. He took with him Alvarado and Olid, and entrusted the charge of the garrison to Sandoval. Cortés had had practical acquaintance with the incompetence of the first of these cavaliers for so delicate a post, during his short, but disastrous, rule in Mexico.

But all his precautions had not availed to shroud his designs from the vigilant foe, whose eye was on all his movements; who seemed even to divine his thoughts, and to be prepared to thwart their execution. He had advanced but a few leagues, when he was met by a considerable body of Mexicans, drawn up to dispute his progress. A sharp skirmish took place, in which the enemy were driven from the ground, and the way was left open to the Christians. They held a circuitous route to the north, and their first point of attack was the insular town of Xaltocan, situated on the northern extremity of the lake of that name, now called San Christobal. The town was entirely surrounded by water, and communicated with the main land by means of causeways, in the same manner as the Mexican capital. Cortés, riding at the head of his cavalry, advanced along the dike, till he was brought to a stand by finding a wide opening in it, through which the waters poured so as to be altogether impracticable, not only for horse, but for infantry. The lake was covered with canoes, filled with Aztec warriors, who, anticipating the movement of the Spaniards, had come to the aid of the city. They now began a furious discharge of stones and arrows on the assailants, while they were themselves tolerably well protected from the musketry of their enemy by the light bulwarks, with which, for that purpose, they had fortified their canoes.

The severe volleys of the Mexicans did some injury to the Spaniards and their allies, and began to throw them into disorder, crowded as they were on the narrow causeway, without the means of advancing, when Cortés ordered a retreat. This was followed by renewed tempests of missiles, accompanied by taunts and fierce yells of defiance. The battle-cry of the Aztec, like the war-whoop of the North American Indian, was an appalling note, according to the Conqueror's own acknowledgment, in the ears of the Spaniards. At this juncture, the general fortunately obtained information from a deserter, one of the Mexican allies, of a ford, by which the army might traverse the shallow lake, and penetrate the place. He instantly detached the greater part of the infantry on the service, posting himself with the remainder, and with the horse, at the entrance of the passage, to cover the attack and prevent any interruption in the rear.

The soldiers, under the direction of the Indian guide, forded the lake without much difficulty, though in some places the water came above their girdles. During the passage they were annoyed by the enemy's missiles; but when they had gained the dry level, they took ample revenge, and speedily put all who resisted to the sword. The greater part, together with the townsmen, made their escape in the boats. The place was now abandoned to pillage. The troops found in it many women, who had been left to their fate; and these, together with a considerable quantity of cotton stuffs, gold, and articles of food, fell into the hands of the victors, who, setting fire to the deserted city, returned in triumph to their comrades.

Continuing his circuitous route, Cortés presented himself successively before three other places, each of which had been deserted by the inhabitants in anticipation of his arrival. The principal of these, Azcapozalco, had once been the capital of an independent state. It was now the great slave-market of the Aztecs, where their unfortunate captives were brought, and disposed of at public sale. It was also the quarter occupied by the jewellers; and the place whence the Spaniards obtained the goldsmiths who melted down the rich treasures received from Montezuma. But they found there only a small supply of the precious metals, or, indeed, of anything else of value, as the people had been careful to remove their effects. They spared the buildings, however, in consideration of their having met with no resistance.

During the nights, the troops bivouacked in the open fields, maintaining the strictest watch, for the country was all in arms, and beacons were flaming on every hill-top, while dark masses of the enemy were occasionally descried in the distance. The Spaniards were now traversing the most opulent region of Anahuac. Cities and villages were scattered over hill and valley, with cultivated environs blooming around them, all giving token of a dense and industrious population. In the centre of this brilliant circumference stood the Indian metropolis, with its gorgeous tiara of pyramids and temples, attracting the eye of the soldier from every other object, as he wound round the borders of the lake. Every inch of ground which the army trod was familiar to them—familiar as the scenes of childhood, though with very different associations, for it had been written on their memories in characters of blood. On the right rose the Hill of Montezuma, crowned by the *teocalli,* under the roof of which the shattered relics of the army had been gathered on the day following the flight from the capital. In front lay the city of Tacuba, through whose inhospitable streets they had hurried in fear and consternation; and away to the east of it stretched the melancholy causeway.

It was the general's purpose to march at once on Tacuba, and establish his quarters in that ancient capital for the present. He found a strong force encamped under its walls, prepared to dispute his entrance. Without waiting for their advance, he rode at full gallop against them with his little body of horse. The arquebuses and crossbows opened a lively volley on their extended wings, and the infantry, armed with their swords and copper-headed lances, and supported by the Indian battalions, followed up the attack of the horse with an alacrity which soon put the enemy to flight. The Spaniards usually opened the combat with a charge of cavalry. But, had the science of the Aztecs been equal to their courage, they might with their long spears have turned the scale of battle, sometimes at least, in their own favour; for it was with the same formidable weapon that the Swiss mountaineers, but a few years before this period of our history, broke and completely foiled the famous *ordonnance* of Charles the Bold, the best appointed cavalry of their day. But the barbarians were ignorant of the value of this weapon when opposed to cavalry. And, indeed, the appalling apparition of the war-horse and his rider still held a mysterious power over their imagination, which contributed, perhaps, quite as much as the effective force of the cavalry itself, to their discomfiture. Cortés led his troops without further opposition into the suburbs of Tacuba, the ancient Tlacopan, where he established himself for the night.

On the following morning, he found the indefatigable Aztecs again under arms, and, on the open ground before the city, prepared to give him battle. He marched out against them, and, after an action hotly contested, though of no long duration, again routed them. They fled towards the town, but were driven through the streets at the point of the lance, and were compelled, together with the inhabitants, to evacuate the place. The city was then delivered over to pillage; and the Indian allies, not content with plundering the houses of everything portable within them, set them on fire, and in a short time a quarter of the town—the poorer dwellings, probably, built of light, combustible materials—was in flames. Cortés and his troops did all in their power to stop the conflagration, but the Tlascalans were a fierce race, not easily guided at any time and, when their passions were once kindled, it was impossible, even for the general himself, to control them. They were a terrible auxiliary, and, from their insubordination, as terrible sometimes to friend as to foe.

Cortés proposed to remain in his present quarters for some days, during which time he established his own residence in the ancient palace of the lords of Tlacopan. It was a long range of low buildings, like most of the royal residences in the country, and offered good accommodations for the Spanish forces. During his halt here, there was not a day on which the army was not engaged in one or more rencontres with the enemy. They terminated almost uniformly in favour of the Spaniards, though with more or less injury to them and to their allies. One encounter, indeed, had nearly been attended with more fatal consequences.

The Spanish general, in the heat of pursuit, had allowed himself to be decoyed upon the great causeway—the same which had once been so fatal to his army. He followed the flying foe, until he had gained the further side of the nearest bridge, which had been repaired since the disastrous action of the *noche triste*. When thus far advanced the Aztecs, with the rapidity of lightning, turned on him, and he beheld a large reinforcement in their rear, all fresh on the field, prepared to support their countrymen. At the same time, swarms of boats, unobserved in the eagerness of the chase, seemed to start up as if by magic, covering the waters around. The Spaniards were now exposed to a perfect hailstorm of missiles, both from the causeway and the lake; but they stood unmoved amidst the tempest, when Cortés, too late perceiving his error, gave orders for the retreat. Slowly, and with admirable coolness, his men receded, step by step, offering a resolute front to the enemy. The Mexicans came on with their usual vociferation, making the shores echo to their war-cries, and striking at the Spaniards with their long pikes, and with poles, to which the swords taken from the Christians had been fastened. A cavalier, named Volante, bearing the standard of Cortés, was felled by one of their weapons, and, tumbling into the lake, was picked up by the Mexican boats. He was a man of a muscular frame, and, as the enemy were dragging him off, he succeeded in extricating himself from their grasp, and clenching his colours in his hand, with a desperate effort sprang back upon the causeway. At length, after some hard fighting, in which many of the Spaniards were wounded, and many of their allies slain, the troops regained the land, where Cortés, with a full heart, returned thanks to Heaven for what he might well regard as a providential deliverance. It was a salutary lesson; though he should scarcely have needed one, so soon after the affair of Iztapalapan, to warn him of the wily tactics of his enemy.

It had been one of Cortés' principal objects in this expedition to obtain an interview, if possible, with the Aztec emperor, or with some of the great lords at his court, and to try if some means for an accommodation could not be found, by which he might avoid the appeal to arms. An occasion for such a parley presented itself, when his forces were one day confronted with those of the enemy, with a broken bridge interposed between them. Cortés, riding in advance of his people, intimated by signs his peaceful intent, and that he wished to confer with the Aztecs. They respected the signal, and, with the aid of his interpreter, he requested that, if there were any great chief among them, he would come forward and hold a parley with him. The Mexicans replied, in derision, they were all chiefs, and bade him speak openly whatever he had to tell them. As the general returned no answer, they asked why he did not make another visit to the capital, and tauntingly added, "Perhaps Malintzin does not expect to find there another Montezuma, as obedient to his command as the former." Some of them complimented the Tlascalans with the epithet of *women,* who, they said, would never have ventured so near the capital, but for the protection of the white men.

The animosity of the two nations was not confined to these harmless, though bitter jests, but showed itself in regular cartels of defiance, which daily passed between the principal chieftains. These were followed by combats, in which one or more champions fought on a side, to vindicate the honour of their respective countries. A fair field of fight was given to the warriors, who conducted those combats, *à l'outrance,* with the punctilio of a European tourney; displaying a valour worthy of the two boldest of the races of Anahuac, and a skill in the management of their weapons, which drew forth the admiration of the Spaniards.

Cortés had now been six days in Tacuba. There was nothing further to detain him, as he had accomplished the chief objects of his expedition. He had humbled several of the places which had been most active in their hostility; and he had revived the credit of the Castilian arms, which had been much tarnished by their former reverses in this quarter of the valley. He had also made himself acquainted with the condition of the capital, which he found in a better posture of defence than he had imagined. All the ravages of the preceding year seemed to be repaired, and there was no evidence, even to his experienced eye, that the wasting hand of war had so lately swept over the land. The Aztec troops, which swarmed through the valley, seemed to be well appointed, and showed an invincible spirit, as if prepared to resist to the last. It is true, they had been beaten in every encounter. In the open field they were no match for the Spaniards, whose cavalry they could never comprehend, and whose firearms easily penetrated the cotton mail, which formed the stoutest defence of the Indian warrior. But, entangled in the long streets and narrow lanes of the metropolis, where every house was a citadel, the Spaniards, as experience had shown, would lose much of their superiority. With the Mexican emperor, confident in the strength of his preparations, the general saw there was no probability of effecting an accommodation. He saw, too, the necessity of the most careful preparations on his own part—indeed, that he must strain his resources to the utmost, before he could safely venture to rouse the lion in his lair.

The Spaniards returned by the same route by which they had come. Their retreat was interpreted into a flight by the natives, who hung on the rear of the army, uttering vainglorious vaunts, and saluting the troops with showers of arrows, which did some mischief. Cortés resorted to one of their own stratagems to rid himself of this annoyance. He divided his cavalry into two or three small parties, and concealed them among some thick shrubbery, which fringed both sides of the road. The rest of the army continued its march. The Mexicans followed, unsuspicious of the ambuscade, when the horse, suddenly darting from their place of concealment, threw the enemy's flanks into confusion, and the retreating columns of infantry, facing about suddenly, commenced a brisk attack, which completed their consternation. It was a broad and level plain, over which the panic-struck Mexicans made the best of their way, without attempting resistance; while the cavalry, riding them down and piercing the fugitives with their lances, followed up the chase for several miles, in what Cortés calls a truly beautiful style. The army experienced no further annoyance from the enemy.

On their arrival at Tezcuco, they were greeted with joy by their comrades, who had received no tidings of them during the fortnight which had elapsed since their departure. The Tlascalans, immediately on their return, requested the general's permission to carry back to their own country the valuable booty which they had gathered in their foray— a request which, however unpalatable, he could not refuse.

The troops had not been in quarters more than two or three days, when an embassy arrived from Chalco, again soliciting the protection of the Spaniards against the Mexicans, who menaced them from several points in their neighbourhood. But the soldiers were so much exhausted by unintermitted vigils, forced marches, battles, and wounds, that Cortés wished to give them a breathing-time to recruit, before engaging in a new expedition. He answered the application of the Chalcans, by sending his missives to the allied cities, calling on them to march to the assistance of their confederate. It is not to be supposed that they could comprehend the import of his despatches. But the paper, with its mysterious characters, served for a warrant to the officer who bore it, as the interpreter of the general's commands.

But, although these were implicitly obeyed, the Chalcans felt the danger so pressing, that they soon repeated their petition for the Spaniards to come in person to their relief. Cortés no longer hesitated; for he was well aware of the importance of Chalco, not merely on its own account, but from its position, which commanded one of the great avenues to Tlascala, and to Vera Cruz, the intercourse with which should run no risk of interruption. Without further loss of time, therefore, he detached a body of three hundred Spanish foot and twenty horse, under the command of Sandoval, for the protection of the city.

That active officer soon presented himself before Chalco, and, strengthened by the reinforcement of its own troops and those of the confederate towns, directed his first operations against Huaxtepec, a place of some importance, lying two leagues or more to the south among the mountains. It was held by a strong Mexican force, watching their opportunity to make a descent upon Chalco. The Spaniards found the enemy drawn up at a distance from the town, prepared to receive them. The ground was broken and tangled with bushes, unfavourable to the cavalry, which in consequence soon fell into disorder; and Sandoval, finding himself embarrassed by their movements, ordered them, after sustaining some loss, from the field. In their place he brought up his musketeers and crossbow-men, who poured a rapid fire into the thick columns of the Indians. The rest of the infantry, with sword and pike, charged the flanks of the enemy, who, bewildered by the shock, after sustaining considerable slaughter, fell back in an irregular manner, leaving the field of battle to the Spaniards.

The victors proposed to bivouac there for the night. But, while engaged in preparations for their evening meal, they were aroused by the cry of "To arms, to arms! the enemy is upon us!" In an instant the trooper was in his saddle, the soldier grasped his musket or his good toledo, and the action was renewed with greater fury than before. The Mexicans had received a reinforcement from the city. But their second attempt was not more fortunate than their first; and the victorious Spaniards, driving their antagonists before them, entered and took possession of the town itself, which had already been evacuated by the inhabitants.

Sandoval took up his quarters in the dwelling of the lord of the place, surrounded by gardens, which rivalled those of Iztapalapan in magnificence, and surpassed them in extent. They are said to have been two leagues in circumference, having pleasure-houses, and numerous tanks stocked with various kinds of fish; and they were embellished with trees, shrubs, and plants, native and exotic, some selected for their beauty and fragrance, others for their medicinal properties. They were scientifically arranged; and the whole establishment displayed a degree of horticultural taste and knowledge, of which it would not have been easy to find a counterpart, at that day, in the more civilised communities of Europe. Such is the testimony not only of the rude Conquerors, but of men of science, who visited these beautiful repositories in the day of their glory.

After halting two days to refresh his forces in this agreeable spot, Sandoval marched on Jacapichtla, about six miles to the eastward. It was a town, or rather fortress, perched on a rocky eminence, almost inaccessible from its steepness. It was garrisoned by a Mexican force, who rolled down on the assailants, as they attempted to scale the heights, huge fragments of rock, which, thundering over the sides of the precipice, carried ruin and desolation in their path. The Indian confederates fell back in dismay from the attempt. But Sandoval, indignant that any achievement should be too difficult for a Spaniard, commanded his cavaliers to dismount, and, declaring that he "would carry the place or die in the attempt," led on his men with the cheering cry of "St. Iago." With renewed courage, they now followed their gallant leader up the ascent, under a storm of lighter missiles, mingled with huge masses of stone, which, breaking into splinters, overturned the assailants, and made fearful havoc in their ranks. Sandoval, who had been wounded on the preceding day, received a severe contusion on the head, while more than one of his brave comrades were struck down by his side. Still they clambered up, sustaining themselves by the bushes or projecting pieces of rock, and seemed to force themselves onward as much by the energy of their wills, as by the strength of their bodies.

After incredible toil, they stood on the summit, face to face with the astonished garrison. For a moment they paused to recover breath, then sprang furiously on their foes. The struggle was short but desperate. Most of the Aztecs were put to the sword. Some were thrown headlong over the battlements, and others, letting themselves down the precipice, were killed on the borders of a little stream that wound round its base, the waters of which were so polluted with blood that the victors were unable to slake their thirst with them for a full hour!

Sandoval, having now accomplished the object of his expedition, by reducing the strongholds which had so long held the Chalcans in awe, returned in triumph to Tezcuco. Meanwhile, the Aztec emperor, whose vigilant eye had been attentive to all that had passed, thought that the absence of so many of its warriors afforded a favourable opportunity for recovering Chalco. He sent a fleet of boats for this purpose across the lake, with a numerous force under the command of some of his most valiant chiefs. Fortunately the absent Chalcans reached their city before the arrival of the enemy; but, though supported by their Indian allies, they were so much alarmed by the magnitude of the hostile array, that they sent again to the Spaniards invoking their aid.

The messengers arrived at the same time with Sandoval and his army. Cortés was much puzzled by the contradictory accounts. He suspected some negligence in his lieutenant, and, displeased with his precipitate return in this unsettled state of the affair, ordered him back at once, with such of his forces as were in fighting condition. Sandoval felt deeply injured by this proceeding, but he made no attempt at exculpation, and, obeying his commander in silence, put himself at the head of his troops, and made a rapid countermarch on the Indian city.

Before he reached it, a battle had been fought between the Mexicans and the confederates, in which the latter, who had acquired unwonted confidence from their recent successes, were victorious. A number of Aztec nobles fell into their hands in the engagement, whom they delivered to Sandoval to be carried off as prisoners to Tezcuco. On his arrival there, the cavalier, wounded by the unworthy treatment he had received, retired to his own quarters without presenting himself before his chief.

During his absence, the inquiries of Cortés had satisfied him of his own precipitate conduct, and of the great injustice he had done his lieutenant. There was no man in the army on whose services he set so high a value, as the responsible situations in which he had placed him plainly showed; and there was none for whom he seems to have entertained a greater personal regard. On Sandoval's return, therefore, Cortés instantly sent to request his attendance; when, with a soldier's frankness, he made such an explanation as soothed the irritated spirit of the cavalier—a matter of no great difficulty, as the latter had too generous a nature, and too earnest a devotion to his commander and the cause in which they were embarked, to harbour a petty feeling of resentment in his bosom.

During the occurrence of these events, the work was going forward actively on the canal, and the brigantines were within a fortnight of their completion. The greatest vigilance was required, in the meantime, to prevent their destruction by the enemy, who had already made three ineffectual attempts to burn them on the stocks. The precautions which Cortés thought it necessary to take against the Tezcucans themselves, added not a little to his embarrassment.

At this time he received embassies from different Indian states, some of them on the remote shores of the Mexican Gulf, tendering their allegiance and soliciting his protection. For this he was partly indebted to the good offices of Ixtlilxochitl, who, in consequence of his brother's death, was now advanced to the sovereignty of Tezcuco. This important position greatly increased his consideration and authority through the country, of which he freely availed himself to bring the natives under the dominion of the Spaniards.

The general received also at this time the welcome intelligence of the arrival of three vessels at Villa Rica, with two hundred men on board, well provided with arms and ammunition, and with seventy or eighty horses. It was a most seasonable reinforcement. From what quarter it came is uncertain; most probably from Hispaniola. Cortés, it may be remembered, had sent for supplies to that place; and the authorities of the island, who had general jurisdiction over the affairs of the colonies, had shown themselves, on more than one occasion, well inclined towards him, probably considering him, under all circumstances, as better fitted than any other man to achieve the conquest of the country.

The new recruits soon found their way to Tezcuco; as the communications with the port were now open and unobstructed. Among them were several cavaliers of consideration, one of whom, Julian de Alderete, the royal treasurer, came over to superintend the interests of the crown.

There was also in the number a Dominican friar, who brought a quantity of pontifical bulls, offering indulgences to those engaged in war against the infidel. The soldiers were not slow to fortify themselves with the good graces of the Church; and the worthy father, after driving a prosperous traffic with his spiritual wares, had the satisfaction to return home, at the end of a few months, well freighted, in exchange, with the more substantial treasures of the Indies.

CHAPTER III

Second Reconnoitring Expedition—Engagements on the Sierra —Capture of Cuernavaca—Battles at Xochimilco—Narrow Escape of Cortés—He Enters Tacuba

1521

NOTWITHSTANDING THE RELIEF which had been afforded to the people of Chalco, it was so ineffectual that envoys from that city again arrived at Tezcuco, bearing a hieroglyphical chart, on which were depicted several strong places in their neighbourhood, garrisoned by the Aztecs, from which they expected annoyance. Cortés determined this time to take the affair into his own hands, and to scour the country so effectually as to place Chalco, if possible, in a state of security. He did not confine himself to this object, but proposed, before his return, to pass quite round the great lakes, and reconnoitre the country to the south of them, in the same manner as he had before done to the west. In the course of his march, he would direct his arms against some of the strong places from which the Mexicans might expect support in the siege. Two or three weeks must elapse before the completion of the brigantines; and, if no other good resulted from the expedition, it would give active occupation to his troops, whose turbulent spirits might fester into discontent in the monotonous existence of a camp.

He selected for the expedition thirty horse and three hundred Spanish infantry, with a considerable body of Tlascalan and Tezcucan warriors. The remaining garrison he left in charge of the trusty Sandoval, who, with the friendly lord of the capital, would watch over the construction of the brigantines, and protect them from the assaults of the Aztecs.

On April 5 he began his march, and on the following day arrived at Chalco, where he was met by a number of the confederate chiefs. With the aid of his faithful interpreters, Doña Marina and Aguilar, he explained to them the objects of his present expedition; stated his purpose soon to enforce the blockade of Mexico, and required their co-operation with the whole strength of their levies. To this they readily assented; and he soon received a sufficient proof of their friendly disposition in the forces which joined him on the march, amounting, according to one of the army, to more than had ever before followed his banner.

Taking a southerly direction, the troops, after leaving Chalco, struck into the recesses of the wild sierra, which, with its bristling peaks, serves as a formidable palisade to fence round the beautiful valley; while, within its rugged arms, it shuts up many a green and fruitful pasture of its own. As the Spaniards passed through its deep gorges, they occasionally wound round the base of some huge cliff or rocky eminence, on which the inhabitants had built their towns in the same manner as was done by the people of Europe in the feudal ages; a position which, however favourable to the picturesque, intimates a sense of insecurity as the cause of it, which may reconcile us to the absence of this striking appendage of the landscape in our own more fortunate country.

The occupants of these airy pinnacles took advantage of their situation to shower down stones and arrows on the troops, as they defiled through the narrow passes of the sierra. Though greatly annoyed by their incessant hostilities, Cortés held on his way, till, winding round the base of a castellated cliff, occupied by a strong garrison of Indians, he was so severely pressed that he felt to pass on without chastising the aggressors would imply a want of strength, which must disparage him in the eyes of his allies. Halting in the valley, therefore, he detached a small body of light troops to scale the heights, while he remained with the main body of the army below, to guard against surprise from the enemy.

The lower region of the rocky eminence was so steep that the soldiers found it no easy matter to ascend, scrambling, as well as they could, with hand and knee. But, as they came into the more exposed view of the garrison, the latter rolled down huge masses of rock, which, bounding along the declivity, and breaking into fragments, crushed the foremost assailants, and mangled their limbs in a frightful manner. Still they strove to work their way upward, now taking advantage of some gulley, worn by the winter torrent, now sheltering themselves behind a projecting cliff, or some straggling tree, anchored among the crevices of the mountain. It was all in vain. For no sooner did they emerge again into open view than the rocky avalanche thundered on their heads with a fury against which steel helm and cuirass were as little defence as gossamer. All the party were more or less wounded. Eight of the number were killed on the spot—a loss the little band could ill afford—and the gallant ensign Corral, who led the advance, saw the banner in his hand torn into shreds. Cortés, at length convinced of the impracticability of the attempt, at least without a more severe loss than he was disposed to incur, commanded a retreat. It was high time; for a large body of the enemy were on full march across the valley to attack him.

He did not wait for their approach, but gathering his broken files together, headed his cavalry, and spurred boldly against them. On the level plain the Spaniards were on their own ground. The Indians, unable to sustain the furious onset, broke, and fell back before it. The fight soon became a rout, and the fiery cavaliers, dashing over them at full gallop, or running them through with their lances, took some revenge for their late discomfiture. The pursuit continued for some miles, till the nimble foe made their escape into the rugged fastnesses of the sierra, where the Spaniards did not care to follow. The weather was sultry, and, as the country was nearly destitute of water, the men and horses suffered extremely. Before evening they reached a spot overshadowed by a grove of wild mulberry trees, in which some scanty springs afforded a miserable supply to the army.

Near the place rose another rocky summit of the sierra, garrisoned by a stronger force than the one which they had encountered in the former part of the day; and at no great distance stood a second fortress at a still greater height, though considerably smaller than its neighbour. This was also tenanted by a body of warriors, who, as well as those of the adjoining cliff, soon made active demonstration of their hostility by pouring down missiles on the troops below. Cortés, anxious to retrieve the disgrace of the morning, ordered an assault on the larger, and, as it seemed, more practicable eminence. But, though two attempts were made with great resolution, they were repulsed with loss to the assailants. The rocky sides of the hill had been artificially cut and smoothed, so as greatly to increase the natural difficulties of the ascent. The shades of evening now closed around; and Cortés drew off his men to the mulberry grove, where he took up his bivouac for the night, deeply chagrined at having been twice foiled by the enemy on the same day.

During the night, the Indian force, which occupied the adjoining height, passed over to their brethren, to aid them in the encounter, which they foresaw would be renewed on the following morning. No sooner did the Spanish general, at the break of day, become aware of this manœuvre than, with his usual quickness, he took advantage of it. He detached a body of musketeers and crossbow-men to occupy the deserted eminence, purposing, as soon as this was done, to lead the assault in person against the other. It was not long before the Castilian banner was seen streaming from the rocky pinnacle, when the general instantly led up his men to the attack. And, while the garrison were meeting them resolutely on that quarter, the detachment on the neighbouring heights poured into the place a well-directed fire, which so much distressed the enemy that, in a very short time, they signified their willingness to capitulate.

On entering the place, the Spaniards found that a plain of some extent ran along the crest of the sierra, and that it was tenanted, not only by men, but by women and their families, with their effects. No violence was offered by the victors to the property or persons of the vanquished, and the knowledge of this lenity induced the Indian garrison, who had made so stout a resistance on the morning of the preceding day, to tender their submission.

After a halt of two days in this sequestered region, the army resumed its march in a south-westerly direction on Huaxtepec, the same city which had surrendered to Sandoval. Here they were kindly received by the cacique, and entertained in his magnificent gardens, which Cortés and his officers, who had not before seen them, compared with the best in Castile. Still threading the wild mountain mazes, the army passed through Juahtepec and several other places which were abandoned at their approach. As the inhabitants, however, hung in armed bodies on their flanks and rear, doing them occasionally some mischief, the Spaniards took their revenge by burning the deserted towns.

Thus holding on their fiery track, they descended the bold slope of the Cordilleras, which, on the south, are far more precipitous than on the Atlantic side. Indeed, a single day's journey is sufficient to place the traveller on a level several thousand feet lower than that occupied by him in the morning; thus conveying him in a few hours through the climates of many degrees of latitude. The route of the army led them across many an acre, covered with lava and blackened scoriæ, attesting the volcanic character of the region: though this was frequently relieved by patches of verdure, and even tracts of prodigal fertility, as if nature were desirous to compensate by these extraordinary efforts for the curse of barrenness, which elsewhere had fallen on the land. On the ninth day of their march, the troops arrived before the strong city of Quauhnahuac, or Cuernavaca, as since called by the Spaniards. It was the ancient capital of the Tlahui-cas, and the most considerable place for wealth and population in this part of the country. It was tributary to the Aztecs, and a garrison of this nation was quartered within its walls. The town was singularly situated on a projecting piece of land, encompassed by *barrancas,* or formidable ravines, except on one side, which opened on a rich and well cultivated country. For, though the place stood at an elevation of between five and six thousand feet above the level of the sea, it had a southern exposure so sheltered by the mountain barrier on the north that its climate was as soft and genial as that of a much lower region.

The Spaniards, on arriving before this city, the limit of their southerly progress, found themselves separated from it by one of the vast barrancas before noticed, which resembled one of those frightful rents not unfre-quent in the Mexican Andes, the result, no doubt, of some terrible con-vulsion in earlier ages. The rocky sides of the ravine sank perpendicularly down, and so bare as scarcely to exhibit even a vestige of the cactus, or of the other hardy plants with which nature in these fruitful regions so gracefully covers up her deformities. The bottom of the chasm, however, showed a striking contrast to this, being literally choked up with a rich and spontaneous vegetation; for the huge walls of rock, which shut in these barrancas, while they screen them from the cold winds of the Cordilleras, reflect the rays of a vertical sun, so as to produce an almost suffocating heat in the inclosure, stimulating the soil to the rank fertility of the *tierra caliente.* Under the action of this forcing apparatus—so to speak—the inhabitants of the towns on their margin above may with ease obtain the vegetable products which are to be found on the sultry level of the lowlands.

At the bottom of the ravine was seen a little stream, which, oozing from the stony bowels of the sierra, tumbled along its narrow channel, and contributed by its perpetual moisture to the exuberant fertility of the valley. This rivulet, which at certain seasons of the year was swollen to a torrent, was traversed at some distance below the town, where the sloping sides of the barranca afforded a more practicable passage, by two rude bridges, both of which had been broken in anticipation of the coming of the Spaniards. The latter had now arrived on the brink of the chasm, which intervened between them and the city. It was, as has been re-marked, of no great width, and the army drawn up on its borders was directly exposed to the archery of the garrison, on whom its own fire made little impression, protected as they were by their defences.

The general, annoyed by his position, sent a detachment to seek a passage lower down, by which the troops might be landed on the other side. But although the banks of the ravine became less formidable as they descended, they found no means of crossing the river, till a path unexpectedly presented itself, on which, probably, no one before had ever been daring enough to venture.

From the cliffs on the opposite sides of the barranca, two huge trees shot up to an enormous height, and, inclining towards each other, interlaced their boughs so as to form a sort of natural bridge. Across this avenue, in mid air, a Tlascalan conceived it would not be difficult to pass to the opposite bank. The bold mountaineer succeeded in the attempt, and was soon followed by several others of his countrymen, trained to feats of agility and strength among their native hills. The Spaniards imitated their example. It was a perilous effort for an armed man to make his way over this aerial causeway, swayed to and fro by the wind, where the brain might become giddy, and where a single false movement of hand or foot would plunge him into the abyss below. Three of the soldiers lost their hold and fell. The rest, consisting of some twenty or thirty Spaniards, and a considerable number of Tlascalans, alighted in safety on the other bank. There hastily forming, they marched with all speed on the city. The enemy, engaged in their contest with the Castilians on the opposite brink of the ravine, were taken by surprise—which, indeed, could scarcely have been exceeded if they had seen their foe drop from the clouds on the field of battle.

They made a brave resistance, however, when fortunately the Spaniards succeeded in repairing one of the dilapidated bridges in such a manner as to enable both cavalry and foot to cross the river, though with much delay. The horse under Olid and Andrés de Tapia instantly rode up to the succour of their countrymen. They were soon followed by Cortés at the head of the remaining battalions; and the enemy, driven from one point to another, were compelled to evacuate the city, and to take refuge among the mountains. The buildings in one quarter of the town were speedily wrapt in flames. The place was abandoned to pillage, and, as it was one of the most opulent marts in the country, it amply compensated the victors for the toil and danger they had encountered. The trembling caciques, returning soon after to the city, appeared before Cortés, and deprecating his resentment by charging the blame, as usual, on the Mexicans, threw themselves on his mercy. Satisfied with their submission, he allowed no further violence to the inhabitants.

Having thus accomplished the great object of his expedition across the mountains, the Spanish commander turned his face northwards, to recross the formidable barrier which divided him from the valley. The ascent, steep and laborious, was rendered still more difficult by fragments of rock and loose stones which encumbered the passes. The mountain sides and summits were shaggy with thick forests of pine and stunted oak, which threw a melancholy gloom over the region, still further heightened at the present day by its being a favourite haunt of banditti.

The weather was sultry, and, as the stony soil was nearly destitute of water, the troops suffered severely from thirst.

Several of them, indeed, fainted on the road, and a few of the Indian allies perished from exhaustion. The line of march must have taken the army across the eastern shoulder of the mountain, called the *Cruz del Marques,* or Cross of the Marquess, from a huge stone cross, erected there to indicate the boundary of the territories granted by the crown to Cortés, as Marquess of the Valley. Much, indeed, of the route lately traversed by the troops lay across the princely domain subsequently assigned to the Conqueror.

The Spaniards were greeted from these heights with a different view from any which they had before had of the Mexican Valley, made more attractive in their eyes, doubtless, by contrast with the savage scenery in which they had lately been involved. It was its most pleasant and populous quarter, for nowhere did its cities and villages cluster together in such numbers as round the lake of sweet water. From whatever quarter seen, however, the enchanting region presented the same aspect of natural beauty and cultivation, with its flourishing villas, and its fair lake in the centre, whose dark and polished surface glistened like a mirror, deep set in the huge framework of porphyry in which nature had enclosed it.

The point of attack selected by the general was Xochimilco, or the "field of flowers," as its name implies, from the floating gardens which rode at anchor, as it were, on the neighbouring waters. It was one of the most potent and wealthy cities in the valley, and a staunch vassal of the Aztec crown. It stood, like the capital itself, partly in the water, and was approached in that quarter by causeways of no great length. The town was composed of houses like those of most other places of like magnitude in the country, mostly of cottages or huts made of clay and the light bamboo, mingled with aspiring *teocallis,* and edifices of stone, belonging to the more opulent classes.

As the Spaniards advanced, they were met by skirmishing parties of the enemy, who, after dismissing a light volley of arrows, rapidly retreated before them. As they took the direction of Xochimilco, Cortés inferred that they were prepared to resist him in considerable force. It exceeded his expectations.

On traversing the principal causeway, he found it occupied, at the further extremity, by a numerous body of warriors, who, stationed on the opposite side of a bridge, which had been broken, were prepared to dispute his passage. They had constructed a temporary barrier of palisades, which screened them from the fire of the musketry. But the water in its neighbourhood was very shallow, and the cavaliers and infantry, plunging into it, soon made their way, swimming or wading, as they could, in face of a storm of missiles, to the landing near the town. Here they closed with the enemy, and, hand to hand, after a sharp struggle, drove them back on the city; a few, however, taking the direction of the open country, were followed up by the cavalry. The great mass hotly pursued by the infantry, were driven through street and lane, without much further resistance. Cortés, with a few followers, disengaging himself from the tumult, remained near the entrance of the city. He had not been there long, when he was assailed by a fresh body of Indians, who suddenly poured into the place from a neighbouring dike. The general, with his usual fearlessness, threw himself into the midst, in hopes to check their advance. But his own followers were too few to support him, and he was overwhelmed by the crowd of combatants. His horse lost his footing and fell; and Cortés, who received a severe blow on the head before he could rise, was seized and dragged off in triumph by the Indians. At this critical moment, a Tlascalan, who perceived the general's extremity, sprang, like one of the wild ocelots of his own forests, into the midst of the assailants, and endeavoured to tear him from their grasp. Two of the general's servants also speedily came to the rescue, and Cortés, with their aid and that of the brave Tlascalan, succeeded in regaining his feet and shaking off his enemies. To vault into the saddle and brandish his good lance was but the work of a moment. Others of his men quickly came up, and the clash of arms reaching the ears of the Spaniards who had gone in pursuit, they returned, and, after a desperate conflict, forced the enemy from the city. Their retreat, however, was intercepted by the cavalry returning from the country, and, thus hemmed in between the opposite columns, they were cut to pieces, or saved themselves only by plunging into the lake.

This was the greatest personal danger which Cortés had yet encountered. His life was in the power of the barbarians, and, had it not been for their eagerness to take him prisoner, he must undoubtedly have lost it. To the same cause may be frequently attributed the preservation of the Spaniards in these engagements. The next day he sought, it is said, for the Tlascalan who came so boldly to his rescue, and, as he could learn nothing of him, he gave the credit of his preservation to his patron, St. Peter. He may well be excused for presuming the interposition of his good Genius, to shield him from the awful doom of the captive—a doom not likely to be mitigated in his case. That heart must have been a bold one, indeed, which, from any motive, could voluntarily encounter such a peril! Yet his followers did as much, and that, too, for a much inferior reward.

The period which we are reviewing was still the age of chivalry; that stirring and adventurous age of which we can form little conception in the present day of sober, practical reality. The Spaniard, with his nice point of honour, high romance, and proud, vainglorious vaunt, was the true representative of that age. The Europeans, generally, had not yet learned to accommodate themselves to a life of literary toil, or to the drudgery of trade, or the patient tillage of the soil. They left these to the hooded inmate of the cloister, the humble burgher, and the miserable serf. Arms was the only profession worthy of gentle blood—the only career which the high-mettled cavalier could tread with honour. The New World, with its strange and mysterious perils, afforded a noble theatre for the exercise of his calling; and the Spaniard entered on it with all the enthusiasm of a paladin of romance.

Other nations entered on it also, but with different motives. The French set forth their missionaries to take up their dwelling among the heathen, who, in the good work of winning souls to Paradise, were content to wear—nay, sometimes seemed to court—the crown of martyrdom. The Dutch, too, had their mission, but it was one of worldly lucre, and they found a recompense for toil and suffering in their gainful traffic with the natives. While our own Puritan fathers, with the true Anglo-Saxon spirit, left their pleasant homes across the waters, and pitched their tents in the howling wilderness, that they might enjoy the sweets of civil and religious freedom. But the Spaniard came over to the New World in the true spirit of a knight-errant, courting adventure however perilous; wooing danger, as it would seem, for its own sake. With sword and lance, he was ever ready to do battle for the Faith; and, as he raised his old war-cry of "St. Jago," he fancied himself fighting under the banner of the military apostle, and felt his single arm a match for more than a hundred infidels! It was the expiring age of chivalry; and Spain, romantic Spain, was the land where its light lingered longest above the horizon.

It was not yet dusk when Cortés and his followers re-entered the city; and the general's first act was to ascend a neighbouring *teocalli* and reconnoitre the surrounding country. He there beheld a sight which might have troubled a bolder spirit than his. The surface of the salt lake was darkened with canoes, and the causeway, for many a mile, with Indian squadrons, apparently on their march towards the Christian camp. In fact, no sooner had Guatemozin been apprised of the arrival of the white men at Xochimilco than he mustered his levies in great force to relieve the city. They were now on their march, and, as the capital was but four leagues distant, would arrive soon after nightfall.

Cortés made active preparations for the defence of his quarters. He stationed a corps of pikemen along the landing where the Aztecs would be likely to disembark. He doubled the sentinels, and, with his principal officers, made the rounds repeatedly in the course of the night. In addition to other causes for watchfulness, the bolts of the crossbow-men were nearly exhausted, and the archers were busily employed in preparing and adjusting shafts to the copper heads, of which great store had been provided for the army. There was little sleep in the camp that night.

It passed away, however, without molestation from the enemy. Though not stormy, it was exceedingly dark. But, although the Spaniards on duty could see nothing, they distinctly heard the sound of many oars in the water, at no great distance from the shore. Yet those on board the canoes made no attempt to land, distrusting, or advised, it may be, of the preparations made for their reception. With early dawn, they were under arms, and, without waiting for the movement of the Spaniards, poured into the city and attacked them in their own quarters.

The Spaniards, who were gathered in the area round one of the *teocallis,* were taken at a disadvantage in the town, where the narrow lanes and streets, many of them covered with a smooth and slippery cement, offered obvious impediments to the manœuvres of cavalry. But Cortés hastily formed his musketeers and crossbow-men, and poured such a lively, well-directed fire into the enemy's ranks, as threw him into disorder, and compelled him to recoil. The infantry, with their long pikes, followed up the bow; and the horse, charging at full speed, as the retreating Aztecs emerged from the city, drove them several miles along the main land.

At some distance, however, they were met by a strong reinforcement of their countrymen, and rallying, the tide of battle turned, and the cavaliers, swept along by it, gave the rein to their steeds, and rode back at full gallop towards the town. They had not proceeded very far, when they came upon the main body of the army, advancing rapidly to their support. Thus strengthened, they once more returned to the charge, and the rival hosts met together in full career, with the shock of an earthquake. For a time, victory seemed to hang in the balance, as the mighty press reeled to and fro under the opposite impulse, and a confused shout rose up towards heaven, in which the war-whoop of the savage was mingled with the battle-cry of the Christian—a still stranger sound on these sequestered shores. But, in the end, Castilian valour, or rather Castilian arms and discipline, proved triumphant. The enemy faltered, gave way, and, recoiling step by step, the retreat soon terminated in a rout, and the Spaniards, following up the flying foe, drove them from the field with such dreadful slaughter that they made no further attempt to renew the battle.

The victors were now undisputed masters of the city. It was a wealthy place, well stored with Indian fabrics, cotton, gold, featherwork, and other articles of luxury and use, affording a rich booty to the soldiers. While engaged in the work of plunder, a party of the enemy, landing from their canoes, fell on some of the stragglers laden with merchandise, and made four of them prisoners. It created a greater sensation among the troops than if ten times that number had fallen on the field. Indeed, it was rare that a Spaniard allowed himself to be taken alive. In the present instance the unfortunate men were taken by surprise. They were hurried to the capital, and soon after sacrificed; when their arms and legs were cut off, by the command of the ferocious young chief of the Aztecs, and sent round to the different cities, with the assurance that this should be the fate of the enemies of Mexico!

From the prisoners taken in the late engagement, Cortés learned that the forces already sent by Guatemozin formed but a small part of his levies; that his policy was to send detachment after detachment, until the Spaniards, however victorious they might come off from the contest with each individual, would, in the end, succumb from mere exhaustion, and thus be vanquished, as it were, by their own victories.

The soldiers having now sacked the city, Cortés did not care to await further assaults from the enemy in his present quarters. On the fourth morning after his arrival he mustered his forces on a neighbouring plain. They came many of them reeling under the weight of their plunder. The general saw this with uneasiness. They were to march, he said, through a populous country, all in arms to dispute their passage. To secure their safety, they should move as light and unencumbered as possible. The sight of so much spoil would sharpen the appetite of their enemies, and draw them on, like a flock of famished eagles after their prey. But his eloquence was lost on his men; who plainly told him they had a right to the fruit of their victories, and that what they had won with their swords, they knew well enough how to defend with them.

Seeing them thus bent on their purpose, the general did not care to baulk their inclinations. He ordered the baggage to the centre, and placed a few of the cavalry over it; dividing the remainder between the front and rear, in which latter post, as that most exposed to attack, he also stationed his arquebusiers and crossbow-men. Thus prepared, he resumed his march; but first set fire to the combustible buildings of Xochimilco, in retaliation for the resistance he had met there. The light of the burning city streamed high into the air, sending its ominous glare far and wide across the waters, and telling the inhabitants on their margin that the fatal strangers so long predicted by their oracles had descended like a consuming flame upon their borders.

Small bodies of the enemy were seen occasionally at a distance, but they did not venture to attack the army on its march, which before noon brought them to Cojohuacan, a large town about two leagues distant from Xochimilco. One could scarcely travel that distance in this populous quarter of the valley without meeting with a place of considerable size, oftentimes the capital of what had formerly been an independent state. The inhabitants, members of different tribes, and speaking dialects somewhat different, belonged to the same great family of nations who had come from the real or imaginary region of Aztlan, in the far north-west. Gathered round the shores of their Alpine sea, these petty communities continued, after their incorporation with the Aztec monarchy, to maintain a spirit of rivalry in their intercourse with one another—which—as with the cities on the Mediterranean, in the feudal ages—quickened their mental energies, and raised the Mexican Valley higher in the scale of civilisation than most other quarters of Anahuac.

The town at which the army had now arrived was deserted by its inhabitants; and Cortés halted two days there to restore his troops, and give the needful attention to the wounded. He made use of the time to reconnoitre the neighbouring ground, and taking with him a strong detachment, descended on the causeway which led from Cojohuacan to the great avenue of Iztapalapan. At the point of intersection, called Xoloc, he found a strong barrier or fortification, behind which a Mexican force was intrenched. Their archery did some mischief to the Spaniards, as they came within bow-shot. But the latter, marching intrepidly forward in face of the arrowy shower, stormed the works, and, after an obstinate struggle, drove the enemy from their position. Cortés then advanced some way on the great causeway of Iztapalapan; but he beheld the further extremity darkened by a numerous array of warriors, and as he did not care to engage in unnecessary hostilities, especially as his ammunition was nearly exhausted, he fell back and retreated to his own quarters.

The following day, the army continued its march, taking the road to Tacuba, but a few miles distant. On the way it experienced much annoyance from straggling parties of the enemy, who, furious at the sight of the booty which the invaders were bearing away, made repeated attacks on their flanks and rear. Cortés retaliated, as on the former expedition, by one of their own stratagems, but with less success than before; for, pursuing the retreating enemy too hotly, he fell with his cavalry into an ambuscade, which they had prepared for him in their turn. He was not yet a match for their wily tactics. The Spanish cavaliers were enveloped in a moment by their subtle foe, and separated from the rest of the army. But, spurring on their good steeds, and charging in a solid column together, they succeeded in breaking through the Indian array, and in making their escape, except two individuals, who fell into the enemy's hands. They were the general's own servants, who had followed him faithfully through the whole campaign, and he was deeply affected by their loss; rendered the more distressing by the consideration of the dismal fate that awaited them. When the little band rejoined the army, which had halted in some anxiety at their absence, under the walls of Tacuba, the soldiers were astonished at the dejected mien of their commander, which too visibly betrayed his emotion.

The sun was still high in the heavens, when they entered the ancient capital of the Tepanecs. The first care of Cortés was to ascend the principal *teocalli,* and survey the surrounding country. It was an admirable point of view, commanding the capital, which lay but little more than a league distant, and its immediate environs. Cortés was accompanied by Alderete, the treasurer, and some other cavaliers, who had lately joined his banner. The spectacle was still new to them; and, as they gazed on the stately city, with its broad lake covered with boats and barges hurrying to and fro, some laden with merchandise, or fruits and vegetables, for the markets of Tenochtitlan, others crowded with warriors, they could not withhold their admiration at the life and activity of the scene, declaring that nothing but the hand of Providence could have led their countrymen safe through the heart of this powerful empire.

In the midst of the admiring circle, the brow of Cortés alone was observed to be overcast, and a sigh, which now and then stole audibly from his bosom, showed the gloomy working of his thoughts. "Take comfort," said one of the cavaliers, approaching his commander, and wishing to console him in his rough way for his recent loss, "you must not lay these things so much to heart; it is, after all, but the fortune of war." The general's answer showed the nature of his meditations. "You are my witness," said he, "how often I have endeavoured to persuade yonder capital peacefully to submit. It fills me with grief, when I think of the toil and the dangers my brave followers have yet to encounter before we can call it ours. But the time is come when we must put our hands to the work."

There can be no doubt that Cortés, with every other man in his army, felt he was engaged in a holy crusade, and that, independently of personal considerations, he could not serve Heaven better than by planting the Cross on the bloodstained towers of the heathen metropolis. But it was natural that he should feel some compunction, as he gazed on the goodly scene, and thought of the coming tempest, and how soon the opening blossoms of civilisation which there met his eye must wither under the rude breath of war. It was a striking spectacle, that of the great Conqueror, thus brooding in silence over the desolation he was about to bring on the land! It seems to have made a deep impression on his soldiers, little accustomed to such proofs of his sensibility; and it forms the burden of some of those *romances,* or national ballads, with which the Castilian minstrel, in the olden time, delighted to commemorate the favourite heroes of his country, and which, coming midway between oral tradition and chronicle, have been found as imperishable a record as chronicle itself.

Tacuba was the point which Cortés had reached on his former expedition round the northern side of the valley. He had now, therefore, made the entire circuit of the great lake; had reconnoitred the several approaches to the capital, and inspected with his own eyes the dispositions made on the opposite quarters for its defence. He had no occasion to prolong his stay in Tacuba, the vicinity of which to Mexico must soon bring on him its whole warlike population.

Early on the following morning, he resumed his march, taking the route pursued in the former expedition, north of the small lakes. He met with less annoyance from the enemy than on the preceding days; a circumstance owing in some degree, perhaps, to the state of the weather, which was exceedingly tempestuous. The soldiers, with their garments heavy with moisture, ploughed their way with difficulty through the miry roads flooded by the torrents. On one occasion, as their military chronicler informs us, the officers neglected to go the rounds of the camp at night, and the sentinels to mount guard, trusting to the violence of the storm for their protection. Yet the fate of Narvaez might have taught them not to put their faith in the elements.

At Acolman, in the Acolhuan territory, they were met by Sandoval, with the friendly cacique of Tezcuco, and several cavaliers, among whom were some recently arrived from the islands. They cordially greeted their countrymen, and communicated the tidings that the canal was completed, and that the brigantines, rigged and equipped, were ready to be launched on the bosom of the lake. There seemed to be no reason, therefore, for longer postponing operations against Mexico. With this welcome intelligence, Cortés and his victorious legions made their entry for the last time into the Acolhuan capital, having consumed just three weeks in completing the circuit of the valley.

CHAPTER IV

Conspiracy in the Army—Brigantines Launched—Muster of
Forces—Execution of Xicotencatl—March of the Army
—Beginning of the Siege

1521

AT THE VERY TIME when Cortés was occupied with reconnoitring the
the valley, preparatory to his siege of the capital, a busy faction in Castile
was labouring to subvert his authority and defeat his plans of conquest
altogether. The fame of his brilliant exploits had spread not only through
the isles, but to Spain, and many parts of Europe, where a general admiration was felt for the invincible energy of the man, who, with his
single arm as it were, could so long maintain a contest with the powerful
Indian empire. The absence of the Spanish monarch from his dominions,
and the troubles of the country, can alone explain the supine indifference
shown by the government to the prosecution of this great enterprise. To
the same causes it may be ascribed that no action was had in regard to
the suits of Velasquez and Narvaez, backed as they were by so potent an
advocate as Bishop Fonseca, president of the Council of the Indies. The
reins of government had fallen into the hands of Adrian of Utrecht,
Charles' preceptor, and afterwards Pope—a man of learning, and not
without sagacity, but slow and timid in his policy, and altogether incapable of that decisive action which suited the bold genius of his predecessor, Cardinal Ximenes.

In the spring of 1521, however, a number of ordinances passed the
Council of the Indies, which threatened an important innovation in the
affairs of New Spain. It was decreed that the Royal Audience of Hispaniola should abandon the proceedings already instituted against Narvaez, for his treatment of the commissioner Ayllon; that that unfortunate
commander should be released from his confinement at Vera Cruz; and
that an arbitrator should be sent to Mexico, with authority to investigate
the affairs and conduct of Cortés, and to render ample justice to the

governor of Cuba. There were not wanting persons at court, who looked with dissatisfaction on these proceedings, as an unworthy requital of the services of Cortés, and who thought the present moment, at any rate, not the most suitable for taking measures which might discourage the general, and, perhaps, render him desperate. But the arrogant temper of the Bishop of Burgos overruled all objections; and the ordinances having been approved by the Regency, were signed by that body, April 11, 1521. A person named Tapia, one of the functionaries of the Audience of St. Domingo, was selected as the new commissioner to be despatched to Vera Cruz. Fortunately circumstances occurred which postponed the execution of the design for the present, and permitted Cortés to go forward unmolested in his career of conquest.

But, while thus allowed to remain, for the present at least, in possession of authority, he was assailed by a danger nearer home, which menaced not only his authority, but his life. This was a conspiracy in the army, of a more dark and dangerous character than any hitherto formed there. It was set on foot by a common soldier, named Antonio Villafaña, a native of Old Castile, of whom nothing is known but his share in this transaction. He was one of the troop of Narvaez—that leaven of disaffection, which had remained with the army, swelling with discontent on every light occasion, and ready at all times to rise into mutiny. They had voluntarily continued in the service after the secession of their comrades at Tlascala; but it was from the same mercenary hopes with which they had originally embarked in the expedition—and in these they were destined still to be disappointed. They had little of the true spirit of adventure, which distinguished the old companions of Cortés; and they found the barren laurels of victory but a sorry recompense for all their toils and sufferings.

With these men were joined others, who had causes of personal disgust with the general; and others, again, who looked with disgust on the result of the war. The gloomy fate of their countrymen, who had fallen into the enemy's hands, filled them with dismay. They felt themselves the victims of a chimerical spirit in their leader, who, with such inadequate means, was urging to extremity so ferocious and formidable a foe; and they shrank with something like apprehension from thus pursuing the enemy into his own haunts, where he would gather tenfold energy from despair.

These men would have willingly abandoned the enterprise, and returned to Cuba; but how could they do it? Cortés had control over the whole route from the city to the sea-coast; and not a vessel could leave its ports without his warrant. Even if he were put out of the way, there were others, his principal officers, ready to step into his place, and avenge the death of their commander. It was necessary to embrace these, also, in the scheme of destruction; and it was proposed, therefore, together with Cortés, to assassinate Sandoval, Olid, Alvarado, and two or three others most devoted to his interests. The conspirators would then raise the cry of liberty, and doubted not that they should be joined by the greater part of the army, or enough, at least, to enable them to work their own pleasure. They proposed to offer the command, on Cortés' death, to Francisco Verdugo, a brother-in-law of Velasquez. He was an honourable cavalier, and not privy to their design. But they had little doubt that he would acquiesce in the command thus, in a manner, forced upon him, and this would secure them the protection of the governor of Cuba, who, indeed, from his own hatred of Cortés, would be disposed to look with a lenient eye on their proceedings.

The conspirators even went so far as to appoint the subordinate officers, an *alguacil mayor,* in place of Sandoval, a quartermaster-general to succeed Olid, and some others. The time fixed for the execution of the plot was soon after the return of Cortés from his expedition. A parcel, pretended to have come by a fresh arrival from Castile, was to be presented to him while at table, and, when he was engaged in breaking open the letters, the conspirators were to fall on him and his officers, and despatch them with their poniards. Such was the iniquitous scheme devised for the destruction of Cortés and the expedition. But a conspiracy, to be successful, especially when numbers are concerned, should allow but little time to elapse between its conception and its execution.

On the day previous to that appointed for the perpetration of the deed, one of the party, feeling a natural compunction at the commission of the crime, went to the general's quarters, and solicited a private interview with him. He threw himself at his commander's feet, and revealed all the particulars relating to the conspiracy, adding that in Villafaña's possession a paper would be found, containing the names of his accomplices. Cortés, thunderstruck at the disclosure, lost not a moment in profiting by it. He sent for Alvarado, Sandoval, and one or two other officers marked out by the conspirator, and, after communicating the affair to them, went at once with them to Villafaña's quarters, attended by four *alguacils.*

They found him in conference with three or four friends, who were instantly taken from the apartment, and placed in custody. Villafaña, confounded at this sudden apparition of his commander, had barely time to snatch a paper, containing the signatures of the confederates, from his bosom, and attempt to swallow it. But Cortés arrested his arm, and seized the paper. As he glanced his eye rapidly over the fatal list, he was much moved at finding there the names of more than one who had some claim to consideration in the army. He tore the scroll in pieces, and ordered Villafaña to be taken into custody. He was immediately tried by a military court hastily got together, at which the general himself presided. There seems to have been no doubt of the man's guilt. He was condemned to death, and, after allowing him time for confession and absolution, the sentence was executed by hanging him from the window of his own quarters.

Those ignorant of the affair were astonished at the spectacle; and the remaining conspirators were filled with consternation, when they saw that their plot was detected, and anticipated a similar fate for themselves. But they were mistaken. Cortés pursued the matter no further. A little reflection convinced him that to do so would involve him in the most disagreeable, and even dangerous, perplexities. And, however much the parties implicated in so foul a deed might deserve death, he could ill afford the loss even of the guilty, with his present limited numbers. He resolved, therefore, to content himself with the punishment of the ring-leader.

He called his troops together, and briefly explained to them the nature of the crime for which Villafaña had suffered. He had made no confession, he said, and the guilty secret had perished with him. He then expressed his sorrow that any should have been found in their ranks capable of so base an act, and stated his own unconsciousness of having wronged any individual among them; but, if he had done so, he invited them frankly to declare it, as he was most anxious to afford them all the redress in his power. But there was no one of his audience, whatever might be his grievances, who cared to enter his complaint at such a moment; least of all were the conspirators willing to do so, for they were too happy at having, as they fancied, escaped detection, to stand forward now in the ranks of the malcontents. The affair passed off, therefore, without further consequences.

The conduct of Cortés, in this delicate conjuncture, shows great coolness and knowledge of human nature. Had he suffered his detection, or even his suspicion, of the guilty parties to take air, it would have placed him in hostile relations with them for the rest of his life. It was a disclosure of this kind, in the early part of Louis the Eleventh's reign, to which many of the troubles of his later years were attributed. The mask once torn away, there is no longer occasion to consult even appearances. The door seems to be closed against reform. The alienation, which might have been changed by circumstances, or conciliated by kindness, settles into a deep and deadly rancour; and Cortés would have been surrounded by enemies in his own camp, more implacable than those in the camp of the Aztecs.

As it was, the guilty soldiers had suffered too serious apprehensions to place their lives hastily in a similar jeopardy. They strove, on the contrary, by demonstrations of loyalty, and the assiduous discharge of their duties, to turn away suspicion from themselves. Cortés, on his part, was careful to preserve his natural demeanour, equally removed from distrust, and—what was perhaps more difficult—that studied courtesy which intimates, quite as plainly, suspicion of the party who is the object of it. To do this required no little address. Yet he did not forget the past. He had, it is true, destroyed the scroll containing the list of the conspirators; but the man that has once learned the names of those who have conspired against his life has no need of a written record to keep them fresh in his memory. Cortés kept his eye on all their movements, and took care to place them in no situation, afterwards, where they could do him injury.

This attempt on the life of their commander excited a strong sensation in the army, with whom his many dazzling qualities and brilliant military talents had made him a general favourite. They were anxious to testify their reprobation of so foul a deed coming from their own body, and they felt the necessity of taking some effectual measures for watching over the safety of one, with whom their own destinies, as well as the fate of the enterprise, were so intimately connected. It was arranged, therefore, that he should be provided with a guard of soldiers, who were placed under the direction of a trusty cavalier named Antonio de Quiñones. They constituted the general's bodyguard during the rest of the campaign, watching over him day and night, and protecting him from domestic treason, no less than from the sword of the enemy.

As was stated at the close of the last chapter, the Spaniards, on their return to quarters, found the construction of the brigantines completed, and that they were fully rigged, equipped, and ready for service. The canal, also, after having occupied eight thousand men for nearly two months, was finished.

It was a work of great labour; for it extended half a league in length, was twelve feet wide, and as many deep. The sides were strengthened by palisades of wood, or solid masonry. At intervals dams and locks were constructed, and part of the opening was through the hard rock. By this avenue the brigantines might now be safely introduced on the lake.

Cortés was resolved that so auspicious an event should be celebrated with due solemnity. On April 28 the troops were drawn up under arms, and the whole population of Tezcuco assembled to witness the ceremony. Mass was performed, and every man in the army, together with the general, confessed and received the sacrament. Prayers were offered up by Father Olmedo, and a benediction invoked on the little navy, the first worthy of the name ever launched on American waters. The signal was given by the firing of a cannon, when the vessels, dropping down the canal one after another, reached the lake in good order; and as they emerged on its ample bosom, with music sounding, and the royal ensign of Castile proudly floating from their masts, a shout of admiration arose from the countless multitudes of spectators, which mingled with the roar of artillery and musketry from the vessels and the shore! It was a novel spectacle to the simple natives; and they gazed with wonder on the gallant ships, which, fluttering like sea-birds on their snowy pinions, bounded lightly over the waters, as if rejoicing in their element. It touched the stern hearts of the Conquerors with a glow of rapture, and, as they felt that Heaven had blessed their undertaking, they broke forth, by general accord, into the noble anthem of the *Te Deum*. But there was no one of that vast multitude for whom the sight had deeper interest than their commander. For he looked on it as the work, in a manner, of his own hands; and his bosom swelled with exultation, as he felt he was now possessed of a power strong enough to command the lake, and to shake the haughty towers of Tenochtitlan.

The general's next step was to muster his forces in the great square of the capital. He found they amounted to eighty-seven horse, and eight hundred and eighteen foot, of which one hundred and eighteen were arquebusiers and crossbow-men. He had three large field-pieces of iron, and fifteen lighter guns or falconets of brass. The heavier cannon had been transported from Vera Cruz to Tezcuco, a little while before, by the faithful Tlascalans. He was well supplied with shot and balls, with about ten hundredweight of powder, and fifty thousand copperheaded arrows, made after a pattern furnished by him to the natives. The number and appointments of the army much exceeded what they had been at any time since the flight from Mexico, and showed the good effects of the late arrivals from the islands. Indeed, taking the fleet into the account, Cortés had never before been in so good a condition for carrying on his operations. Three hundred of the men were sent to man the vessels, thirteen, or rather twelve, in number, one of the smallest having been found, on trial, too dull a sailer to be of service. Half of the crews were required to navigate the ships. There was some difficulty in finding hands for this, as the men were averse to the employment. Cortés selected those who came from Palos, Moguer, and other maritime towns, and notwithstanding their frequent claims of exemption, as hidalgos, from this menial occupation, he pressed them into the service. Each vessel mounted a piece of heavy ordnance, and was placed under an officer of respectability, to whom Cortés gave a general code of instructions for the government of the little navy, of which he proposed to take the command in person.

He had already sent to his Indian confederates, announcing his purpose of immediately laying siege to Mexico, and called on them to furnish their promised levies within the space of ten days at furthest. The Tlascalans he ordered to join him at Tezcuco; the others were to assemble at Chalco, a more convenient place of rendezvous for the operations in the southern quarter of the valley. The Tlascalans arrived within the time prescribed, led by the younger Xicotencatl, supported by Chichemecatl, the same doughty warrior who had convoyed the brigantines to Tezcuco. They came fifty thousand strong, according to Cortés, making a brilliant show with their military finery, and marching proudly forward under the great national banner, emblazoned with a spread eagle, the arms of the republic. With as blithe and manly a step as if they were going to the battle-ground, they defiled through the gates of the capital, making its walls ring with the friendly shouts of "Castile and Tlascala."

The observations which Cortés had made in his late tour of *reconnaissance* had determined him to begin the siege by distributing his forces into three separate camps, which he proposed to establish at the extremities of the principal causeways. By this arrangement the troops would be enabled to move in concert on the capital, and be in the best position to intercept its supplies from the surrounding country. The first of these points was Tacuba, commanding the fatal causeway of the *noche triste*. This was assigned to Pedro de Alvarado, with a force consisting, according to Cortés' own statement, of thirty horse, one hundred and sixty-eight Spanish infantry, and five and twenty thousand Tlascalans. Christoval de

Olid had command of the second army, of much the same magnitude, which was to take up its position at Cojohuacan, the city, it will be remembered, overlooking the short causeway connected with that of Iztapalapan. Gonzalo de Sandoval had charge of the third division, of equal strength with each of the two preceding, but which was to draw its Indian levies from the forces assembled at Chalco. This officer was to march on Iztapalapan, and complete the destruction of that city, begun by Cortés soon after his entrance into the valley. It was too formidable a post to remain in the rear of the army. The general intended to support the attack with his brigantines, after which the subsequent movements of Sandoval would be determined by circumstances.

Having announced his intended dispositions to his officers, the Spanish commander called his troops together, and made one of these brief and stirring harangues with which he was wont on great occasions to kindle the hearts of his soldiery. "I have taken the last step," he said; "I have brought you to the goal for which you have so long panted. A few days will place you before the gates of Mexico—the capital from which you were driven with so much ignominy. But we now go forward under the smiles of Providence. Does any one doubt it? Let him but compare our present condition with that in which we found ourselves not twelve months since, when, broken and dispirited, we sought shelter within the walls of Tlascala; nay, with that in which we were but a few months since, when we took up our quarters in Tezcuco. Since that time our strength has been nearly doubled. We are fighting the battles of the Faith, fighting for our honour, for riches, for revenge. I have brought you face to face with your foe. It is for you to do the rest."

The address of the bold chief was answered by the thundering acclamations of his followers, who declared that every man would do his duty under such a leader; and they only asked to be led against the enemy. Cortés then caused the regulations for the army, published at Tlascala, to be read again to the troops, with the assurance that they should be enforced to the letter.

It was arranged that the Indian forces should precede the Spanish by a day's march, and should halt for their confederates on the borders of the Tezcucan territory. A circumstance occurred soon after their departure, which gave bad augury for the future. A quarrel had arisen in the camp at Tezcuco between a Spanish soldier and a Tlascalan chief, in which the latter was badly hurt. He was sent back to Tlascala, and the matter was hushed up, that it might not reach the ears of the general, who, it was known, would not pass it over lightly. Xicotencatl was a near relative of the injured party, and on the first day's halt he took the opportunity to leave the army, with a number of his followers, and set off for Tlascala. Other causes are assigned for his desertion. It is certain that, from the first, he looked on the expedition with an evil eye, and had predicted that no good would come of it. He came into it with reluctance, as, indeed, he detested the Spaniards in his heart.

His partner in the command instantly sent information of the affair to the Spanish general, still encamped at Tezcuco. Cortés, who saw at once the mischievous consequences of this defection at such a time, detached a party of Tlascalan and Tezcucan Indians after the fugitive, with instructions to prevail on him, if possible, to return to his duty. They overtook him on the road, and remonstrated with him on his conduct, contrasting it with that of his countrymen generally, and of his own father in particular, the steady friend of the white men. "So much the worse," replied the chieftain; "if they had taken my counsel, they would never have become the dupes of the perfidious strangers." Finding their remonstrances received only with anger or contemptuous taunts, the emissaries returned without accomplishing their object.

Cortés did not hesitate on the course he was to pursue. "Xicotencatl," he said, "had always been the enemy of the Spaniards, first in the field, and since in the council-chamber; openly, or in secret, still the same—their implacable enemy. There was no use in parleying with the false-hearted Indian." He instantly despatched a small body of horse with an *alguacil* to arrest the chief, wherever he might be found, even though it were in the streets of Tlascala, and to bring him back to Tezcuco. At the same time he sent information of Xicotencatl's proceedings to the Tlascalan senate, adding that desertion among the Spaniards was punished with death.

The emissaries of Cortés punctually fulfilled his orders. They arrested the fugitive chief—whether in Tlascala or in its neighbourhood is uncertain—and brought him a prisoner to Tezcuco, where a high gallows, erected in the great square, was prepared for his reception. He was instantly led to the place of execution; his sentence and the cause for which he suffered were publicly proclaimed, and the unfortunate cacique expiated his offence by the vile death of a malefactor. His ample property, consisting of lands, slaves, and some gold, was all confiscated to the Castilian crown.

Thus perished Xicotencatl, in the flower of his age—as dauntless a warrior as ever led an Indian army to battle. He was the first chief who successfully resisted the arms of the invaders; and, had the natives of Anahuac generally been animated with a spirit like his, Cortés would probably never have set foot in the capital of Montezuma. He was gifted with a clearer insight into the future than his countrymen; for he saw that the European was an enemy far more to be dreaded than the Aztec. Yet, when he consented to fight under the banner of the white men, he had no right to desert it, and he incurred the penalty prescribed by the code of savage as well as of civilised nations. It is said, indeed, that the Tlascalan senate aided in apprehending him, having previously answered Cortés that his crime was punishable with death by their own laws. It was a bold act, however, thus to execute him in the midst of his people; for he was a powerful chief, heir to one of the four seigniories of the republic. His chivalrous qualities made him popular, especially with the younger part of his countrymen; and his garments were torn into shreds at his death, and distributed as sacred relics among them. Still, no resistance was offered to the execution of the sentence, and no commotion followed it. He was the only Tlascalan who ever swerved from his loyalty to the Spaniards.

According to the plan of operations settled by Cortés, Sandoval, with his division, was to take a southern direction; while Alvarado and Olid would make the northern circuit of the lakes. These two cavaliers, after getting possession of Tacuba, were to advance to Chapultepec, and demolish the great aqueduct there, which supplied Mexico with water. On May 10, they commenced their march; but at Acolman, where they halted for the night, a dispute arose between the soldiers of the two divisions, respecting their quarters. From words they came to blows, and a defiance was even exchanged between the leaders, who entered into the angry feelings of their followers. Intelligence of this was soon communicated to Cortés, who sent at once to the fiery chiefs, imploring them, by their regard for him and the common cause, to lay aside their differences, which must end in their own ruin, and that of the expedition. His remonstrance prevailed, at least, so far as to establish a show of reconciliation between the parties. But Olid was not a man to forget, or easily to forgive; and Alvarado, though frank and liberal, had an impatient temper, much more easily excited than appeased. They were never afterwards friends.

The Spaniards met with no opposition on their march. The principal towns were all abandoned by the inhabitants, who had gone to strengthen the garrison of Mexico, or taken refuge with their families among the mountains. Tacuba was in like manner deserted, and the troops once more established themselves in their old quarters in the lordly city of the Tepanecs.

Their first undertaking was to cut off the pipes that conducted the water from the royal streams of Chapultepec to feed the numerous tanks and fountains which sparkled in the courtyards of the capital. The aqueduct, partly constructed of brickwork, and partly of stone and mortar, was raised on a strong, though narrow, dike which transported it across an arm of the lake; and the whole work was one of the most pleasing monuments of Mexican civilisation. The Indians, well aware of its importance, had stationed a large body of troops for its protection. A battle followed, in which both sides suffered considerably, but the Spaniards were victorious. A part of the aqueduct was demolished, and during the siege no water found its way again to the capital through this channel.

On the following day the combined forces descended on the fatal causeway, to make themselves masters, if possible, of the nearest bridge. They found the dike covered with a swarm of warriors, as numerous as on the night of their disaster, while the surface of the lake was dark with the multitude of canoes. The intrepid Christians strove to advance under a perfect hurricane of missiles from the water and the land, but they made slow progress. Barricades thrown across the causeway embarrassed the cavalry, and rendered it nearly useless. The sides of the Indian boats were fortified with bulwarks, which shielded the crews from the arquebuses and crossbows; and, when the warriors on the dike were hard pushed by the pikemen, they threw themselves fearlessly into the water, as if it were their native element, and reappearing along the sides of the dike, shot off their arrows and javelins with fatal execution. After a long and obstinate struggle, the Christians were compelled to fall back on their own quarters with disgrace, and—including the allies—with nearly as much damage as they had inflicted on the enemy. Olid, disgusted with the result of the engagement, inveighed against his companion, as having involved them in it by his wanton temerity, and drew off his forces the next morning to his own station at Cojohuacan.

The camps, separated by only two leagues, maintained an easy communication with each other. They found abundant employment in foraging the neighbouring country for provisions, and in repelling the active sallies of the enemy; on whom they took their revenge by cutting off his supplies. But their own position was precarious, and they looked with impatience for the arrival of the brigantines under Cortés. It was in the latter part of May that Olid took up his quarters at Cojohuacan; and from that time may be dated the commencement of the siege of Mexico.

CHAPTER V

*Indian Flotilla Defeated—Occupation of the Causeways—
Desperate Assaults—Firing of the Palaces—Spirit of the
Besieged—Barracks for the Troops*

1521

No sooner had Cortés received intelligence that his two officers had established themselves in their respective posts, than he ordered Sandoval to march on Iztapalapan. The cavalier's route led him through a country for the most part friendly; and at Chalco his little body of Spaniards was swelled by the formidable muster of Indian levies, who awaited there his approach. After this junction, he continued his march without opposition till he arrived before the hostile city, under whose walls he found a large force drawn up to receive him. A battle followed, and the natives, after maintaining their ground sturdily for some time, were compelled to give way, and to seek refuge either on the water or in that part of the town which hung over it. The remainder was speedily occupied by the Spaniards.

Meanwhile Cortés had set sail with his flotilla, intending to support his lieutenant's attack by water. On drawing near the southern shore of the lake, he passed under the shadow of an insulated peak, since named from him the "Rock of the Marquess." It was held by a body of Indians, who saluted the fleet, as it passed, with showers of stones and arrows. Cortés, resolving to punish their audacity, and to clear the lake of his troublesome enemy, instantly landed with a hundred and fifty of his followers. He placed himself at their head, scaled the steep ascent, in the face of a driving storm of missiles, and, reaching the summit, put the garrison to the sword. There were a number of women and children, also, gathered in the place, whom he spared.

On the top of the eminence was a blazing beacon, serving to notify to the inhabitants of the capital when the Spanish fleet weighed anchor. Before Cortés had regained his brigantine, the canoes and *piraguas* of the enemy had left the harbours of Mexico, and were seen darkening the lake for many a rood. There were several hundred of them, all crowded with warriors, and advancing rapidly by means of their oars over the calm bosom of the waters.

Cortés, who regarded his fleet, to use his own language, as "the key of the war," felt the importance of striking a decisive blow in the first encounter with the enemy. It was with chagrin, therefore, that he found his sails rendered useless by the want of wind. He calmly waited the approach of the Indian squadron, which, however, lay on their oars, at something more than musket-shot distance, as if hesitating to encounter these leviathans of their waters. At this moment, a light air from land rippled the surface of the lake; it gradually freshened into a breeze, and Cortés, taking advantage of the friendly succour, which he may be excused, under all the circumstances, for regarding as especially sent him by Heaven, extended his line of battle, and bore down, under full press of canvas, on the enemy.

The latter no sooner encountered the bows of their formidable opponents, than they were overturned and sent to the bottom by the shock, or so much damaged that they speedily filled and sank. The water was covered with the wreck of broken canoes, and with the bodies of men struggling for life in the waves, and vainly imploring their companions to take them on board their overcrowded vessels. The Spanish fleet, as it dashed through the mob of boats, sent off its volleys to the right and left with a terrible effect, completing the discomfiture of the Aztecs. The latter made no attempt at resistance, scarcely venturing a single flight of arrows, but strove with all their strength to regain the port from which they had so lately issued. They were no match in the chase, any more than in the fight, for their terrible antagonist, who, borne on the wings of the wind, careered to and fro at his pleasure, dealing death widely around him, and making the shores ring with the thunders of his ordnance. A few only of the Indian flotilla succeeded in recovering the port, and, gliding up the canals, found a shelter in the bosom of the city, where the heavier burden of the brigantines made it impossible for them to follow. This victory, more complete than even the sanguine temper of Cortés had prognosticated, proved the superiority of the Spaniards, and left them, henceforth, undisputed masters of the Aztec sea.

It was nearly dusk when the squadron, coasting along the great southern causeway, anchored off the point of junction, called xoloc, where the branch from Cojohuacan meets the principal dike. The avenue widened at this point, so as to afford room for two towers, or turreted temples, built of stone, and surrounded by walls of the same material, which presented altogether a position of some strength, and, at the present moment, was garrisoned by a body of Aztecs. They were not numerous; and Cortés, landing with his soldiers, succeeded without much difficulty in dislodging the enemy, and in getting possession of the works.

It seems to have been originally the general's design to take up his own quarters with Olid at Cojohuacan. But, if so, he now changed his purpose, and wisely fixed on this spot, as the best position for his encampment. It was but half a league distant from the capital; and, while it commanded its great southern avenue, had a direct communication with the garrison at Cojohuacan, through which he might receive supplies from the surrounding country. Here, then, he determined to establish his headquarters. He at once caused his heavy iron cannon to be transferred from the brigantines to the causeway, and sent orders to Olid to join him with half his force, while Sandoval was instructed to abandon his present quarters, and advance to Cojohuacan, whence he was to detach fifty picked men of his infantry to the camp of Cortés. Having made these arrangements, the general busily occupied himself with strengthening the works at Xoloc, and putting them in the best posture of defence.

During the first five or six days after their encampment, the Spaniards experienced much annoyance from the enemy, who too late endeavoured to prevent their taking up a position so near the capital, and which, had they known much of the science of war, they would have taken better care themselves to secure. Contrary to their usual practice, the Indians made their attacks by night as well as by day. The water swarmed with canoes, which hovered at a distance in terror of the brigantines, but still approached near enough, especially under cover of the darkness, to send showers of arrows into the Christian camp, that fell so thick as to hide the surface of the ground, and impede the movements of the soldiers. Others ran along the western side of the causeway, unprotected, as it was, by the Spanish fleet, and plied their archery with such galling effect that the Spaniards were forced to make a temporary breach in the dike, wide enough to admit two of their own smaller vessels, which, passing through, soon obtained an entire command of the interior basin, as they before had of the outer. Still, the bold barbarians, advancing along the causeway, marched up within bow-shot of the Christian ramparts, sending forth such yells and discordant battle-cries that it seemed, in the words of Cortés, "as if heaven and earth were coming together." But they were severely punished for their temerity, as the batteries, which commanded the approaches to the camp, opened a desolating fire that scattered the assailants, and drove them back in confusion to their own quarters.

The two principal avenues to Mexico, those on the south and the west, were now occupied by the Christians. There still remained a third, the great dike of Tepejacac, on the north, which, indeed, taking up the principal street that passed in a direct line through the heart of the city, might be regarded as a continuation of the dike of Iztapalapan. By this northern route a means of escape was still left open to the besieged, and they availed themselves of it, at present, to maintain their communications with the country, and to supply themselves with provisions. Alvarado, who observed this from his station at Tacuba, advised his commander of it, and the latter instructed Sandoval to take up his position on the causeway. That officer, though suffering at the time from a severe wound received from a lance in one of the late skirmishes, hastened to obey; and thus, by shutting up its only communication with the surrounding country, completed the blockade of the capital.

But Cortés was not content to wait patiently the effects of a dilatory blockade, which might exhaust the patience of his allies, and his own resources. He determined to support it by such active assaults on the city as should still further distress the besieged, and hasten the hour of surrender. For this purpose he ordered a simultaneous attack, by the two commanders at the other stations, on the quarters nearest their encampments.

On the day appointed, his forces were under arms with the dawn. Mass, as usual, was performed; and the Indian confederates, as they listened with grave attention to the stately and imposing service, regarded with undisguised admiration the devotional reverence shown by the Christians, whom, in their simplicity, they looked upon as little less than divinities themselves. The Spanish infantry marched in the van, led on by Cortés, attended by a number of cavaliers, dismounted like himself. They had not moved far upon the causeway, when they were brought to a stand by one of the open breaches, that had formerly been traversed by a bridge. On the further side a solid rampart of stone and lime had been erected, and behind this a strong body of Aztecs were posted, who discharged on the Spaniards, as they advanced, a thick volley of arrows. The latter vainly endeavoured to dislodge them with their firearms and crossbows; they were too well secured behind their defences.

Cortés then ordered two of the brigantines, which had kept along, one on each side of the causeway, in order to co-operate with the army, to station themselves so as to enfilade the position occupied by the enemy. Thus placed between two well-directed fires, the Indians were compelled to recede. The soldiers on board the vessels, springing to land, bounded like deer up the sides of the dike. They were soon followed by their countrymen under Cortés, who, throwing themselves into the water, swam the undefended chasm, and joined in pursuit of the enemy. The Mexicans fell back, however, in something like order, till they reached another opening in the dike, like the former, dismantled of its bridge, and fortified in the same manner by a bulwark of stone, behind which the retreating Aztecs, swimming across the chasm, and reinforced by fresh bodies of their countrymen, again took shelter.

They made good their post till, again assailed by the cannonade from the brigantines, they were compelled to give way. In this manner breach after breach was carried, and, at every fresh instance of success, a shout went up from the crews of the vessels, which, answered by the long files of the Spaniards and their confederates on the causeway, made the valley echo to its borders.

Cortés had now reached the end of the great avenue, where it entered the suburbs. There he halted to give time for the rear-guard to come up with him. It was detained by the labour of filling up the breaches in such a manner as to make a practicable passage for the artillery and horse, and to secure one for the rest of the army on its retreat. This important duty was intrusted to the allies, who executed it by tearing down the ramparts on the margins, and throwing them into the chasms, and, when this was not sufficient—for the water was deep around the southern causeway—by dislodging the great stones and rubbish from the dike itself, which was broad enough to admit of it, and adding them to the pile, until it was raised above the level of the water.

The street on which the Spaniards now entered was the great avenue that intersected the town from north to south, and the same by which they had first visited the capital. It was broad and perfectly straight, and, in the distance, dark masses of warriors might be seen gathering to the support of their countrymen, who were prepared to dispute the further progress of the Spaniards. The sides were lined with buildings, the terraced roofs of which were also crowded with combatants, who, as the army advanced, poured down a pitiless storm of missiles on their heads, which glanced harmless, indeed, from the coat of mail, but too often found their way through the more common *escaupil* of the soldier, already

gaping with many a ghastly rent. Cortés, to rid himself of this annoyance
for the future, ordered his Indian pioneers to level the principal buildings, as they advanced; in which work of demolition, no less than in the
repair of the breaches, they proved of inestimable service.

The Spaniards, meanwhile, were steadily, but slowly, advancing, as
the enemy recoiled before the rolling fire of musketry, though turning at
intervals to discharge their javelins and arrows against their pursuers. In
this way they kept along the great street, until their course was interrupted by a wide ditch or canal, once traversed by a bridge, of which
only a few planks now remained. These were broken by the Indians the
moment they had crossed, and a formidable array of spears was instantly
seen bristling over the summit of a solid rampart of stone, which protected the opposite side of the canal. Cortés was no longer supported by
his brigantines, which the shallowness of the canals prevented from penetrating into the suburbs. He brought forward his arquebusiers, who, protected by the targets of their comrades, opened a fire on the enemy. But
the balls fell harmless from the bulwarks of stone; while the assailants
presented but too easy a mark to their opponents.

The general then caused the heavy guns to be brought up, and opened
a lively cannonade, which soon cleared a breach in the works, through
which the musketeers and crossbow-men poured in their volleys thick
as hail. The Indians now gave way in disorder, after having held their
antagonists at bay for two hours. The latter, jumping into the shallow
water, scaled the opposite bank without further resistance, and drove
the enemy along the street towards the square, where the sacred
pyramid reared its colossal bulk high over the other edifices of the city.

It was a spot too familiar to the Spaniards. On one side stood the
palace of Axayacatl, their old quarters, the scene to many of them
of so much suffering. Opposite was the pile of low, irregular buildings,
once the residence of the unfortunate Montezuma; while the third side
of the square was flanked by the *Coatepantli,* or Wall of Serpents,
which encompassed the great *teocalli* with its little city of holy edifices.
The Spaniards halted at the entrance of the square, as if oppressed, and
for a moment overpowered, by the bitter recollections that crowded on
their minds. But their intrepid leader, impatient at their hesitation,
loudly called on them to advance before the Aztecs had time to rally;
and grasping his target in one hand, and waving his sword high above
his head with the other, he cried his war-cry of "St. Jago," and led
them at once against the enemy.

The Mexicans, intimidated by the presence of their detested foe, who, in spite of all their efforts had again forced his way into the heart of their city, made no further resistance, but retreated, or rather fled, for refuge into the sacred inclosure of the *teocalli,* where the numerous buildings scattered over its ample area afforded many good points of defence. A few priests, clad in their usual wild and blood-stained vestments, were to be seen lingering on the terraces which wound round the stately sides of the pyramid, chanting hymns in honour of their god, and encouraging the warriors below to battle bravely for his altars.

The Spaniards poured through the open gates into the area, and a small party rushed up the winding corridors to its summit. No vestige now remained there of the Cross, or of any other symbol of the pure faith to which it had been dedicated. A new effigy of the Aztec war-god had taken the place of the one demolished by the Christians, and raised its fantastic and hideous form in the same niche which had been occupied by its predecessor. The Spaniards soon tore away its golden mask and the rich jewels with which it was bedizened, and hurling the struggling priests down the sides of the pyramid, made the best of their way to their comrades in the area. It was full time.

The Aztecs, indignant at the sacrilegious outrage perpetrated before their eyes, and gathering courage from the inspiration of the place, under the very presence of their deities, raised a yell of horror and vindictive fury, as, throwing themselves into something like order, they sprang, by a common impulse, on the Spaniards. The latter, who had halted near the entrance, though taken by surprise, made an effort to maintain their position at the gateway. But in vain; for the headlong rush of the assailants drove them at once into the square, where they were attacked by other bodies of Indians, pouring in from the neighbouring streets. Broken, and losing their presence of mind, the troops made no attempt to rally, but, crossing the square, and abandoning the cannon planted there to the enemy, they hurried down the great street of Iztapalapan. Here they were soon mingled with the allies, who choked up the way, and who, catching the panic of the Spaniards, increased the confusion, while the eyes of the fugitives, blinded by the missiles that rained on them from the *azoteas,* were scarcely capable of distinguishing friend from foe. In vain Cortés endeavoured to stay the torrent, and to restore order. His voice was drowned in the wild uproar, as he was swept away, like driftwood, by the fury of the current.

All seemed to be lost—when suddenly sounds were heard in an adjoining street, like the distant tramp of horses galloping rapidly over the pavement. They drew nearer and nearer, and a body of cavalry soon emerged on the great square. Though but a handful in number, they plunged boldly into the thick of the enemy. We have often had occasion to notice the superstitious dread entertained by the Indians of the horse and his rider. And, although the long residence of the cavalry in the capital had familiarised the natives, in some measure, with their presence, so long a time had now elapsed since they had beheld them, that all their former mysterious terrors revived in full force; and, when thus suddenly assailed in flank by the formidable apparition, they were seized with a panic, and fell into confusion. It soon spread to the leading files, and Cortés, perceiving his advantage, turned with the rapidity of lightning, and, at this time supported by his followers, succeeded in driving the enemy with some loss back into the inclosure.

It was now the hour of vespers, and, as night must soon overtake them, he made no further attempt to pursue his advantage. Ordering the trumpets, therefore, to sound a retreat, he drew off his forces in good order, taking with him the artillery which had been abandoned in the square. The allies first went off the ground, followed by the Spanish infantry, while the rear was protected by the horse, thus reversing the order of march on their entrance. The Aztecs hung on the closing files, and though driven back by frequent charges of the cavalry, still followed in the distance, shooting off their ineffectual missiles, and filling the air with wild cries and howlings, like a herd of ravenous wolves disappointed of their prey. It was late before the army reached its quarters at Xoloc.

Cortés had been well supported by Alvarado and Sandoval in this assault on the city; though neither of these commanders had penetrated the suburbs, deterred, perhaps, by the difficulties of the passage, which, in Alvarado's case, were greater than those presented to Cortés, from the greater number of breaches with which the dike in his quarter was intersected. Something was owing, too, to the want of brigantines, until Cortés supplied the deficiency by detaching half of his little navy to the support of his officers. Without their co-operation, however, the general himself could not have advanced so far, nor, perhaps, have succeeded at all in setting foot within the city. The success of this assault spread consternation, not only among the Mexicans, but their vassals, as they saw that the formidable preparations for defence were to avail little against the white man, who had so soon, in spite of them, forced his way into the very heart of the capital. Several of the neighbouring places, in consequence, now showed a willingness to shake off their allegiance, and claimed the protection of the Spaniards. Among these were the territory of Xochimilco, so roughly treated by the invaders, and some tribes of Otomies, a rude but valiant people, who dwelt on the western confines of the valley. Their support was valuable, not so much from the additional reinforcements which it brought, as from the greater security it gave to the army, whose outposts were perpetually menaced by these warlike barbarians.

The most important aid which the Spaniards received at this time was from Tezcuco, whose prince, Ixtlilxochitl, gathered the whole strength of his levies, to the number of fifty thousand, if we are to credit Cortés, and led them in person to the Christian camp. By the general's orders they were distributed among the three divisions of the besiegers.

Thus strengthened, Cortés prepared to make another attack upon the capital, and that before it should have time to recover from the former. Orders were given to his lieutenants on the other causeways, to march at the same time, and co-operate with him, as before, in the assault. It was conducted in precisely the same manner as on the previous entry, the infantry taking the van, and the allies and cavalry following. But, to the great dismay of the Spaniards, they found two-thirds of the breaches restored to their former state, and the stones and other materials, with which they had been stopped, removed by the indefatigable enemy. They were again obliged to bring up the cannon, the brigantines ran alongside, and the enemy was dislodged, and driven from post to post, in the same manner as on the preceding attack. In short, the whole work was to be done over again. It was not till an hour after noon that the army had won a footing in the suburbs.

Here their progress was not so difficult as before; for the buildings from the terraces of which they had experienced the most annoyance had been swept away. Still it was only step by step that they forced a passage in face of the Mexican militia, who disputed their advance with the same spirit as before. Cortés, who would willingly have spared the inhabitants, if he could have brought them to terms, saw them with regret, as he says, thus desperately bent on a war of extermination. He conceived that there would be no way more likely to affect their minds, than by destroying at once some of the principal edifices, which they were accustomed to venerate as the pride and ornament of the city.

Marching into the great square, he selected, as the first to be destroyed, the old palace of Axayacatl, his former barracks. The ample range of low buildings was, it is true, constructed of stone; but the interior, as well as the outworks, its turrets, and roofs, were of wood. The Spaniards, whose associations with the pile were of so gloomy a character, sprang to the work of destruction with a satisfaction like that which the French mob may have felt in the demolition of the Bastile. Torches and fire-brands were thrown about in all directions; the lower parts of the building were speedily on fire, which, running along the inflammable hangings and woodwork of the interior, rapidly spread to the second floor. There the element took freer range, and, before it was visible from without, sent up from every aperture and crevice a dense column of vapour, that hung like a funereal pall over the city. This was dissipated by a bright sheet of flame, which enveloped all the upper regions of the vast pile, till, the supporters giving way, the wide range of turreted chambers fell, amidst clouds of dust and ashes, with an appalling crash that for a moment stayed the Spaniards in the work of devastation.

It was but for a moment. On the other side of the square, adjoining Montezuma's residence, were several buildings, as the reader is aware, appropriated to animals. One of these was now marked for destruction—the House of Birds, filled with specimens of all the painted varieties which swarmed over the wide forests of Mexico. It was an airy and elegant building, after the Indian fashion, and, viewed in connection with its object, was undoubtedly a remarkable proof of refinement and intellectual taste in a barbarous monarch. Its light, combustible materials of wood and bamboo formed a striking contrast to the heavy stone edifices round it, and made it obviously convenient for the present purpose of the invaders. The torches were applied, and the fanciful structure was soon wrapped in flames that sent their baleful splendours far and wide over city and lake. Its feathered inhabitants either perished in the fire, or those of stronger wing, bursting the burning lattice-work of the aviary, soared high into the air, and, fluttering for a while over the devoted city, fled with loud screams to their native forests beyond the mountains.

The Aztecs gazed with inexpressible horror on this destruction of the venerable abode of their monarchs, and of the monuments of their luxury and splendour. Their rage was exasperated almost to madness, as they beheld their hated foes, the Tlascalans, busy in the work of

desolation, and aided by the Tezcucans, their own allies, and not unfrequently their kinsmen. They vented their fury in bitter execrations,
especially on the young prince Ixtlilxochitl, who, marching side by side
with Cortés, took his full share in the dangers of the day. The warriors
from the housetops poured the most opprobrious epithets on him as he
passed, denouncing him as a false-hearted traitor; false to his country
and his blood—reproaches not altogether unmerited, as his kinsman,
who chronicles the circumstance, candidly confesses. He gave little heed
to their taunts, however, holding on his way with the dogged resolution
of one true to the cause in which he was embarked; and, when he
entered the great square, he grappled with the leader of the Aztec forces,
wrenched a lance from his grasp, won by the latter from the Christians,
and dealt him a blow with his mace, or *maquahuitl,* which brought him
lifeless to the ground.

The Spanish commander, having accomplished the work of destruction, sounded a retreat, sending on the Indian allies, who blocked up
the way before him. The Mexicans, maddened by their losses, in wild
transports of fury hung close on his rear, and though driven back by
the cavalry, still returned, throwing themselves desperately under the
horses, striving to tear the riders from their saddles, and content to
throw away their own lives for one blow at their enemy. Fortunately
the greater part of their militia was engaged with the assailants on the
opposite quarters of the city; but, thus crippled, they pushed the
Spaniards under Cortés so vigorously that few reached the camp that
night without bearing on their bodies some token of the desperate
conflict.

On the following day, and, indeed, on several days following, the
general repeated his assaults with as little care for repose, as if he
and his men had been made of iron. On one occasion he advanced some
way down the street of Tacuba, in which he carried three of the
bridges, desirous, if possible, to open a communication with Alvarado,
posted on the contiguous causeway. But the Spaniards in that quarter
had not penetrated beyond the suburbs, still impeded by the severe
character of the ground, and wanting, it may be, somewhat of that fiery
impetuosity which the soldier feels who fights under the eyes of his chief.

In each of these assaults, the breaches were found more or less restored to their original state by the pertinacious Mexicans, and the materials, which had been deposited in them with so much labour, again
removed. It may seem strange that Cortés did not take measures to

guard against the repetition of an act which caused so much delay and embarrassment to his operations. He notices this in his letter to the emperor, in which he says that to do so would have required either that he should have established his quarters in the city itself, which would have surrounded him with enemies, and cut off his communications with the country; or that he should have posted a sufficient guard of Spaniards—for the natives were out of the question—to protect the breaches by night, a duty altogether beyond the strength of men engaged in so arduous a service through the day.

Yet this was the course adopted by Alvarado; who stationed, at night, a guard of forty soldiers for the defence of the opening nearest to the enemy. This was relieved by a similar detachment in a few hours, and this again by a third, the two former still lying on their post; so that, on an alarm, a body of one hundred and twenty soldiers was ready on the spot to repel an attack. Sometimes, indeed, the whole division took up their bivouac in the neighbourhood of the breach, resting on their arms, and ready for instant action.

But a life of such incessant toil and vigilance was almost too severe even for the stubborn constitutions of the Spaniards. "Through the long night," exclaims Diaz, who served in Alvarado's division, "we kept our dreary watch; neither wind, nor wet, nor cold availing anything. There we stood, smarting, as we were, from the wounds we had received in the fight of the preceding day." It was the rainy season, which continues in that country from July to September; and the surface of the causeways, flooded by the storms, and broken up by the constant movement of such large bodies of men, was converted into a marsh, or rather quagmire, which added inconceivably to the distresses of the army.

The troops under Cortés were scarcely in a better situation. But few of them could find shelter in the rude towers that garnished the works of Xoloc. The greater part were compelled to bivouac in the open air, exposed to all the inclemency of the weather. Every man, unless his wounds prevented it, was required by the camp regulations to sleep on his arms; and they were often roused from their hasty slumbers by the midnight call to battle. For Guatemozin, contrary to the usual practice of his countrymen, frequently selected the hours of darkness to aim a blow at the enemy. "In short," exclaims the veteran soldier above quoted, "so unintermitting were our engagements, by day and by night, during the three months in which we lay before the capital, that to recount them all would but exhaust the reader's patience, and make him to fancy he was perusing the incredible feats of a knight errant of romance."

The Aztec emperor conducted his operations on a systematic plan, which showed some approach to military science. He not unfrequently made simultaneous attacks on the three several divisions of the Spaniards established on the causeways, and on the garrisons at their extremities. To accomplish this, he enforced the service not merely of his own militia of the capital, but of the great towns in the neighbourhood, who all moved in concert, at the well-known signal of the beacon-fire, or of the huge drum struck by the priests on the summit of the temple. One of these general attacks, it was observed, whether from accident or design, took place on the eve of St. John the Baptist, the anniversary of the day on which the Spaniards made their second entry into the Mexican capital.

Notwithstanding the severe drain on his forces by this incessant warfare, the young monarch contrived to relieve them in some degree by different detachments, who took the place of one another. This was apparent from the different uniforms and military badges of the Indian battalions, who successively came and disappeared from the field. At night a strict guard was maintained in the Aztec quarters, a thing not common with the nations of the plateau. The outposts of the hostile armies were stationed within sight of each other. That of the Mexicans was usually placed in the neighbourhood of some wide breach, and its position was marked by a large fire in front. The hours for relieving guard were intimated by the shrill Aztec whistle, while bodies of men might be seen moving behind the flame, which threw a still ruddier glow over the cinnamon-coloured skins of the warriors.

While thus active on land, Guatemozin was not idle on the water. He was too wise, indeed, to cope with the Spanish navy again in open battle; but he resorted to stratagem, so much more congenial to Indian warfare. He placed a large number of canoes in ambuscade among the tall reeds which fringed the southern shores of the lake, and caused piles, at the same time, to be driven into the neighbouring shallows. Several *piraguas,* or boats of a larger size, then issued forth, and rowed near the spot where the Spanish brigantines were moored. Two of the smallest vessels, supposing the Indian barks were conveying provisions to the besieged, instantly stood after them, as had been foreseen. The Aztec boats fled for shelter to the reedy thicket, where their companions lay in ambush. The Spaniards, following, were soon entangled among the palisades under the water. They were instantly surrounded by the whole swarm of Indian canoes, most of the men were wounded, several, including the two commanders, slain, and one of the brigantines fell—a useless prize—into the hands of the victors. Among the slain was Pedro Barba, captain of the crossbow-men, a gallant officer, who had highly distinguished himself in the Conquest. This disaster occasioned much mortification to Cortés. It was a salutary lesson that stood him in good stead during the remainder of the war.

Thus the contest was waged by land and by water—on the causeway, the city, and the lake. Whatever else might fail, the capital of the Aztec empire was true to itself; and, mindful of its ancient renown, opposed a bold front to its enemies in every direction. As in a body, whose extremities have been struck with death, life still rallied in the heart, and seemed to beat there for the time, with even a more vigorous pulsation than ever.

It may appear extraordinary that Guatemozin should have been able to provide for the maintenance of the crowded population now gathered in the metropolis, especially as the avenues were all in the possession of the besieging army. But, independently of the preparations made with this view before the siege and of the loathsome sustenance daily furnished by the victims for sacrifice, supplies were constantly obtained from the surrounding country across the lake. This was so conducted, for a time, as in a great measure to escape observation; and even when the brigantines were commanded to cruise day and night, and sweep the waters of the boats employed in this service, many still contrived, under cover of the darkness, to elude the vigilance of the cruisers, and brought their cargoes into port. It was not till the great towns in the neighbourhood cast off their allegiance that the supply began to fail, from the failure of its sources. This defection was more frequent, as the inhabitants became convinced that the government, incompetent to its own defence, must be still more so to theirs: and the Aztec metropolis saw its great vassals fall off, one after another, as the tree, over which decay is stealing, parts with its leaves at the first blast of the tempest.

The cities, which now claimed the Spanish general's protection, supplied the camp with an incredible number of warriors; a number which, if we admit Cortés' own estimate, one hundred and fifty thousand, could have only served to embarrass his operations on the long extended causeways. Yet it is true that the valley, teeming with towns and villages, swarmed with a population—and one, too, in which every man was a warrior—greatly exceeding that of the present day. These levies were distributed among the three garrisons at the terminations of the causeways; and many found active employment in foraging the country for provisions, and yet more in carrying on hostilities against the places still unfriendly to the Spaniards.

Cortés found further occupation for them in the construction of barracks for his troops, who suffered greatly from exposure to the incessant rains of the season, which were observed to fall more heavily by night than by day. Quantities of stone and timber were obtained from the buildings that had been demolished in the city. They were transported in the brigantines to the causeway, and from these materials a row of huts or barracks was constructed, extending on either side of the works of Xoloc. It may give some idea of the great breadth of the causeway at this place, one of the deepest parts of the lake, to add that, although the barracks were erected in parallel lines on the opposite sides of it, there still remained space enough for the army to defile between.

By this arrangement, ample accommodations were furnished for the Spanish troops and their Indian attendants, amounting in all to about two thousand. The great body of the allies, with a small detachment of horse and infantry, were quartered at the neighbouring post of Cojohuacan, which served to protect the rear of the encampment, and to maintain its communications with the country. A similar disposition of forces took place in the other divisions of the army, under Alvarado and Sandoval, though the accommodations provided for the shelter of the troops on their causeways were not so substantial as those for the division of Cortés.

The Spanish camp was supplied with provisions from the friendly towns in the neighbourhood, and especially from Tezcuco. They consisted of fish, the fruits of the country, particularly a sort of fig borne by the *tuna* (*cactus opuntia*), and a species of cherry, or something much resembling it, which grew abundant at this season. But their principal food was the *tortillas,* cakes of Indian meal, still common in Mexico, for which bakehouses were established, under the care of the natives, in the garrison towns commanding the causeways. The allies, as appears too probable, reinforced their frugal fare with an occasional banquet on human flesh, for which the battlefield unhappily afforded them too much facility, and which, however shocking to the feelings of Cortés, he did not consider himself in a situation at that moment to prevent.

Thus the tempest, which had been so long mustering, broke at length in all its fury on the Aztec capital. Its unhappy inmates beheld the hostile legions encompassing them about with their glittering files stretching as far as the eye could reach. They saw themselves deserted by their allies and vassals in their utmost need; the fierce stranger penetrating into their secret places, violating their temples, plundering their palaces, wasting the fair city by day, firing its suburbs by night, and intrenching himself in solid edifices under their walls, as if determined never to withdraw his foot while one stone remained upon another. All this they saw, yet their spirits were unbroken; and, though famine and pestilence were beginning to creep over them, they still showed the same determined front to their enemies. Cortés, who would gladly have spared the town and its inhabitants, beheld this resolution with astonishment. He intimated more than once, by means of the prisoners whom he released, his willingness to grant them fair terms of capitulation. Day after day, he fully expected his proffers would be accepted. But day after day he was disappointed. He had yet to learn how tenacious was the memory of the Aztecs; and that, whatever might be the horrors of their present situation, and their fears for the future, they were all forgotten in their hatred of the white man.

CHAPTER VI

General Assault on the City—Defeat of the Spaniards—Their Disastrous Condition—Sacrifice of the Captives—Defection of the Allies—Constancy of the Troops

1521

FAMINE was now gradually working its way into the heart of the beleaguered city. It seemed certain that, with this strict blockade, the crowded population must in the end be driven to capitulate, though no arm should be raised against them. But it required time; and the Spaniards, though constant and enduring by nature, began to be impatient of hardships scarcely inferior to those experienced by the besieged. In some respects their condition was even worse, exposed, as they were, to the cold, drenching rains, which fell with little intermission, rendering their situation dreary and disastrous in the extreme.

In this state of things there were many who would willingly have shortened their sufferings, and taken the chance of carrying the place by a *coup de main*. Others thought it would be best to get possession of the great market of Tlatelolco, which, from its situation in the northwestern part of the city, might afford the means of communication with the camps of both Alvarado and Sandoval. This place, encompassed by spacious porticos, would furnish accommodations for a numerous host; and, once established in the capital, the Spaniards would be in a position to follow up the blow with far more effect than at a distance.

These arguments were pressed by several of the officers, particularly by Alderete, the royal treasurer, a person of much consideration, not only from his rank, but from the capacity and zeal he had shown in the service. In deference to their wishes, Cortés summoned a council of war, and laid the matter before it. The treasurer's views were espoused by most of the high-mettled cavaliers, who looked with eagerness to any change of their present forlorn and wearisome life; and Cortés, thinking it probably more prudent to adopt the less expedient course, than to enforce a cold and reluctant obedience to his own opinion, suffered himself to be overruled.

A day was fixed for the assault, which was to be made simultaneously by the two divisions under Alvarado and the commander-in-chief. Sandoval was instructed to draw off the greater part of his forces from the northern causeway, and to unite himself with Alvarado, while seventy picked soldiers were to be detached to the support of Cortés.

On the appointed morning, the two armies, after the usual celebration of Mass, advanced along their respective causeways against the city. They were supported, in addition to the brigantines, by a numerous fleet of Indian boats, which were to force a passage up the canals, and by a countless multitude of allies, whose very numbers served in the end to embarrass their operations. After clearing the suburbs, three avenues presented themselves, which all terminated in the square of Tlatelolco. The principal one, being of much greater width than the other two, might rather be called a causeway than a street, since it was flanked by deep canals on either side. Cortés divided his force into three bodies. One of them he placed under Alderete, with orders to occupy the principal street. A second he gave in charge to Andrés de Tapia and Jorge de Alvarado; the former a cavalier of courage and capacity, the latter a younger brother of Don Pedro, and possessed of the intrepid spirit which belonged to that chivalrous family. These were to penetrate by one of the parallel streets, while the general himself, at the head of the third division, was to occupy the other. A small body of cavalry, with two or three field-pieces, was stationed as a reserve in front of the great street of Tacuba, which was designated as the rallying point for the different divisions.

Cortés gave the most positive instructions to his captains not to advance a step without securing the means of retreat, by carefully filling up the ditches, and the openings in the causeway. The neglect of this precaution by Alvarado, in an assault which he had made on the city but a few days before, had been attended with such serious consequences to his army that Cortés rode over, himself, to his officer's quarters, for the purpose of publicly reprimanding him for his disobedience of orders. On his arrival at the camp, however, he found that his offending captain had conducted the affair with so much gallantry that the intended reprimand—though well deserved—subsided into a mild rebuke.

The arrangements being completed, the three divisions marched at once up the several streets. Cortés, dismounting, took the van of his own squadron, at the head of his infantry. The Mexicans fell back as he advanced, making less resistance than usual. The Spaniards pushed on, carrying one barricade after another, and carefully filling up the gaps with rubbish, so as to secure themselves a footing. The canoes supported the attack, by moving along the canals, and grappling with those of the enemy; while numbers of the nimble-footed Tlascalans, scaling the terraces, passed on from one house to another, where they were connected, hurling the defenders into the streets below. The enemy, taken apparently by surprise, seemed incapable of withstanding for a moment the fury of the assault; and the victorious Christians, cheered on by the shouts of triumph which arose from their companions in the adjoining streets, were only the more eager to be first at the destined goal.

Indeed, the facility of his success led the general to suspect that he might be advancing too fast; that it might be a device of the enemy to draw them into the heart of the city, and then surround or attack them in the rear. He had some misgivings, moreover, lest his too ardent officers, in the heat of the chase, should, notwithstanding his commands, have overlooked the necessary precaution of filling up the breaches. He accordingly brought his squadron to a halt, prepared to baffle any insidious movement of his adversary. Meanwhile he received more than one message from Alderete, informing him that he had nearly gained the market. This only increased the general's apprehension that, in the rapidity of his advance, he might have neglected to secure the ground. He determined to trust no eyes but his own, and, taking a small body of troops, proceeded at once to reconnoitre the route followed by the treasurer.

He had not proceeded far along the great street, or causeway, when his progress was arrested by an opening ten or twelve paces wide, and filled with water, at least two fathoms deep, by which a communication was formed between the canals on the opposite sides. A feeble attempt had been made to stop the gap with the rubbish of the causeway, but in too careless a manner to be of the least service; and a few straggling stones and pieces of timber only showed that the work had been abandoned almost as soon as begun. To add to his consternation, the general observed that the sides of the causeway in this neighbourhood had been pared off, and, as was evident, very recently. He saw in all this the artifice of the cunning enemy; and had little doubt that his hot-headed officer had rushed into a snare deliberately laid for him. Deeply alarmed, he set about repairing the mischief as fast as possible, by ordering his men to fill up the yawning chasm.

But they had scarcely begun their labours, when the hoarse echoes of conflict in the distance were succeeded by a hideous sound of mingled yells and war-whoops that seemed to rend the very heavens. This was followed by a rushing noise, as of the tread of thronging multitudes, showing that the tide of battle was turned back from its former course, and was rolling on towards the spot where Cortés and his little band of cavaliers were planted.

His conjecture proved too true. Alderete had followed the retreating Aztecs with an eagerness which increased with every step of his advance. He had carried the barricades, which had defended the breach, without much difficulty, and, as he swept on, gave orders that the opening should be stopped. But the blood of the high-spirited cavaliers was warmed by the chase, and no one cared to be detained by the ignoble occupation of filling up the ditches, while he could gather laurels so easily in the fight; and they all pressed on, exhorting and cheering one another with the assurance of being the first to reach the square of Tlatelolco. In this way they suffered themselves to be decoyed into the heart of the city; when suddenly the horn of Guatemozin—the sacred symbol, heard only in seasons of extraordinary peril—sent forth a long and piercing note from the summit of a neighbouring *teocalli*. In an instant, the flying Aztecs, as if maddened by the blast, wheeled about, and turned on their pursuers. At the same time, countless swarms of warriors from the adjoining streets and lanes poured in upon the flanks of the assailants, filling the air with the fierce, unearthly cries which had reached the ears of Cortés, and drowning, for a moment, the wild dissonance which reigned in the other quarters of the capital.

The army, taken by surprise, and shaken by the fury of the assault, were thrown into the utmost disorder. Friends and foes, white men and Indians, were mingled together in one promiscuous mass; spears, swords, and war-clubs were brandished together in the air. Blows fell at random. In their eagerness to escape, they trod down one another. Blinded by the missiles, which now rained on them from the *azoteas,* they staggered on, scarcely knowing in what direction, or fell, struck down by hands which they could not see. On they came like a rushing torrent sweeping along some steep declivity, and rolling in one confused tide towards the open breach, on the further side of which stood Cortés and his companions, horror-struck at the sight of the approaching ruin. The foremost files soon plunged into the gulf, treading one another under the flood, some striving ineffectually to swim, others, with more success, to clamber over the heaps of their suffocated comrades. Many, as they attempted to scale the opposite sides of the slippery dike, fell into the water, or were hurried off by the warriors in the canoes, who added to the horrors of the rout by the fresh storm of darts and javelins which they poured on the fugitives.

Cortés, meanwhile, with his brave followers, kept his station undaunted on the other side of the breach. "I had made up my mind," he says, "to die rather than desert my poor followers in their extremity!" With outstretched hands he endeavoured to rescue as many as he could from the watery grave, and from the more appalling fate of captivity. He as vainly tried to restore something like presence of mind and order among the distracted fugitives. His person was too well known to the Aztecs, and his position now made him a conspicuous mark for their weapons. Darts, stones, and arrows fell around him as thick as hail, but glanced harmless from his steel helmet and armour of proof. At length a cry of "Malintzin, Malintzin!" arose among the enemy; and six of their number, strong and athletic warriors, rushing on him at once, made a violent effort to drag him on board their boat. In the struggle he received a severe wound in the leg, which, for the time, disabled it. There seemed to be no hope for him; when a faithful follower, Christoval de Olea, perceiving his general's extremity, threw himself on the Aztecs, and with a blow cut off the arm of one savage, and then plunged his sword in the body of another. He was quickly supported by a comrade named Lerma, and by a Tlascalan chief, who, fighting over the prostrate body of Cortés, despatched three more of the assailants, though the heroic Olea paid dearly for his self-devotion, as he fell mortally wounded by the side of his general.

The report soon spread among the soldiers that their commander was taken; and Quiñones, the captain of his guard, with several others pouring in to the rescue, succeeded in disentangling Cortés from the grasp of his enemies who were struggling with him in the water, and raising him in their arms, placed him again on the causeway. One of his pages,

meanwhile, had advanced some way through the press, leading a horse
for his master to mount. But the youth received a wound in the throat
from a javelin, which prevented him from effecting his object. Another
of his attendants was more successful. It was Guzman, his chamberlain;
but, as he held the bridle, while Cortés was assisted into the saddle, he
was snatched away by the Aztecs, and with the swiftness of thought,
hurried off by their canoes. The general still lingered, unwilling to leave
the spot, whilst his presence could be of the least service. But the
faithful Quiñones, taking his horse by the bridle, turned his head from
the breach, exclaiming at the same time that his master's life was "too
important to the army to be thrown away there."

Yet it was no easy matter to force a passage through the press. The
surface of the causeway, cut up by the feet of men and horses, was knee-
deep in mud, and in some parts was so much broken, that the water
from the canals flowed over it. The crowded mass, in their efforts to
extricate themselves from their perilous position, staggered to and fro
like a drunken man. Those on the flanks were often forced by the lateral
pressure of their comrades down the slippery sides of the dike, where
they were picked up by the canoes of the enemy; whose shouts of triumph
proclaimed the savage joy with which they gathered in every new victim
for the sacrifice. Two cavaliers, riding by the general's side, lost their
footing, and rolled down the declivity into the water. One was taken and
his horse killed; the other was happy enough to escape. The valiant
ensign, Corral, had a similar piece of good fortune. He slipped into the
canal, and the enemy felt sure of their prize, when he again succeeded
in recovering the causeway with the tattered banner of Castile still flying
above his head. The barbarians set up a cry of disappointed rage, as they
lost possession of a trophy, to which the people of Anahuac attached, as
we have seen, the highest importance, hardly inferior in their eyes to the
capture of the commander-in-chief himself.

Cortés at length succeeded in regaining the firm ground, and reaching
the open place before the great street of Tacuba. Here, under a sharp fire
of the artillery, he rallied his broken squadrons, and charging at the head
of the little body of horse, which, not having been brought into action,
were still fresh, he beat off the enemy. He then commanded the retreat
of the two other divisions. The scattered forces again united; and the
general, sending forward his Indian confederates, took the rear with a
chosen body of cavalry to cover the retreat of the army, which was
effected with but little additional loss.

Andrés de Tapia was despatched to the western causeway to acquaint Alvarado and Sandoval with the failure of the enterprise. Meanwhile the two captains had penetrated far into the city. Cheered by the triumphant shouts of their countrymen in the adjacent streets, they had pushed on with extraordinary vigour, that they might not be outstripped in the race of glory. They had almost reached the market-place, which lay nearer to their quarters than to the general's, when they heard the blast from the dread horn of Guatemozin, followed by the overpowering yell of the barbarians, which had so startled the ears of Cortés; till at length the sounds of the receding conflict died away in the distance. The two captains now understood that the day must have gone hard with their countrymen. They soon had further proof of it, when the victorious Aztecs, returning from the pursuit of Cortés, joined their forces to those engaged with Sandoval and Alvarado, and fell on them with redoubled fury. At the same time they rolled on the ground two or three of the bloody heads of the Spaniards, shouting the name of "Malintzin." The captains, struck with horror at the spectacle—though they gave little credit to the words of the enemy—instantly ordered a retreat. Indeed, it was not in their power to maintain their ground against the furious assaults of the besieged, who poured on them swarm after swarm, with a desperation, of which, says one who was there, "although it seems as if it were now present to my eyes, I can give but a faint idea to the reader. God alone could have brought us off safe from the perils of that day." The fierce barbarians followed up the Spaniards to their very intrenchments. But here they were met, first by the cross fire of the brigantines, which, dashing through the palisades planted to obstruct their movements, completely enfiladed the causeway, and next by that of the small battery erected in front of the camp, which, under the management of a skilful engineer, named Medrano, swept the whole length of the defile. Thus galled in front and on flank, the shattered columns of the Aztecs were compelled to give way and take shelter under the defences of the city.

The greatest anxiety now prevailed in the camp, regarding the fate of Cortés; for Tapia had been detained on the road by scattered parties of the enemy, whom Guatemozin had stationed there to interrupt the communications between the camps. He arrived, at length, however, though bleeding from several wounds. His intelligence, while it reassured the Spaniards as to the general's personal safety, was not calculated to allay their uneasiness in other respects.

Sandoval, in particular, was desirous to acquaint himself with the actual state of things, and the further intentions of Cortés. Suffering as he was from three wounds, which he had received in that day's fight, he resolved to visit in person the quarters of the commander-in-chief. It was midday—for the busy scenes of the morning had occupied but a few hours—when Sandoval remounted the good steed, on whose strength and speed he knew he could rely. It was a noble animal, well known throughout the army, and worthy of its gallant rider, whom it had carried safe through all the long marches and bloody battles of the Conquest. On the way he fell in with Guatemozin's scouts, who gave him chase, and showered around him volleys of missiles, which fortunately found no vulnerable point in his own harness, or that of his well-barbed charger.

On arriving at the camp, he found the troops there much worn and dispirited by the disaster of the morning. They had good reason to be so. Besides the killed, and a long file of wounded, sixty-two Spaniards, with a multitude of allies, had fallen alive into the hands of the enemy—an enemy who was never known to spare a captive. The loss of two field-pieces and seven horses crowned their own disgrace and the triumphs of the Aztecs. This loss, so insignificant in European warfare, was a great one here, where both horses and artillery, the most powerful arms of war against the barbarians, were not to be procured without the greatest cost and difficulty.

Cortés, it was observed, had borne himself throughout this trying day with his usual trepidity and coolness. The only time he was seen to falter was when the Mexicans threw down before him the heads of several Spaniards, shouting at the same time, "Sandoval," "Tonatiuh," the well-known epithet of Alvarado. At the sight of the gory trophies he grew deadly pale—but, in a moment recovering his usual confidence, he endeavoured to cheer up the drooping spirits of his followers. It was with a cheerful countenance that he now received his lieutenant; but a shade of sadness was visible through this outward composure, showing how the catastrophe of the *puente cuidada,* "the sorrowful bridge," as he mournfully called it, lay heavy at his heart.

To the cavalier's anxious inquiries, as to the cause of the disaster, he replied: "It is for my sins that it has befallen me, son Sandoval"; for such was the affectionate epithet with which Cortés often addressed his best-beloved and trusty officer. He then explained to him the immediate cause, in the negligence of the treasurer. Further conversation followed, in which the general declared his purpose to forego active hostilities for a few days. "You must take my place," he continued, "for I am too much crippled at present to discharge my duties. You must watch over the safety of the camps. Give especial heed to Alvarado's. He is a gallant soldier, I know it well; but I doubt the Mexican hounds may, some hour, take him at disadvantage." These few words showed the general's own estimate of his two lieutenants; both equally brave and chivalrous; but the one uniting with these qualities the circumspection so essential to success in perilous enterprises, in which the other was signally deficient. The future conqueror of Guatemala had to gather wisdom, as usual, from the bitter fruits of his own errors. It was under the training of Cortés that he learned to be a soldier. The general, having concluded his instructions, affectionately embraced his lieutenant, and dismissed him to his quarters.

It was late in the afternoon when he reached them; but the sun was still lingering above the western hills, and poured his beams wide over the valley, lighting up the old towers and temples of Tenochtitlan with a mellow radiance that little harmonised with the dark scenes of strife in which the city had so lately been involved. The tranquillity of the hour, however, was on a sudden broken by the strange sounds of the great drum in the temple of the war-god—sounds which recalled the *noche triste,* with all its terrible images, to the minds of the Spaniards, for that was the only occasion on which they had ever heard them. They intimated some solemn act of religion within the unhallowed precincts of the *teocalli;* and the soldiers, startled by the mournful vibrations, which might be heard for leagues across the valley, turned their eyes to the quarter whence they proceeded. They there beheld a long procession winding up the huge sides of the pyramid; for the camp of Alvarado was pitched scarcely a mile from the city, and objects are distinctly visible, at a great distance, in the transparent atmosphere of the tableland.

As the long file of priests and warriors reached the flat summit of the *teocalli,* the Spaniards saw the figures of several men stripped to their waists, some of whom, by the whiteness of their skins, they recognised as their own countrymen. They were the victims for sacrifice. Their heads were gaudily decorated with coronals of plumes, and they carried fans in their hands. They were urged along by blows, and compelled to take part in the dances in honour of the Aztec war-god. The unfortunate captives, then stripped of their sad finery, were stretched one after another on the great stone of sacrifice. On its convex surface, their breasts were heaved up conveniently for the diabolical purpose of the priestly executioner, who cut asunder the ribs by a strong blow with his sharp razor of *itztli,* and thrusting his hand into the wound, tore away the heart, which, hot and reeking, was deposited on the golden censer before the idol. The body of the slaughtered victim was then hurled down the steep stairs of the pyramid, which, it may be remembered, were placed at the same angle of the pile, one flight below another; and the mutilated remains were gathered up by the savages beneath, who soon prepared with them the cannibal repast which completed the work of abomination!

We may imagine with what sensations the stupefied Spaniards must have gazed on this horrid spectacle, so near that they could almost recognise the persons of their unfortunate friends, see the struggles and writhings of their bodies, hear—or fancy that they heard—their screams of agony! yet so far removed that they could render them no assistance. Their limbs trembled beneath them as they thought what might one day be their own fate; and the bravest among them, who had hitherto gone to battle, as careless and light-hearted, as to the banquet or the ballroom, were unable, from this time forward, to encounter their ferocious enemy without a sickening feeling, much akin to fear, coming over them.

Such was not the effect produced by this spectacle on the Mexican forces, gathered at the end of the causeway. Like vultures maddened by the smell of distant carrion, they set up a piercing cry, and, as they shouted that, "such should be the fate of all their enemies," swept along in one fierce torrent over the dike. But the Spaniards were not to be taken by surprise; and, before the barbarian horde had come within their lines, they opened such a deadly fire from their battery of heavy guns, supported by the musketry and crossbows, that the assailants were compelled to fall back slowly, but fearfully mangled, to their former position.

The five following days passed away in a state of inaction, except indeed, so far as was necessary to repel the *sorties,* made from time to time, by the militia of the capital. The Mexicans, elated with their success, meanwhile abandoned themselves to jubilee; singing, dancing and feasting on the mangled relics of their wretched victims. Guatemozin sent several heads of the Spaniards, as well as of the horses, round the country, calling on his old vassals to forsake the banners of the white men, unless they would share the doom of the enemies of Mexico. The priests now cheered the young monarch and the people with the declaration that the dread Huitzilopotchli, their offended deity, appeased by the sacrifices offered up on his altars, would again take the Aztecs under his protection, and deliver their enemies, before the expiration of eight days, into their hands.

This comfortable prediction, confidently believed by the Mexicans, was thundered in the ears of the besieging army in tones of exultation and defiance. However it may have been contemned by the Spaniards, it had a very different effect on their allies. The latter had begun to be disgusted with a service so full of peril and suffering, and already protracted far beyond the usual term of Indian hostilities. They had less confidence than before in the Spaniards. Experience had shown that they were neither invincible nor immortal, and their recent reverses made them even distrust the ability of the Christians to reduce the Aztec metropolis. They recalled to mind the ominous words of Xicotencatl, that "so sacrilegious a war could come to no good for the people of Anahuac." They felt that their arm was raised against the gods of their country. The prediction of the oracle fell heavy on their hearts. They had little doubt of its fulfilment, and were only eager to turn away the bolt from their own heads by a timely secession from the cause.

They took advantage, therefore, of the friendly cover of night to steal away from their quarters. Company after company deserted in this manner, taking the direction of their respective homes. Those belonging to the great towns of the valley, whose allegiance was the most recent, were the first to cast it off. Their example was followed by the older confederates, the militia of Cholula, Tepeaca, Tezcuco, and even the faithful Tlascala. There were, it is true, some exceptions to these, and among them, Ixtlilxochitl, the younger lord of Tezcuco, and Chichemecatl, the valiant Tlascalan chieftain, who, with a few of their immediate followers, still remained true to the banner under which they had enlisted. But their number was insignificant. The Spaniards beheld with dismay the mighty array, on which they relied for support, thus silently melting away before the breath of superstition. Cortés alone maintained a cheerful countenance. He treated the prediction with contempt, as an invention of the priests, and sent his messengers after the retreating squadrons, beseeching them to postpone their departure, or at least to halt on the road, till the time, which would soon elapse, should show the falsehood of the prophecy.

The affairs of the Spaniards, at this crisis, must be confessed to have worn a gloomy aspect. Deserted by their allies, with their ammunition nearly exhausted, cut off from the customary supplies from the neighbourhood, harassed by unintermitting vigils and fatigues, smarting under wounds, of which every man in the army had his share, with an unfriendly country in their rear, and a mortal foe in front, they might well be excused for faltering in their enterprise. They found abundant occupation by day in foraging the country, and in maintaining their position on the causeways against the enemy, now made doubly daring by success and by the promises of their priests; while at night their slumbers were disturbed by the beat of the melancholy drum, the sounds of which, booming far over the waters, tolled the knell of their murdered comrades. Night after night fresh victims were led up to the great altar of sacrifice; and while the city blazed with the illuminations of a thousand bonfires on the terraced roofs of the dwellings, and in the areas of the temples, the dismal pageant, showing through the fiery glare like the work of the ministers of hell, was distinctly visible from the camp below. One of the last of the sufferers was Guzman, the unfortunate chamberlain of Cortés, who lingered in captivity eighteen days before he met his doom.

Yet in this hour of trial the Spaniards did not falter. Had they faltered, they might have learned a lesson of fortitude from some of their own wives, who continued with them in the camp, and who displayed a heroism, on this occasion, of which history has preserved several examples. One of these, protected by her husband's armour, would frequently mount guard in his place, when he was wearied. Another, hastily putting on a soldier's *escaupil* and seizing a sword and lance, was seen, on one occasion, to rally her retreating countrymen, and lead them back against the enemy. Cortés would have persuaded these Amazonian dames to remain at Tlascala; but they proudly replied, "It was the duty of Castilian wives not to abandon their husbands in danger, but to share it with them—and die with them, if necessary." And well did they do their duty.

Amidst all the distresses and multiplied embarrassments of their situation, the Spaniards still remained true to their purpose. They relaxed in no degree the severity of the blockade. Their camps still occupied the only avenues to the city; and their batteries, sweeping the long defiles at every fresh assault of the Aztecs, mowed down hundreds of the assailants. Their brigantines still rode on the waters, cutting off the communication with the shore. It is true, indeed, the loss of the auxiliary canoes left a passage open for the occasional introduction of supplies to the capital. But the whole amount of these supplies was small; and its crowded population, while exulting in their temporary advantage, and the delusive assurances of their priests, were beginning to sink under the withering grasp of an enemy within, more terrible than the one which lay before their gates.

CHAPTER VII

Success of the Spaniards—Fruitless Offers to Guatemozin—
Buildings Razed to the Ground—Terrible Famine—The
Troops Gain the Market-Place—Battering Engine

1521

THUS PASSED AWAY the eight days prescribed by the oracle; and the sun, which rose upon the ninth, beheld the fair city still beset on every side by the inexorable foe. It was a great mistake of the Aztec priests— one not uncommon with false prophets, anxious to produce a startling impression on their followers—to assign so short a term for the fulfilment of their prediction.

The Tezcucan and Tlascalan chiefs now sent to acquaint their troops with the failure of the prophecy, and to recall them to the Christian camp. The Tlascalans, who had halted on the way, returned, ashamed of their credulity, and with ancient feelings of animosity, heightened by the artifice of which they had been the dupes. Their example was followed by many of the other confederates, with the levity natural to a people whose convictions are the result, not of reason, but of superstition. In a short time the Spanish general found himself at the head of an auxiliary force, which, if not so numerous as before, was more than adequate to all his purposes. He received them with politic benignity; and, while he reminded them that they had been guilty of a great crime in thus abandoning their commander, he was willing to overlook it in consideration of their past services. They must be aware that these services were not necessary to the Spaniards, who had carried on the siege with the same vigour during their absence as when they were present. But he was unwilling that those who had shared the dangers of the war with him should not also partake of its triumphs, and be present at the fall of their enemy, which he promised, with a confidence better founded than that of the priests in their prediction, should not be long delayed.

Yet the menaces and machinations of Guatemozin were still not without effect in the distant provinces. Before the full return of the confederates, Cortés received an embassy from Cuernavaca, ten or twelve leagues distant, and another from some friendly towns of the Otomies, still further off, imploring his protection against their formidable neighbours, who menaced them with hostilities as allies of the Spaniards. As the latter were then situated, they were in a condition to receive succour much more than to give it. Most of the officers were accordingly opposed to granting a request, the compliance with which must still further impair their diminished strength. But Cortés knew the importance, above all, of not betraying his own inability to grant it. "The greater our weakness," he said, "the greater need have we to cover it under a show of strength."

He immediately detached Tapia with a body of about a hundred men in one direction, and Sandoval with a somewhat larger force in the other, with orders that their absence should not in any event be prolonged beyond ten days. The two captains executed their commission promptly and effectually. They each met and defeated his adversary in a pitched battle; laid waste the hostile territories, and returned within the time prescribed. They were soon followed by ambassadors from the conquered places, soliciting the alliance of the Spaniards; and the affair terminated by an accession of new confederates, and, what was more important, a conviction in the old, that the Spaniards were both willing and competent to protect them.

Fortune, who seldom dispenses her frowns or her favours single-handed, further showed her good will to the Spaniards at this time, by sending a vessel into Vera Cruz laden with ammunition and military stores. It was part of the fleet destined for the Florida coast by the romantic old knight, Ponce de Leon. The cargo was immediately taken by the authorities of the port, and forwarded, without delay, to the camp, where it arrived most seasonably, as the want of powder, in particular, had begun to be seriously felt. With strength thus renovated, Cortés determined to resume active operations, but on a plan widely differing from that pursued before.

In the former deliberations on the subject, two courses, as we have seen, presented themselves to the general. One was to intrench himself in the heart of the capital, and from this point carry on hostilities; the other was the mode of proceeding hitherto followed. Both were open to serious objections, which he hoped would be obviated by the one now adopted. This was to advance no step without securing the entire safety of the army, not only on its immediate retreat, but in its future inroads. Every breach in the causeway, every canal in the streets, was to be filled up in so solid a manner that the work should not be again disturbed. The materials for this were to be furnished by the buildings, every one of which, as the army advanced, whether public or private, hut, temple, or palace, was to be demolished! Not a building in their path was to be spared. They were all indiscriminately to be levelled, until, in the Conqueror's own language, "the water should be converted into dry land," and a smooth and open ground be afforded for the manœuvres of the cavalry and artillery.

Cortés came to this terrible determination with great difficulty. He sincerely desired to spare the city, "the most beautiful thing in the world," as he enthusiastically styles it, and which would have formed the most glorious trophy of his conquest. But, in a place where every house was a fortress, and every street was cut up by canals so embarrassing to his movements, experience proved it was vain to think of doing so, and becoming master of it. There was as little hope of a peaceful accommodation with the Aztecs, who, so far from being broken by all they had hitherto endured, and the long perspective of future woes, showed a spirit as haughty and implacable as ever.

The general's intentions were learned by the Indian allies with unbounded satisfaction; and they answered his call for aid by thousands of pioneers, armed with their *coas,* or hoes of the country, all testifying the greatest alacrity in helping on the work of destruction. In a short time the breaches in the great causeways were filled up so effectually that they were never again molested. Cortés himself set the example by carrying stones and timber with his own hands. The buildings in the suburbs were then thoroughly levelled, the canals were filled up with the rubbish, and a wide space around the city was thrown open to the manœuvres of the cavalry, who swept over it free and unresisted. The Mexicans did not look with indifference on these preparations to lay waste their town, and leave them bare and unprotected against the enemy. They made incessant efforts to impede the labours of the besiegers, but the latter, under cover of their guns, which kept up an unintermitting fire, still advanced in the work of desolation.

The gleam of fortune, which had so lately broken out on the Mexicans, again disappeared; and the dark mist, after having been raised for a moment, settled on the doomed capital more heavily than before.

Famine, with all her hideous train of woes, was making rapid strides among its accumulated population. The stores provided for the siege were exhausted. The casual supply of human victims, or that obtained by some straggling pirogue from the neighbouring shores, was too inconsiderable to be widely felt. Some forced a scanty sustenance from a mucilaginous substance, gathered in small quantities on the surface of the lake and canals. Others appeased the cravings of appetite by devouring rats, lizards, and the like loathsome reptiles, which had not yet deserted the starving city. Its days seemed to be already numbered. But the page of history has many an example, to show that there are no limits to the endurance of which humanity is capable, when animated by hatred and despair.

With the sword thus suspended over it, the Spanish commander, desirous to make one more effort to save the capital, persuaded three Aztec nobles, taken in one of the late actions, to bear a message from him to Guatemozin; though they undertook it with reluctance, for fear of the consequences to themselves. Cortés told the emperor that all had now been done that brave men could do in defence of their country. There remained no hope, no chance of escape for the Mexicans. Their provisions were exhausted; their communications were cut off; their vassals had deserted them; even their gods had betrayed them. They stood alone, with the nations of Anahuac banded against them. There was no hope, but in immediate surrender. He besought the young monarch to take compassion on his brave subjects, who were daily perishing before his eyes; and on the fair city, whose stately buildings were fast crumbling into ruins. "Return to the allegiance," he concludes, "which you once proffered to the sovereign of Castile. The past shall be forgotten. The persons and property—in short, all the rights of the Aztecs —shall be respected. You shall be confirmed in your authority, and Spain will once more take your city under her protection."

The eyes of the young monarch kindled, and his dark cheeks flushed with sudden anger, as he listened to proposals so humiliating. But though his bosom glowed with the fiery temper of the Indian, he had the qualities of a "gentle cavalier," says one of his enemies, who knew him well. He did no harm to the envoys; but, after the heat of the moment had passed off, he gave the matter a calm consideration, and called a council of his wise men and warriors to deliberate upon it. Some were for accepting the proposals, as offering the only chance of preservation. But the priests took a different view of the matter. They knew that the ruin of their own order must follow the triumph of Christianity. "Peace was good," they said, "but not with the white men." They reminded Guatemozin of the fate of his uncle Montezuma, and the requital he had met with for all his hospitality: of the seizure and imprisonment of Cacama, the cacique of Tezcuco; of the massacre of the nobles by Alvarado; of the insatiable avarice of the invaders, which had stripped the country of its treasures; of their profanation of the temples; of the injuries and insults which they had heaped without measure on the people and their religion. "Better," they said, "to trust in the promises of their own gods, who had so long watched over the nation. Better, if need be, give up our lives at once for our country, than drag them out in slavery and suffering among the false strangers."

The eloquence of the priests, artfully touching the various wrongs of his people, roused the hot blood of Guatemozin. "Since it is so," he abruptly exclaimed, "let us think only of supplying the wants of the people. Let no man, henceforth, who values his life, talk of surrender. We can at least die like warriors."

The Spaniards waited two days for the answer to their embassy. At length, it came in a general sortie of the Mexicans, who, pouring through every gate of the capital, like a river that has burst its banks, swept on, wave upon wave, to the very entrenchments of the besiegers, threatening to overwhelm them by their numbers! Fortunately, the position of the latter on the dikes secured their flanks, and the narrowness of the defile gave their small battery of guns all the advantages of a larger one. The fire of artillery and musketry blazed without intermission along the several causeways, belching forth volumes of sulphurous smoke, that, rolling heavily over the waters, settled dark around the Indian city, and hid it from the surrounding country. The brigantines thundered, at the same time, on the flanks of the columns, which, after some ineffectual efforts to maintain themselves, rolled back in wild confusion, till their impotent fury died away in sullen murmurs within the capital.

Cortés now steadily pursued the plan he had laid down for the devastation of the city. Day after day the several armies entered by their respective quarters; Sandoval probably directing his operations against the north-eastern district. The buildings made of the porous *tetzontli,* though generally low, were so massy and extensive, and the canals were so numerous, that their progress was necessarily slow. They, however, gathered fresh accessions of strength every day from the numbers who

flocked to the camp from the surrounding country, and who joined in
the work of destruction with a hearty good will, which showed their
eagerness to break the detested yoke of the Aztecs. The latter raged with
impotent anger as they beheld their lordly edifices, their temples, all they
had been accustomed to venerate, thus ruthlessly swept away; their
canals, constructed with so much labour, and what to them seemed
science, filled up with rubbish; their flourishing city, in short, turned
into a desert, over which the insulting foe now rode triumphant. They
heaped many a taunt on the Indian allies. "Go on," they said, bitterly;
"the more you destroy, the more you will have to build up again
hereafter. If we conquer, you shall build for us; and if your white
friends conquer, they will make you do as much for them." The event
justified the prediction.

In their rage they rushed blindly on the corps which covered the
Indian pioneers. But they were as often driven back by the impetuous
charge of the cavalry, or received on the long pikes of Chinantla, which
did good service to the besiegers in their operations. At the close of day,
however, when the Spaniards drew off their forces, taking care to send
the multitudinous host of confederates first from the ground, the Mexicans usually rallied for a more formidable attack. Then they poured out
from every lane and by-way, like so many mountain streams, sweeping
over the broad level cleared by the enemy, and falling impetuously on
their flanks and rear. At such times they inflicted considerable loss in
their turn, till an ambush, which Cortés laid for them among the
buildings adjoining the great temple, did them so much mischief, that
they were compelled to act with more reserve.

At times the war displayed something of a chivalrous character, in the
personal rencontres of the combatants. Challenges passed between them,
and especially between the native warriors. These combats were usually
conducted on the *azoteas,* whose broad and level surface afforded a
good field of fight. On one occasion, a Mexican of powerful frame,
brandishing a sword and buckler which he had won from the Christians,
defied his enemies to meet him in single fight. A young page of Cortés,
named Nuñez, obtained his master's permission to accept the vaunting
challenge of the Aztec; and, springing on the *azotea,* succeeded after a
hard struggle in discomfiting his antagonist, who fought at a disadvantage with weapons in which he was unpractised, and, running him
through the body, brought off his spoils in triumph, and laid them at
the general's feet.

The division of Cortés had now worked its way as far north as the great street of Tacuba, which opened a communication with Alvarado's camp, and near which stood the palace of Guatemozin. It was a spacious stone pile that might well be called a fortress. Though deserted by its royal master, it was held by a strong body of Aztecs, who made a temporary defence, but of little avail against the battering enginery of the besiegers. It was soon set on fire, and its crumbling walls were levelled in the dust, like those other stately edifices of the capital, the boast and admiration of the Aztecs, and some of the fairest fruits of their civilisation. "It was a sad thing to witness their destruction," exclaims Cortés; "but it was part of our plan of operations, and we had no alternative."

These operations had consumed several weeks, so that it was now drawing towards the latter part of July. During this time, the blockade had been maintained with the utmost rigour, and the wretched inhabitants were suffering all the extremities of famine. Some few stragglers were taken, from time to time, in the neighbourhood of the Christian camp, whither they had wandered in search of food. They were kindly treated by command of Cortés, who was in hopes to induce others to follow their example, and thus to afford a means of conciliating the inhabitants, which might open the way to their submission. But few were found willing to leave the shelter of the capital, and they preferred to take their chance with their suffering countrymen, rather than trust themselves to the mercies of the besiegers.

From these few stragglers, however, the Spaniards heard a dismal tale of woe, respecting the crowded population in the interior of the city. All the ordinary means of sustenance had long since failed, and they now supported life as they could, by means of such roots as they could dig from the earth, by gnawing the bark of trees, by feeding on the grass— on anything, in short, however loathsome, that could allay the craving of appetite. Their only drink was the brackish water of the soil, saturated with the salt lake. Under this unwholesome diet, and the diseases engendered by it, the population was gradually wasting away. Men sickened and died every day, in all the excruciating torments produced by hunger, and the wan and emaciated survivors seemed only to be waiting for their time.

The Spaniards had visible confirmation of all this, as they penetrated deeper into the city, and approached the district of Tlatelolco, now occupied by the besieged. They found the ground turned up in quest of roots and weeds, the trees stripped of their green stems, their foliage, and their bark. Troops of famished Indians flitted in the distance, gliding like ghosts among the scenes of their former residence. Dead bodies lay unburied in the streets and courtyards, or filled up the canals. It was a sure sign of the extremity of the Aztecs; for they held the burial of the dead as a solemn and imperative duty. In the early part of the siege, they had religiously attended to it. In its later stages, they were still careful to withdraw the dead from the public eye, by bringing their remains within the houses. But the number of these, and their own sufferings, had now so fearfully increased, that they had grown indifferent to this, and they suffered their friends and their kinsmen to lie and moulder on the spot where they drew their last breath!

As the invaders entered the dwellings, a more appalling spectacle presented itself—the floors covered with the prostrate forms of the miserable inmates, some in the agonies of death, others festering in their corruption; men, women, and children, inhaling the poisonous atmosphere, and mingling promiscuously together; mothers, with their infants in their arms perishing of hunger before their eyes, while they were unable to afford them the nourishment of nature; men crippled by their wounds, with their bodies frightfully mangled, vainly attempting to crawl away, as the enemy entered. Yet, even in this state, they scorned to ask for mercy, and glared on the invaders with the sullen ferocity of the wounded tiger that the huntsmen have tracked to his forest cave. The Spanish commander issued strict orders that mercy should be shown to these poor and disabled victims. But the Indian allies made no distinction. An Aztec, under whatever circumstances, was an enemy; and, with hideous shouts of triumph, they pulled down the burning buildings on their heads, consuming the living and the dead in one common funeral pile!

Yet the sufferings of the Aztecs, terrible as they were, did not incline them to submission. There were many, indeed, who, from greater strength of constitution, or from the more favourable circumstances in which they were placed, still showed all their wonted energy of body and mind, and maintained the same undaunted and resolute demeanour as before. They fiercely rejected all the overtures of Cortés, declaring they would rather die than surrender, and, adding with a bitter tone of exultation that the invaders would be at least disappointed in their expectations of treasure, for it was buried where they could never find it!

The women, it is said, shared in this desperate—it should rather be called *heroic*—spirit. They were indefatigable in nursing the sick, and dressing their wounds; they aided the warriors in battle, by supplying them with the Indian ammunition of stones and arrows, prepared their slings, strung their bows, and displayed, in short, all the constancy and courage shown by the noble maidens of Saragossa in our day, and by those of Carthage in the days of antiquity.

Cortés had now entered one of the great avenues leading to the market-place of Tlatelolco, the quarter towards which the movements of Alvarado were also directed. A single canal only lay in his way, but this was of great width and stoutly defended by the Mexican archery. At this crisis, the army one evening, while in their entrenchments on the causeway, were surprised by an uncommon light, that arose from the huge *teocalli* in that part of the city, which, being at the north, was the most distant from their own position. This temple, dedicated to the dread war-god, was inferior only to the pyramid in the great square; and on it the Spaniards had more than once seen their unhappy countrymen led to slaughter. They now supposed that the enemy were employed in some of their diabolical ceremonies, when the flame, mounting higher and higher, showed that the sanctuaries themselves were on fire. A shout of exultation at the sight broke forth from the assembled soldiers, as they assured one another that their countrymen under Alvarado had got possession of the building.

It was indeed true. That gallant officer, whose position on the western causeway placed him near the district of Tlatelolco, had obeyed his commander's instructions to the letter, razing every building to the ground in his progress, and filling up the ditches with their ruins. He, at length, found himself before the great *teocalli* in the neighbourhood of the market. He ordered a company, under a cavalier named Gutierre de Badajoz, to storm the place, which was defended by a body of warriors, mingled with priests, still more wild and ferocious than the soldiery. The garrison, rushing down the winding terraces, fell on the assailants with such fury, as compelled them to retreat in confusion, and with some loss. Alvarado ordered another detachment to their support. This last was engaged, at the moment, with a body of Aztecs, who hung on its rear as it wound up the galleries of the *teocalli*. Thus hemmed in between two enemies, above and below, the position of the Spaniards was critical. With sword and buckler, they plunged desperately on the ascending Mexicans, and drove them into the courtyard below, where Alvarado plied them with such lively volleys of musketry, as soon threw them into disorder and compelled them to abandon the ground. Being thus rid of annoyance in the rear, the Spaniards returned to the charge. They drove the enemy up the heights of the pyramid, and, reaching the broad summit, a fierce encounter followed in mid air—such an encounter as takes place where death is the certain consequence of defeat. It ended, as usual, in the discomfiture of the Aztecs, who were either slaughtered on the spot still wet with the blood of their own victims, or pitched headlong down the sides of the pyramid.

The area was covered with the various symbols of the barbarous worship of the country, and with two lofty sanctuaries, before whose grinning idols were displayed the heads of several Christian captives, who had been immolated on their altars. Although overgrown by their long, matted hair and bushy beards, the Spaniards could recognise, in the livid countenances, their comrades who had fallen into the hands of the enemy. Tears fell from their eyes, as they gazed on the melancholy spectacle, and thought of the hideous death which their countrymen had suffered. They removed the sad relics with decent care, and after the Conquest, deposited them in consecrated ground, on a spot since covered by the Church of the Martyrs.

They completed their work by firing the sanctuaries, that the place might be no more polluted by these abominable rites. The flame crept slowly up the lofty pinnacles, in which stone was mingled with wood, till, at length, bursting into one bright blaze, it shot up its spiral volume to such a height that it was seen from the most distant quarters of the valley. It was this which had been hailed by the soldiery of Cortés, and it served as the beacon-light to both friend and foe, intimating the progress of the Christian arms.

The commander-in-chief and his division, animated by the spectacle, made, in their entrance on the following day, more determined efforts to place themselves alongside of their companions under Alvarado. The broad canal, above noticed as the only impediment now lying in his way, was to be traversed; and on the further side, the emaciated figures of the Aztec warriors were gathered in numbers to dispute the passage, like the gloomy shades that wander—as ancient poets tell us—on the banks of the infernal river. They poured down, however, a storm of missiles, which were no shades, on the heads of the Indian labourers, while occupied with filling up the wide gap with the ruins of the surrounding buildings. Still they toiled on in defiance of the arrowy shower, fresh numbers taking the place of those who fell. And when at length the work was completed, the cavalry rode over the rough plain at full charge against the enemy, followed by the deep array of spearmen, who bore down all opposition with their invincible phalanx.

The Spaniards now found themselves on the same ground with Alvarado's division. Soon afterwards that chief, attended by several of his staff, rode into their lines, and cordially embraced his countrymen and companions in arms, for the first time since the beginning of the siege. They were now in the neighbourhood of the market. Cortés, taking with him a few of his cavaliers, galloped into it. It was a vast inclosure, as the reader has already seen, covering many an acre. Its dimensions were suited to the immense multitudes who gathered there from all parts of the valley in the flourishing days of the Aztec monarchy. It was surrounded by porticos and pavilions for the accommodation of the artisans and traders, who there displayed their various fabrics and articles of merchandise. The flat roofs of the piazzas were now covered with crowds of men and women, who gazed in silent dismay on the steel-clad horsemen that profaned these precincts with their presence for the first time since their expulsion from the capital. The multitude, composed for the most part, probably, of unarmed citizens, seemed taken by surprise; at least, they made no show of resistance; and the general, after leisurely viewing the ground, was permitted to ride back unmolested to the army.

On arriving there, he ascended the *teocalli,* from which the standard of Castile, supplanting the memorials of Aztec superstition, was now triumphantly floating. The Conqueror, as he strode among the smoking embers on the summit, calmly surveyed the scene of desolation below. The palaces, the temples, the busy marts of industry and trade, the glittering canals, covered with their rich freights from the surrounding country, the royal pomp of groves and gardens, all the splendours of the imperial city, the capital of the Western World, for ever gone—and in their place a barren wilderness! How different the spectacle which the year before had met his eye, as it wandered over the scenes from the heights of the neighbouring *teocalli,* with Montezuma at his side! Seven-eighths of the city were laid in ruins, with the occasional exception, perhaps, of some colossal temple, that it would have required too much time to demolish. The remaining eighth, comprehending the district of Tlatelolco, was all that now remained to the Aztecs, whose population—still large after all its losses—was crowded into a compass that would hardly have afforded accommodations for a third of their numbers. It was the quarter lying between the great northern and western causeways, and is recognised in the modern capital as the *Barrio de San Jago* and its vicinity. It was the favourite residence of the Indians after the Conquest, though at the present day thinly covered with humble dwellings, forming the straggling suburbs, as it were, of the metropolis. Yet it still affords some faint vestiges of what it was in its prouder days; and the curious antiquary, and occasionally the labourer, as he turns up the soil, encounters a glittering fragment of obsidian, or the mouldering head of a lance, or arrow, or some other warlike relic, attesting that on this spot the retreating Aztecs made their last stand for the independence of their country.

On the day following, Cortés, at the head of his battalions, made a second entry into the great *tianguez*. But this time the Mexicans were better prepared for his coming. They were assembled in considerable force in the spacious square. A sharp encounter followed; but it was short. Their strength was not equal to their spirit, and they melted away before the rolling fire of musketry, and left the Spaniards masters of the inclosure.

The first act was to set fire to some temples of no great size within the market-place, or more probably on its borders. As the flames ascended, the Aztecs, horror-struck, broke forth into piteous lamentations at the destruction of the deities on whom they relied for protection.

The general's next step was at the suggestion of a soldier named Sotelo, a man who had served under the Great Captain in the Italian wars, where he professed to have gathered knowledge of the science of engineering, as it was then practised. He offered his services to construct a sort of catapult, a machine for discharging stones of great size, which might take the place of the regular battering-train, in demolishing the buildings. As the ammunition, notwithstanding the liberal supplies which, from time to time, had found their way into the camp, now began to fail, Cortés eagerly acceded to a proposal so well suited to his exigencies. Timber and stone were furnished, and a number of hands were employed, under the direction of the self-styled engineer, in constructing the ponderous apparatus, which was erected on a solid platform of masonry, thirty paces square, and seven or eight feet high, that covered the centre of the market-place. It was the work of the Aztec princes, and was used as a scaffolding on which mountebanks and jugglers might exhibit their marvellous feats for the amusement of the populace, who took great delight in these performances.

The erection of the machine consumed several days, during which hostilities were suspended, while the artisans were protected from interruption by a strong corps of infantry. At length the work was completed; and the besieged, who, with silent awe, had beheld from the neighbouring *azoteas,* the progress of the mysterious engine, which was to lay the remainder of their capital in ruins, now looked with terror for its operation. A stone of huge size was deposited on the timber. The machinery was set in motion; and the rocky fragment was discharged with a tremendous force from the catapult. But, instead of taking the direction of the Aztec buildings, it rose high and perpendicularly into the air, and, descending whence it sprung, broke the ill-omened machine into splinters! It was a total failure. The Aztecs were released from their apprehensions, and the soldiery made many a merry jest on the catastrophe, somewhat at the expense of their commander, who testified no little vexation at the disappointment, and still more at his own credulity.

CHAPTER VIII

*Dreadful Sufferings of the Besieged—Spirit of Guatemozin—
Murderous Assault—Capture of Guatemozin—Evacuation of the City—Termination of the Siege—Reflections*

1521

THERE WAS NO OCCASION to resort to artificial means to precipitate the
ruin of the Aztecs. It was accelerated every hour by causes more potent
than those arising from mere human agency. There they were—pent up
in their close and suffocating quarters, nobles, commoners, and slaves,
men, women, and children, some in houses, more frequently in hovels—
for this part of the city was not the best—others in the open air in
canoes, or in the streets, shivering in the cold rains of night, and
scorched by the burning heat of day. An old chronicler mentions the
fact of two women of rank remaining three days and nights up to their
necks in the water among the reeds, with only a handful of maize for
their support. The ordinary means of sustaining life were long since
gone. They wandered about in search of anything, however unwholesome or revolting, that might mitigate the fierce gnawings of hunger.
Some hunted for insects and worms on the borders of the lake, or
gathered the salt weeds and moss from its bottom, while at times they
might be seen casting a wistful look at the green hills beyond, which
many of them had left to share the fate of their brethren in the capital.

To their credit, it is said by the Spanish writers that they were not
driven in their extremity to violate the laws of nature by feeding on one
another. But unhappily this is contradicted by the Indian authorities,
who state that many a mother, in her agony, devoured the offspring
which she had no longer the means of supporting. This is recorded of
more than one siege in history; and it is the more probable here, where
the sensibilities must have been blunted by familiarity with the brutal
practices of the national superstition.

471

But all was not sufficient, and hundreds of famished wretches died every day from extremity of suffering. Some dragged themselves into the houses, and drew their last breath alone, and in silence. Others sank down in the public streets. Wherever they died, there they were left. There was no one to bury or to remove them. Familiarity with the spectacle made men indifferent to it. They looked on in dumb despair, waiting for their own turn. There was no complaint, no lamentation, but deep, unutterable woe.

If in other quarters of the town the corpses might be seen scattered over the streets, here they were gathered in heaps. "They lay so thick," said Bernal Diaz, "that one could not tread except among the bodies." "A man could not set his foot down," says Cortés, yet more strongly, "unless on the corpse of an Indian!" They were piled one upon another, the living mingled with the dead. They stretched themselves on the bodies of their friends, and lay down to sleep there. Death was every-where. The city was a vast charnel-house, in which all was hastening to decay and decomposition. A poisonous steam arose from the mass of putrefaction, under the action of alternate rain and heat, which so tainted the whole atmosphere, that the Spaniards, including the general himself, in their brief visits to the quarter, were made ill by it, and it bred a pestilence that swept off even greater numbers than the famine.

Men's minds were unsettled by these strange and accumulated horrors. They resorted to all the superstitious rites prescribed by their religion, to stay the pestilence. They called on their priests to invoke the gods in their behalf. But the oracles were dumb, or gave only gloomy responses. Their deities had deserted them, and in their place they saw signs of celestial wrath, telling of still greater woes in reserve. Many, after the siege, declared that, among other prodigies, they beheld a stream of light, of a blood-red colour, coming from the north in the direction of Tepejacac, with a rushing noise, like that of a whirlwind, which swept round the district of Tlatelolco, darting out sparkles and flakes of fire till it shot far into the centre of the lake! In the disordered state of their nerves, a mysterious fear took possession of their senses. Prodigies were of familiar occurrence, and the most familiar phenomena of nature were converted into prodigies. Stunned by their calamities, reason was bewildered, and they became the sport of the wildest and most superstitious fancies.

In the midst of these awful scenes, the young emperor of the Aztecs remained, according to all accounts, calm and courageous. With his fair capital laid in ruins before his eyes, his nobles and faithful subjects dying around him, his territory rent away, foot by foot, till scarce enough remained for him to stand on, he rejected every invitation to capitulate, and showed the same indomitable spirit as at the commencement of the siege. When Cortés, in the hope that the extremities of the besieged would incline them to listen to an accommodation, persuaded a noble prisoner to bear to Guatemozin his proposals to that effect; the fierce young monarch, according to the general, ordered him at once to be sacrificed. It is a Spaniard, we must remember, who tells the story.

Cortés, who had suspended hostilities for several days, in the vain hope that the distresses of the Mexicans would bend them to submission, now determined to drive them to it by a general assault. Cooped up, as they were, within a narrow quarter of the city, their position favoured such an attempt. He commanded Alvarado to hold himself in readiness, and directed Sandoval—who, besides the causeway, had charge of the fleet, which lay off the Tlatelolcan district—to support the attack by a cannonade on the houses near the water. He then led his forces into the city, or rather across the horrid waste that now encircled it.

On entering the Indian precincts, he was met by several of the chiefs, who, stretching forth their emaciated arms, exclaimed, "You are the children of the Sun. But the Sun is swift in his course. Why are you, then, so tardy? Why do you delay so long to put an end to our miseries? Rather kill us at once, that we may go to our god Huitzilopotchli, who waits for us in Heaven to give us rest from our sufferings!"

Cortés was moved by their piteous appeal, and answered that he desired not their death, but their submission. "Why does your master refuse to treat with me," he said, "when a single hour will suffice for me to crush him and all his people?" He then urged them to request Guatemozin to confer with him, with the assurance that he might do it in safety, as his person should not be molested.

The nobles, after some persuasion, undertook the mission; and it was received by the young monarch in a manner which showed—if the anecdote before related of him be true—that misfortune had, at length, asserted some power over his haughty spirit. He consented to the interview, though not to have it take place on that day, but the following, in the great square of Tlatelolco. Cortés, well satisfied, immediately withdrew from the city, and resumed his position on the causeway.

The next morning he presented himself at the place appointed, having previously stationed Alvarado there with a strong corps of infantry to guard against treachery. The stone platform in the centre of the square was covered with mats and carpets, and a banquet was prepared to refresh the famished monarch and his nobles. Having made these arrangements, he awaited the hour of the interview.

But Guatemozin, instead of appearing himself, sent his nobles, the same who had brought to him the general's invitation, and who now excused their master's absence on the plea of illness. Cortés, though disappointed, gave a courteous reception to the envoys, considering that it might still afford the means of opening a communication with the emperor. He persuaded them without much entreaty to partake of the good cheer spread before them, which they did with a voracity that told how severe had been their abstinence. He then dismissed them with a seasonable supply of provisions for their master, pressing him to consent to an interview, without which it was impossible their differences could be adjusted.

The Indian envoys returned in a short time, bearing with them a present of fine cotton fabrics, of no great value, from Guatemozin, who still declined to meet the Spanish general. Cortés, though deeply chagrined, was unwilling to give up the point. "He will surely come," he said to the envoys, "when he sees that I suffer you to go and come unharmed, you who have been my steady enemies, no less than himself, throughout the war. He has nothing to fear from me." He again parted with them, promising to receive their answer the following day.

On the next morning, the Aztec chiefs, entering the Christian quarters, announced to Cortés that Guatemozin would confer with him at noon in the market-place. The general was punctual at the hour; but without success. Neither monarch nor ministers appeared there. It was plain that the Indian prince did not care to trust the promises of his enemy. A thought of Montezuma may have passed across his mind. After he had waited three hours, the general's patience was exhausted, and, as he learned that the Mexicans were busy in preparations for defence, he made immediate dispositions for the assault.

The confederates had been left without the walls, for he did not care to bring them in sight of the quarry, before he was ready to slip the leash. He now ordered them to join him; and, supported by Alvarado's division, marched at once into the enemy's quarters. He found them prepared to receive him. Their most able-bodied warriors were thrown into the van, covering their feeble and crippled comrades. Women were seen occasionally mingling in the ranks, and, as well as children, thronged the *azoteas,* where, with famine-stricken visages, and haggard eyes, they scowled defiance and hatred on their invaders.

As the Spaniards advanced, the Mexicans set up a fierce war-cry, and sent off clouds of arrows with their accustomed spirit, while the women and boys rained down darts and stones from their elevated position on the terraces. But the missiles were sent by hands too feeble to do much damage; and, when the squadrons closed, the loss of strength became still more sensible in the Aztecs. Their blows fell feebly and with doubtful aim; though some, it is true, of stronger constitution, or gathering strength from despair, maintained to the last a desperate fight.

The arquebusiers now poured in a deadly fire. The brigantines replied by successive volleys in the opposite quarter. The besieged, hemmed in, like deer surrounded by the huntsmen, were brought down on every side. The carnage was horrible. The ground was heaped up with slain, until the maddened combatants were obliged to climb over the human mounds to get at one another. The miry soil was saturated with blood, which ran off like water, and dyed the canals themselves with crimson. All was uproar and terrible confusion. The hideous yells of the barbarians; the oaths and execrations of the Spaniards; the cries of the wounded; the shrieks of women and children; the heavy blows of the Conquerors; the death-struggle of their victims; the rapid, reverberating echoes of musketry; the hissing of innumerable missiles; the crash and crackling of blazing buildings, crushing hundreds in their ruins; the blinding volumes of dust and sulphurous smoke shrouding all in their gloomy canopy—made a scene appalling even to the soldiers of Cortés, steeled as they were by many a rough passage of war, and by long familiarity with blood and violence. "The piteous cries of the women and children, in particular," says the general, "were enough to break one's heart." He commanded that they should be spared, and that all, who asked it, should receive quarter. He particularly urged this on the confederates, and placed men among them to restrain their violence. But he had set an engine in motion too terrible to be controlled. It were as easy to curb the hurricane in its fury, as the passions of an infuriated horde of savages. "Never did I see so pitiless a race," he exclaims, "or any thing wearing the form of man so destitute of humanity." They made no distinction of sex or age, and in this hour of vengeance seemed to be requiting the hoarded wrongs of a century. At length, sated with slaughter, the Spanish commander sounded a retreat. It was full time, if, according to his own statement—we may hope it is an exaggeration—

forty thousand souls had perished! Yet their fate was to be envied, in comparison with that of those who survived.

Through the long night which followed, no movement was perceptible in the Aztec quarter. No light was seen there, no sound was heard, save the low moaning of some wounded or dying wretch, writhing in his agony. All was dark and silent—the darkness of the grave. The last blow seemed to have completely stunned them. They had parted with hope, and sat in sullen despair, like men waiting in silence the stroke of the executioner. Yet, for all this, they showed no disposition to submit. Every new injury had sunk deeper into their souls, and filled them with a deeper hatred of their enemy. Fortune, friends, kindred, home—all were gone. They were content to throw away life itself, now that they had nothing more to live for.

Far different was the scene in the Christian camp, where, elated with their recent successes, all was alive with bustle, and preparation for the morrow. Bonfires were seen blazing along the causeways, lights gleamed from tents and barracks, and the sounds of music and merriment, borne over the waters, proclaimed the joy of the soldiers at the prospect of so soon terminating their wearisome campaign.

On the following morning the Spanish commander again mustered his forces, having decided to follow up the blow of the preceding day before the enemy should have time to rally, and at once to put an end to the war. He had arranged with Alvarado, on the evening previous, to occupy the market-place of Tlatelolco; and the discharge of an arquebuse was to be the signal for a simultaneous assault. Sandoval was to hold the northern causeway, and, with the fleet, to watch the movements of the Indian emperor, and to intercept the flight to the main land, which Cortés knew he meditated. To allow him to effect this would be to leave a formidable enemy in his own neighbourhood, who might at any time kindle the flame of insurrection throughout the country. He ordered Sandoval, however, to do no harm to the royal person, and not to fire on the enemy at all, except in self-defence.

It was on the memorable 15th of August 1521, the day of St. Hypolito —from this circumstance selected as the patron saint of Modern Mexico —that Cortés led his warlike array for the last time across the black and blasted environs which lay around the Indian capital. On entering the Aztec precincts, he paused, willing to afford its wretched inmates one more chance of escape, before striking the fatal blow. He obtained an interview with some of the principal chiefs, and expostulated with them on the conduct of their prince. "He surely will not," said the general, "see you all perish, when he can so easily save you." He then urged them to prevail on Guatemozin to hold a conference with him, repeating the assurances of his personal safety.

The messengers went on their mission, and soon returned with the *cihuacoatl* at their head, a magistrate of high authority among the Mexicans. He said, with a melancholy air, in which his own disappointment was visible, that "Guatemozin was ready to die where he was, but would hold no interview with the Spanish commander"; adding in a tone of resignation, "It is for you to work your pleasure." "Go, then," replied the stern Conqueror, "and prepare your countrymen for death. Their hour is come."

He still postponed the assault for several hours. But the impatience of his troops at this delay was heightened by the rumour that Guatemozin and his nobles were preparing to escape with their effects in the *piraguas* and canoes which were moored on the margin of the lake. Convinced of the fruitlessness and impolicy of further procrastination, Cortés made his final dispositions for the attack, and took his own station on an *azotea,* which commanded the theatre of operations.

When the assailants came into presence of the enemy, they found them huddled together in the utmost confusion, all ages and sexes, in masses so dense that they nearly forced one another over the brink of the causeways into the water below. Some had climbed on the terraces, others feebly supported themselves against the walls of the buildings. Their squalid and tattered garments gave a wildness to their appearance, which still further heightened the ferocity of their expression, as they glared on their enemy with eyes in which hate was mingled with despair. When the Spaniards had approached within bow-shot, the Aztecs let off a flight of impotent missiles, showing to the last the resolute spirit, though they had lost the strength, of their better days. The fatal signal was then given by the discharge of an arquebuse—speedily followed by peals of heavy ordnance, the rattle of firearms, and the hellish shouts of the confederates, as they sprang upon their victims. It is unnecessary to stain the page with a repetition of the horrors of the preceding day. Some of the wretched Aztecs threw themselves into the water, and were picked up by the canoes. Others sank and were suffocated in the canals. The number of these became so great that a bridge was made of their dead bodies, over which the assailants could climb to the opposite banks. Others again, especially the women, begged for mercy, which, as the chroniclers assure us, was everywhere granted by the Spaniards, and, contrary to the instructions and entreaties of Cortés, everywhere refused by the confederates.

While this work of butchery was going on, numbers were observed pushing off in the barks that lined the shore, and making the best of their way across the lake. They were constantly intercepted by the brigantines, which broke through the flimsy array of boats; sending off their volleys to the right and left, as the crews of the latter hotly assailed them. The battle raged as fiercely on the lake as on the land. Many of the Indian vessels were shattered and overturned. Some few, however, under cover of the smoke, which rolled darkly over the waters, succeeded in clearing themselves of the turmoil, and were fast nearing the opposite shore.

Sandoval had particularly charged his captains to keep an eye on the movements of any vessel in which it was at all probable that Guatemozin might be concealed. At this crisis, three or four of the largest *piraguas* were seen skimming over the water, and making their way rapidly across the lake. A captain named Garci Holguin, who had command of one of the best sailers in the fleet, instantly gave them chase. The wind was favourable, and every moment he gained on the fugitives, who pulled their oars with a vigour that despair alone could have given. But it was in vain; and, after a short race, Holguin, coming alongside of one of the *piraguas*, which, whether from its appearance, or from information he had received, he conjectured might bear the Indian emperor, ordered his men to level their crossbows at the boat. But, before they could discharge them, a cry arose from those in it that their lord was on board. At the same moment, a young warrior, armed with buckler and *maquahuitl*, rose up, as if to beat off the assailants. But, as the Spanish captain ordered his men not to shoot, he dropped his weapons, and exclaimed, "I am Guatemozin; lead me to Malintzin, I am his prisoner; but let no harm come to my wife and my followers."

Holguin assured him that his wishes should be respected, and assisted him to get on board the brigantine, followed by his wife and attendants. These twenty in number, consisting of Coanoca, the deposed lord of Tezcuco, the lord of Tlacopan, and several other caciques and dignitaries, whose rank, probably, had secured them some exemption from the general calamities of the siege. When the captives were seated on the deck of his vessel, Holguin requested the Aztec prince to put an end to the combat by commanding his people in the other canoes to surrender.

But, with a dejected air, he replied, "It is not necessary. They will fight no longer, when they see that their prince is taken." He spoke truth. The news of Guatemozin's capture spread rapidly through the fleet, and on shore, where the Mexicans were still engaged in conflict with their enemies. It ceased, however, at once. They made no further resistance; and those on the water quickly followed the brigantines, which conveyed their captive monarch to land. It seemed as if the fight had been maintained thus long, the better to divert the enemy's attention, and cover their master's retreat.

Meanwhile Sandoval, on receiving tidings of the capture, brought his own brigantine alongside of Holguin's, and demanded the royal prisoner to be surrendered to him. But his captain claimed him as his prize. A dispute arose between the parties, each anxious to have the glory of the deed, and perhaps the privilege of commemorating it on his escutcheon. The controversy continued so long that it reached the ears of Cortés, who, in his station on the *azotea,* had learned, with no little satisfaction, the capture of his enemy. He instantly sent orders to his wrangling officers to bring Guatemozin before him, that he might adjust the difference between them. He charged them, at the same time, to treat their prisoner with respect. He then made preparations for the interview; caused the terrace to be carpeted with crimson cloth and matting, and a table to be spread with provisions of which the unhappy Aztecs stood so much in need. His lovely Indian mistress, Doña Marina, was present to act as interpreter. She had stood by his side through all the troubled scenes of the Conquest, and she was there now to witness its triumphant termination.

Guatemozin, on landing, was escorted by a company of infantry to the presence of the Spanish commander. He mounted the *azotea* with a calm and steady step, and was easily to be distinguished from his attendant nobles, though his full, dark eyes were no longer lighted up with their accustomed fire, and his features wore an expression of passive resignation that told little of the fierce and fiery spirit that burned within. His head was large, his limbs well proportioned, his complexion fairer than those of his bronze-coloured nation, and his whole deportment singularly mild and engaging.

Cortés came forward with a dignified and studied courtesy to receive him. The Aztec monarch probably knew the person of his conqueror, for he first broke silence by saying: "I have done all that I could to defend myself and my people. I am now reduced to this state. You will deal with me, Malintzin, as you list." Then, laying his hand on the hilt of a poniard, stuck in the general's belt, he added, with vehemence, "Better despatch me with this, and rid me of life at once." Cortés was filled with admiration at the proud bearing of the young barbarian, showing in his reverses a spirit worthy of an ancient Roman. "Fear not," he replied, "you shall be treated with all honour. You have defended your capital like a brave warrior. A Spaniard knows how to respect valour even in an enemy." He then inquired of him where he had left the princess, his wife; and, being informed that she still remained under protection of a Spanish guard on board the brigantine, the general sent to have her escorted to his presence.

She was the youngest daughter of Montezuma; and was hardly yet on the verge of womanhood. On the accession of her cousin, Guatemozin, to the throne, she had been wedded to him as his lawful wife. She is celebrated by her contemporaries for her personal charms; and the beautiful princess, Tecuichpo, is still commemorated by the Spaniards, since from her, by a subsequent marriage, are descended some of the illustrious families of their own nation. She was kindly received by Cortés, who showed her the respectful attentions suited to her rank. Her birth, no doubt, gave her an additional interest in his eyes, and he may have felt some touch of compunction, as he gazed on the daughter of the unfortunate Montezuma. He invited his royal captives to partake of the refreshments which their exhausted condition rendered so necessary. Meanwhile the Spanish commander made his dispositions for the night, ordering Sandoval to escort the prisoners to Cojohuacan, whither he proposed himself immediately to follow. The other captains, Olid and Alvarado, were to draw off their forces to their respective quarters. It was impossible for them to continue in the capital, where the poisonous effluvia from the unburied carcases loaded the air with infection. A small guard only was stationed to keep order in the wasted suburbs. It was the hour of vespers when Guatemozin surrendered, and the siege might be considered as then concluded. The evening set in dark, and the rain began to fall, before the several parties had evacuated the city.

During the night, a tremendous tempest, such as the Spaniards had rarely witnessed, and such as is known only within the tropics, burst over the Mexican Valley. The thunder, reverberating from the rocky amphitheatre of hills, bellowed over the waste of waters, and shook the *teocallis* and crazy tenements of Tenochtitlan—the few that yet survived —to their foundations. The lightning seemed to cleave asunder the vault of Heaven, as its vivid flashes wrapped the whole scene in a ghastly glare, for a moment, to be again swallowed up in darkness. The war of elements was in unison with the fortunes of the ruined city. It seemed as if the deities of Anahuac, scared from their ancient abodes, were borne along shrieking and howling in the blast, as they abandoned the fallen capital to its fate!

On the day following the surrender, Guatemozin requested the Spanish commander to allow the Mexicans to leave the city, and to pass unmolested into the open country. To this Cortés readily assented, as, indeed, without it, he could take no steps for purifying the capital. He gave his orders, accordingly, for the evacuation of the place, commanding that no one, Spaniard or confederate, should offer violence to the Aztecs, or in any way obstruct their departure. The whole number of these is variously estimated at from thirty to seventy thousand, besides women and children, who had survived the sword, pestilence, and famine. It is certain they were three days in defiling along the several causeways—a mournful train; husbands and wives, parents and children, the sick and the wounded, leaning on one another for support, as they feebly tottered along, squalid, and but half covered with rags, that disclosed at every step hideous gashes, some recently received, others festering from long neglect, and carrying with them an atmosphere of contagion. Their wasted forms and famine-stricken faces told the whole history of the siege; and as the straggling files gained the opposite shore, they were observed to pause from time to time, as if to take one more look at the spot so lately crowned by the imperial city, once their pleasant home, and endeared to them by many a glorious recollection.

On the departure of the inhabitants, measures were immediately taken to purify the place, by means of numerous fires kept burning day and night, especially in the infected quarter of Tlatelolco, and by collecting the heaps of dead, which lay mouldering in the streets, and consigning them to the earth. Of the whole number who perished in the course of the siege, it is impossible to form any probable computation. The accounts range widely from one hundred and twenty thousand, the lowest estimate, to two hundred and forty thousand. The number of the Spaniards who fell was comparatively small, but that of the allies must have been large, if the historian of Tezcuco is correct in asserting that thirty thousand perished of his own countrymen alone. That the number of those destroyed within the city was immense cannot be doubted, when we consider that, besides its own redundant population, it was thronged with that of the neighbouring towns, who, distrusting their strength to resist the enemy, sought protection within its walls.

The booty found there—that is, the treasures of gold and jewels, the only booty of much value in the eyes of the Spaniards—fell far below their expectations. It did not exceed, according to the general's statement, a hundred and thirty thousand *castellanos* of gold, including the sovereign's share, which, indeed, taking into account many articles of curious and costly workmanship, voluntarily relinquished by the army, greatly exceeded his legitimate fifth. Yet the Aztecs must have been in possession of a much larger treasure, if it were only the wreck of that recovered from the Spaniards on the night of the memorable flight from Mexico. Some of the spoil may have been sent away from the capital; some spent in preparations for defence, and more of it buried in the earth, or sunk in the water of the lake. Their menaces were not without a meaning. They had, at least, the satisfaction of disappointing the avarice of their enemies.

Cortés had no further occasion for the presence of his Indian allies. He assembled the chiefs of the different squadrons, thanked them for their services, noticed their valour in flattering terms, and, after distributing presents among them, with the assurance that his master, the emperor, would recompense their fidelity yet more largely, dismissed them to their own homes. They carried off a liberal share of the spoils, of which they had plundered the dwellings—not of a kind to excite the cupidity of the Spaniards—and returned in triumph, short-sighted triumph! at the success of their expedition, and the downfall of the Aztec dynasty.

Great also was the satisfaction of the Spaniards at this brilliant termination of their long and laborious campaign. They were, indeed, disappointed at the small amount of treasure found in the conquered city. But the soldier is usually too much absorbed in the present to give much heed to the future; and, though their discontent showed itself afterwards in a more clamorous form, they now thought only of their triumph, and abandoned themselves to jubilee. Cortés celebrated the event by a banquet, as sumptuous as circumstances would permit, to which all the cavaliers and officers were invited. Loud and long was their revelry, which was carried to such an excess, as provoked the animadversion of Father Olmedo, who intimated that this was not the fitting way to testify their sense of the favours shown them by the Almighty. Cortés admitted the justice of the rebuke, but craved some indulgence for a soldier's licence in the hour of victory. The following day was appointed for the commemoration of their successes in a more suitable manner.

A procession of the whole army was then formed with Father Olmedo at its head. The soiled and tattered banners of Castile, which had waved over many a field of battle, now threw their shadows on the peaceful array of the soldiery, as they slowly moved along, rehearsing the litany, and displaying the image of the Virgin and the blessed symbol of man's redemption. The reverend father pronounced a discourse, in which he briefly reminded the troops of their great cause for thankfulness to Providence for conducting them safe through their long and perilous pilgrimage; and, dwelling on the responsibility incurred by their present position, he besought them not to abuse the rights of conquest, but to treat the unfortunate Indians with humanity. The sacrament was then administered to the commander-in-chief and the principal cavaliers, and the services concluded with a solemn thanksgiving to the God of battles, who had enabled them to carry the banner of the Cross triumphant over this barbaric empire.

Thus, after a siege of nearly three months' duration, unmatched in history for the constancy and courage of the besieged, seldom surpassed for the severity of its sufferings, fell the renowned capital of the Aztecs. Unmatched, it may be truly said, for constancy and courage, when we recollect that the door of capitulation on the most honourable terms was left open to them throughout the whole blockade, and that, sternly rejecting every proposal of their enemy, they, to a man, preferred to die rather than surrender. More than three centuries had elapsed since the Aztecs, a poor and wandering tribe from the far north-west, had come on the plateau. There they built their miserable collection of huts on the spot—as tradition tells us—prescribed by the oracle. Their conquests, at first confined to their immediate neighbourhood, gradually covered the valley, then crossing the mountains, swept over the broad extent of the tableland, descended its precipitous sides, and rolled onwards to the Mexican Gulf, and the distant confines of Central America. Their wretched capital, meanwhile, keeping pace with the enlargement of territory, had grown into a flourishing city, filled with buildings, monuments of art, and a numerous population that gave it the first rank among the capitals of the Western World. At this crisis, came over another race from the remote East, strangers like themselves, whose coming had also been predicted by the oracle, and, appearing on the plateau, assailed them in the very zenith of their prosperity, and blotted them out from the map of nations for ever! The whole story has the air of fable rather than of history! a legend of romance—a tale of the genii!

Yet we cannot regret the fall of an empire which did so little to promote the happiness of its subjects, or the real interests of humanity. Notwithstanding the lustre thrown over its latter days by the glorious defence of its capital, by the mild munificence of Montezuma, by the dauntless heroism of Guatemozin, the Aztecs were emphatically a fierce and brutal race, little calculated, in their best aspects, to excite our sympathy and regard. Their civilisation, such as it was, was not their own, but reflected, perhaps imperfectly, from a race whom they had succeeded in the land. It was, in respect to the Aztecs, a generous graft on a vicious stock, and could have brought no fruit to perfection. They ruled over their wide domains with a sword, instead of a sceptre. They did nothing to ameliorate the condition, or in any way promote the progress, of their vassals. Their vassals were serfs, used only to minister to their pleasure, held in awe by armed garrisons, ground to the dust by imposts in peace, by military conscriptions in war. They did not, like the Romans, whom they resembled in the nature of their conquests, extend the rights of citizenship to the conquered. They did not amalgamate them into one great nation, with common rights and interests. They held them as aliens—even those who in the valley were gathered round the very walls of the capital. The Aztec metropolis, the heart of the monarchy, had not a sympathy, not a pulsation, in common with the rest of the body politic. It was a stranger in its own land.

The Aztecs not only did not advance the condition of their vassals, but morally speaking, they did much to degrade it. How can a nation, where human sacrifices prevail, and especially when combined with cannibalism, further the march of civilisation? How can the interests of humanity be consulted where man is levelled to the rank of the brutes that perish? The influence of the Aztecs introduced their gloomy superstition into lands before unacquainted with it, or where, at least, it was not established in any great strength. The example of the capital was contagious. As the latter increased in opulence, the religious celebrations were conducted with still more terrible magnificence. In the same manner as the gladiatorial shows of the Romans increased in pomp with the increasing splendour of the capital, men became familiar with scenes of horror and the most loathsome abominations; women and children— the whole nation—became familiar with, and assisted at them. The

heart was hardened, the manners were made ferocious, the feeble light
of civilisation, transmitted from a milder race, was growing fainter
and fainter, as thousands and thousands of miserable victims throughout
the empire were yearly fattened in its cages, sacrificed on its altars,
dressed and served at its banquets! The whole land was converted into a
vast human shambles! The empire of the Aztecs did not fall before its
time.

Whether these unparalleled outrages furnish a sufficient plea to the
Spaniards for their invasion, whether, with the Protestant, we are
content to find a warrant for it in the natural rights and demands of
civilisation, or, with the Roman Catholic, in the good pleasure of the
Pope—on the one or other of which grounds, the conquests by most
Christian nations in the East and the West have been defended—it is
unnecessary to discuss, as it has already been considered in a former
chapter. It is more material to inquire, whether, assuming the right, the
conquest of Mexico was conducted with a proper regard to the claims
of humanity. And here we must admit that, with all allowance for the
ferocity of the age and the laxity of its principles, there are passages
which every Spaniard, who cherishes the fame of his countrymen, would
be glad to see expunged from their history; passages not to be vindicated
on the score of self-defence, or of necessity of any kind, and which must
for ever leave a dark spot on the annals of the Conquest. And yet, taken
as a whole, the invasion, up to the capture of the capital, was conducted
on principles less revolting to humanity than most, perhaps than any, of
the other conquests of the Castilian crown in the New World.

It may seem slight praise to say that the followers of Cortés used no
bloodhounds to hunt down their wretched victims, as in some other parts
of the Continent, nor exterminated a peaceful and submissive population
in mere wantonness of cruelty, as in the islands. Yet it is something that
they were not so far infected by the spirit of the age, and that their
swords were rarely stained with blood unless it was indispensable to the
success of their enterprise. Even in the last siege of the capital, the
sufferings of the Aztecs, terrible as they were, do not imply any unusual
cruelty in the victors; they were not greater than those inflicted on their
own countrymen at home, in many a memorable instance, by the most
polished nations, not merely of ancient times but of our own. They were
the inevitable consequences which follow from war, when, instead of
being confined to its legitimate field, it is brought home to the hearth-
stone, to the peaceful community of the city—its burghers untrained to

arms, its women and children yet more defenceless. In the present instance, indeed, the sufferings of the besieged were in a great degree to be charged on themselves—on their patriotic, but desperate, self-devotion. It was not the desire, as certainly it was not the interest, of the Spaniards to destroy the capital, or its inhabitants. When any of these fell into their hands, they were kindly entertained, their wants supplied, and every means taken to infuse into them a spirit of conciliation; and this, too, it should be remembered, in despite of the dreadful doom to which they consigned their Christian captives. The gates of a fair capitulation were kept open, though unavailingly, to the last hour.

The right of conquest necessarily implies that of using whatever force may be necessary for overcoming resistance to the assertion of that right. For the Spaniards to have done otherwise than they did would have been to abandon the siege, and, with it, the conquest of the country. To have suffered the inhabitants, with their high-spirited monarch, to escape, would but have prolonged the miseries of war by transferring it to another and more inaccessible quarter. They literally, as far as the success of the expedition was concerned, had no choice. If our imagination is struck with the amount of suffering in this, and in similar scenes of the Conquest, it should be borne in mind that it is a natural result of the great masses of men engaged in the conflict. The amount of suffering does not in itself show the amount of cruelty which caused it; and it is but justice to the Conquerors of Mexico to say that the very brilliancy and importance of their exploits have given a melancholy celebrity to their misdeeds, and thrown them into somewhat bolder relief than strictly belongs to them. It is proper that thus much should be stated, not to excuse their excesses, but that we may be enabled to make a more impartial estimate of their conduct, as compared with that of other nations under similar circumstances, and that we may not visit them with peculiar obloquy for evils which necessarily flow from the condition of war. I have not drawn a veil over these evils; for the historian should not shrink from depicting, in their true colours, the atrocities of a condition over which success is apt to throw a false halo of glory, but which, bursting asunder the strong bonds of human fellowship, purchases its triumphs by arming the hand of man against his brother, makes a savage of the civilised, and kindles the fires of hell in the bosom of the savage.

Whatever may be thought of the Conquest in a moral view, regarded as a military achievement, it must fill us with astonishment. That a handful of adventurers, indifferently armed and equipped, should have landed on the shores of a powerful empire, inhabited by a fierce and warlike race, and in defiance of the reiterated prohibitions of its sovereign, have forced their way into the interior; that they should have done this, without knowledge of the language or of the land, without chart or compass to guide them, without any idea of the difficulties they were to encounter, totally uncertain whether the next step might bring them on a hostile nation, or on a desert, feeling their way along in the dark, as it were; that though nearly overwhelmed by their first encounter with the inhabitants, they should have still pressed on to the capital of the empire, and, having reached it, thrown themselves unhesitatingly into the midst of their enemies; that, so far from being daunted by the extraordinary spectacle there exhibited of power and civilisation, they should have been but the more confirmed in their original design; that they should have seized the monarch, have executed his ministers before the eyes of his subjects, and, when driven forth with ruin from the gates, have gathered their scattered wreck together, and, after a system of operations pursued with consummate policy and daring, have succeeded in overturning the capital, and establishing their sway over the country; that all this should have been so effected by a mere handful of indigent adventurers is in fact little short of the miraculous, too startling for the probabilities demanded by fiction, and without a parallel in the pages of history.

Yet this must not be understood too literally; for it would be unjust to the Aztecs themselves, at least to their military prowess, to regard the Conquest as directly achieved by the Spaniards alone. This would indeed be to arm the latter with the charmed shield of Ruggiero, and the magic lance of Astolfo, overturning its hundreds at a touch. The Indian empire was in a manner conquered by Indians. The first terrible encounter of the Spaniards with the Tlascalans, which had nearly proved their ruin, did in fact insure their success. It secured to them a strong native support, on which to retreat in the hour of trouble, and round which they could rally the kindred races of the land for one great and overwhelming assault. The Aztec monarchy fell by the hands of its own subjects, under the direction of European sagacity and science. Had it been united, it might have bidden defiance to the invaders. As it was, the capital was dissevered from the rest of the country; and the bolt, which might have passed off comparatively harmless, had the empire been cemented by a common principle of loyalty and patriotism, now found its way into every crack and crevice of the ill-compacted fabric, and buried it in its own ruins. Its fate may serve as a striking proof that a government, which does not rest on the sympathies of its subjects, cannot long abide; that human institutions, when not connected with human prosperity and progress, must fall—if not before the increasing light of civilisation, by the hand of violence; by violence from within, if not from without. And who shall lament their fall?